T0287784

I HOPE THIS REACHES YOU

Great Lakes Books Series

Series Editor
Thomas Klug

Sterling Heights, Michigan

A complete listing of the books in this series can be found
online at wsupress.wayne.edu

I HOPE THIS REACHES YOU

AN AMERICAN SOLDIER'S ACCOUNT OF WORLD WAR I

HILARY CONNOR

Prologue by Elizabeth Field Connor

WAYNE STATE UNIVERSITY PRESS
DETROIT

© 2020 by Hilary Connor. All rights reserved. No part of this book may be reproduced without formal permission.

ISBN 978-0-8143-4707-2 (paperback)
ISBN 978-0-8143-4708-9 (ebook)

Library of Congress Control Number: 2020938744

Wayne State University Press
Leonard N. Simons Building
4809 Woodward Avenue
Detroit, Michigan 48201-1309

Visit us online at wsupress.wayne.edu

Beware the toils of war ... the mesh of the huge
dragnet sweeping up the world.

> Homer, *The Iliad*

Alas! I hoped, the toils of war o'ercome, to
meet soft quiet and repose at home.

> Homer, *The Odyssey*

The story of men at war is a timeless saga that is shared by every soldier who has marched off to war. It is a journey seldom understood by those who have never had to take that path—to know it one has to experience it. And therein lies the trap. War is a tragedy in two parts. Surviving it is but the first act. Being able to ever fully return from it presents a far more complicated ordeal. No soldier's story is complete without recounting both. This book is dedicated to all who have gone into harm's way in service of country.

CONTENTS

PROLOGUE

Elizabeth Field Connor

The basement of my father's house was thick with the smell of must. It was also filled with a lifetime's worth of clutter. My father had been dead for several years, yet one aspect of his life remained the same—whenever it poured, rainwater continued to seep through cracks in the cellar walls, pooling on the concrete floor beneath all of the things he had left in his wake.

Over the years, my stepmother had talked wistfully about wanting to wade into that morass to try to get a grip on what was down there, and then throw some of it out. And over the years, just as hopefully, I had agreed to help.

Finally, in the spring of 2011, I made good on that promise. After escorting my stepmother to a matinee performance of *War Horse* on Broadway, my husband Hilary and I returned to their house in New Jersey, where the three of us rolled up our sleeves and got to work, digging into the past. Buried in a corner was a heavy wooden box that my husband uncovered and dragged into the light.

"What's that?" I asked.

My stepmother shook her head slowly, indicating she had never seen it before. Remnants of two faded shipping labels didn't offer any clues.

"Looks like an army footlocker," my husband said, eyeing the stenciled lettering on the trunk's olive green top. Above the black silhouette of a caduceus, the trunk was marked:

BYRON F FIELD
1st AMB. CO. "MICH."
117th Sanitary Train
42nd Division

"Your father never mentioned anything about an army footlocker," my stepmother said doubtfully.

My father, Byron Fiske Field Jr., had served in the Army Air Corps in World War II as the navigator of a B-25. After being shot down by a Japanese Zero, his plane crash-landed in Russia. He'd been lucky and survived with only minor injuries. Others in the plane weren't as fortunate. His ordeal was far from over, though—because of Russia's neutrality with Japan, my father spent the remainder of the war in a Siberian camp of internment.

Other than those brief facts, he'd never talked much about the war. Most vets didn't. But something told me this footlocker didn't contain my father's story.

"Let's see what's inside," my husband suggested.

An old brass lock was fastened to a metal hasp that secured the lid of the trunk. It looked formidable. Hilary gave it a tug anyway, and unexpectedly it wobbled. Apparently, someone else hadn't had a key either, and so had popped the latch pin to free the lid. But that was long ago. Now a thick growth of dust webs sealed the crack beneath the lid. I watched expectantly as my husband slipped his fingertips into the crack. The hinges creaked as the trunk opened. In the dim light, we leaned in. Immediately, I jerked my head back. The odor of mildew was overwhelming.

But the wonder that confronted me was truly staggering. Like a necromancer's spell, it reached out and grabbed me. Taking a deep breath, I moved closer—and found myself staring at a trove of artifacts layered up to the lip of the trunk. What I saw brought me to my knees.

I tried not to breathe too deeply as I began to sort through the carefully organized sections. Items stacked on the bottom were contaminated by mold from moisture that had seeped into the trunk each time the basement had flooded. Fortunately, most of what was packed away was still high and dry. Treasures—ranging from the yellowed pages of a diary kept by my grandfather during World War I to sepia-tinged photographs and daguerreotype pictures of distant relatives—were pure gold to my eyes.

Suddenly, the risk of inhaling mold spores no longer seemed important. Instead, my focus was on breathing new life into the past as I tried to divine the meaning and purpose of each artifact that I extracted from the trunk. Hundreds of picture postcards of villages in France and Germany were meticulously maintained in a card file. Dozens of war letters, written to a woman whose name I didn't recognize, were neatly tied in bundles. Four books on the Great War and high school and college yearbooks from the early 1900s were brittle to the touch but otherwise still intact. A copy of the New Testament given to my grandfather at the age of seven and a family Bible from 1888 had been reverentially packed away for safekeeping. A family photo album, songbooks, reams of piano sheet music, Masonic Temple aprons, and other bits and pieces of my grandfather's life were sprinkled here and there like jewels in a treasure chest.

After taking stock of the items, I stood up, still clutching a framed photograph of my grandfather taken somewhere in the trenches of France. I studied the young face—eyes old beyond their years stared back.

It was a lot to absorb in one sitting. Yet a portrait had begun to emerge—of an articulate and promising young man who, like thousands of other patriotic Americans, had set aside his hopes and dreams to answer his country's call to duty by enlisting and fighting in the war to end all wars—World War I. Growing up in the Midwest, I'd never gotten to know that man. My grandfather had visited occasionally but mostly he'd lived on the West Coast—a distant and mysterious figure in the eyes of a small child. I'd been told that he was an exceptionally intelligent man but had suffered recurring bouts of alcoholism that cost him prestigious jobs in private industry and universities, eventually ruining his marriage and straining his relationship with his son and daughter.

At the age of seventy, he died alone in a Veterans Administration hospital in San Francisco. A letter I had written to him when he was hospitalized there was among the keepsakes I found in the trunk. In that letter, dated December 13, 1967, I told him how sorry I was to hear that he was ill. Then, hoping to cheer him up, I asked him what he'd like for Christmas. He never replied. Seven weeks later he died.

Maybe this trunk was his belated answer.

As a gift to both him and me, I took it home—where I went through it carefully, examining closely the telltale clues of a life now gone. An undertaking dealing with artifacts one hundred years old is not so easily done, and is at times especially challenging when the subject of the postmortem happens to be a relative. Fortunately, Hilary, a published writer and retired investigative prosecutor, helped me to put these newly discovered items in their proper historical perspective, which in turn afforded me the unique opportunity to view my grandfather in a new light, instead of through the time-thickened haze of family lore. This trunk, full of his World War I letters, books, and writings, serves as a resurrection of sorts in that regard—allowing Byron to return from the past to narrate his own odyssey of war, in his own words.

What follows is his story.

A NOTE ON THE TEXT

In recounting Byron F. Field's story, I have relied primarily on four principal sources of information found in the footlocker that was issued to Byron as a member of the 168th Ambulance Company in the 42nd Division—or, as it was famously known, the Rainbow Division. The first of these sources is a diary kept by Byron from February 1918 to July 1919, 214 pages handwritten during the war.

The second cache of firsthand information is contained in two books that were coauthored by Byron F. Field in the late winter and early spring of 1919. The first, *The History of Ambulance Company 168*, was written by select members of the Ambulance Company, recounting events and personal experiences that occurred during the war. In addition to writing the memoriam to fallen comrades and "The Dawn of Peace" chapter, Byron also served as the book's editor. The second book, *Iodine and Gasoline*, was written by select members of the 117th Sanitary Train, of which the 168th Ambulance Company was part, and it also recounts events and experiences during the war. Byron wrote the "Champagne" chapter of this book.

Perhaps the most extraordinary source of information found in the trunk is a collection of over three hundred letters written by Byron during the war to his parents and his college sweetheart, Estelle M. Cozine. Interleaved with many of the letters are mementos: flower petals, flowers, musical programs, army, YMCA, and Red Cross notices, newspaper and magazine clippings, train tickets, church service programs, and other bits and pieces of everyday life. These proved invaluable to me in creating a broader and richer historical context. Of the 308 letters written by Byron, the 156 that were addressed to Estelle are especially poignant. It is apparent from the notations written in red ink on the outside of envelopes and in the margins of pages that in July 1969 (one year after Byron's death) Estelle reviewed and categorized the contents of each letter, annotating the pages and initialing each envelope *E '69*. Estelle's annotations are often as informative as the contents of the letters themselves.

The last category of primary source material is a voluminous collection of personal papers, including professional letters, academic articles, speech notes, opinion pieces, and essays that were written by Byron in the decades after the war. Several of these writings were penned under the pseudonym *Homer Fiske*—a *nom de guerre* that Byron reserved for all of his war-related writings. The fact that Byron chose to adopt this ominous echo of the great poet of war on first being discharged from the army evidences his awareness of the epic struggles that were waiting to confront him in the years that followed the war.

Two additional sources of information found in the trunk are first-hand accounts written by other members of the Rainbow Division: *Rainbow Bright*, by infantryman Lawrence O. Stewart in 1923; and *Men of the Rainbow*, by artilleryman Leslie Langille in 1933. These books were helpful in providing a day-to-day portrait of life and death in the trenches of France. Whether Byron knew the authors personally is unknown—that he valued their attempt to put into words what was basically an indescribable experience is evidenced by his having kept these books among his own belongings.

At appropriate junctures in the book, relevant portions of these sources are referenced in the notes section for each chapter. All of the people and occurrences depicted in this book are real. In the interest of historical accuracy, the facts and circumstances surrounding the events described here have been meticulously researched. In order to make the people who populate the pages of Byron's diary, books, letters, and other writings come to life in a more intimate and animated fashion, in some scenes, a narrative technique has been employed to better relate the events that propelled these individuals through history. Byron's quotations are taken verbatim from his diary, books, letters, and personal papers. The narrative tenor in certain scenes, however, is mine—fashioned from whole cloth woven from the content, setting, and spirit of the original documents.

1
ANSWERING THE CALL

May 24, 1917. After five days of continuous rain, clear skies had conspired with waterlogged ground and a faint breeze to envelop the Jackson Railroad Station in a cloud of fog. Although somewhat unexpected, for southern Michigan this was nothing new. According to legend, a young Indian brave who had gone out on a hunt was the first to disappear in such a mist. Ever since, this phenomenon had been called the Potawatomi Curtain.

As the morning train bound for Detroit pulled into the station, Byron Fiske Field waited his turn to board. No sooner had he entrained than the shrill blast of the conductor's whistle set the wheels in motion. After clearing the station, the train picked up speed and glimpses of downtown Jackson flashed by in the window like so many street scenes in a hand-cranked stereopticon. Before long, there was nothing left to look at but endless acres of Michigan farmland.

It had been an exceptionally cool spring—the most unpromising in thirty-one years. The fields of wheat and sugar beets were still an uncertain mixture of green and brown. Whether this year's crop would be able to make up for lost time was the cause of much concern. At the age of nineteen, though, hope springs eternal regardless of circumstance. Byron was no exception to that rule. By the time the train passed an orchard of cherry trees, the morning fog had lifted, and clusters of pink floated against a bright blue sky. To Byron, the future looked limitless.

On April 6, Congress had declared war on Germany. Byron was eager to answer his country's call to duty. Others he knew had already enlisted, but Byron's options were limited. Plagued with bad eyesight, Byron knew that he'd almost certainly be rejected for military service. On earlier forays into Detroit, army, navy and Marine Corps recruiters had told him so. Which wasn't entirely bad news—a pacifist at heart, Byron had other plans.

Byron had just finished his freshman year at Albion College, where he was studying to be a Methodist missionary. Although the idea of killing another human being was at odds with his Christian beliefs, like other Americans he was convinced of the righteousness of this war, the war to end all wars, and he was determined to do his part. Given his limited vision, Byron figured that his best chance of getting overseas was to volunteer to serve in a medical unit where the physical requirements to enlist were less stringent and he wouldn't be expected to fire a gun. He'd heard that the Red Cross corps was looking for volunteers.

Still, Byron was leaving nothing to chance. In an abundance of caution he had come armed with a letter from the family doctor attesting to his general fitness, and he had even memorized eye charts down to the smallest type. At five feet, eleven inches tall and a solid 190 pounds, Byron was an impressive physical specimen. Not to mention bright. More important, though, he wasn't particular about the type of work he'd be asked to do. He was more than willing to serve in any position, from orderly to litter bearer to ambulance driver, just to be in the thick of it—supremely confident that his innate talent would be readily apparent to superior officers and that he'd soon be given greater responsibility. Maybe even a promotion.

Byron was not alone in his enthusiasm. The train was loaded with it—passenger cars filled with the resolve of young men eager to enlist. This groundswell of support represented a recent change. Prior to America's declaration of war, most citizens had viewed the conflict in Europe as a far-off, ill-defined affair of little significance to their lives. As Byron recollected in an essay written after the war:

> We were at play—or work—at study. The days were filled
> with hours in the classroom, the chambers, and along the
> river in canoes. Spring suns had barely melted the last snows
> into the grass. Already we were thinking of the summer days

when vacation would be with us, and we wouldn't have to go a-hurrying to "eight o'clocks," or give answer for too frequent cuts from classes.

Oh yes, we read the newspapers, in the same detached way that any college boy scans the news for information about what is doing in the outside world. Our chief source of outside information however was the letter from home, and that was confined chiefly to remarks about the health and financial condition of our own family.

We did read of the war—off there in Europe. Yes, we even heard occasional reference made to it in our class in European History, although the professor was more concerned in our knowledge of the significance of the Battle of Tours or Poitiers than Verdun or the Somme. The latter was too recent to be of immediate historical significance to him—it hadn't been seasoned in foolscap and leather binding yet.

We read of "atrocities," of White Papers and Red Papers, of the Russian revolt, of Gallipoli—but for the most part they were "outside our world." Spring was coming, and the annual class games, the walks which had been deprived us through the fields and woods, alone, or with our damozels.

Then came April 6—and war. Still remote. As a high school boy, I had watched the Princess Pats being recruited in 1914. They had seemed just like any other "soldiers"—they were going over to Europe to get into a war about something or other. Some acquaintances had been filled with a spirit of adventure, or, thinking deeply, of a desire to do the right thing, as they saw it, and had gone over to Windsor, opposite Detroit, and joined up with the Canucks.

But here we were in it. Newspaper reading took on a new significance. "Platitudinous" remarks of President Wilson were now accepted as too coldly matter-of-fact. We were pledged to support a Cause—"to help make the world safe for democracy." We were involved directly, it seemed, because we refused to be dictated about when and where ships flying our flags could go—sort of a War of 1812 attitude. We were on the side of Right too—there could be no doubt about it—the other side had committed atrocities, had violated international law, had tried to take advantage of certain innocent peoples. We were a kind of eleventh hour "defenders of the faith."

For Byron and other self-fashioned crusaders on the train that morning, it would be just two short hours and nine more stops on the Michigan Central Railroad line before they reached Detroit, and destiny. To pass the time Byron engaged in small talk with the girlfriend of a former high school classmate. She'd recognized him on boarding the train and had taken the open seat beside him. Despite not being able to recall her name, Byron managed to hold up his end of the conversation. Just before reaching downtown Detroit, the train stopped and the young lady departed. Byron began to talk with a passenger seated opposite him, explaining that he was on his way to Detroit to enlist in any medical unit that would have him in order to fight in the Great War.

It was then that a man seated across the aisle spoke up, saying that he was already enrolled in one of the units. Byron smiled back, somewhat surprised. The man explained that he couldn't help but overhear Byron, then asked if he might be of some assistance. The man affected a sleek, almost elegant, bearing—Byron sized him up as a "Michigan Man." Before continuing, the man politely waited to be invited into the conversation. Byron didn't hesitate—as the son of a general business agent, Byron had been schooled in the importance of cultivating connections in life no matter how inconsequential they might at first appear to be. After following up with a firm handshake and proper introduction, Byron went on to explain that he was hoping to enroll in an ambulance company—although, truth be told, he had no idea what his prospects for success were. For better or worse, Byron had decided to go it alone. He had not spoken to anyone about wanting to enlist; if his parents were acquainted with any of the officers in charge of an ambulance company, he was in no position to avail himself of their contacts. Byron's parents didn't have the slightest idea that he was even thinking about enlistment—much less on his way to Detroit to actually do it. If they had, they would have done everything in their power to prevent it. Byron knew that the prospect of another family tragedy in the making would have been too much for them to endure.

Years before, Byron's parents had had to commit his older brother, Ralph, to the Michigan Home for the Feebleminded. The possibility that they could lose their only other child in a war that many viewed as one of choice, not necessity, was a risk that they were not willing to assume. To the extent that any young man filled with patriotic zeal was capable of understanding this, Byron did. Still, he was determined to answer his country's call to duty and until that deed was done, Byron was prepared to keep his own counsel.

In his quest to enlist, Byron had not entirely forsaken his parents, though. College tuition was a costly family expense. Byron appreciated that and had waited for the semester to end before he made any attempt to enlist in an ambulance company. He just hoped that in doing so he hadn't left it too late—college credits didn't carry much weight in the army, and save unbridled patriotism, Byron knew that he possessed no skills of particular interest or use to a medical unit. In their stead, he had come armed with a packet of letters attesting to his good character, and in a sleight of hand that would have done a magician proud, he quickly produced those letters from his briefcase, then waited patiently while the man looked them over. Handing the letters back, the man seemed suitably impressed, remarking that Byron appeared to be "the boy" then.

For the remainder of the trip, Byron asked endless questions, and to the best of his ability the man attempted to provide answers down to the smallest detail—of which there were plenty. Each ambulance company would be comprised of a captain, four lieutenants, one top cutter plus six additional sergeants, and some 120 privates, in addition to cooks, wagoners, and saddlers. Routine tasks would be shared equally—all of the enlisted men being required to wear a lot of different hats. Which suited Byron just fine. Given that many of the American ambulance companies would be motorized, and that Byron was an experienced driver, he hoped that his familiarity with automobiles would set him apart from other recruits whose families couldn't afford to buy a motorcar, though he was more than willing to work as a litter bearer if need be.

As Byron would soon learn, getting the wounded out of the line of fire was just the first part of a very dangerous and arduous job.

"Can You Drive a Car?" American Field Service recruiting poster, illustrated by Charles Dana Gibson, 1917. (Library of Congress.)

Student driver. Front cover of *Leslie's Weekly*, January 18, 1917.

"Knowledge Is Power." Front cover of *Leslie's Weekly*, January 6, 1916.

"How Long Must This Continue?" Front cover of *Leslie's Weekly*, January 25, 1917.

"The Call." Front cover of *Leslie's Weekly*, April 19, 1917.

Before the broken and bloodied bodies of wounded soldiers could be extracted from the field of battle, they would have to be treated—with splints, bandages, or whatever it took—then carried by litter to a dressing station, which could be thousands of yards away. In the mud and mayhem at the front, yards would seem like miles, the dead and dying everywhere. On finally reaching a dressing station, the next order of business for medical personnel was to triage the wounded—an emergency assessment procedure in which the worst battlefield casualties with the best chance of survival were prioritized, then given stopgap medical treatment to stabilize their condition so that they could be driven to a base hospital where they would be operated on—assuming they were still alive. The rest of the wounded would have to wait their turn—or die.

For Byron, all this was yet to come. At this point, he was no more capable of envisioning the unimaginable than anyone else who had never been subjected to the horrors of war—especially this war. There had never been anything like it. To truly know it, one had to experience it. Simply doing that would prove to be the challenge of a lifetime.

As the train pulled into the depot in Detroit, the two men made arrangements to meet after Byron had checked into his room at the Library Park Hotel. After that, the man would take Byron over to meet Mr. Jones, the supervisor in charge of the state Red Cross.

From Byron's perspective, limited vision notwithstanding, it appeared to be a hopeful start.

THE WORLD'S GREATEST
ADVERTISING ADVENTURE

The Michigan Central train station was the newest jewel in a resplendent downtown Detroit. In the decade leading up to the war, the city that was putting the country on wheels had almost doubled in population as Americans flocked to Detroit to work in its factories. The railroad tycoon William Vanderbilt, owner of the Michigan Central Railroad, thought it was only proper that a station befitting Detroit's new stature in the world should be built to receive the city's many visitors. In 1914, that station had opened to great fanfare.

On the morning of May 24, as Byron departed the train from Jackson, the long finger of Uncle Sam pointed out from a recruiting poster. Placards imploring citizens to invest in war bonds or do their patriotic duty in other ways were fastened to stanchions that ran the length of the platform. On entering the grand hall, the clamor of commotion echoed off the station's polished marble floors and vaulted tile ceiling. Byron craned his neck to admire the ornate surroundings, barely keeping an eye out for impending collisions and other forms of misadventure in the vast churning crowd. Others, however, were doing a much better job of that—uniformed soldiers had been posted at the station doors and platforms.

After the United States had officially declared war on Germany, security at strategic locations had been heightened. In the previous three years, there had been no shortage of mysterious fires and industrial mishaps at plants and factories that were providing equipment

"I Want You for U.S. Army." Recruiting poster, illustrated by James Montgomery Flagg, 1917. (Library of Congress.)

Will you be ready to-morrow to make munitions for Germany? If not

INVEST IN

LIBERTY BONDS TO-DAY

Louis Raemaekers's poster for Liberty Bonds, 1917, Liberty Loan Committee, Brown Robertson Co., New York.

and provisions to England and France. At the time of their occurrence, those incidents were viewed as more of a nuisance than a threat to national security—the sporadic work of a handful of German American sympathizers. Now that America was arming itself to march off to war, though, it was thought that Detroit's manufacturing prowess and burgeoning railroad traffic with Canada would be prime targets for trained saboteurs.

As it turned out, those fears were not far-fetched. Little more than two months after Byron detrained in Detroit, authorities uncovered a plot to blow up the nearby Port Huron railway tunnel connecting the United States and Canada. Albert Kaltschmidt, a German national who was the leader of a German American bund in Detroit, would be arrested with others for conspiring to pack high explosives aboard a passenger car headed into the tunnel, as well as other acts of sabotage aimed at factories in Detroit and Canada. At the moment, though, it was business as usual at the train station. As Byron exited through the terminal's brass doors and boarded a streetcar for the Library Park Hotel, for him, at least, the world was still a peaceful place.

In a letter written that night to his college sweetheart, Estelle Cozine, Byron said that he was "really in luck," as evidenced by his having checked into room number 245 on the 24th of May, following his chance encounter on the train with an ambulance corps volunteer who had introduced him to Mr. Jones of the Red Cross. According to Byron, Mr. Jones had immediately recognized his "budding genius" and "warmed up" to him, promising to take him to "the men who are at the head of this new unit" the following morning at 10:00.

Estelle had just completed her freshman year at Albion College, and like Byron, she too was devoutly Methodist. Unlike Byron, however, she still questioned the necessity of the United States entering the war. In his letter to Estelle that night, Byron good-naturedly teased her about "maying" with another beau while he was in Detroit. Then he suggested that she take in the silent movie *The Eagle's Wing*, knowing full well that neither was a realistic possibility—Estelle was completely taken with Byron, and she was much too smart to be swayed by the melodramatics of a thinly veiled war propaganda film. Other Americans, however, were not nearly so discerning.

ESTELLE COZINE, "Birdie" (Sorosis) . Albion
One of the best examples of the all-around woman—prominent in social circles, vice-president of the Y. W., and active in all religious work. Jumping center on the Senior girls' champ. team, and last but not least, winner of the state oratorical contest. P. S.—She is the first girl to have her name on the Mildred Chappel Memorial Cup.

Estelle M. Cozine in the *Albion College Yearbook*, 1918.

Released in late 1916, *The Eagle's Wing* warned of the inherent danger of being unprepared for war, depicting the sinister work of foreign agents who were actively plotting with nearby countries to attack the United States. In one of those rare instances in which life really does imitate art—even if it's bad art—the movie became a popular hit by sheer coincidence. On January 16, 1917, the so-called Zimmermann telegram was intercepted and decrypted by British intelligence agents. In the telegram, German foreign secretary Arthur Zimmermann proposed that Mexico ally itself with Germany in the event that the U.S. Congress declared war on Germany. As the spoils of war, a victorious Germany would then give portions of the southwestern United States to Mexico. On March 1, 1917, the contents of that telegram were made public by the *New York Times*. Not surprisingly, ensuing news accounts read like the pages of a sensational movie script. The truth, however, was more complicated than that. The entreaty to Mexico was born of Germany's continued frustration over the British naval blockade and an anticipated resumption of unrestricted submarine warfare in February, due in part to the United States' refusal to cease exporting armaments and other war supplies to England and France, even on passenger ships.

The subtleties of this political brinksmanship were lost on the American public, whose outrage over the telegram was immediate and widespread. To some extent this reaction was not unforeseen, given that Britain had been subtly but persistently laying the groundwork for such an eventuality from the very outset of the war. Within hours of declaring war on August 4, 1914, Great Britain severed Germany's

"On Guard." Front cover of *Leslie's Weekly*, February 22, 1917.

five transatlantic cables, stifling its ability to communicate with the outside world—and, most important, influence public opinion in the United States. Not only did this leave the only European transatlantic cables to North America in English hands, it also enabled Britain to monitor and exercise a great degree of control over the information that was transmitted from Europe concerning the war. Germany had been relegated to communicating with North America through U.S. diplomatic channels which, unknown to both countries at the time, were surreptitiously intercepted and decoded by Britain.

The use of propaganda as a weapon of war was hardly unique to this conflict. Its dissemination on such a massive scale, however, was wholly unprecedented. In large part, it was this widespread use of propaganda by both sides that made it difficult, if not impossible, for many trusting but relatively uninformed Americans to discern fact from fiction in deciding whether the United States should remain neutral or declare war on Germany. This onslaught of propaganda began almost immediately after war was declared—the first media salvo having been fired by the German government when it established a department of propaganda to influence popular opinion in neutral countries. Not to be outmaneuvered on this emerging new front, the British government set up a similar agency, the War Propaganda Bureau. In the ensuing fog of misinformation that was generated by the propaganda machines of both sides, unvarnished facts were hard to find. As noted by Hiram Warren Johnson, the isolationist senator from California, "The first casualty when war comes is truth."

The accuracy of that statement is perhaps best exemplified by the public relations battle that ensued between Great Britain and Germany in the aftermath of the sinking of the RMS *Lusitania*. The buildup to that battle, although somewhat tortuous, began as follows. In the early fall of 1914, as fighting on the western front settled into a prolonged and entrenched affair, the use of ordnance intensified as each side tried to pummel the other into submission. It quickly became apparent to both sides that the ever-increasing demand for munitions would soon exceed the ability of armament manufacturers to meet that demand. And, to the great consternation of the Allies, at this point in the war, German munitions producers were able to manufacture more than double the combined output of their British and French counterparts, which created a critical munitions gap between the two sides. In an attempt to close that gap, the Allies turned to American manufacturers, and from the start merchant vessels were used to ferry that contraband from ports in the United States to Europe. To augment that merchant fleet, ocean liners like the *Lusitania* were often used to carry munitions and other war supplies in their hold.

At the outset of the war, the rules of engagement as to what constituted contraband and by what means it could be confiscated on the high seas were governed by the Hague Convention and the so-called Cruiser Rules. According to those rules, only warships and merchant ships that presented a real threat to the attacker could be sunk without warning. In all other circumstances, civilian vessels could not be fired on without the attacker first providing fair warning, and then a reasonable opportunity for the ship's crew to surrender. In November 1914, implementation of this rule became more difficult when Great Britain imposed an embargo on Germany, declaring the North Sea to be a war zone—which dictated that merchant ships bound for ports in Germany were first required to put into British ports for inspection before proceeding. The situation was further complicated on February 4, 1915, when Germany countered by imposing a blockade of its own, claiming

British reproduction of the Lusitania Medal purchased by Byron in Edinburgh, 1919.

"The Golden Shower." Front cover of *Leslie's Weekly*, December 28, 1916, drawn by E. Flohri. The sale of munitions and supplies to Great Britain and France was good for the U.S. economy.

"Fact and Fiction." Front cover of *Leslie's Weekly*, January 11, 1917, illustrated by Norman Rockwell. Women's suffrage and the call to war—a gender-based difference in perspective?

that the waters adjacent to Great Britain and Ireland were also a war zone. In practical terms, imposition of these decrees meant that any vessel sailing through these troubled waters was subject to being impounded or, worse yet, attacked with little or no warning.

To lessen the risk of being sunk by a German U-boat, British merchant vessels often resorted to sailing under false colors in an attempt to disguise their identity, a clear violation of the Cruiser Rules. For additional good measure, the British Admiralty had instructed the captains of merchant ships to ram U-boats on sight if possible—which only served to foreclose the possibility that a U-boat captain would actually risk surfacing to give fair warning. Despite these countermeasures, sailing through war-zone waters was an extremely hazardous endeavor—not so perilous, however, as to deter the owners of ocean liners from continuing to court disaster by agreeing to transport contraband in their hold. There were, after all, profits to be made and a patriotic duty to help the war effort—in which particular order of importance shipowners held each is open to speculation.

For ocean liner captains who were charged with ensuring the safe passage of civilian passengers traveling aboard contraband-laden ships, it was a nerve-wracking experience. Captain Daniel Dow of the RMS *Lusitania* was proof positive of this disquieting fact—on March 8, 1915, after having completed his seventh transatlantic run through submarine-infested waters, Dow asked to be relieved of command. The reason given by owners of the Cunard Steamship Company was mental exhaustion. On the *Lusitania*'s next voyage from New York City to Liverpool, disaster finally struck. On May 7, 1915, a German U-boat sank the *Lusitania* in waters off the southern coast of Ireland. Nearly twelve hundred civilian passengers and crew members were killed, many of them American citizens.

In the wake of the disaster, the criticism directed toward Germany was prompt and severe. Germany's response was no less staunch—asserting that its actions were justified because the *Lusitania* had been carrying munitions manufactured by American suppliers in her hold, and that she was officially classified as an auxiliary battle cruiser of the British Navy. The fact that the *Lusitania* was not equipped with mounted deck guns or any other type of armament was an irksome detail that German authorities had conveniently ignored in issuing their rebuttal.

In an effort to further defend its actions, Germany pointed out that it had made a good-faith effort to give unsuspecting civilians fair warning as to the risk they could incur by booking passage on the *Lusitania*. To wit, in the days immediately preceding the ship's departure from New York City, the German embassy had placed a notice in numerous newspapers in the United States warning civilian passengers not to travel on "vessels flying the flag of Great Britain." In New York City in particular, this notice had been prominently printed in newspapers adjacent to and directly below the Cunard Line advertisement listing the departure date for the *Lusitania*'s voyage.

Although Germany's interpretation of its obligation under international law may arguably have been correct, when weighed against the staggering loss of innocent life, it fell on deaf ears. In the court of public opinion, Germany's after-the-fact explanation rang empathetically hollow—from this point forward, whether it actually deserved to or not, Great Britain would own the moral high ground in this unfortunate affair. British authorities, no doubt realizing this, flatly denied that the *Lusitania* had been transporting contraband, relying in part on falsified shipping manifests to substantiate their claim.

In an ill-advised attempt to promote Germany's version of events and place the blame on Great Britain for having set the stage for such needless loss of life, in August a renowned German medalist, Karl Goetz, produced the infamous "Lusitania Medal." The medal was a macabre work of art in which a skeleton is depicted working as a merchant of death for the Cunard Line, selling tickets to unsuspecting passengers on the ill-fated voyage. Within days of its issuance, the medal became a public relations disaster for Germany when the British propaganda machine shifted into high gear, pointing to the medal as yet another example of German cruelty and cynicism in making a mockery of such a tragic event. The British didn't confine themselves to simply pointing to the medal, however—they mass-produced it, circulating over three hundred thousand copies in an effort to further demonize Germany in the eyes of the world. Ultimately, the British propaganda campaign carried the day. In the face of worldwide condemnation, in September

1915, Germany modified its use of sink-on-sight submarine tactics to henceforth exclude ocean liners. This initial restriction, and the total moratorium that would soon follow, lasted for eighteen months.

Decades later it would be proven beyond all doubt that the *Lusitania* was in fact carrying munitions in her hold. In the immediate aftermath of the disaster, however, this unsettling information was unknown to the public at large, having come to rest at the bottom of the Atlantic Ocean. In the absence of such dispositive proof, it is likely that many Americans misinterpreted Germany's subsequent curtailment of its submarine activity as a tacit admission of guilt—that Bryon seems to have subscribed to this point of view is evidenced by an essay he wrote after the war as well as a copy of the British-produced Lusitania Medal found among his personal belongings.

It was hardly surprising, then, that after three years of being exposed to such carefully crafted and largely uncontroverted British propaganda, so many Americans would be so willing to accept the Zimmermann telegram as further proof that Germany was willing to resort to any means necessary to win the war. Still, there were those who remained doubtful of their country's official resolve to abandon its long-standing policy of isolationism and declare war on Germany. Apparently, Byron numbered among them, deeming President Wilson's most recent pronouncements concerning German malevolence as merely "platitudinous." His skepticism would be short-lived, however. Any lingering doubts about the sincerity of Wilson's evolving pro-war position were soon dispelled—that tipping point came in March 1917 with the latest spate of U-boat attacks on American merchant ships. In Byron's words, the circumstances engendered "sort of a War of 1812 attitude" "about when and where ships flying our flags could go"—recasting Wilson's call to arms as "coldly matter-of-fact." That Congress was overwhelmingly of the same mind is reflected in the Senate vote to declare war on Germany by a margin of 82-6, and in the House of Representatives on April 6, 1917, by a vote of 373-50.

Such a change of heart was indeed reflective of the rapidly changing mood in the country—a sentiment that would gain further momentum due to the intensity of the homegrown propaganda campaign to which Byron and others were suddenly subjected once war had been declared.

This public relations campaign began in earnest on April 13, 1917, with the empanelment of the Committee on Public Information. The mandate of the committee was simple—use any means necessary to drum up support for the war. In subsequently selling the war to the American people, the machinations of the committee were all-encompassing—no communication medium, advertising artifice, pool of applicants, or audience of listeners went unutilized or unaddressed. In the words of the committee's chairman, George Creel, it was "a vast enterprise in salesmanship, the world's greatest advertising adventure."

Notwithstanding any previous religious objections Byron held concerning the shedding of blood in battle, he was apparently one of many who got swept away in the ensuing torrent of pro-war propaganda. In attempting to reconcile the relative ease with which Byron had been persuaded to enlist, it is certainly possible that in the run-up to war he was simply overwhelmed by the committee's pro-war sales pitch, and got sold a bill of goods. To some extent this conclusion may be warranted. After all, at this point in life, Byron was still relatively young and impressionable. That is not to imply, however, that he could be categorized as a bewildered buyer—or that he ever exhibited buyer's remorse once he had decided to enter the fray. To the contrary, as reflected in his writings both before and during the war, he was a well-informed and discerning young man. And once he had made up his mind that "we were on the side of Right," Byron was unwavering in that belief, never hesitating to advance that position with others.

Nor was he alone in his newfound enmity for Germany and unabashed enthusiasm for America's involvement in the war. Such beliefs were the all too predictable and frequent results of the committee's extraordinary exertions—especially with younger men like Byron. Not only was he in patriotic lockstep with many of his youthful brethren, he was in the vanguard of those who would ultimately rush off to enlist—taking the first step at 10:00 the following morning. Then, as promised, Mr. Jones made good on his offer to introduce Byron to the men "at the head of this new unit."

From there, Byron moved on to quickly achieve his objective—by the end of the day, he was officially enlisted in the 1st Michigan Ambulance Company.

3
MARKING TIME

At the time of its founding in 1821, Jackson, Michigan, was a typical midwestern town, located in the heart of Michigan's Lower Peninsula. Fertile soil was the marrow of Jackson's existence, agriculture its lifeblood.

In 1841, all that changed. With the arrival of the railroad, Jackson suddenly found itself infused with the pulse and vitality of a young nation on the move. Quickly outgrowing its local roots, Jackson became a regional rail hub with branch lines that spread far afield. By the end of the century, an ever-expanding array of goods, people, and ideas flowed through the streets of Jackson, making it second only to Detroit in terms of manufacturing, commerce, and influence in the area.

Home to forty thousand hard-working, God-fearing citizens, Jackson embodied the very essence of the American dream, with peace, prosperity, and religious freedom its cherished ideals. What distinguished Jackson from most other towns of its time, though, was the enduring belief among its citizens that those inalienable rights belonged to all Americans, not just a privileged few. It was in this egalitarian spirit that the party of Lincoln first took root "under the oaks" at a statewide convention of abolitionists in Jackson in 1854. And it was into this cradle of American idealism and midwestern progressive thought that Byron Fiske Field was born.

At the time of his birth in 1897, Byron was but the latest offshoot of one of the most prodigious family trees in the New World—the first Fields emigrated from England to Boston in 1629 as part of the great

Puritan diaspora. Soon thereafter, Fields spread out across the American landscape—migrating from Boston to Connecticut, then New York and Ohio, before reaching Michigan in the early 1800s. Prominent among those who had left their mark along the way were the Congregationalist minister Dudley David Field and his four sons: Stephen J. Field, U.S. Supreme Court justice; Cyrus W. Field, founder of the Atlantic Telegraph Company (constructor of the first transatlantic cable); Henry M. Field, Presbyterian pastor and editor of the *Evangelist*; and David D. Field, noted jurist and leading authority on American civil procedure. Following closely on their heels were Marshall Field, merchandizing magnate in Chicago; and Eugene Field, renowned poet.

In Frontier, Michigan, where Fields were among the first pioneers to stake their claim to the unsettled land, a primitive crossroads still bears the sign Field Corner. And deservedly so. In a cemetery nearby, row upon row of headstones bear testament to the long-standing connection between Fields and their country. The family's legacy is nothing short of remarkable. Not fewer than 154 Fields and their progeny took part in the American Revolution, the most notable being Thomas Jefferson, grandson of Mary Field. Scores more fought in the Civil War. Now it was Byron's turn to carry that standard in battle.

After returning from Detroit, Byron had to convince his parents to let him honor that obligation. It was not going to be easy. As he recounted in an essay titled "An Interlude," written after the war, his parents' reaction on first learning of his enlistment was anything but supportive.

> I got in just as they were sitting down for the evening meal.
>
> "Well, I've done it!"
>
> "What?" from both of them.
>
> "Enlisted!"
>
> "Oh, no you haven't."
>
> "Yes, sure enough—in Detroit—in the First Michigan Ambulance Company."
>
> "Why did you do it?"
>
> "Well, it seemed like the thing to do; we're in the war aren't we?"
>
> "Yes, but why did you have to enlist?"

"I didn't have to, but I thought I better."

There were some tears, some recrimination, but there was a glow in their eyes through the tears—"Yes, perhaps he should have done it." But he was only 19, and "I didn't raise my boy to be a soldier" hadn't been sung millions of times not to produce an effect in parents of only sons.

Eventually, Byron's parents reconciled themselves to the fact that their son was adamant about serving in the war, which must have been especially difficult for his mother, Birdie Ella, to accept. Not only was she being asked to allow her only able-minded son to march off to war, she was doing so in contravention of her religious background. She was, after all, a Power by birth. And unlike the Fields, who had a long and storied history of having fought in all of the country's prior wars, the Power family did not hold courage in combat as a time-honored tradition. And with good cause—the Powers were one of the oldest families of Quakers in Michigan. Birdie Ella's great-grandfather Arthur Power exhibited his own special brand of courage in being among the first wave of pioneers to migrate from New York to the wilds of Michigan in 1823, where he founded the Quaker village of Farmington, later known as Quakertown.

Although the Friends Society in Farmington disbanded just prior to Birdie's birth in 1867, no doubt her reluctance to allow Byron to march off to war was grounded in the bedrock of that long-standing peaceable tradition. The fact that she was able to finally set aside her own qualms about war and allow her son to go into harm's way proved how much she loved him—even if it did mean risking the ultimate sacrifice as a parent.

Byron's father also managed to see past whatever reservations he may have had concerning his son's decision to enlist; he accompanied Byron on a trip to Detroit to speak to the officers in charge of the ambulance company at an orientation meeting for new recruits. He was apparently satisfied that Byron was in good hands. Father and son returned to Jackson, where Byron spent the next few weeks at home waiting for orders to report for duty. In the interim, his parents found no shortage of chores around the house to occupy his time.

In a letter to Estelle dated June 27, Byron talked about "taking time by the forelock" to tackle all of "the things which have been saved for me to do." During the week, he "shingled a building," "carried in five tons of coal," "washed whole stores full of dishes," and helped his father write "some insurance." In his spare time, Byron applied himself to studying French grammar and military tactics, which he hoped would stand him in good stead when it came time for advancement later.

As always, Friday nights were reserved for choir practice. Although Byron was a much better piano player than a vocalist, that fact did not discourage him from singing in the choir—no doubt Birdie Ella (a graduate of the Music Conservatory at Albion College) had helped to nurture his interest in both endeavors. In his letter to Estelle on June 27, Byron proudly related that he sang two solos in practice that drew particular praise from Mrs. Weber, the choir director, who inquired if he'd been taking lessons. After replying that he hadn't, Byron joked that he'd "been going around with the Professor's daughter" lately, which must have accounted for the improvement.

In some small measure that response was actually true. An unintended benefit of courting Estelle came about as a result of the strict etiquette of the time—which required that Byron spend evenings at the Cozine household if he wanted to see Estelle. And since Estelle's father, Harlan Cozine, was the director of the Music Conservatory at Albion College and Estelle was an accomplished soprano, it was only natural that many of those evenings found Byron and her family gathered around the piano in the parlor singing late into the night. As it turned out, Byron would find great solace in music and the memory of those carefree evenings during the dark days that lay ahead.

In the Field household, Sunday belonged to the Lord. After attending church on the morning of June 24, Byron went to a meeting of young Methodists at the Epworth League, then spent the afternoon reading the Sunday paper and socializing with company at home as usual. But these were extraordinary times, and even on the Lord's Day, the drums of war continued to beat. At 6:00 that evening, Byron and his father stepped out of the family residence on the corner of First and High Streets and headed off to a special assembly at the Masonic Temple. The featured speaker was Dr. Samuel Dickie: long-standing president of Albion College, former mayor of the city of Albion, chairman of the National Prohibition Party, and above all else, citizen-patriot extraordinaire.

Byron's father, James, was an active member of the Jackson Lodge, but the assembly to hear Dr. Dickie speak would be open to male members of the public generally, and even though the meeting room of the lodge was large, seating was expected to be in short supply. According to Byron, "[T]here must have been fully fifteen-hundred men there."

At this point in a long and distinguished career, Dr. Dickie was a public figure of almost mythical proportions. His skill as an orator was legendary—as an ordained deacon of the Methodist Church, he had delivered countless sermons and other church-related speeches, and as chairman of the National Prohibition Party for twelve years, it was said that he'd traveled the entire span of the country, railing against the evils of alcohol in practically every city with a population over ten thousand citizens. A reverential hush fell over the crowd as Dr. Dickie strode purposefully across the stage. No introduction was necessary; Dickie commanded center stage like he owned it. His swept-back silver hair and neatly trimmed moustache glistened under the lights over the podium. Dressed in a black suit, Dickie stood silent for what seemed like an eternity while he fixed the waiting congregation with his piercing blue eyes. Then, in a baritone voice that seemed to resonate from on high, his words poured forth with the conviction of scripture.

Dr. Dickie began by relating that he had been in Germany at the outbreak of the war, and had personally suffered the humiliation cast on all foreigners unfortunate enough to be there at that time. After returning from Germany, Dr. Dickie had taken time out from his many duties to travel the length and breadth of the country, delivering essentially the same speech—a dire warning about the evils of Kaiserism and German *Kultur* in Europe. Dr. Dickie's indictment of the German government and people was categorical, describing Germany as "a monster who has outdone Attila." Dickie's condemnation of Germany as a nation of barbarians was purposeful, and in keeping with the Judeo-Christian view of war in its most basic terms: a battle between good and evil. Though overly simplistic, it was a necessary fiction for those with qualms about killing in war, as the demonization of one's enemies made killing them an honorable act in a just cause.

The cause of this war was anything but simple, however. For most Americans at that time, the underlying reasons for the war were a

"Despotism against Democracy." Front cover of *Leslie's Weekly*, May 3, 1917, illustrated by James Montgomery Flagg.

confusing cascade of events brought on by a host of factors of which the average citizen was for the most part ignorant, indifferent, or woefully misinformed. Even with the benefit of one hundred years' hindsight, scholars still debate the list of factors that contributed to the outbreak of hostilities in Europe, and the amount of blame to be apportioned among the war's participants. Among the principal causes of the war generally acknowledged by historians are the assassination of Archduke Franz Ferdinand (presumptive heir to the throne of Austria-Hungary); the internecine web of treaties and alliances among the countries of Europe and Russia that were triggered in the aftermath of the arch-duke's death; the waning power and tenuous relationship between the principal monarchs of Europe and Russia; wounded French pride over the loss of Alsace-Lorraine in the Franco-Prussian War of 1870; bur-geoning German nationalism; the economic status and imperialistic ambitions of Germany, France, Great Britain, Italy, Russia, and Austria-Hungary; and the persistent saber-rattling of European generals, poli-ticians, and arms manufacturers.

In practical terms, most of these factors had little or no impact on the everyday affairs of the average American. That speakers like Dr. Dickie were able to convince many U.S. citizens otherwise is one of the great examples of the persuasive power of propaganda. For nearly three years, Dickie had been cautiously but persistently advo-cating that the United States enter the war, being careful, though, not to use incendiary language that would unnecessarily alienate Ameri-cans opposed to the war. Dr. Dickie was mindful of the fact that many Christian Americans questioned whether the conflict in Europe was a just war. After all, the United States had not been directly attacked, and it was only months earlier that Woodrow Wilson had been reelected to a second term as the president who had kept the United States out of the war.

Antiwar sentiment was particularly strong in the Midwest, where German American immigrants were sympathetic to Germany's plight. But now that Germany's renewed submarine tactics had provided the justification for the U.S. Congress to declare war, patriotism ran high, and Dr. Dickie seized the opportunity to pick up the tempo and sharpen the rhetoric of his speeches, tackling the issue of misplaced German sympathy head-on. According to Dickie, the first three days after Germany declared war were filled with murder. French students who were touring, visiting, or working among "these modern vandals" were led out in squads and deliberately shot. Dr. Dickie talked about his many years of traveling throughout Germany, often on foot, as proof of his great familiarity with the common man. He stated unequivocally that it was impossible for middle-class Germans not to show their contempt for any other nationality than German.

Incredulity dripped from Dr. Dickie's voice as he recounted a German minister who'd had the temerity to claim that atrocities described in the press were exaggerated or entirely wrong. Dickie said that, not being a minister himself, he "told that minister a thing or two"—having just returned from Europe where he'd witnessed indescribable horrors and heard of others from Christian officers whose eyes were filled with tears of anger as they recounted them.

Dickie's disagreement with the German minister was by no means an isolated incident. In 1917, there was still much debate in America whether German troops had committed atrocities in Belgium and France during the first days of the war. Rumors ran rampant. Firsthand accounts like Dickie's were few and far between. It is now known that German soldiers did in fact execute over six thousand innocent Belgian and French civilians whom invading troops suspected of being resistance fighters (called *franc tireurs*, or free shooters), or those who were deemed unduly sympathetic to the Allied cause. It is also equally clear, however, that German soldiers did not eat babies, cut off children's arms and feet as tokens of war, or summarily execute the elderly, as some reports had wildly claimed.

Dickie was aware that most of those who listened to him were dependent on the observations of others as to the state of affairs in Europe, and he sought to press his advantage in that regard by using personal anecdotes to promote his case for war against Germany—telling of yet another German sympathizer who was so badly misinformed he claimed that Germany was as much a democracy as the United States. Dickie wagged his head in disbelief. A few men joined in, grumbling at the comparison.

"Gentlemen, do you understand the system of German government?"

Dickie let the question hang in the air dramatically before continuing on to explain that Germany was governed by a king, the Kaiser, who appointed representatives to serve in two legislative bodies in a system that was nothing more than a "pseudo-democracy." In reality, this assertion by Dickie was a pseudo-truth—although Germany was not a republic by American democratic standards, it was not an absolute monarchy either. Suffrage existed for men over the age of twenty-five, and popular elections were held to select representatives to serve in the Reichstag. Dickie was not about to let those inconvenient details stop him from overegging the pudding, though—he had a concoction to bake.

"The greatest example of a centralized one-man power government in the world is held in the hollow of Wilhelm's hand," Dickie proclaimed, holding out a cupped hand as if to offer proof.

If there were any German Americans in the audience, none looked ready to debate the issue with him. In a room where most of the men had never ventured further afield than Chicago, the vast knowledge and worldly experience of Dr. Dickie carried the force of law. And not just in a figurative sense—once the United States had declared war on Germany, speaking out against that decision was fraught with legal peril. Only three weeks earlier, on June 5, 1917, Congress had enacted the Espionage Act. This law and its successor, the Sedition Act of 1918, would be used as tools to stifle antiwar sentiment. For those with qualms about the righteousness of this war, imposition of these new strictures was no idle concern, as would later be evidenced by the arrest of newspaper editor Victor Berger and Socialist Party labor leader Eugene Debs for espousing views in opposition to the war. On this particular occasion, though, Byron made no mention of any dissent as Dickie continued his assault on all things Teutonic by zeroing in on German elitism as propounded by the present Kaiser and his father before him—describing it as an indoctrination in which ordinary Germans had been taught to believe in the divine right of kings and the superiority of all things German over everything else.

Dickie's anti-German screed didn't stop there, however—he took it one precipitous step further, equating German nationalism with a "delusional obsession" in which an entire nation had apparently gone "insane." Then, in the next breath, he seemingly did the same—losing all apparent sense of equilibrium by openly and unabashedly advocating to his audience that only "wholesale killing" could stop this insanity. It was a startling statement to make in a public forum. Under normal circumstances, Dickie's words would have sounded like the reckless rhetoric of a warmongering lunatic. But these were exceptional times—it seems that the run-up to war always is. And when viewed in that context, his exhortation was perfectly in keeping with the impassioned preaching of others. Even religious leaders who had originally opposed the United States entering the war now favored taking up arms. From the Bible-thumping evangelist Billy Sunday to Charles R. Brown, the staid dean of the Yale University Divinity School, ministers numbered among those who had changed their minds. Some were so zealous in their advocacy for war that they condemned well-intentioned pacifists as "parasites," "cowards," and "traitors."

The reluctance of pacifists to answer the call to arms was not unique to this war. The search for some measure of spiritual equanimity in the face of war had always been a struggle for Christian Americans. As Thomas Paine so succinctly put it many years before, these truly were "the times that try men's souls." Dickie undoubtedly understood this—even though Congress had declared war on Germany, some Americans still needed to be convinced that the conflict in Europe was a just war. For many in the audience that night, Dickie's words, though extreme, provided that moral justification.

As always, Dickie's delivery was masterful, his logic seemingly unassailable. After laying out his case for war against Germany, Dickie paused to catch his breath. A sea of determined faces looked back.

"Gentlemen." Dickie's voice was grave with purpose. "The great business of this country and her allies today is to kill Germans! The German Empire must be dismembered or our grandchildren will have to fight another war!"

Any pretense at measured response got swept from the room by the force of Dickie's words. Men sprang to their feet in unison. The applause was thunderous. Byron's hands ached from clapping. Byron would later write to Estelle that "they listened for an hour and a half to a wonderful speech . . . mainly the same as the Commencement speech" that Dr. Dickie had delivered at Albion College only weeks earlier. It was a speech that he would deliver many times more in the months to come. Speakers of Dr. Dickie's ilk were in great demand, especially now that the United States needed to raise an army. By European standards, the U.S. Army was relatively small—a mere 120,000 strong at the time war was declared. It was estimated that an additional 1 million men would be needed to field an adequate fighting force. By the time Byron enlisted on May 25, only 73,000 men had volunteered for service. To remedy that, on May 18 Congress enacted the Selective Service Act of 1917. For additional good measure, a Committee on Public Information had been empaneled to launch a national propaganda campaign to drum up support for the war. In the months to come, 75,000 speakers called "Four Minute Men" would deliver over 750,000 four-minute speeches at public assemblies totaling more than 314 million people. But nobody was better at it than Dr. Dickie, especially with a receptive audience of earnest young listeners like Byron.

Rousing speeches delivered to assembled throngs were nothing new in the annals of war. Old men had been exhorting youth to take up arms since time immemorial. On college campuses, town squares, and even at church camp meetings, young men were being called upon to do their patriotic duty. Byron was in the first wave of American men to answer the call. By the fall of 1917, college enrollment would plummet over 40 percent as college-aged men rushed off to enlist. Patriotic fervor became so acute that the War Department and American educators established the Student Army Training Corps (SATC) as a way to keep young men on college campuses. Under Dr. Dickie, Albion College had already formulated plans to include a military training program as part of the curriculum. The following year, Albion would be made into an SATC military post with barracks housing over two hundred student soldiers. All that was still to be realized, though. For Byron, the future was already at hand.

By the time the meeting was over, darkness had fallen. Under the thin light of a first-quarter moon, Byron and his father walked home in quiet reflection. After the experience, Byron was thoroughly convinced that he had made the right decision.

The time for action was now.

4
PASSING MUSTER

From the time of its inception as the Michigan Legion, the Michigan National Guard had compiled a long and distinguished record of service to the country. Like other National Guard units, the Michigan National Guard could trace its roots back to Article I, Section 8 of the U.S. Constitution, which recognized the existence of state militia and the power of Congress to call "forth the Militia to execute the Laws of the Union, suppress Insurrections and repel Invasions." It was under this authority that the Michigan Legion was first mustered into service during the War of 1812 to protect Michigan settlers from attacks by Shawnee warriors and British regulars. Since then, Michigan militiamen had never failed to answer the call to duty.

Beginning with the American Revolution, state militias had provided the bulk of troops in all of the country's wars—the War of 1812, the Mexican War, the first days of the Civil War, and most recently the Spanish-American War. In 1903, this time-honored tradition was formally mandated with the passage of the Militia Act, whereby state militias were designated National Guard units to be used as the primary reserve force of the U.S. Army. In 1916, this commitment was further strengthened by congressional enactment of the National Defense Act, which enabled the president to mobilize National Guard units during time of war.

On Friday, July 12, 1917, in keeping with that grand tradition, and by invoking this newly vested authority, President Woodrow Wilson issued an order federalizing National Guard units in New York, Ohio, West Virginia, Michigan, Wisconsin, Iowa, Nebraska, North and South

Dakota, and Minnesota. In accordance with that order, guardsmen from the 31st Infantry Regiment and the 1st Michigan Ambulance Company were told to report to their home station at the Detroit Armory the following Monday.

At 9:00 that morning, Byron arrived in Detroit on the train from Jackson. By the time he'd hustled over to the armory, fifteen hundred men were already packed inside. On the train ride in, Byron had wondered what he would find at the armory. He wasn't entirely sure but it certainly wasn't this—the most noticeable thing about this group was its utter lack of uniformity. The conglomeration of men appeared to be from all walks of life except for the grizzled veterans who'd served in the recent Pancho Villa Expedition on the Mexican border. In their pointed campaign hats and drab olive uniforms, the "Border Rats" stuck out like clusters of cactus in a vegetable patch. The atmosphere in the armory was an uneasy mixture of feigned nonchalance by the veterans and nervous chatter from the rookies. Each company had been allowed to recruit in excess of the usual war strength of 150 men in order to fill vacancies that were anticipated from the imposition of new federal medical standards. Byron was one of those in question—whether his eyesight would pass muster with army doctors remained to be seen. Until then, Byron told himself, his fate was in God's hands, and he turned his attention to taking care of the things he could control.

Judging by the other men in the room, Byron was confident that he belonged—that he had the right stuff. What he didn't have at the moment, though, was a uniform. Most of the other recruits didn't either, but that hadn't stopped some of them from improvising. Here and there, military hats and caps of varying shapes and colors bobbed on the surface of the crowd. A few of the men wore uniform ensembles that were mostly mixed but seldom matched. Blouses, breeches, and leggings that came from different eras and branches of the service were sprinkled throughout. Shoes came in all styles and colors. What was consistent among all of the men, though, was their enthusiasm and pride. Uniformed or not, it was truly an army of citizen soldiers.

Roll call was held at 10:00 for both units. After the infantry regiment fell in and marched off, Captain Robert Baskerville addressed the members of the 1st Michigan Ambulance Company separately. Baskerville was the company's commanding officer. In Byron's estimation, he looked to be in his forties, with the stern demeanor of a school principal. He was in fact a practicing physician in Detroit who'd been a member of the Michigan National Guard since 1906. In establishing his bona fides, he told the men that he'd served in the Mexican Border War.

Baskerville informed the company that the initial training regimen would be rudimentary, lasting only a few weeks before the unit moved out to a basic training camp. Training in Detroit would be held daily from Monday to Friday, with Saturday a half day and nights and Sundays off. Mornings would be devoted to drills conducted by Captain Frederick McAfee, Lieutenant Arlington Lecklider, and Sergeant First Class Frank Gallagher. Afternoons were to be focused on medical lectures, anatomy classes at the morgue, and a hands-on emergency clinic at the hospital. The company would be rationed at the Henry Clay Hotel, where breakfast would be served at 7, lunch at 11, and dinner at 5. Because they would not be sleeping overnight in barracks, attendance at meals, except for lunch, wasn't mandatory.

The next morning at 7:00 sharp, Byron was seated in the makeshift mess hall at the Henry Clay Hotel. In order to do that, however, he had to become a Methodist circuit rider of sorts. Because his parents could not afford to put him up at a hotel in Detroit, and he wouldn't be able to commute from Jackson each morning and still get to the mess hall on time, other accommodations would have to be found on very short notice. Even in times of war, though, the Good Lord works in mysterious ways.

For years Byron's father had been the superintendent of the adult Sunday school program at the Methodist Church in Jackson, and as an attendee of many regional church conferences, he'd developed a network of contacts in the Detroit area, a couple of whom had agreed to put Byron up for a few days. On Monday night Byron bunked at Stan Silby's house in Wayne, a suburb of Detroit. For the next few nights, he stayed at Frank Benish's place on Twenty-Fifth Street in the city. The small one-story houses made for tight quarters, but the company was good. On Saturday afternoon Byron rushed back to Jackson for the weekend.

Other than attending Albion College, which was only a stone's throw from Jackson, Byron had never been away from home for an extended period of time. Although he had never considered himself a homebody, for the first time in his life Byron was out of his comfort zone. As he confessed to Estelle in a letter earlier that week, he'd never "spent such lonesome days." The following week, Byron rented a room at the YMCA in Detroit. Bob Gerholz from Jackson was also staying there. The son of German immigrants, Bob had no qualms about fighting in the war and had enlisted in the army as an infantryman. Bob's unit would move out shortly for Fort Sheridan.

Byron's stay at the Y wouldn't be for long either. Rumor had it the company would be moving out on August 1. Until then, to pass the time in the evening, Bryon went to Sunday school classes at the Central Methodist Church downtown, and meetings of the Epworth League at the Methodist Episcopal Church on Grand Avenue, where Frank Benish and Stan Silby introduced him to other churchgoing young men and women. Byron found the meetings a godsend, writing to Estelle that "I hear so much cussing and swearing and smell so much smoke . . . that the sound and odor of a prayer meeting is actually refreshing. I've chewed gum till my mouth aches trying to overcome the tobacco smoke."

Byron's days were filled with more than just foul language and the stench of cigarette smoke. When the men weren't busy drilling, they were listening to lectures. The first lecture the company heard was "Military Courtesy," an army euphemism for the strict rules of engagement between enlisted men and officers, and the fines and punishments that went along with disobeying them. It was Lieutenant Lecklider's job to reinforce those rules, in addition to toughening the men up, which he did every morning from 8:00 until 10:30, marching and drilling the men into a state of near exhaustion.

Medical lectures proved to be even more taxing. Coming after lunch, the pungent odor and grisly specter of corpses at the morgue were difficult for some of the men to stomach. For others, it was the sight of fresh blood in the operating room that left them limp and pale. With Byron, it was the agony of patients in pain that was most unnerving. In a letter to Estelle's father dated July 23, Byron recounted:

Our work here consists of drills and hikes in the morning and medical school in the afternoon. Today we had school for two hours straight—one lecture—on fractures and breaks to various bones especially those of the head. The work will perhaps be a little hard at first for me as I have a bit too much sympathy for the suffering and am inclined to let my feelings unnerve me. Nor do I intend to let this service render me harsh, but rather more gentle, only my ministrations can be directed now.

Helping to guide Byron in those ministrations was Dr. Max Ballin, the chief of surgery at Harper Hospital. Captain Baskerville had asked Dr. Ballin to instruct the men on the types of trauma they would encounter at the front, and the basic emergency procedures they'd need to treat them. Byron and Ballin were kindred spirits of a sort—both were determined to do no harm. Yet only one of them was still naive enough to believe that America's declaration of war was the simple answer to a very complex problem.

Like many other German Americans, Dr. Ballin was still tied to the country of his origin. Ballin had graduated from the University of Berlin in 1892 and was widely recognized as a brilliant surgeon, but he was Jewish, which meant that he was unable to rise above a certain level in the medical hierarchy of Germany without first renouncing his faith and converting to Christianity. Ballin was prepared to do neither. Instead, he chose to immigrate to the United States, where his career flourished. He had three brothers and other relatives who still lived in Germany, however, and he worried deeply about their safety, in addition to the well-being of many other good people there: Jewish or not. War killed indiscriminately. Unlike Byron, Ballin understood this.

Dr. Ballin had been a colleague and mentor of Captain Baskerville's at Harper Hospital, and Baskerville was a devoted disciple of Ballin's teaching method. Ballin painstakingly took the time to explain to his students every detail of what he did in the operating room and why he was doing it. Then he would make his students roll up their sleeves and do it too—which left some of the men woozy. Compared to the chaos and carnage that awaited them at the front, the sterile conditions of Dr. Ballin's operating room would soon be nothing more than a fond memory.

Indeed, the memory of Ballin's enthusiasm and dedication to his work would continue to influence many of the men long after the war had ended. In his letter to Estelle's father, Byron remarked almost presciently, "The medical training which we are having is very valuable, and those who do survive the war are surely going to have a fine asset." Many of the men Ballin helped to train would apply their medical training when they returned from the war. In 1931, while working for the Commonwealth Edison Company in Chicago, Byron coauthored a book on employee health and first aid in the workplace. Byron's friend and tent mate Horace J. Sprague later became director of the American Red Cross services for the Midwest.

At that moment, the immediate focus for Byron and the rest of the men was on passing muster with the army. In his letter to Estelle's father, Byron talked about the unit being inspected by federal mustering officers. A few days later, word finally came down that the 1st Michigan Ambulance Company had been officially accepted in federal service. But Byron had still not received a decision from the army doctors concerning his eyesight. In the interim he continued to think positively, if not romantically. In a letter to Estelle's father, after Byron finished extolling Estelle's maidenly virtues, he closed with an almost chivalrous flourish: "I hope so much that nothing may happen to harm her or to in any other way molest your happy home. I count none outside my family circle as better friends than you and yours. As you have no sons to fight, I'd like to fight for you, too. God must be near us. We must win, and cannot if we cannot rightly claim His aid. Pray for me often my friend, that I may come back or go Home—whichever—spotless."

When viewed in the harsh light of today's world, such idealism about war would seem unabashedly melodramatic, if not totally misguided. In the context of this particular time in history, however, Byron's words were entirely appropriate and undoubtedly viewed by Estelle's father as heartfelt and selfless. Most important, though, they were principled. In Christian theology, the set of principles that legitimized the shedding of blood in a just war was hardly new. First articulated by St. Augustine in AD 400 and then nine hundred years later by Thomas Aquinas, this ethos was commonly understood and accepted by devout Christians as an important and necessary prerequisite to engaging in war. For a war to be just in the eyes of the Lord, it must first be an unavoidable response to an unprovoked act of aggression. Then, the level of violence used in response to that aggression must be proportional to the threat presented. And last, that violence must discriminate between combatants and civilians. What was new about this war, however, were the weapons of mass destruction being unleashed on the world for the very first time. Whether Byron or anyone else would be able to withstand their indiscriminate fury and return from the war in one piece, much less "spotless," was cause for grave concern.

On Sunday, July 29, Byron's mother and father accompanied Estelle's family to Detroit, where they all attended services at the Central Methodist Church, after which they enjoyed a picnic supper on Belle Isle. It was on this visit that Estelle's younger sister, Ruth, gave Byron a pocket-sized edition of the New Testament that he would carry with him throughout the war. Tucked inside the Bible were two small typewritten pages containing Psalms 1 and 23—"The Lord is my Shepherd" from the Old Testament. At the bottom of Psalm 1, the parenthetical question "Do you know the Psalm by memory and experience?" was also typed in. In the harrowing months to come, Byron would do his best to answer that question faithfully.

On August 1, Byron finally got the word he'd been waiting for—he was medically approved for service. Others in the unit were not. In a letter to Estelle on this date, Byron noted that 18 men out of 130 in the company had been rejected for various medical reasons, with the fate of 20 others still to be determined. As the final composition of the unit began to solidify, Byron noticed that discipline was stiffening as well. Officers had started to distance themselves from enlisted men, telling them that they'd soon be leaving for basic training camp at Grayling, Michigan. In preparation for their departure, uniforms were issued to the men. A second set of inoculations and vaccinations for typhoid and smallpox were also dispensed.

Rumor that a third series of shots was in store came as no surprise. Over the centuries, war and pestilence had gone hand in hand. This war was no exception. Recent outbreaks of smallpox in Germany, Austria, France, Poland, and Russia had been well publicized. Estelle's

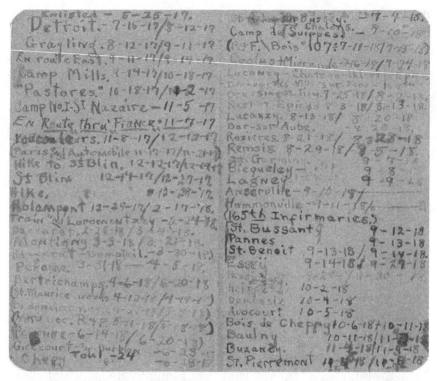

Inside cover of the pocket Bible Ruth Cozine gave to Byron on July 29, 1917. Here Byron wrote a chronology of his post of assignments during the war.

concern about this was evident in Byron's letters. Other contagions were waiting for the men in the trenches of France as well—tetanus, trench fever, dysentery, and diphtheria—for which there were no known antidotes other than good hygiene and even better luck. The worst scourge of all, however, had yet to make its dramatic and deadly entrance on the world stage. The great influenza had been slowly and quietly incubating in isolated pockets around the globe—like army training camps. By the time the Armistice was declared in November 1918, this horrific disease and the pneumonia that often accompanied it would end up killing more American soldiers than the Great War itself, and over 20 million people worldwide.

On August 12, all that was yet to come—the threat of death and disease still as remote as the dark side of moon. In the bright glow of the afternoon sun, an aura of supreme confidence seemed to envelop

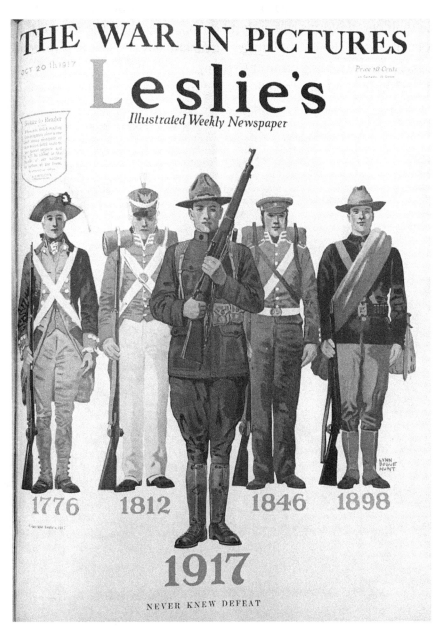

"Never Knew Defeat." Front cover of *Leslie's Weekly*, October 20, 1917.

the men as they paraded through the streets of downtown Detroit in their new uniforms and perfect health. On reaching the Third Street Depot, the Michigan Ambulance Company eagerly boarded railroad cars for basic training camp at Grayling.

Their long odyssey had finally begun.

5
THIS IS NO SUNDAY SCHOOL

The train ride north was more of a stag party on wheels than a military expedition. With the men crammed eight to a compartment, spirits ran high, the enthusiasm contagious. Around midnight, as the gravity of exhaustion began to take hold, things finally quieted down. By the time the train reached Grayling, most of the men had dozed off.

The men had been told that Camp Grayling was in the middle of nowhere, but that didn't begin to describe the desolation that greeted them when they awoke. Overnight a cold rain had blown in from the north. In the thin light of early morning, the men looked out on the scorched remains of what once were miles of pristine forest. The fire-blackened earth stretched clear to Lake Margrethe, where a stiff wind could be seen whipping white caps on the slate-gray water. Some of the men joked about deserting.

As the train pulled into Grayling, the rain slackened. In the distance, a tree-covered ridge stretched across the western horizon. Nestled at the foot of the hills was Camp Grayling—a vast expanse of tents seeming to sprout from the ground like mushrooms. By the time the company had detrained and tramped its way through the mud to reach camp, the rain had stopped completely. Men immediately set about pitching tents on waterlogged platforms. Stoves, cots, and blankets arrived in short order. It would take a lot more than that, though, to cut the chill. They were in the North Country now. For most of the men, it seemed very far from home.

After a long first day, each soldier was rewarded with a cold roast beef sandwich. Some of the men groused, but Byron was a happy camper.

In a letter to Estelle that evening, Byron wrote that "the place is ideal" with "dozens of mess halls and new buildings." Byron wasn't entirely mistaken about the relative merits of the camp. Established in 1913 on a grant of land from lumber baron Rasmus Hanson, Camp Grayling was one of the largest and newest National Guard training camps in the country. Although its rustic accommodations would never be mistaken for the Ritz, with its permanent wooden structures that housed mess halls, an administration building, and an infirmary, it was a relatively desirable base at which to train. Military units from other states and Canada often sought to use its facilities.

The next day, clear skies brought noticeably warmer weather, and things began to look up as the men settled into a regular routine. After a hot breakfast at the mess hall, mornings were consumed with three hours of close-order drills, calisthenics, and double-timing it around camp. Afternoons were devoted to litter-bearing exercises and first aid instructions. In the evenings, the men entertained themselves playing cards and other games of chance, or listening and singing along to soldiers playing guitars, mandolins, and a cornet. At the end of his first night in camp, Byron wrote to Estelle that he had "retired early using Ruth's testament for the first time. War orders or compelling sickness not preventing, I

1st Michigan Ambulance Corps of Detroit at Grayling Camp, *Detroit Free Press*, September 2, 1917. Note Byron's notations in the margin identifying himself and other members of the unit.

shall read the Book every night. I can see that much prayer and reading of this Book will be of great help to myself and pure action and speech of more help to my fellows." Like attending church on the Sabbath, reading the Bible was a practice that Byron would do his best to observe.

On Wednesday evening, a feast was held around a roaring bonfire to celebrate the unit's induction into the newly created 42nd Division. The Rainbow Division, as it would soon be called, was a compilation of the best National Guard units from across the country. In recognition of its extraordinary service in the Mexican Border War, the 1st Michigan Ambulance Company had been selected to be part of the new division and would henceforth be redesignated the 168th Ambulance Company—one of four ambulance companies assigned to the division's 117th Sanitary Train. In addition to the four ambulance companies, the sanitary train was composed of four field hospitals whose medical personnel would be responsible for tending to all of the division's ailments, from sniffles to deadly wounds.

Grateful rookies showered the veterans with praise. In a show of mock appreciation, the veterans reciprocated by holding an impromptu kangaroo court that immediately handed down a verdict requiring the rookies to submit to rites of initiation. As part of the initiation ceremony, each rookie was made to run a gauntlet of forty-two veterans, who swatted them with small straps of hide. After which the esteemed jurists reconvened and ruled that the men had to crawl through a second time just to ensure that each man received a full fifty swats. It was all in good fun; no man was worse for the wear.

Byron shared a tent with nine other rookies. A square space only fifteen feet wide, the tent barely left room for the men to wiggle. According to a diagram Byron included in a letter to Estelle, a narrow aisle ran down the spine of the tent from the front door to the back flap. Ten cots were spaced out evenly, five ribs on either side. In the center sat a potbellied stove. One man's Victrola was perched on a small table between two of the cots. A wooden gearbox anchored the aisle at the back of the tent. It was extremely close quarters, but it was a good group of men. Over time, they'd end up sharing just about everything in their lives, including germs. Byron would get especially

Cover page of the sheet music for "Over There," George M. Cohan's popular wartime song, 1918. The illustration is by Norman Rockwell. (Library of Congress.)

close to two of the men, only one of whom would return from the war alive.

At night when Byron wasn't playing checkers or writing letters home to Estelle and his parents, he was quietly reading passages from the pocket Bible that Ruth had given him. Others gambled. Herbert Jackson, whom Byron befriended, played romantic songs on his Victrola. Most of the men had wives or sweethearts back home, and as the days passed thoughts of home grew stronger. Some of the men hoped for weekend passes, others talked about taking "French leave." A few of the men took to sneaking into town to get drunk.

In an effort to keep the men entertained, boxing and wrestling competitions between the units were staged at night. When compared to the lure of sweethearts and the comforts of home, however, the satisfaction derived from watching exhibitions of the manly arts took lonely soldiers only so far. Before men started to go AWOL, the higher-ups started doling out weekend passes, a few at a time. On August 23, Byron got a forty-eight-hour pass for home. He was one of the lucky ones; others would have to wait their turn. That didn't stop some of them from slipping away, though. As Byron caught the train home, Herbert Jackson and three other men from his tent climbed aboard too—all sneaking out on French leave.

That Sunday night, after spending a wonderful weekend at home with his parents and Estelle, Byron returned to camp as ordered. His only regret was not being able to kiss Estelle, even though he got to hold her in his arms. The four men from his tent who'd gone AWOL returned from leave a bit disappointed too—all had been tracked down by Captain Baskerville in Detroit. It ended up costing each man a thirty-day stint in the guardhouse. In a letter to Estelle written on September 2, Byron included an article from the *Detroit News* recounting the exploits of Herbert Jackson and the other fugitives from his tent. One of the escapees had actually managed to get married before being apprehended. Another man was intercepted at the altar by Captain Baskerville. In the presence of the bride and the wedding party, Baskerville made it clear that if the groom went ahead and tied the knot, not only would he be severing his ties to the ambulance company, he'd also be roping himself into an immediate transfer to an infantry regiment. On carefully considering his options, the groom decided to postpone the ceremony.

By no means did Byron's tent contain the only group of homesick delinquents. For the next few days, Baskerville continued to round up more strays, corralling an additional thirteen rookies in the guard-house. By week's end, all but six were back in the fold. Eventually everyone returned, but all was not forgiven. Seven of the men were immediately discharged for a host of reasons. Good replacements would have to be found on short notice—rumor had it the unit would be heading east for Camp Mills on Long Island, New York, in just one week. To discourage any further defections, additional guards were posted at the camp perimeter. In drawing guard duty several nights that week, Byron became his brother's keeper.

In a letter to Estelle on September 6, Byron wrote that he hoped she would be able to visit him along with his parents that Sunday. He talked about his tentmate Jackson playing romantic songs on the Vic-trola and how homesick all of the men were. Byron also included a humorous magazine clipping on the great popularity and joy derived from the new fad of kissing. Although Bryon hoped that Estelle would appreciate it as a joke and not think less of him, it was clear from his letters that he was desperately lonely.

In the next few days, a sense of impending departure began to build as additional equipment was distributed to the men. A lecture on the need for censorship and the use of preprinted postcards was given. The postcards contained a series of authorized sentences to choose from, reading: "I am quite well"; "I have been admitted to hospital—sick—or wounded"; "I am being sent down to the base"; "I have received no letter from you." The sender scratched out the messages that didn't apply. British troops at the front had been using these cards to eliminate leaks of information in the event that letters inadvertently fell into German hands. At this point, it was still unclear if American troops would be required to use these cards or simply rely on offi-cers to censor their letters. Either way, Byron was taking no chances. On Friday, September 7, while he was still capable of communicating freely, Byron went into town and dashed off a short telegram to Estelle informing her that they were departing on "Monday at the latest. . . . Send lots of letters."

On the 8th, Byron followed up with a letter containing inside information he'd gotten from a transportation sergeant on the route to Long Island the company would take. After mentioning that Jackson was one of the stops the train would make along the way, Byron closed by saying, "I would give almost anything to see you once more before we go." Monday the 10th found Byron still at Grayling, however. In a letter written to Estelle that day, Byron apologized for getting everyone's hopes up needlessly, noting that the company "may not go the Jackson route at all." At the time of writing the letter, Byron was unaware that Estelle was probably the most disappointed person of all—having waited the entire day at the Jackson rail depot for a troop train that never came.

As it turned out, Byron's latest hunch was correct—ultimately, their route would not take them through Jackson. On the afternoon of September 11, the company abruptly broke camp and moved out for Camp Mills. As the men boarded the train, the exact route the company would take was the subject of much speculation. If the route took them through Detroit, the men wanted to at least wave good-bye to relatives as the train rolled through. By the time the train pulled into the rail yard at Bay City, it was already dusk. During the brief stop, a few of the men detrained and managed to locate the yardmaster, who confided that the train was scheduled to pull into Detroit between 2:00 and 3:00 in the morning. On hearing this, Byron and a group of men immediately detrained and dashed off telegrams to loved ones nearby. It was terribly short notice, but a few parents and relatives did manage to make it to the Detroit rail depot—Byron's father among them. The stop lasted only fifteen minutes. Still, Byron made good use of that time, giving his father hugs to pass on to his mother, Estelle, and others.

After leaving Detroit, the train entered Canada through a tunnel under the Detroit River. For the better part of the following day, the train traveled across lower Ontario, reentering the United States over the Whirlpool Rapids Bridge, a mile above Niagara Falls. As Byron later recounted to Estelle, the train barreled on to Syracuse, Schenectady, Utica, and Albany. At Jersey City, the train finally came to a halt. Byron awoke and peered out through the window. Barely visible in the early morning fog was the Singer Tower in Lower Manhattan. For the time being, though, this was as close to seeing "New Yawk" as Byron would get—from there, the train entered a tunnel that crossed under the Hudson and East Rivers before resurfacing in Brooklyn, where it headed on to Long Island. After forty-two restless hours, the company finally reached Mineola, where they waited on a sidetrack for three hours while troop trains ahead of them unloaded legions of men and tons of equipment.

Detraining with their equipment, Byron and the company marched from the train depot into camp. Camp Mills was located on a tract of land in the middle of the Hempstead Plains on Long Island. Named in honor of Spanish-American War hero Albert L. Mills, the base was established as a temporary camp to assemble and mobilize the 42nd Division. The flat farmland was the perfect spot on which to pitch a tent—thousands of them, in fact. On August 20 the first unit to arrive at Camp Mills had been the Field Hospital from Washington, DC. In the next three weeks, an additional thirty thousand soldiers from National Guard units in twenty-six states would descend on the quaint village of Hempstead. The 168th Ambulance Company was one of the last units to enter camp. By that time, all the good real estate was spoken for, so the unit staked its claim on a small ridge next to the Oklahoma Ambulance Company. As fellow midwesterners, members of the two units became fast friends. It was a close working relationship that would serve them well during the war.

As it turned out, one of the few advantages to the sloping patch of ground on which the company had encamped was that it afforded the men an unobstructed view of the enormous sprawling camp and aerodrome nearby. In a letter to Estelle on September 17, Bryon wrote that "it takes twenty minutes fast walking to go across the camp proper. . . . Already the aeroplanes have become so common to us that we hardly notice them. The sound of their engines is very loud, and continues from morning until night. If it is possible I am certainly going to take a ride in one before we leave." Byron was almost certainly not alone in his flights of fancy—for a foot soldier, the appeal of being able to soar high above the daily grind was understandable, especially in 1917, when "aeroplanes" were still newfangled machines. It was an allure that would continue to tempt Byron throughout the war.

For the duration of his time at the camp, however, Byron's days would be grounded in the hard reality of basic training. As noted in a letter to Estelle, this was real camp, not like Grayling. The days were long and the work hard. Discipline was stricter. Old equipment dating back to the Spanish-American War was recalled until the latest equipment could be issued as the 42nd Division readied itself for a new kind of warfare. The men were kept on the go from reveille to taps—doing calisthenics, close-order drills, ten-mile marches with sixty-five-pound packs, litter-bearing exercises, inspections, and formal battalion reviews.

Camp facilities were as rugged as the training. There were no permanent mess halls. Men sat and ate wherever they could. Makeshift kitchens were set up in each company, requiring the men to stand in long lines waiting to be served unappetizing army fare. Many soldiers supplemented their meals on "Robber's Row," where civilian sutlers sold extra victuals at exorbitant prices. Outdoor cold-water showers were rigged between units. Although the days were a bit warmer than at Grayling, during the night a cool fog rolled in on the breeze from Long Island Sound, soaking the men to the bone. To make matters worse, the army was strictly enforcing a medical order that required soldiers to sleep with the flaps of their tents open to prevent the spread of consumption. With only two wool blankets per soldier and no stoves to heat the tents, the cure was possibly worse than the disease, nearly killing the men from exposure. Two months later, the camp would be shut down after governors complained that guardsmen from their states were being unnecessarily and dangerously exposed to the elements. It was a raw experience for sure, but it was nothing compared to the conditions that awaited the men in France.

As inhospitable as conditions in camp were, the surrounding towns couldn't have been more accommodating. On September 30, forty thousand spectators turned out to cheer three brigades of the Rainbow Division as they marched by on review. Whenever soldiers wandered into town, the citizens welcomed them with a mixture of warmth and curiosity. By 1917, the provincial nature of the country was already beginning to change with the introduction of the telephone, automobile, and airplane. But it was the Great War that provided the catalyst for even greater change as it brought together large numbers of disparate peoples, suddenly shrinking the country and the world in a way not seen before. As East met West in the towns that surrounded Camp Mills, a typical encounter might unfold as follows:

> "Where are you from young man?"
>   "Nebraska, ma'am."
>   "There are lots of men here from Nebraska."
>   "Yes, quite a few, ma'am."
>   "Well, Nebraska must be a good sized town then, what part of New York is it in?"

At night, gracious Long Islanders were anxious to do their patriotic duty, hosting parties in the villages nearby. Byron went to his share, even one at the exclusive Meadow Brook Country Club. Estelle, understandably concerned, discreetly inquired if any of the young ladies had caught Byron's fancy. Bryon assured her that he had eyes only for her. Not that she had reason to doubt his affection. He wrote often. His letters were filled with words of love and expressed how very much he missed her. It was the first time he'd been "away from home when the gladiolas were in bloom."

On the 19th the men got paid and "excitement reigned," which for the most part meant that the men got to settle their outstanding debts, drink, smoke, and gamble—none of which Byron wanted or needed to do. Byron had led a relatively sheltered existence in Jackson and remained steadfast to the principles that had been instilled in him by strict parents. Not in a self-righteous way, however: Byron wore his religious conviction as inconspicuously as the lightly penciled notation on the inside cover of the Bible that Estelle's sister Ruth had given him—"I.Cor. 10:14—Temptation Defeated." Byron had been hoping that Camp Mills would "be all business from the word go": that there would be less opportunity for idle mischief, and that discipline in the company would improve. He would be sorely disappointed. In a letter written on the 20th, he lamented, "This is no Sunday School." Indeed, it was becoming apparent to Byron that, like a good many other institutions, the army had an arbitrary set of rules and practices, and these weren't necessarily based on merit, or even fairly applied. In a letter to Estelle on October 12, Byron began to let his disillusionment show.

> It is a peculiar thing—this army and camp life—one cannot explain it to an outsider appreciatively. Here are a lot of men who before had nothing in common except their sex. Here they come, in our company three fourths are volunteers—now all have some things in common. We all fight a common enemy, we all serve under the same commander, and are governed by exactly the same iron rules. And the idea of iron rules cannot be appreciated. The soldier goes through his daily routine, the bugle calls him—he is lying in his bunk—he must get up and "fall in." Why not sleep, or just omit this roll call? There would be extra duty, perhaps a small fine, and a poor impression made in the eyes of officers. And the officers—a very arbitrary group, more so because they are drawn from as many kinds of people as there are in the army, and because it is hard for men of one group to be commanded by men of another group. Here, for example is a college man, or a successful young businessman who is being bossed around by some fellow who has never done any more than loaf around, or at best menial labor. Then there is the vice versa case of the fellows not appreciating an unusually good officer. And yet through it all, the inferior can never talk back to the superior, must do his bidding. Thus arises another current in the camp stream—groups of men get together for mutual protection against an obdurate officer, and resist him in every way possible short of open violation of rules. And officers in turn have their lists of men whom they are determined to "break." All this is part of army experience.

Byron wasn't the only camper whose spirits were beginning to droop. It was no small task keeping thirty thousand men distracted, much less happy in the face of war. Vaudeville entertainers and singers were brought in by the YMCA to put on free concerts and shows for the men. On October 16, the day after the World Series ended, Shoeless Joe Jackson and the world champions, the Chicago White Sox, played an exhibition game against John McGraw's New York Giants and Jim Thorpe in Garden City. Six hundred men from the sanitary train were in attendance. Eventually, though, it was decided that the best cure for the blues was to simply turn the men loose on weekend passes, and hope that they didn't go AWOL. Officers began to issue passes for the men to visit the bright lights of New York City.

On September 26, Byron got an unexpected visit from his parents, who had traveled east to see him one last time before he went overseas. In a letter written to Estelle on the 28th, Byron said that he'd obtained a weekend pass to go to New York City with his parents, where they hoped to hear John McCormack sing "Macushla" at a benefit concert for New York's storied Irish regiment—"The Fighting 69th." McCormack was the great Irish tenor of his time. There was scarcely a household in America with a talking machine that didn't have a recording of McCormack's "Mother Machree." Despite his enormous popularity in this country, however, the fact that McCormack had just become a naturalized U.S. citizen in 1917 exposed him to the suspect status that was reserved for all "hyphenated Americans." That term first gained currency in the late 1800s and reached fever pitch in 1915 when former president Theodore Roosevelt declared that "there is no room in this country for hyphenated Americanism." German American and Irish American immigrants were the obvious intended targets of this warning. By the turn of the century, the demographics of the country had changed greatly. According to the 1910 census, one in three Americans had either been born abroad or had a parent who had been. Questions and suspicions concerning loyalty to the United States were smoldering concerns to the old guard. President Woodrow Wilson did nothing to dampen those doubts. To the contrary, he continued to fan the flames of suspicion regarding hyphenated Americans: "Any man who carries a hyphen about with him carries a dagger that he is ready to plunge into the vitals of this Republic."

As an outspoken supporter of Irish nationalism, McCormack went to great lengths to assuage any fears concerning his patriotism and his support for the war. McCormack and other Irish American entertainers, like George M. Cohan, gave numerous benefit concerts and shows to help raise funds for the Red Cross and sell Liberty Bonds. There is no indication that Byron and his parents were able to obtain tickets to hear McCormack sing that Sunday in New York. The fact that many others did, however, and that McCormack was able to raise $11,000 at the concert was prominently documented in the *New York Times* the following day.

On another trip to New York City on October 2, Byron and tentmate Horace Sprague attended the lavish extravaganza *Cheer Up* at the Hippodrome. In a letter to Estelle, Byron marveled at "the 500 people in the cast, besides elephants, camels, etc. a most wonderful piece" featuring catchy songs like "a soldier's farewell, 'Cheer Up Liza.'"

On October 7, for the first time in over two months, Byron was able to attend church services. In a letter written to Estelle that afternoon, Byron included the church program, then made mention of a special songbook that he was compiling.

> I have a little red notebook in which I have copied words of a few songs which I like so that I may sing them when I want to. I have "Just Awearyin' for You," "I Hear You Calling Me," "Sunshine of Your Smile," "O Dry Those Tears," and I would like to get a few more. I wish when you get the time you would write out for me "Believe Me If All Those Endearing Young Charms," "In The Gloaming," and "Gray Days." You may smile at the ones selected, but they are some of those I most enjoy singing when I'm lonesome or thinking of you.

Byron was right—Estelle was no doubt smiling at his selection of songs. It was an indication of how very much he missed her, and fifty years later she would still be moved by his words, highlighting this paragraph in red ink. In the very next paragraph, however, Byron ceased to indulge in any further self-pity, noting with apparent satisfaction: "Hurrah, all soldiers in the ranks are to receive 20% additional pay while in foreign service. That means $36 for a regular 'buck' private and $39.60 for a first class private. That's better."

"Not Too Proud to Fight." Front cover of *Leslie's Weekly*, July 27, 1916.

It may have been marginally better pay, but it was still very little compensation for assuming such great risk. Despite Byron's apparent satisfaction at having received this raise, the overall inequity of the situation could not have been lost on him. After all, only two years earlier he had been paid $40 a month to work as a primary unit teacher in a one-room schoolhouse in Jackson, Michigan—where the most unpleasant conditions he was likely to be subjected to were spitballs and sass from mischievous students. Still, the fact that Byron was more than willing to overlook the indignity of being undervalued as a soldier about to enter combat was no doubt grounded in his unwavering belief in the righteousness of this war, and his patriotic resolve to serve despite whatever misfortune might befall him.

As to the longer-term financial well-being of men who were about to enter battle, in anticipation of the worst-case scenario, Congress had recently amended the War Risk Insurance Act to provide a means for soldiers to acquire life and disability insurance at affordable rates. Byron immediately signed up for a government-issued policy with a face value of $10,000, arranging for the $6.50 monthly premium to be deducted from his pay. Reasonable rate or not, it was still a costly expense for a buck private on a monthly stipend of only $36. And when coupled with the additional $10 per pay that Byron was having sent home to his parents as part of an automatic savings plan, it left him with limited funds to spend on leisure activities. Which was exactly the result that Congress had intended when it further enacted a provision requiring that a mandatory $15 family allowance be deducted from each month's pay for enlisted men who had dependents at home to support. Army administrators believed that with less discretionary income for idle mischief (like gambling, drinking, and patronizing prostitutes), there would be better discipline in the ranks, and a reliable source of income for the families of enlisted men. Given that Byron was a bachelor with no vices to indulge or dependents at home to support, he was able to afford a few modest excursions into New York City and the towns that surrounded Camp Mills.

On his final trip to the big city on October 9, Byron and two other men from camp threw financial caution to the wind—with the trenches of France awaiting them, they could hardly be blamed for putting on

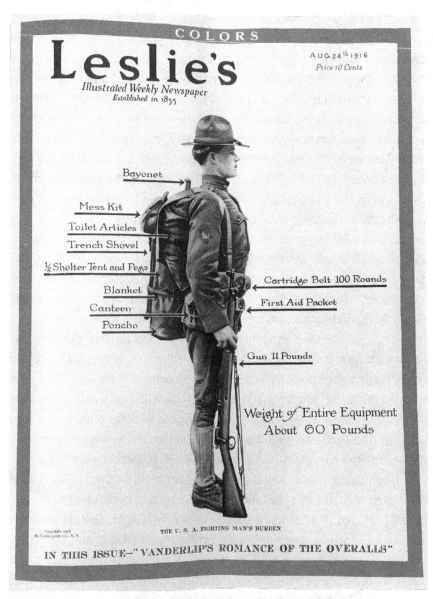

"The U.S.A. Fighting Man's Burden." Front cover of *Leslie's Weekly*, August 24, 1916.

the Ritz. Byron would later write to Estelle that they began the night by catching the P. G. Wodehouse Broadway hit *Riviera Girl*, after which they "went down to The Eldorado, a smart restaurant famous for its whole roasted chickens . . . , before closing out the night with ginger-ales at swanky Rector's Cabaret . . . the meeting place for the easy rich . . . [with] jeweled women drunk and smoking, and champagne at $10 a bottle flowing like water."

After returning from leave, Byron noticed that things had tightened up at camp. Captain Baskerville told the men that the company would be getting ready to move out on three hours' notice. In a letter written to Estelle on the 12th, Byron said, "I'm so uneasy I can't get down to work on anything definite." Neither could most of the other men. The usual banter between soldiers disappeared as a somber mood descended on the camp. Men worried a great deal about the voyage overseas. In an era when most people couldn't swim, the grim prospect of falling prey to a German U-boat and drowning at sea was a real concern. Since the resumption of unrestricted submarine warfare in February, the number of ships sunk by German U-boats had increased alarmingly.

In a letter to Estelle, Byron did his best to assuage those fears, writing that a veterinary lieutenant who had already made several trips across the Atlantic "sees no more danger in crossing the pond than in crossing a city street. And we have boat and life belt drills every day. There can be no lights at night, keyholes are plugged up, and not even a match can be lit on deck." Then, in an apparent attempt to keep Estelle from unduly worrying about whether he had arrived safely in France from lack of timely news, Byron cautioned her that it often takes "nearly a month for war mail to get from one end to the other." As it turned out, the army had already taken steps to expedite the transmission of news to loved ones at home: before boarding ships, the men were told to address preprinted cards to relatives announcing their safe landing in France. The cards were then collected and would be mailed from New York as soon as word was cabled back that the men had safely disembarked at Saint-Nazaire.

In preparation for that landing, everything got packed away. Each man kept only a blanket roll containing a half-tent, long underwear (known as suit-underwear or Union suits), socks, towels, and toilet kit. The rest of their personal gear was stowed in barracks bags that would catch up with them in France. Cots were disassembled. The men slept in clothes on the cold ground. On the 17th, the men weren't allowed to leave their company street. No mail went in or out. From this point on, all correspondence would be subject to the scrutiny of censors. Byron had foreseen that possibility and worked out a system of code with Estelle in advance: "Remember when I mean the opposite of what I say I'll misspell the first or second word in the sentence. Of course you can judge by the context when I may accidentally misspell such a word. And another scheme which sounds easy would be to write in a P.S. or P.S.S. things which I mean exactly the opposite. This last seems quite the better scheme."

In a hurried letter to Estelle on the evening of the 17th, Byron closed with a Shakespearean flourish: "[S]ometime during the night we expect to be awakened to start—on this—the longest lap of our journey. Only one journey could be longer than this—the one—'to that borne from which no traveler returns'—but we are all full of hope and enthusiasm." To circumvent the censors, Byron asked one of the men who was staying behind at Camp Mills to mail the letter from Hemp-stead. That night, under cover of darkness, the 117th Sanitary Train slipped out of camp. It was one of the first units to depart for France. Leaving their tents still standing, the men of the company marched in silence to Garden City, where they entrained for Long Island City. From there, a short ferry ride took them to the piers of Hoboken, New Jersey, where the ambulance company boarded the USS *Pastores*.

A tug pushed the ship down the Hudson River past the Statue of Liberty and out through the Verrazano Narrows, where it joined six other troop ships waiting off Sandy Hook. Escorted by a battle cruiser and two destroyers, the convoy got underway. It would take two long weeks to make port at Saint-Nazaire, France.

Soldiers came topside, watching until land disappeared from sight. For many, it was their last glimpse of home.

"Goodbye, sweetheart!!" Front cover of *Leslie's Weekly*, June 8, 1918, illustrated by Griswold Tyng.

6
OVER THERE

On May 6, 1916, one year after the sinking of the RMS *Lusitania*, Germany finally curtailed its use of unrestricted submarine warfare on mercantile shipping for fear of provoking the United States to enter the war. This reluctant shift in tactics represented a sea change in the balance of power between Great Britain and Germany in the ongoing battle of embargoes. With German U-boats no longer preying on merchant ships carrying much-needed foodstuffs and supplies to Great Britain, the people there were able to obtain some measure of relief.

For the citizens of Germany, no similar reprieve was forthcoming. The British embargo continued unabated—the resulting impact on the quality of life was devastating. After three years of severe privation, the people of Germany were desperate for an end to the war. And by early 1917, the Kaiser was willing to gamble in order to attain it.

The German high command believed that by unleashing its submarine fleet and throwing a stranglehold on the British Isles, it would be able to force Britain to sue for peace before the United States could train and mobilize an army. In a war where very little had gone according to plan so far, the Kaiser's gambit represented a high-risk move. Continuing on in a deadlock, however, was no longer a viable option. So, on January 31, 1917, the Kaiser threw diplomatic caution to the wind and ordered the German Navy to set sail once again into the maelstrom that was all but certain to follow the resumption of its unrestricted submarine tactics.

The impact of the blockade on Great Britain was immediate and severe. In February and March, U-boats sank an alarming number of ships bringing food and war-related materiel to England. By the end of April, Britain's stored wheat had been reduced to a mere six weeks' supply. Although the monthly tonnage of shipping lost to U-boats would eventually level off during the summer months, the British people still suffered greatly. This was not nearly enough, however, to weaken England's resolve, and at great cost the war dragged on.

In the summer of 1917, the Vatican tried to break the deadly stalemate by attempting to broker a peace settlement. Both sides politely but briefly considered Pope Benedict's proposal before rejecting its terms. The Allies were confident that with the United States about to enter the war, the balance would soon tip in their favor. Germany, on the other hand, viewed itself as winning the war of attrition and wanted more favorable terms, convinced that its submarine strategy would be able to extract them.

Germany's U-boat fleet was comprised of approximately one hundred submarines, fifty of which patrolled the seas through which American convoys would have to sail in order to reach France. Although Germany possessed several long-range U-boats, the fleet generally concentrated its efforts in the so-called danger zone—an area that extended no farther west than twenty degrees longitude, which in practical terms meant that for the first week of a voyage from the United States, the risk of encountering a U-boat was relatively low. On entering the danger zone, however, the prospect of the convoy being attacked was all too real. Most of the men in Byron's company didn't need to be reminded of that fact. Despite General John J. Pershing's attempt to censor the news coming out of France, reports of U-boat sightings and attacks on American ships had been well publicized. In late June, the first American convoy carrying troops to France was attacked twice by German submarines—the last attack coming only two days from safe harbor in Saint-Nazaire.

In an effort to thwart U-boat attacks, different strategies had been tried, with varying degrees of success. These included onboard blackouts, running zigzag courses, and even painting ships in dazzle (zebra-striped) camouflage that made it more difficult for U-boat captains to fix the speed and distance of a convoy. Ultimately, though, it was simply moving with the herd that proved to be the best way of reducing a ship's chance of being attacked. The one significant downside to that tactic was that a convoy could only move as fast as its slowest ship, and the odd collection of ships that headed out to sea on October 18 was a perfect example of that discomforting truth.

The armored cruiser USS *Seattle* and the two destroyers assigned to escort the convoy were built for speed and combat, although that fact alone was by no means any guarantee of safe passage. The captain and crew of the *Seattle* learned that lesson firsthand in June, having had to fend off repeated U-boat attacks on the first American convoy to sail for France. Not all warship encounters with submarines ended nearly as well, however—Britain had already lost several warships to U-boat attacks, the most recent being the armored cruiser HMS *Drake* on October 2 off the coast of Ireland.

Five of the troop ships in the convoy—the USS *President Lincoln*, the *President Grant*, the *Mount Vernon*, the *DeKalb*, and the *Covington*—were originally passenger liners belonging to German steamship companies that had been interned by the United States at the start of the war in August 1914. Once the United States had declared war, all five were officially confiscated and converted to troopships. As part of their refitting, the ships were equipped with multiple deck guns—the *President Lincoln* and the *DeKalb* being the most heavily armed. The *Lincoln* boasted four impressive six-inch guns and two rapid-fire three-pound cannons. The *DeKalb* was armed with a complement of twenty-six guns. The two remaining troop ships were banana boats—literally. Prior to the war, the USS *Pastores* and the USS *Tenadores* had been used by the United Fruit Company to ship bananas from South America. Soldiers were but the latest perishables to be carried in the hold.

The *Mount Vernon* was capable of stretching her sea legs and running with the naval escort at speeds of twenty-two knots or more. The rest of the convoy could manage only fifteen knots under a good head of steam, if they were lucky. Even at that modest speed, however, they would at least be on par with U-boats, which could cruise only at fourteen to fifteen knots when surfaced—which wasn't an ideal option for U-boat captains, as any attempt by a U-boat to stalk a well-guarded convoy on the surface for a prolonged period of time ran the considerable risk of leaving itself exposed and vulnerable to counterattack.

Moreover, given the limited range and underwater speed of U-boats, any attempt to pursue their prey while submerged presented even greater difficulties. In practical application, speed was important to a U-boat only in being able to get out to the hunting grounds in a timely manner, not in the hunt itself. Aside from its torpedoes, a U-boat's most valuable asset was its ability to submerge and lie in wait in a position of opportunity—like the Bay of Biscay leading to Saint-Nazaire, where an unsuspecting troop ship might appear in its crosshairs.

Oddly, it was the lumbering banana boats that would make it through the war unscathed. Three of the troop ships in the convoy would eventually fall victim to deadly U-boat attacks, including the speedy *Mount Vernon* and the heavily armed *President Lincoln*. Others would have close calls. In the final telling, misfortune at sea seemed simply a matter of being in the wrong place at the wrong time.

Byron and the rest of the ambulance company were relegated to the ship's hold on the fifth and lowest deck of the *Pastores*. As the men descended the final rung of iron steps, the lingering smell of overripe fruit hung thick in the air. Makeshift canvas bunks had been rigged three and four tiers high, extending the full length and width of the compartment. A mere eighteen inches separated the tiers of bunks. Other than men squeezing past one another, nothing else stirred in the hold—the hull of the ship had been built to be waterproof and airtight. Below the crew's quarters on the second deck, the ship had no ventilation, and with heat radiating from the boiler room nearby, the stagnant air quickly became stifling. The men had been told that there would be regular shifts topside to catch the breeze, but Byron was taking no chances. He immediately grabbed a top bunk—not that the air up there would be any fresher, but in a boat full of seasick men, it could prove to be a whole lot drier.

The first day at sea was relatively peaceful. The weather was balmy. As the ships sliced through the warm water of the Gulfstream, the men strolled on deck in shirtsleeves or sat in the sun using life vests as cushions. At night, the men continued to congregate on deck, some quietly marveling at the crystal-clear stars set against a jet-black sky, others watching the splashes of phosphorescent green algae that sparkled in the ship's wake. No one smoked or lit a match. Other than the mist-thin blue light that seeped from the passageways below deck, the ships were cloaked in total darkness.

The days that followed were rough. As the ships entered the cold gray water of the North Atlantic, soldiers came topside to ride the ship's railing as they retched into the pitching sea. The men got little sympathy from the crew. Any seasick soldier desperate enough to ask how far it was to land got the same smart answer, "Three miles, mister—straight down." As the ships continued to bludgeon their way through the seemingly endless swells, most of the nauseous men found their sea legs. For those who didn't, "A torpedo from a German sub would be welcome" was a commonly heard sentiment.

Byron was among those wracked by seasickness. It took seven days for him to regain some measure of intestinal equanimity. A calm stomach was no guarantee of a renewed appetite, however—and with good cause. The food served in the enlisted men's mess was exactly that—a nauseating mess consisting of a cheap cut of meat slopped on a tin tray with vegetables and potatoes that had been steamed beyond recognition. The men grumbled that blacksmiths and boilermakers were better suited to prepare hot food than navy cooks. For those who were desperate enough to try to take a bite, it often ended up on the deck anyway. As the ship pitched in the deep swells, pots, tables, and trashcans frequently overturned in the tumult, sending the unsavory slop sloshing across the floor—and on occasion down the hatchway into the hold where the men slept. After a few days in rough seas, the lion house at the zoo smelled better.

Before long, most of the men were ravenous for anything edible. A few men, like Byron, lived off the Hershey bars and other snacks they had stocked up on before leaving Hempstead. For those who hadn't, the only appetizing option available was to buy apples, oranges, and candy from unscrupulous stewards who reaped outlandish profits. Like the civilian sutlers who had preyed on the men at Camp Mills, profiteers were a parasitic presence that would continue to plague the soldiers for the duration of the war.

The men aboard the *Pastores*, however, got their revenge— Halloween was nigh. On Mischief Night, one intrepid soldier discovered a crawl space between the bulkheads that led to the cooks' and stewards' storeroom. After bribing the guards, man after man crawled into the storeroom to claim his booty. Anything and everything that could fit through the narrow crawlspace got lifted from the officers' foodstuffs—pickles, pears, apples, peaches, figs, salmon, brandy, lobster, and shrimp were devoured in an enlisted men's orgy that lasted well into the night. At the end of the feast, any incriminating remains were tossed overboard.

The following morning outraged navy stewards discovered the theft, and an ensuing investigation pegged the loss at over $2,000. There was no shortage of smiling suspects, but with no evidence to support charges, commanding officers didn't see any point in pursuing the matter further. Under the circumstances the men could hardly be blamed—for young soldiers in the middle of a long, tension-filled voyage through submarine-infested waters, such high-spirited shenanigans were relatively harmless fun and a much-needed diversion.

The first indication that this voyage was destined to be a nerve-racking affair occurred after only three days at sea—when the USS *Grant* suddenly developed engine trouble. After trying unsuccessfully to keep pace with the other ships in the convoy, on October 21, the *Grant* dropped from the pack and headed back to New York. It was an unfortunate turn of events but not entirely unexpected. At the outbreak of the war, German crews assigned to vessels that had been impounded in U.S. ports received orders from their superior officers to destroy or otherwise disable the machinery and equipment on board those ships prior to surrendering them to U.S. authorities. When the vessels were later refitted as transport ships for U.S. troops, naval repair crews did their best to restore them to serviceable condition, but on ships as large as the *Grant* it was practically impossible to uncover every hidden defect.

As inopportune as the *Grant*'s misfortune was, it would have been much worse if the mishap had occurred in the danger zone, where the ship would have been a sitting duck for U-boats. No sooner had the *Grant* steamed from sight than word began to circulate among the men that German mechanics had sabotaged the *Grant*'s engine by drilling small holes in the boiler that wouldn't be detected until the ship was well out to sea and proceeding under a full head of steam. As always in times of stress, rumor hardened into fact—to most of the men, the incident underscored the need to be vigilant at all times.

Life belts were worn above and below deck. At any time of day or night, abandon-ship drills were held without warning. The men were never told if the alert was a drill or not, causing them to spring to their assigned stations on deck with a sense of urgency, nervously scanning the surface of the ocean for a periscope until finally being told to stand down. The repetition of the drills was exasperating but served its purpose. Long before the ships entered the danger zone, the men were as adept at navigating the ship's crowded decks and passageways as the crew.

The drills also proved to be valuable in ways totally unanticipated. During one of the drills, lifeboats were lowered into the water for the first time. It was only then that the crew discovered that some of the boats were held together with glue instead of screws. After the bottom fell out of one of the boats, spilling two sailors into the sea, all the remaining lifeboats and rafts were immediately inspected to ensure that others hadn't been tampered with as well. Still, it was impossible to uncover every bit of German deviltry, and the men knew that it was only a matter of time before the next sabotage made itself known.

Two days before reaching the danger zone, the ships undertook gunnery practice for the last time—rotating into position to fire at a barrel towed behind one of the ships. The unerring accuracy of the navy gunners on a rolling sea was an impressive sight. The true test of proficiency, however, would come in being able to spot a U-boat before it spotted the convoy—and the answer to that question remained to be seen. As soon as the convoy entered the danger zone, drills slacked off. The demeanor of the crew stiffened noticeably as the ships began to tack a zigzag course. For the remainder of the voyage, soldiers were brusquely told, "Don't sit here" and "Don't loiter there" as sailors went about their business.

The *President Lincoln* was the next ship to fall prey to mechanical failure—coming to a dead stop in potentially troublesome waters. The remaining ships could ill afford to wait so they swept on, leaving only one destroyer behind for protection while mechanics worked feverishly to correct the problem. Tension filled the air as thousands of soldiers stood ready to abandon ship should the worst-case scenario present itself—in that event, with only limited space available in lifeboats, most of the men would have had to cling to rafts in water temperatures that hovered between forty-five to fifty degrees Fahrenheit. Under such forbidding conditions, the prospects for survival were unlikely at best. After two interminable hours of waiting, the crisis finally passed when mechanics got the *Lincoln* underway again. It was an uncomfortably close call.

An even more menacing threat might have become a full-blown catastrophe. As related by Captain W. E. Talbot of the 117th Supply Train, whose duties included permanent officer of the day on board the *Mount Vernon*, a few days after departing Hoboken, the *Mount Vernon* had begun to receive reports from other ships in the convoy that at night a light could be seen emanating from a location below deck. At the very least, this constituted a negligent breach of the convoy's blackout protocol—at worst, it was a deliberate act of treachery. Either way, it placed the entire convoy in grave danger, and Talbot and his detail of men set out to catch the offender as quickly as possible.

With multiple decks to traverse and dozens of portholes to cover, it soon became apparent that catching the culprit would not be easily done. The best vantage point from which to detect the illicit activity was on other ships, whose spotters then relayed word to the *Mount Vernon*. In terms of rapid response, this means of communication was hardly ideal—by the time Talbot and his men were able to spring into action and navigate the dimly lit passageways of the ship to get to the general area of the deck from which the light was last seen shining, the offending party had already vanished into the night. Until one fateful occasion when the ship's master-at-arms stumbled across a barefooted suspect skulking in the dark. In the struggle that ensued, the suspect escaped, bashing in his would-be captor's skull with a blackjack and killing him.

The following night, when another display of light was detected, Talbot and his detail of men closed in faster, nabbing their man this time. He appeared to be an unassuming civilian passenger. Ample proof of his murderous intent was found on him, however: a blackjack, a long-bladed knife, and a garrote. A monkey wrench and a can of oil used to unfasten bolts and silently open porthole covers were also found nearby. It was later determined that the passenger was a German spy, traveling under cover as a Swiss attaché. He was executed by the French when the ship reached port.

In an effort to distract the men from such worrisome events, when weather permitted impromptu boxing matches and concerts were held on deck. The *President Lincoln* had the luxury of being entertained by the Indiana National Guard band. The men on board the *Pastores* had to rely on the steady voices of singers like Byron to lead them in song. On occasion, Byron was also required to play the piano in the officers' quarters. "Sweet Adeline," "Pack Up Your Troubles in Your Old Kit Bag," "Keep the Home Fires Burning" and "It's a Long Way to Tipperary" were company favorites. "Drunk Last Night" was also a big hit. But the song that brought out the best in the men was George M. Cohan's "Over There"—even the sailors joined in, the ship seeming to surge with Yankee pride as it headed over the bounding main.

When the men weren't taking part in drills or enjoying diversions, the days were long and monotonous. To pass the time, Byron began to read and answer Estelle's "steamer letters." In addition to their regular correspondence, Estelle had written a series of letters for Byron to read on the long voyage. Each letter was meant to provide "a bright spot in the day's events." The letters were pure Estelle—funny, newsy, flirtatious, filled with love, and thought provoking. Read today, the letters provide a glimpse into a world in the midst of great social and political reform—moving from the well-established norms of the horse-drawn Edwardian period to the fast-paced challenges and rewards of a new age, the Progressive Era. As reflected in their letters, Byron and Estelle embodied the youthful enthusiasm and confidence of that new order. And in some regards, it was Estelle who was more willing to embrace that change.

On October 25, Byron began crafting a response to Estelle's steamer letters. In a long letter written over the course of several days, Byron addressed many of the progressive ideals discussed in Estelle's letters. On the issue of women's suffrage, Byron acknowledged that he had been mistaken: "Yes, the day may come before we're very old when another Victoria—only a Yankee Queen—may rise to be our president. I didn't agree in Suffrage until a year or so ago, but now I must agree—as it seems must every reasonable man—that equal suffrage is not only right, but best."

In an earlier letter of September 28, Byron and Estelle seemed to be in perfect accord on another reform issue—workers' rights. It is clear that Estelle often sought and valued Byron's advice; in this letter he advised her on how to develop this topic for a paper and oral presentation at school:

> I wish I could talk with you about your oration, and the one I would have written. This "poverty" is such a general topic that you will certainly need to confine your speech to a very definite kind. I take it from what you say that yours will be probably, "industrial poverty." Both of your plans have been tried out and you ought to find some very good practical illustrations. For example, in the Hayes Wheel Co. in Jackson, each week a certain part of each week's pay is kept from the employees envelope, and put into a "sick and accident" fund. The men elect certain officers from among themselves to see to the amount of money to be paid in each case, altho they are governed by a certain schedule.
>
> On the other hand, I believe our states are working harder all the time, and making more strict laws about factory sanitation, adequate machine guards, lots of light, and all of the other things needed to make men less likely to become injured or sick. The Sparks-Withington Co. in Jackson, the Ford plant, and many others have special rooms for the men to eat in, have shower baths, steel lockers. It seems to me this latter way is better for the very reason you mentioned—it is a prevention instead of the cure. I wish I knew more about it to tell you, but I know you can get lots of material.

The fact that Byron and Estelle were in lockstep concerning many of the social reform issues of the day was reflective of their religious upbringing—as practicing Methodists, both subscribed to a code of conduct called the Social Creed. The Creed was a doctrine of social responsibility that had been incorporated into the Methodist Book of Discipline in 1908. It was part of a larger progressive movement in Protestantism called Social Gospel—which sought to eradicate the onerous living and working conditions brought on by the rapid urbanization and industrialization of American cities. As originally set forth, the Social Creed stood for the following principles: equal rights and complete justice for all men in all stations of life; the principle of conciliation and arbitration in industrial dissensions; the protection of the worker from dangerous machinery, occupational diseases, injuries and mortality; the abolition of child labor; such regulation of the conditions of labor for women as shall safeguard the physical and moral health of the community; the suppression of the sweating system; the gradual and reasonable reduction of the hours of labor to the lowest point, with work for all, and for that degree of leisure for all which is the condition of the highest human life; a release from work one day in seven; a living wage in every industry; the highest wage that each industry can afford, and for the most equitable division of the products of industry that can be ultimately devised; and, recognition of the Golden Rule and the mind of Christ as the supreme law of society and the sure remedy of all social ills.

It was a very ambitious agenda. Even today, a seemingly basic human right like the ability to earn a living wage in all forms of employment is not fully realized. That a more complex and utopian ideal like the equitable division of the products of industry was never able to gain serious political traction is hardly surprising. In the years that followed the war, the Social Gospel movement would lose its momentum as a force for change. Though somewhat regrettable, it was entirely understandable—with the onset of the Great Depression, people were more concerned with hanging onto any job they could possibly find than the attainment of perfection in the workplace. Still, for Byron and Estelle this was a formative period in their lives, and the lofty ideals embodied in the Social Creed would continue to have a profound and lasting impact on their thoughts and actions for decades to come.

On other matters, like the necessity of having to march off to war, Byron and Estelle were not always of the same mind. In a passage from a letter written on October 25, Byron conceded that Estelle's faith in the power of Christian kindness wasn't totally misplaced, even if he didn't share that view unconditionally, "There certainly wouldn't be any war—as you say—if everyone got from another 'be it the slightest contact—one gleam of faith.'" Despite this obvious difference, Estelle's love and support for Byron are evident in their many letters, though her continued reservations about the war show through in different passages. In a telling response to one of Estelle's steamer letters, Byron seemed pleased that Estelle had been so moved by a newspaper account of displaced French villagers and children that she was finally able to express anger: "I'm glad to see your 'English' finally coming up so that you'd like to kill a German. 'Member how I used to argue that way with you and you couldn't see it? Maybe I'll love some little French ragamuffin so much that I'll bring him home with me."

In dealing with their feelings about the war, as in so many other areas of their lives, Byron and Estelle both looked to their religion and the Bible for spiritual guidance and, considering their difference of opinion on the matter, found differing sources of solace within it. In the October 30 installment of Byron's long response, he wrote that he had turned to the book of Revelation in an attempt to reconcile his Christian beliefs with the antithetical nature of the warpath he was embarking on: "Sunday was the same as the other days. I tried to make it seem a little more religious than the other days by reading more of the Testament than on the weekdays. I've read Revelations last and it certainly is a conundrum. I can't but see how easily great minds have differed on meanings and explanations of various passages. We must take much on faith to be true Christians, trusting to the future to make clear meanings hidden at present." Given their divergent views on the war, it was only logical that Estelle's view of mankind would be less apocalyptic and more spiritually uplifting than Byron's. In an earlier letter of September 17, Byron thanked Estelle for recommending Corinthians 15 to him, writing that he "liked it very much too," although Byron still believed that the resurrection and forgiveness of Christ notwithstanding, it was still necessary for him to go off to war and sacrifice his life if need be.

Unlike Byron and many other Americans at that time, Estelle was still far from convinced that the war with Germany was unavoidable or even necessary. Throughout the duration of their relationship, Estelle would continue to push Byron to consider ideas outside the mainstream. As an officer of the Albion chapter of Sorosis, the first professional society for women, and a state champion college orator, Estelle was a forceful advocate for many of the causes in which she believed. Not surprisingly over the years, Byron would often come out on the short end of their long and spirited discussions.

On the evening of October 28, the convoy suddenly veered to the north at a forty-five-degree angle. The two destroyers that were escorting the ships peeled off and steamed out of sight. With only the cruiser left for protection, the flanks of the troop ships were exposed for the first time since leaving port. They were in the heart of the danger zone. Word spread quickly, and a sense of impending doom gripped the ship like a Jonah. As night fell, some of the men came topside and watched for any telltale sign of the destroyers—or, God forbid, the appearance of a submarine. Alone in the dark on the vast pitching sea, men could hardly be faulted for feeling as if the earth had suddenly begun to wobble on its axis, and that the convoy might slide off it. It soon became apparent to even the most anxious man, though, that continuing to worry was pointless. Eventually most of the men surrendered themselves to fate and returned to their bunks to sleep.

The following dawn, the men awoke to find a squadron of dazzle-striped destroyers surrounding the convoy. Eleven French naval ships darted ahead and to the side of the convoy in intricate patterns, sweeping the sea in search of U-boats. By midmorning, the American destroyers had returned from the hunt. The men soon learned that the destroyers had gone off to intercept a pack of U-boats that had been waiting to ambush the convoy in the Bay of Biscay. While the American destroyers were busy rousting the U-boats, the convoy had managed to steer a course out of harm's way until the French destroyers could arrive from Brittany.

For the next two days, the convoy passed increasing numbers of French fishing vessels headed in and out of the Bay of Biscay. The first sighting of land came at the Belle Isle, nine miles off the coast of Brittany. At the mouth of the Loire River, the cruiser *Seattle* and two American destroyers turned back for home. After the troop ships dropped anchor in the outer harbor of Saint-Nazaire, French pilots came aboard to navigate each ship past the submarine net and into the busy port. At 3:00 on the morning of November 1, the last of the six troopships docked at Saint-Nazaire.

The Rainbow Division was finally over there.

7
CULTURE SHOCK

On the morning of November 1, the men awoke to find that "sunny France" was anything but—all that day, the port of Saint-Nazaire was shrouded in cold gray drizzle. To most of the men it didn't matter. After a two-week voyage through submarine-infested waters, France looked mighty good. For the next twenty-four hours though, a good look was all the men would get.

Legions of soldiers couldn't simply disembark. Space had to be found in base camps. Until then, the men were confined to ships' quarters. Still, that didn't stop the town from turning out. Old men, women, and children came down to the port to wave and welcome the troops. Other than the German POWs, *prisonnier de guerre*, who were working as stevedores under armed guard, the only able-bodied men in sight were dressed in the sky-blue uniform of the French Army—and they were few and far between. The rest of the men were at the front or under gravesites adorned with *fleurs-de-lis*. Many of the villagers wore black dresses, armbands, and mournful faces.

All that day, soldiers lowered hats filled with money down to vendors in exchange for apples and chocolate. Ladies of the night came down too to display their wares, but were careful to stay in the background, just close enough to elicit appreciative catcalls from the men hanging over the ship's railing. At this point, the banter was just harmless fun. If nothing else, though, it underscored the need to reinforce with the men the virtues of abstinence and the perils of contracting a social disease.

For the remainder of the American Expeditionary Force's stay in France, no soldier would be permitted to disembark a ship or otherwise

go on leave without first receiving fair warning. Normally, the responsibility for delivering that message fell to each unit's medical officer.
There is no record of who was actually tasked with that assignment
in the Michigan Ambulance Company, but given that it was a medical
unit, there was certainly no shortage of qualified personnel to assume
that duty. In all likelihood that job fell to First Sergeant Frank Gallagher. As the company's top cutter, it was his responsibility to lay
down the law and discipline those who ran afoul of it. And in this
case, he would have wanted the men to hear it from him, loud and
clear—especially the veterans. With them, the army's new rules were
going to be a hard sell.

Prior to this war, the policy of the U.S. Army regarding the close
association that many soldiers had with prostitutes—and the venereal disease that often resulted—could best be described as "evolving," albeit glacially. At the turn of the century, there simply was no
policy. In 1906, with the development of the Wassermann reaction (a
test for syphilis), army doctors were able to reject recruits who were
afflicted with the disease, which was a good first step toward trying to
cleanse the ranks from the bottom up. It soon became apparent to army

42nd Division marching to Base Camp No. 1, Saint-Nazaire, November 2, 1917.
(Photograph by Army Signal Corps.)

administrators, though, that the problem would not be so easily erad-
icated. In fact, it was increasing—by 1912, the rate of venereal disease
among soldiers had nearly doubled as a result of troops being quartered in Cuba, the Philippines, and Puerto Rico. The War Department
was finally forced to take some form of deterrent action—the issuance
of an order that withheld pay from any soldier who was incapacitated
by the disease. Although it was a sanction with some bite, it was still a
far cry from confronting the problem head-on by addressing the underlying conduct that was actually causing the problem—a problem that
as recently as 1916, the U.S. Army had helped to create; soldiers under
the command of General John J. Pershing were permitted to frequent
army-regulated houses of prostitution during the Mexican Border War.

Under mounting pressure from social reformers at home, Pershing
was determined that the off-duty conduct of American soldiers during
this war was going to be different. In June 1917, he issued edicts to
that effect. They took the form of General Order Nos. 6 and 34, which
Gallagher and other superior officers were required to deliver before
the men could disembark at Saint-Nazaire or other ports of entry. Simply put, Pershing was making the contraction of venereal disease an
offense punishable by court-martial. It was a dire warning that would
be repeatedly delivered in the months to come.

In some units, men were required to sign a pledge promising that
they would behave in a proper manner before being allowed to go on
leave. There is no indication that this was actually done in Byron's
company. For additional good measure, at various times during the
war, circulars were also distributed to the men reminding them not to
engage in conduct that could harm themselves and their country. In
pertinent part, one such leaflet read as follows:

> The United States Government is permitting you to go on leave.
> NOT in order that you may SOW WILD OATS, but to give you an oppor-
> tunity to improve your station in life.

> DO NOT LET BOOZE, A PRETTY FACE, A SHAPELY ANKLE MAKE YOU FORGET! THE
> AEF MUST NOT TAKE EUROPEAN DISEASE TO AMERICA. YOU MUST COME HOME
> CLEAN!!

"Trouble in Mexico." Front cover of *Leslie's Weekly*, October 23, 1913, illustrated by James Montgomery Flagg.

The tenor of these warnings may have been moralistically overbearing, but the substance of the message couldn't have been more timely. The men were about to set foot in France, where a virtual entente cordiale was waiting to overwhelm them. Although the French people had suffered great privation during the war, they were still possessed of enough resources to roll out the red carpet for incoming American troops, offering them a variety of social amenities that included saloons, cafés and, of course, gracious French hospitality. One amenity in particular, however, was to be partaken of only with the utmost discretion—to the extent it was humanly possible, the brothels were to be avoided. And to the extent that it wasn't possible, the men were cautioned to at least do their wives and girlfriends a favor and try to avoid the ones that smelled out loud. Later in the war, soldiers would derisively refer to the city as Stench Nazaire. It was an unkind description but not totally unexpected. Saint-Nazaire was a port town that was treated like a doormat by the hundreds of thousands of soldiers who tramped through its streets. Suffering from the prolonged deprivation of war, Saint-Nazaire didn't have much to offer. Food stocks were limited. Shop windows were bare. A simple cheese sandwich cost the same as a roast chicken dinner in the United States. With all of the able-bodied French men at the front and no one to help support them, women in the town got by any way they could—even prostitution.

In 1917, three new brothels had opened in Saint-Nazaire to accommodate the influx of American troops. Typically, six to eight prostitutes worked in each brothel, servicing forty to fifty customers a day. Needless to say, conditions were more than ripe for disease. Pershing's Order No. 6 did not explicitly prohibit the men from frequenting the brothels—instead, it merely addressed the consequences of engaging in irresponsible sex. Any man who contracted VD would lose his pay and be subject to court-martial. It was a statistical reality that some of the men in the company would contract venereal disease. In August 1917, it was reported that eighty of every one thousand American soldiers suffered from VD. During the month of October, however, the VD rate among American troops had fallen to fifty-four per one thousand—which for the moment, at least, was a hopeful sign that Pershing's order was beginning to gain traction in curbing the disease.

In an attempt to further curtail the spread of the disease, a system of treatment was implemented in which any man who had sexual contact with a prostitute was required to report to a medical officer within three hours of said contact. For any stragglers who were foolhardy enough not to comply with that three-hour window of opportunity, the imposition of disciplinary action was certain. The range of discipline imposed was not so stiff, however, as to deter delinquent soldiers from belatedly complying—on the scale of venereal disease sanctions, this was a subtle but crucial distinction. For the first time, Pershing was making the contraction of venereal disease an offense punishable by court-martial. It was a hard-line position based on Pershing's faith in medical science. He was convinced that timely chemical prophylaxis treatment would be able to cure the disease. In order for the treatment to be most effective, however, he had to set a time limit for the administration of chemical prophylaxis. In an attempt to accomplish both ends, he scaled back the punishment for reporting late. Recognizing that there would always be incorrigible cases of delinquency, Pershing took the additional step of enacting General Order No. 34. For any slacker who thought that by contracting venereal disease he would get a little R&R in the hospital, General Order No. 34 represented Pershing's coup de grâce—venereal disease would be treated on an ambulatory basis.

Before dismissing the men, Gallagher announced that after disembarking the *Pastores* the next day, the company would march straight to Base Camp No. 1. After cleaning up the barracks, the first order of business would be medical inspections. The medical inspections for sexually transmitted diseases were referred to as "dangle parades." They would continue throughout the war.

As it turned out, the rules of engagement were about as clear as the mud that the men would have to march through to get to Base Camp No. 1. The next morning, the Michigan Ambulance Company was the first unit to disembark from the ships. On the way to camp, they passed three brothels—with their red lamps and long lines of men at the door, they were hard to miss.

For Pershing and senior members of his staff, there had never been any doubt that the arrival of the Yanks in France would result in a clash of cultures. It was inevitable. For young Bible-toting midwesterners like Byron, though, it would be nothing short of culture shock, and a confounding one at that. The fact that the situation would become so contentious so early in the war is what caught everyone off guard.

Over the centuries, the English and French had grown intimately familiar with one another's predilections—social and otherwise. The British attitude toward brothels was typical of an empire that had been quartering its troops in other countries for centuries—"When in Rome . . ." But the Americans were strangers in a strange land. In France, prostitution was legal. Brothels (known as *maisons tolérée*) were licensed by the government. The prostitutes who worked in them were inspected by doctors to ensure that they weren't infected with sexually transmitted diseases. The French view was that sexual activity, illicit or not, was as basic to human nature as eating. So it was simply better to regulate it rather than try to repress a natural and necessary urge. Besides, the military hierarchy in France thought that brothels were good for the morale of the men in the trenches—to cure the blues, or *le cafard*, as it was called. Given the harsh reality of this war, it was a rationale that was hard to argue with. For soldiers whose life expectancies could often be measured in weeks, if they were lucky, a few moments of physical intimacy, even with a prostitute, was a powerful attraction when weighed against the seemingly remote risk of contracting venereal disease.

Pershing wasn't nearly as enlightened as the French. In July, less than a week after the first American troops had landed in France, Pershing issued General Order No. 6, even though he knew it would likely ruffle some French feathers. He didn't care—he had social reformers back home to contend with who were fearful that wholesome American boys were being exposed to Old World degeneracy. More important, though, he was well aware of the debilitating effect that venereal disease had already inflicted on French and English troops, and was determined to keep as many American soldiers out of the hospital and on the battlefield as possible.

Despite Pershing's orders, the disease became nearly an epidemic among American troops in early November, rising to a rate of 201 cases per 1,000 men, principally because of the brothels in Saint-Nazaire.

Soldiers returning to base after having visited a brothel often found that the lines of men waiting to be treated at the medical stations were longer than the lines outside the brothels. After personally inspecting the conditions in Saint-Nazaire, Pershing declared it "one of the most disgraceful things that has happened to the American army." The general was forced to take extreme measures.

In December, Pershing issued the infamous Order No. 77. This new directive declared the brothels of Saint-Nazaire off limits to American troops. To further deter even the most incorrigible soldiers, military police were stationed outside the brothels and barbed wire was strung around the base camps. Sentries were posted at the gates with orders that any soldier who returned to camp intoxicated was presumed to have been to a brothel, and taken immediately to a medical station for treatment. This was by no means a simple slap on the wrist. Prophylaxis treatment at that time was quite severe, consisting of laundry soap, scrub brushes, and chemicals injected up the ureter. Its application proved to be as much of a deterrent as it was a cure.

The French reaction to Pershing's measures was a mixture of derision, commercial concern, and indignation. The mayor of Saint-Nazaire complained that the decent women of his city were at risk of being raped by American soldiers who were not being allowed to patronize brothels. A few madames alleged that Pershing's edict was an illegal restraint of trade. At the behest of President Georges Clemenceau, the French surgeon general initiated an investigation and subsequently issued a report implying that the rate of venereal disease among American soldiers was in essence self-inflicted, having come with them from the United States, and that it was the French prostitutes who were at risk of being infected. The report also speculated that Pershing's measures would succeed only in forcing American soldiers to patronize unlicensed and diseased prostitutes, further exacerbating the problem.

Pershing's staff countered that the medical inspections of prostitutes conducted by French doctors were cursory in nature and woefully inadequate as a result, as evidenced by the fact that French doctors had found only five cases of syphilis in the previous five years. They also alleged that France's outrage over the American embargo of its brothels was primarily motivated by economic concerns.

At home, the issue of venereal disease among the soldiers at training camps and abroad had not gone unnoticed. It seemed that reformers were more concerned with the turpitude of soldiers who had gone on "moral holidays" or were engaged in "sex festivals" than the inherent dangers of combat itself. Even the *Literary Digest* opined on the matter, "Unless one comes in contact with a large body of men separated from feminine influence and the social restraints of civilian life, one does not realize how quickly the savage comes to the surface."

That Estelle was aware of the situation and concerned that Byron might succumb to these less than civilized urges is reflected in Byron's letter of December 6. Without explicitly mentioning the brothels, it is clear from Byron's response that he was attempting to assuage her fears in that regard:

> My dearest Birdie, you need not worry that as long as my Strength remains I will give up my ideals. I know too well already how well, as you say, "My folks are wrapped up entirely in their hopes for me." And oh how I love them in return—and all I can say now is a word on paper, what I must do—is to act well. More than once I have said to some fellow when he asked why I didn't do some things that nothing but the faith of "those" at home kept me straight. Of course, I know that in reality it is God, because it is He who prompts and sustains such faith between human beings.

Back in France, President Clemenceau was trying to assuage concerns about the matter also. In a letter to Pershing, Clemenceau asked him to reevaluate his hard-line position and come to some sort of mutually agreeable understanding. Unmoved, Pershing gave a copy of the letter to Raymond Fosdick, a confidant of Woodrow Wilson, who was in France at the time. After returning to the United States, Fosdick gave a copy of Clemenceau's letter to Secretary of War Newton Baker, who remarked, "For God's sake, Raymond, don't show this to the President or he'll stop the war."

Ultimately, Pershing stood his ground and French authorities let him have his way. Not surprisingly, the incidence of venereal disease dropped immediately. The dispute was soon forgotten. France and the United States had a more important conflict to focus on.

8
THE HANDWRITING ON THE WALL

In order to create room for the next wave of soldiers to disembark at Saint-Nazaire, troops had to be moved inland as soon as possible. After four days of washing the sea salt out of their clothing, straightening out their gear, and limbering up their legs on long walks into town or along the sea coast, the 168th Ambulance Company moved out of Base Camp No. 1. It was the first unit of the sanitary train to depart Saint-Nazaire.

Early on the morning of November 6, Byron and other members of the ambulance company boarded train cars for the two-day journey to Vaucouleurs. Enlisted men were assigned to third-class coaches. Officers rode first class. French train cars were considerably smaller than those in the United States. Packing eight men and their equipment into a compartment left no room to stretch out or get comfortable. Disgruntled men slept in the aisle. Equally disgruntled porters and conductors grumbled as they stepped over the men but otherwise let them sleep. Compared to the 8:40 train that the rest of the sanitary train would be taking that evening, though, the Michigan Ambulance Company was riding in the lap of luxury.

The "8:40" was a sobriquet the soldiers had given to the freight trains that carried them to the front. Each locomotive pulled a long string of boxcars—all labeled "*Chevaux*: 8; *Hommes*: 40"—suitable for eight horses, or forty men. At roughly half the size of its counterpart in the United States, a French boxcar was so small that it practically took a cattle prod to get forty men and their equipment on board. And, not unlike the mules that often got shipped in them, the men rode the entire way standing up—being able to eat the straw that covered the floor, however, was not an option for the men. They would have to wait for periodic rest stops to unpack their "iron meals."

For the trip, each man had been given a two-day supply of iron meals—a first-generation emergency field ration that the army would later call an MRE (meal, ready-to-eat). Each ration contained three three-ounce cakes (consisting of a mixture of dried meat, beef bouillon, and parched wheat) and three one-ounce pieces of chocolate packed into a tin container. Their producer, Armour & Co., claimed that each tin had the nutritional value of a well-rounded meal. Whether that claim was actually true or not was of little moment to hungry soldiers—what they knew beyond all doubt was that the unappetizing mélange was a far cry from homemade cooking.

On this trip, some of the men had been lucky enough to be given canned tomatoes and hardtack for breakfast, a relative delicacy under the circumstances. Eventually, though, it would all taste good. In that regard, Byron remarked in a subsequent letter to Estelle, "Say what a difference circumstances make. Last year when the boys came back from the border and I tasted some of the tack, I said 'Never for mine,' and here it tastes like Nabiscoes or better." Another concoction that awaited the men at each rest stop was French coffee. For men used to American coffee, the most redeeming quality of this strange thick brew was its warmth. A few of the fussier men groused that they needed sugar or cream to cut the acrid taste. They were a distinct minority, though—after spending long, cold hours in the drafty boxcars, most of the men would have guzzled hot tar just to stay warm.

The train route started out by tracking the Loire River Valley. The next morning, a bright sun revealed a colorful quilt-work of farms and vineyards that resembled the Hudson Valley in fall. The land between Nantes, Angers, Tours, Bourges, and Nevers was mostly low and fertile. On the sloping hills, well-tended vineyards had already been harvested and pruned for winter. In other places, rows of cropped willow trees lined the fields like armies of broomsticks waiting to be inspected. At Dijon, the train headed north toward Neufchâteau, where the terrain grew more rugged. As the train passed by, women working in the fields waved at the men hanging out of passenger car windows and boxcar doors. For the entire trip, women could be seen working at jobs vacated by *poilus*: men who were fighting at the front. In factories, railroad yards, and depot stations, on locomotives and streetcars, women manned the workforce. At the town of Vaucouleurs, French women had even been known to march off to war—here, at the Chapelle Castrale, Joan of Arc had prayed for guidance before starting out on her fateful journey. Like her, the Rainbow Division would be staying there to prepare itself for combat.

On reaching Vaucouleurs, the men detrained to what they'd become accustomed to as a typical French greeting—it was cold and damp. Vaucouleurs was tucked into the foothills of the Vosges Mountains. Other than Joan of Arc, Vaucouleurs was known for the iron foundry where the Statue of Liberty had been cast and a small munitions factory where women made hand grenades. At 4:00 in the morning, most of the town's twenty-five hundred residents were still fast asleep when the ambulance company marched into town. An advance party had arranged for billeting the men, which in practical terms meant that some of the officers were quartered in rooms while the rest of the men were relegated to sleeping in barn lofts and sheds. As the first troops to arrive in town, it was no small consolation that Byron and the rest of the ambulance company were able to stake their claim to the driest and least drafty of them. For most of the war, weather-beaten barns and sheds would be their usual quarters.

At daybreak, it soon became clear that Vaucouleurs would belie its name—the valley of colors proved to be a dreary collection of buildings. Villagers looked soap deprived and threadbare. The streets were filthy. Piles of rubbish and manure had been left to fester everywhere. Townspeople were seemingly indifferent to the unsanitary conditions. For the next few days, men from the Michigan Ambulance Company assiduously cleaned the streets, clearing up the refuse and scrubbing down the blocks of paving stone that had been laid by Caesar's troops nearly two millennia earlier.

The three hospital companies assigned to the sanitary train continued down the road to the village of Mauvages, where they set up a hospital in an old château. An epidemic of mumps had broken out in the ranks—seventy-four patients would be hospitalized in short order, along with the usual cases of influenza and cold-weather maladies. Treating an army on the move was no small feat considering the shortage of medicine and equipment. In the distance, the rumble of guns warned of far worse challenges to come.

On November 11, a meet-and-greet gathering was held at the newly opened YMCA hut in Vaucouleurs. In a letter to Estelle, Byron described the assemblage:

Last Sunday the local Y.M. was opened. The Y. has leased a small hotel and fixed it up fine with an auditorium, reading & writing room, canteen, etc. etc. The people in charge are very likeable, and also—work very hard. And imagine—a woman is in charge of the whole business here. She is business too. In the afternoon, Sunday, there was held a unique meeting in the auditorium, a French-American meeting. Part of the audience were French townspeople and officers, the other part were Americans. All of the speeches were repeated in English and French. Monsieur Rosaire, an instructor in French at the University of London before the war, a Verdun hero in this war, and now an interpreter on our Divisional Staff (whew!) sang the "Marsaillaise," and the Americans responded with "America." Little Jimmy [a nickname Estelle had given Byron] played the piano. Thereon hangs a tale. Rosaire had no music and so it was up to me to find some. I found the Y.M. interpreter and French instructress, a very amiable young woman, and with her went in search of some music. To make a long story short, our search led us to the home of a jeweler and optician who is at the same time something of a musician, and who has three very agreeable daughters. All of them, and he himself play or sing—piano, violin, etc. True! Well bold Jimmy thought here is an opportunity for adventure not to be winked at, so, a couple of days later he returned with a pair of spectacles he had borrowed, and popped the question. What was the question?—It was—whether he would be too bold in asking to come over some evening to play and sing with the family. "My no," the very motherly mother said—"We should be very pleased to have you." The result is of course that Jimmy will go over some night soon.

Throughout the war, Byron's innate curiosity and intrepid spirit would bring him into contact with people and places not normally encountered by a soldier in the field. For the next few weeks, on evenings when time permitted, Byron would visit Monsieur Filbert and his daughters to sing and socialize. Byron had noticed that M. Filbert's daughters were among but a small number of women his age in the village. On inquiring about this oddity, a villager told him that most of the young women had been shipped off to a convent as a precaution before the American soldiers arrived. In a letter to Estelle on December 3, Byron described a typical soirée at the Filbert household:

> I'm learning all sorts of customs and habits from this French family where I go. They invariably bring out the' [tea], gateau (?) [cake] with crème et sucre. They have a funny habit. Their honey is allowed to sugar in the cold, and they serve it on the table in a small crock. Then they use this in their the' in preference to sugar.
>
> I just learned that M. Filbert's home is up near the firing line—his store being in a town constantly subjected to bombardment. So, he is renting a place here till the lines move forward. I had quite a time talking to them about the significance of the "action de graces," and giving them a list of our national holidays, with their dates. The only map they have of the U.S. is a one page map of the whole of North America. Detroit is shown on it, and I made dots to show Albion, and Jackson. Oh, yes, our town is becoming known way over here. They ask all sorts of questions—are the Indians really red? Are they all over the continent, yet? etc. etc. I tell them all the things I can, and they certainly enjoy hearing it.

As enlightening as some of Byron's evenings were, his days proved to be burdensome. After cleaning up the village streets, Byron and most of the ambulance company were put to work as stevedores. Vaucouleurs was the quartermaster depot for the entire Rainbow Division. Men from the Michigan and Oklahoma ambulance companies spent long, backbreaking days unloading coal, wood, bales of hay, oats, clothes, shoes, foodstuffs, mule teams, wagons, and munitions. In a letter to Estelle dated November 16, Byron remarked: "My present life is far from what would be prescribed in a course for a religious worker—but may all have a very good place. I truly hope so. This week I'm doing steve-dore work at the quarter-master depot. The quantity of supplies is enormous. We are preparing!!—for <u>the</u> day."

Not everyone shared Byron's optimism, however—as forewarned in an age-old proverb about the vicissitudes of war, "for the want of a nail" wars had been lost. Colonel Johnson Hagood was fully aware of that disturbing possibility. Hagood was in charge of the advance section of the army's supply service. In the late fall and early winter of 1917, as supplies and soldiers from the United States streamed into

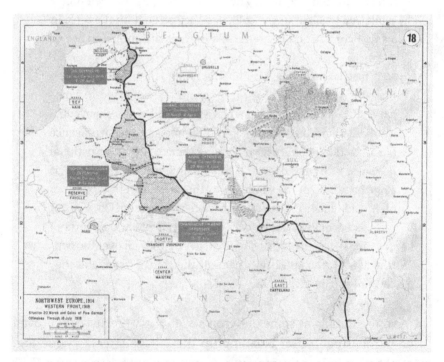

Map of the western front, spring 1918. Vaucouleurs is located in the southeast quadrant, near Lunéville. (From Edward J. Krasnoborski, "Situation 20 March and Gains of Five German Offensives through 18 July 1918," United States Military Academy, Department of History, https://westpoint.edu/sites/default/files/inlineimages/academics/academic_departments/history/WWI/WWOne18.jpg.)

France, getting them to the front proved to be extremely difficult for Hagood and his staff. Although France was interlaced with an elaborate system of railroad lines, at this particular point in time, most of the available railroad equipment was being used to divert French and British resources to the Italian front, where Austro-Hungarian forces had recently broken through Allied lines at the battle of Caporetto. In a scathing letter to General Pershing's chief of staff on November 15, Hagood cautioned, "If the United States does not actually fail, its efficiency is going to be tremendously decreased by the sheer incompetence of its lines of communication." Hagood would later recall that the Rainbow Division's supplies were scattered over a ten-acre field at Vaucouleurs, where they were exposed to the elements and in such a state of disarray that they could not be segregated or used.

Moreover, the division had only six trucks to distribute those supplies. Rural French roads were unpaved and frequently in disrepair, and in inclement weather they were often impassable. Although French, English, and American forces had laid a system of narrow-gauge railroad tracks to expedite the flow of men and equipment to the front lines, as America's involvement in the war intensified, the logistics of moving increasingly larger numbers of men and equipment would become more daunting. In the coming months, nearly 1 million American soldiers would arrive in France. At the moment, though, Hagood's concern was simply to supply the two hundred thousand American soldiers that were already there.

On November 16, the 117th Sanitary Train took matters into its own hands and set out to transport its own equipment. Byron was one of fifty-five men selected by Captain McAfee to go to Meru, a small town northwest of Paris, to pick up thirty-six Ford ambulances and then drive them back to Vaucouleurs. The ambulances were said to be used but otherwise in serviceable condition. On less than an hour's notice the detail of men made it to the railroad station in time to catch the overnight train to Paris. On arriving at Metropolitan Station in Paris the following morning, the men learned that the next train to Meru wouldn't leave until 8:00 that evening from Gare du Nord Station. To pass the time, Captain McAfee gave each man 5 francs and permission to explore Paris.

In a letter to Estelle on November 23, Byron recounted the trip in great detail. A similar letter to his parents would later be published in the *Jackson Patriot News*. In both letters, he described the monuments, gardens, and museums that he and the other men visited while in Paris. In his letter to Estelle, however, Byron took particular note of Napoleon's tomb, remarking: "Here rest the remains of the restless one. The first Kaiser—Napoleon. Why can't Wilhelm, following the same course, see the handwriting on the wall?" Ultimately, Byron would be proven right—the handwriting was already on the wall. The impending tide was slowly, almost imperceptibly, beginning to turn. In his letter to Estelle on the 23rd, Byron talked about the "thousands upon thousands of transports, canon of all size, ammunition dumps, a huge aviation field—and many more evidence of <u>real</u> business" he saw while driving back to Vaucouleurs. It would only be a matter of time before German troops got swept away by the deluge of American soldiers and equipment that was pouring into France.

Notwithstanding Byron's hopeful prophecy, it would be a long time before Kaiser Wilhelm recognized that the end of his reign was inevitable. Whether or not that outcome was divinely preordained, as some like Byron might prefer to believe, was a matter of personal faith—but it is undeniable fact that attaining it would end up costing thousands upon thousands of American soldiers their lives. Any lingering doubts that Byron and the other ambulance drivers may have had about the ferocity and tenacity of the German troops they were about to face in battle were laid to rest on November 11 in the village of Senlis.

In a letter written to Estelle on the 23rd, Byron described the first night's stopover at Senlis on the drive back to Vaucouleurs: "Monday we got the cars tuned up and started out. We slept on the floor of the ambulance on cushions that night in a town held by the Germans in the days of the 'Marne.' We saw the buildings destroyed by the 'Boche,' who came through—as the natives say—'with babies hands in their belts.'"

Many of the gruesome details Byron chose to spare Estelle were later included in one of the books he coauthored after the war:

> Before retiring some of us wandered about the city to see the sights of interest and to buy postcards. In our conversations

with civilians we learned that the 1914 advance of the Germans included this town, and also were informed of some of the Hun atrocities. Children's legs, feet, arms and hands were cut off, babies were rudely taken from mother's arms and cut in two with a slash of sabre or bayonet, also the stories of other horrible mutilations were related to us. We had read all these and it was difficult to believe that the world was infested with a people who committed such horrible and hideous crimes. We must have registered doubt for presently a women brought in a child—a little girl—and we saw for ourselves. The left eye was gone and a scar three inches or more was plainly visible on her cheek where the bayonet had slashed, and her right hand was minus three fingers. The child was eight years old. Imagine the thoughts racing through our minds when we beheld this little girl's plight! God surely couldn't allow such debasement to continue indefinitely.

As it turned out, such debasement would not continue indefinitely. Exactly one year to the day from making it, Byron's fervent wish would be answered.

9
THE VALLEY FORGE HIKE

Vaucouleurs was separated from the frontline trenches by a distance of over twenty-five miles. It was still close enough though to hear the rumble of guns, constant and low. After five weeks of just listening, the men were impatient to be in the thick of it—they had come here to fight Germans, after all, not sweep streets.

Before American troops could be moved to the front, they would first have to be sent to the rear—they still needed to be trained by experienced French soldiers about what to expect once they got there. Their lives would depend on it. The 117th Sanitary Train's training camp was located in the village of Rolampont, sixty-two miles further removed from the action. It would take two thousand boxcars to move the entire 42nd Division to Rolampont—none of which were available in December. So, like other great armies before them, the soldiers of the Rainbow Division would have to pick up stakes, sling on their packs, and make the long trek on foot, crossing over much of the same terrain Roman legions had traveled centuries earlier.

At 10:00 on the morning of December 12, the men hit the road carrying packs loaded with fifty pounds of gear on their backs. All the rest of the company's bags and baggage was loaded onto the ambulances and trucks. Cook wagons rolled ahead of the column in order to set up meals at predesignated stopping points. The hike started out reasonably well. The troops were in good spirits. The weather was seasonably cold but dry. The first day's destination was the village of Maxey-sur-Meuse. The men in front set a pace that would allow the company to get there before sunset. The soldiers who followed sang the usual repertoire of songs.

Fifteen miles a day was an ambitious goal, especially for men who hadn't been on a sustained march since leaving Camp Mills. Although Byron and some of the other men were fit and trim from working as stevedores, none of them was in hiking shape—that required a different sort of stamina and callous-hardened feet. As the men would soon discover, they were as ill equipped to make the long tramp to the rear as they were to enter the trenches at the front. All that would change, incrementally.

Two hours and five miles later, the men were still game—not that anyone complained when the company finally stopped for lunch. Shedding packs, men opened their coats to cool off in the breeze. Then helped themselves to servings of iron rations and hot coffee that went down like ambrosia. After sitting idle for nearly an hour, some of the men started to shiver in their perspiration-soaked clothing. It was time to get moving again. As the company marched on, it wasn't long before the men began to swelter in the afternoon sun. The smiles of the morning were now replaced by grim-faced determination as the soldiers struggled with stiff muscles, blistered feet, and unwieldy packs. Nobody sang. Instead, every epithet imaginable was hurled at the "genius" responsible for designing their backpacks. The infamous M1910 haversack would forever be remembered as one of the most tortuous and useless contraptions ever foisted on a foot soldier. The pack was nothing more than flaps of canvas and straps—into which a half-tent, tent pole and pegs, blankets, overcoat, rain slicker, socks, underwear, iron meals, and kit bag were swaddled. When fully stuffed, the elongated haversack weighed over fifty pounds and looked like an overgrown papoose when strapped on a soldier's back. Unlike its Native American forerunner, however, the army's version didn't have a frame or backboard to help distribute the weight. With no hip support to carry the heavy load, soldiers who tried to march standing upright bore the full weight of the pack on their shoulders—causing the unpadded canvas straps to cut into their skin, leaving shoulders bloodied and bruised. For men who tried to balance the load by marching bent over, a different but equally painful consequence resulted as the muscles of their lower back stiffened and eventually cramped. To add insult to injury, each man wore a medical waist-belt that had eleven pouches filled with bandages and other paraphernalia, plus a canteen and a hatchet that served no purpose other than to get in the way. The effect of having to carry this cumbersome load was debilitating—by late afternoon, the company looked like an army of hunchbacks and cripples as it trudged along.

Darkness had already fallen by the time the company staggered into the village of Maxey-sur-Meuse. The men, completely spent, literally hit the hay in barn lofts and sheds, some not even bothering to eat. In a letter to Estelle written on December 22 Byron described the march:

> It has been ten days since [censored location] where we had been for a month, and may be ten more before we are located in a semi-permanent camp. . . . We used to be disgusted at the seemingly senseless delays in the States, especially after we had been told for days and days that a move was imminent. Over here, the moves come plenty often, with little announcement beforehand. This was a real move, in that we're moving bag and baggage, with fifty plus pounds of it on each of our backs. Yes, really on our backs as we're hiking on this move. We hiked three days from [censored location] landing here [censored location]. On the march, the cook wagons go ahead and have the meals "started," at least when we get up to them. We marched for fifty minute intervals, then rested for ten minutes. We walked approximately 25 kilometers (15 miles) a day for three days.

It took two more days of arduous hiking to complete the first half of the journey. After passing through Joan of Arc's home village, Dom-rémy, and then Neufchâteau, the company spent the second night at Goncourt in demountable quarters called Adrian barracks. From there, they marched on to a temporary encampment in the village of Saint-Blin.

For the next ten days, the sanitary train stayed at Saint-Blin in a complex of Adrian barracks. Named after the French commandant who invented them, Adrian barracks were portable prefabricated sleeping quarters that could be quickly set up and dismantled behind the ever-shifting lines of combat. Constructed of uninsulated panels of wood that barely kept out the wind, each barracks had a wood-burning stove that did precious little to warm the drafty structures. The bunks in each barracks were new and clean but had no bedding. Men bought ticks of straw from local farmers for 2 francs to pad the bunks. The only way to stay warm enough to get some sleep was to hunker down fully clothed under two wool blankets. Some men joined forces by pulling beds together to share blankets and body heat. It was brutally cold at night, but at least the men had a mess hall with tables, chairs, and hot meals to help keep them comfortable during the day.

On December 15, the first heavy snowfall of the winter covered the ground. A freezing rain immediately followed, after which temperatures plummeted even lower, turning the roads and surrounding countryside into an icescape. Instead of avoiding the elements, though, the company instituted a training regimen to harden the men by requiring them to hike five miles each day. The men knew that Saint-Blin was not their ultimate destination, and rumors began to circulate that another move was imminent. With Christmas at hand, for the moment, anyway, men were able to distract themselves by getting ready to celebrate the holiday. In a letter to Estelle written on Christmas Eve, Byron described the anticipation and preparations:

> Of course, like little kids, we're all excited about tomorrow. The pies are all made, and sitting where they tempt us every meal time. The cooks are roasting the turkeys now, so we know we'll have a good feed. We have a mess hall here so we'll be able to sit down to tables for our feed. This morning a dozen of us went out on a hill nearby and collected all the evergreen boughs and mistletoe clumps we could carry back. My, the mistletoe grows in great quantities here. The white balls just fill the green clumps with splotches. Honest, I'd hate to think of the fair damsel's fate who walked down our mistle-toe roofed mess-hall tomorrow.

Then, in a passing reference that was tantamount to a Christmas-related parable on the hardship of a pilgrim's life, Byron mentioned:

"I'll have to spend Christmas without either of my chummies—Sprague had to go over to the hospital today with 'trench fever,' a peculiar swelling—usually in the hands or feet—in his case the hands. It seems to be a comparatively easy thing to remedy but our doctors have not any knowledge of the disease." Trench fever was spread by lice. Notwithstanding the idyllic setting normally associated with the Nativity of Jesus, taking refuge in vermin-infested barns and sheds was less than medically ideal. Given the itinerant lifestyle the men had been relegated to since first arriving in France, it was not surprising that Horace Sprague had contracted the disease. Byron's other "chummie," Herbert Jackson, had previously fallen and broken his leg while exploring the countryside around Vaucouleurs, and would be hospitalized for several more weeks.

A few lucky men had received Christmas packages from home earlier in the week. For Byron and the other men who had not, letters from loved ones would have to suffice as holiday cheer. Mail from home usually arrived in bunches, often four weeks or more after it was written.

On December 21, Byron received a packet of thirteen letters from his parents, Estelle, and others in Michigan. In writing back to Estelle on December 22 about the contents of a letter that he had just received from his parents, Byron remarked on "how busy everyone was [at home] with Liberty Bonds, Y.M.C.A. War Work, Red Cross campaigns, knitting everywhere, and always—war talk and war preparations and war efficiency efforts. Things must be moving back there."

Things were in fact moving on the home front. In October, a second series of Liberty Bonds had been issued by the Treasury Department to help finance the war. Public response to the first series of bonds, issued in April, had been very disappointing, and savvy investors had taken advantage of the situation by purchasing the balance of unsold bonds at subpar value. In an attempt to remedy that situation and encourage investment by the public generally, a second series of bonds was issued in October with an improved rate of return. To help sell those bonds, a promotional campaign, using celebrities like Douglas Fairbanks, Charlie Chaplin, and Mary Pickford, was launched to convince citizens that the purchase of Liberty Bonds was not only

"They Remembered Me!" Front cover of *Leslie's Weekly*, December 22, 1917, illustrated by Norman Rockwell.

a smart investment but a patriotic duty. Byron's father ended up purchasing bonds.

Campaigns in support of the war took other forms as well, one of which was the Red Cross "Knit Your Bit" campaign. Like thousands of other women, Estelle did her patriotic bit, knitting a woolen "helmet" for Byron to wear to bed at night. In a letter written to Estelle on Christmas Eve, Byron addressed other newsy bits of information from the home scene: "The Y.M. has started another fine enterprise. They are having published once a week a 'resume' edition of the leading Parisian newspaper—Le Martin—in English. This is for the benefit of the English-speaking soldiers. It contains a resume of the leading events of each week—in the States, in European countries and—at the front. Then too, there are many interesting articles about cities and battles of the war. The action in taking over the railroad was very interesting to me."

The "action" on railroads referred to by Byron was not only "interesting," it was essential to the war effort. In December, acting on a recommendation from the Interstate Commerce Commission, President Wilson issued an order subjecting the country's troubled railroad system to federal regulation. Thus far the railroads had proven themselves incapable of providing for an expeditious flow of goods and supplies in support of the war. At that time, many of the nation's railroad companies were either in bankruptcy or struggling to avoid it as they tried to cope with the costly effects of inflation and labor unrest. In bringing these long-festering problems to a head, the war gave Wilson and Congress an opportunity to redraw the regulatory map governing interstate commerce and the railroad industry in the interest of national security. In March 1918, the U.S. Railroad Administration was established to enforce these new rules of engagement.

In his letter to Estelle on the 24th, Byron voiced his opinion on another event that would have a much more profound effect on his own life: "[T]he representatives have voted for prohibition again.... I'd be one tickled boy if the whole country could only be dry when we came back. I've seen enough boozing to last a life-time. Anyway, Michigan will be dry." Unlike regulation of the railroads, the war had not served as an impetus for the enactment of Prohibition. The success of the

"The Santa Claus of 1917." Front cover of *Leslie's Weekly*, December 1, 1917, illustrated by James Montgomery Flagg.

temperance movement had been a long time in the making. As a result of many years of dedicated campaigning by countless church groups and civic organizations, Michigan had finally become a dry state in May 1917. In December 1917, the House of Representatives and the U.S. Senate both passed resolutions recommending the enactment of a constitutional amendment that would ban the sale and distribution of alcohol. At this point in his life, Byron was a strict teetotaler, and would remain so for the next decade.

Before ending his letter of the 24th, Byron addressed the rumors of peace negotiations that were continuing to circulate in the trenches and in the press back home. For men whose lives hung in the balance, it was often easier to simply dismiss the rumors as just more posturing by both sides rather than have their hopes raised in vain. In an earlier letter to Estelle, Byron remarked that the men didn't put much stock in the rumors. This time, however, Byron was taking them seriously, and not in a positive way: "We nearly went off our feet a couple of days ago at some rumors of an early peace. An early peace now would be the worst thing that could happen—quitting cold while Germany wasn't yet entirely whipped. We must not quit now—she is still too strong."

Unfortunately, Byron would get his wish. Two weeks later, on January 8, in an attempt to initiate a productive dialogue concerning the settlement of hostilities, President Wilson delivered a speech to Congress outlining a fourteen-point proposal for a fair peace. Although Wilson's proposal would later be considered as a framework for the Treaty of Versailles, at the moment neither side was willing to sit down and negotiate seriously. It would take ten more months of carnage to bring everyone to their senses.

On the morning of December 27, reveille announced the onset of a howling winter storm. In the dim light of dawn, men peered out through barrack windows and shivered at the sight of eight inches of new snow. Temperatures hovered a few degrees above zero.

While men busied themselves packing up gear and getting ready to break camp, large flakes of snow continued to fall, swirling in the stiff wind and piling in drifts against the barrack's walls. It was into these blizzard-like conditions that the men would set out on the second half of their journey—the infamous "Valley Forge Hike." It was the first time since Camp Mills that the sanitary train was intact. The ambulance companies from New Jersey, Tennessee, and Nebraska, which had been aboard the crippled USS *Grant* and were thus delayed in getting to France, had been forced to encamp at LaFouche instead of Vaucouleurs. This meant that for those units to join up with the rest of the sanitary train at Saint-Blin by 10:00 in the morning, they would have to start out from LaFouche at 8, hiking into the teeth of the blizzard. Those men were in no condition to make the march, especially in winter. No one was, really—not even the men from the Michigan and Oklahoma units, who were somewhat acclimated to the weather from having worked outdoors as stevedores. At 10:00, with the New Jersey, Tennessee, and Nebraska units finally back in the fold, the entire sanitary train set out for Rolampont. The road between Saint-Blin and Rolampont was thirty-three miles of glazed ice. As trucks came and went along the route, men were forced to march in deep snow at the edge of the road, doing their best to navigate around the trees and piles of rocks that lined the route, all the while straining to keep their footing in the wind with fifty-pound packs strapped to their backs.

The unshod mules didn't fare much better as they struggled to get traction on the icy inclines. When necessary men pitched in to help the mules pull the wagons up the treacherous hills. At times, though, even this collective effort wasn't enough. On one of the hills Nebraska's kitchen wagon slid off the road into a ditch. It took a team of oxen from a nearby village to right the wagon and get it back on the road.

It didn't take long before the grueling conditions began to exact a heavy toll. By noon, men from New Jersey, Tennessee, and Nebraska started to fall by the wayside. Some of the men simply lay where they fell, too exhausted to move, trusting that ambulances bringing up the rear would be able to pick them up. It was hardly their fault. The men were as ill equipped to cope with the elements as they were poorly conditioned to make the march. By the end of the three-day march, units would be decimated by cases of hypothermia, pneumonia, and influenza. Five men from the sanitary train later died from pneumonia contracted during the long march, two of them from the Michigan Ambulance Company. Due to faulty lines of supply, equipment intended for the Rainbow Division had been redistributed to other

American units in France, leaving the Rainbow Division improperly fitted out for winter campaigning. Everyone seemed to be missing at least one essential article of winter clothing—many of the men were forced to hike in hobnail boots that were totally unfit for the wet conditions in France. In the spring of 1918, the hobnail boot would be replaced with the more durable and water-repellant Pershing boot. For now, however, soldiers resorted to stuffing their shoes with letters from home to help protect their feet from frostbite. As worn shoes gave out, men wrapped their blistered feet in bags, leaving bloody tracks in the snow. Byron would not receive his new boots until later. At least he had a winter overcoat—others did not, many of whom also had no long underwear to insulate them from the wind and snow.

The men of the sanitary train were not alone in their suffering. As noted in diary entries by Major William Donovan, commander of New York's Fighting 69th, lack of proper clothing and footwear during the march hobbled the New Yorkers as well: "One man, today in A Company who wears an 11 size shoe had on five pairs of socks with boards tied to his ankles for the protection of his feet. Cannot get shoes." Then, relating observations made by the division chaplain, Father Francis Duffy, Donovan wrote: "Father Duffy said . . . men on the march from

Rainbow Division's Valley Forge Hike, December 26, 1917. (Photograph by Army Signal Corps.)

Grande had hands frozen to the guns, felt chill-blained and frozen—no shoes. One man walked the last fifteen miles in wooden sabots."

Still, the men soldiered on. By 8:00 that night, all the companies in the sanitary train managed to reach their destination on sheer guts. The men from Nebraska, New Jersey, and Tennessee, who had been on their feet the longest, were allowed to stop at the closest village, Echot, where they stayed in an old château or other buildings with fireplaces.

The Michigan men drew the short straw and marched farther down the road to the village of Forcey, where they slept in barns. In a letter written to Estelle on December 29, Byron described the first day of the hike:

> Why, three mornings ago, Cappy says, "Lets take another little sight-seeing trip," or words to that effect. The 104 of us in that barrack jumped spryly to our feet, carried our straw ticks out, and emptied them, and then went back in and rolled our blanket rolls. Then we monkeyed around at one thing and another until ten when we hied us to our hike. Yes, and we were regular white coated knights of the road too, as the snow pelted down all day. We only had to boom along for an hour and a half. And say, I'll bet you would have wished for a camera if you could have seen us during the rest periods that day and the next. We'd ramble along for fifty minutes, and at the first call of the bugle for the rest, we'd lay down full length in the road or beside it. The packs made an excellent cushion for our backs, and the snow pelting down on our faces would cool them off. That day we had coffee and a roast beef sandwich for dinner, and hiked on in the afternoon for enough to make 25 kilos. Hooray, that night 80 of us had a great bunk, we had hay four feet deep to sleep on, in a big hay loft. I didn't even open up my blanket roll. I plunged my shoes, leggings, and trousers and the parts of my body enclosed therein under a pile of hay, and covered the rest with my over coat and raincoat. Aside from having to get up from 9:00 to 10:30 to be identified for a petty thievery committed by some soldier, I slept soundly till 8 or I guess it was seven the next morning. Fortunately, I bought a fine supper the night of the first day, because

it was so cold the second morning that the bacon had frozen stiff—and we had only coffee and hard tack.

On the first night of the march, all of the men were awakened at ten o'clock and rousted from their berths in haylofts and sheds to stand in line outside a tavern, waiting to be subjected to an impromptu lineup for the alleged theft of money from the proprietor. It was ten degrees below zero. Several soldiers passed out from exhaustion and exposure to the elements. At the end of the grueling ordeal, the tavern owner had failed to identify anyone.

The next morning, men awoke to discover that the breakfast bacon was not the only thing that had frozen stiff during the night. Unlike Byron, many of the men had removed their shoes before going to sleep. It was a painful mistake. On waking, they found that their shoes were frozen solid and that their feet were swollen. Desperate men tried to thaw out their shoes by stuffing them with burning straw and lit candles. Some resorted to chopping and pounding on the frozen leather with hatchets. Eventually, the men were able to force their swollen feet into the rigid shoes—for the rest of the march, though, it was like hiking in shoes carved from blocks of ice.

The second day was more of the same. Temperatures remained below zero as the sanitary train continued to limp through blinding snow and gale force winds. Men too exhausted to keep pace straggled and then dropped by the side of road. By 3:00 in the afternoon, the less hardened men from Nebraska, New Jersey, and Tennessee were completely wrung out and stopped for the night in the village of Mandres, where they stayed in barns and lofts. Michigan and four other companies marched on to Nogent-en-Bassigny. It was their turn for more comfortable accommodations. In his letter of the 29th to Estelle, Byron described the second day of the hike:

> Well, amid some more snow, we hiked along with a couple of hot beef sandwiches for dinner. It was easier that day with only seventeen kilos. We came into quite a little town that night. Some of us happened to put into a deserted house with only a floor for bed and we says—sez we—"Let's hunt for a real place

tonight." And we did. Forgot were the tired backs, and frozen canteens when we got our place. It was the house of a fine old French lady who practically gave over the use of her house to four of us that night. We bought some stuff and brought it in for her to cook. Say little girl—if you only could have been with us, or been a mouse in a corner to have watched us. We had pork steak & egg omellette & French frieds & bread, butter, cheese, jam & hot lemonade. And then we sat around the kitchen stove with our shoes and socks off, so we could dry them, and our 10 and 1/2 hoofies. . . . We did get up and had a fine breakfast of hot coffee & the rest of the bread, cheese and jam. And the woman treated us so fine. She had all her four sons in the battle-lines—one of them under the fleur-de-lis, till all the wars are over.

According to Byron, the next morning was "snapping cold," minus fifteen degrees Fahrenheit, but clear. As the sun rose in the sky so did the temperature. Compared to the blizzard conditions of the previous two days, the relatively calm seven-mile march to Rolampont seemed like a stroll in the park. The Michigan men arrived in Rolampont before dinner; the rest of the sanitary train reached the end of the road by nightfall.

The journey had been a conversion of sorts. In the course of enduring its hardship, the men had learned what it meant to soldier in the face of adversity. More important, though, they had been drawn together as a unit. Individually and collectively, the Rainbow Division would face far greater challenges in the months to come—but for the men who had made the long hard slog, the Valley Forge Hike would always be remembered as the moment that first defined them.

10
REMEMBER JESUS CHRIST

On January 1, the start of a new year ushered in more of the same for the Rainbow Division. In Rolampont, the enlisted men continued to be quartered in drafty Adrian barracks, sheds, and barns, while officers stayed in decent accommodations in town or at a training school in the nearby city of Langres. In Chaumont, only twelve miles away, Pershing and his staff remained comfortably ensconced in a well-appointed château.

After spending one night in a barn, Byron and five of his comrades decided they could do better:

> Our regular billet was a huge barn where there was no heat, or light or anything. So five of us who were in it went out in search of a room. My puppy-French came into good use, and we located a dandy room—with plaster walls and tight floor where we could be fixed up fine. . . . We get the room for a franc a day, and the people are very good to us. We have our straw ticks on the floor. . . . The stove is one of the small army type, but heats well, so we are well satisfied "when we can get wood," which is very scarce. Of course, our light is candles.

In the coming weeks, the men would get down to the primal business of learning how to survive in the trenches. In a letter written to Estelle on New Year's Day, Byron resolved not to lose his ideals in the process:

Howe'er it be, it seems to me,
'Tis only noble to be good,
Kind hearts are more than coronets,
And simple faith than Norman blood.
"Tennyson's idea,—and mine."

Before the men could begin a rigorous regimen of training, however, the first order of business was to get them healthy. It hadn't taken long before the fallout from the grueling march began to manifest itself. As cases of pneumonia, mumps, and influenza began to deplete the ranks, it became necessary to establish a system of triage for the entire division. Every third day, one of the motorized ambulance companies was required to work a twenty-four-hour shift during which orderlies made the rounds of the regimental headquarters to pick up sick patients and ferry them to base hospitals in Chaumont and Neufchâteau. It was an endeavor that would prove to be much easier ordered than actually done in the old Ford ambulances.

It had been decided that Michigan would be one of the motorized companies. That turned out to be a mixed blessing. With no spare parts to be found in France, many of the ambulances had no ignition and/or low or reverse gears. In some cases, the brakes were worn out as well—on one occasion, an ambulance with faulty brakes, failing to hold the curve on an icy road, took an unexpected sleigh ride down a snowy hillside. Until new General Motors Company (GMC) ambulances could finally be obtained in mid-February, Byron and the other drivers would be forced to go about their work on a wing and a prayer.

On days when Byron wasn't flirting with disaster as a jalopy driver, he was in training. At this point, the U.S. Army was totally unprepared for the kind of warfare introduced by World War I. In prior wars, the training regimen for an American infantryman consisted of foot drills and open field tactics. In the trenches of France, however, those outdated maneuvers were absolutely useless—or worse. In the early days of the war, English and French troops had learned that lesson the hard way when German machine guns and artillery had laid that approach to soldiering to rest.

Captain Baskerville was one of several officers who had been sent to French and British training schools to learn the new tactics. On his return in early January, training began in earnest for the rest of the company. The days were long and the discipline was absolute. With the assistance of French and British instructors, the ambulance companies received specialized medical training related to their jobs at the front, as well as other aspects of trench warfare. One way or another, Baskerville claimed, it would improve their ability to save lives—and stay alive. He would be proven right. In a letter written to Estelle on January 3, Byron remarked: "Our Captain and two lieutenants who have been away at officer training school have returned, and have promised us some stiff drills from now on based on the information and experiences they had there. There will be drills with gas masks and with litters, under all conceivable conditions, and much work to get us physically fit for the most strenuous action."

Each day Baskerville put the men through their early-morning paces, which consisted of learning the basics of how to run, duck, and cover in the trenches, as well as the art of avoiding wire entanglements, machine-gun emplacements, and overlapping fields of fire. During these morning sessions, the company was also expected to show its overall versatility as frontline troopers by chopping wood, digging trenches, and shoring up bombproof dugouts. The intricacies of using rifles, pistols, trench mortars, bayonets, and hand grenades were left for the infantry to master.

In the afternoons, the Michigan Ambulance Company was given crash courses by French and British corpsmen on the most common medical procedures in use at the front. Unlike in Dr. Ballin's operating room, in the heat of battle, time and careful deliberation were in short supply—stopgap medicine carried the day. Clinics in splinting shattered limbs, staunching the flow of blood, and bandaging every conceivable wound were held again and again.

As Byron and the others were learning, the treatment of casualties in combat was essentially a relay race against death. The first leg of that race involved the extraction of the wounded from the field of battle by litter bearers, who were tasked with carrying their loads to a battalion aid station, which was usually located 250 to 500 yards behind the front line. These aid stations were manned by one or two doctors and four to six orderlies (medics) who rendered stopgap treatment to the wounded, then passed those patients on to litter bearers who would carry their suffering burdens to a company dressing station, located an additional 3,000 to 6,000 yards to the rear. At that juncture, a system of triage was employed by medical personnel to determine the order in which those incoming casualties would receive further treatment. It was not done on a first-come, first-served basis. Those with the most grievous injuries and best chance of survival were prioritized and immediately evacuated by ambulance to a field hospital for more extensive treatment or surgery. Along the entire route, death was ever present for patients and medical personnel alike. Even field hospitals were not immune from attack by German snipers, airplanes, and artillery.

The survival skill practiced most was gas mask usage. If that were not mastered, all else was lost. By this point in the war, both sides were capable of launching massive gas attacks with devastating effect. As later recounted in *The History of Ambulance Company 168*, a book coauthored by Byron:

> It was vitally necessary to become thoroughly proficient in the use and care of our masks as we later found out. In the casualty lists printed daily throughout the countries [of] England, France, Italy and the United States there appeared under killed in action, names of brave men, who had made the supreme sacrifice, not at the explosion of a shell, not at the sharp, deep, deadly thrust of a bayonet, not because of exposure to the chill blasts of wind, but because of inhalation of great quantities of poisonous gas thrown out by the barbaric horde of Huns. No man has been gassed badly and come forth unmarked. The gas either disfigured its victim temporarily by severe burning to the skin, causing the flesh to become black, or it has gone into his system and by [a] constant eating, corrupting and burning process destroy[ed] the intestines, leaving the soldier a corpse, the lifeless remains of a stalwart hero, a victim of German atrocity and an exponent of the need of Democracy to forever forestall

and crush the doctrines of German Kultur. Sixty percent of all battle casualties was due to gas.

American soldiers were issued both French and English gas masks—neither of which was user-friendly. The French mask was a small contraption with a foul-smelling face pad. The English mask was a cumbersome canister device. To become proficient in the use of both, the men trained each day, tedious hour after tedious hour. They had to be prepared to use them under every imaginable condition—from running in the trenches and across fields in the stifling masks to driving ambulances while peering through breath-fogged lenses on dark and icy roads. Eventually the men were able to put on either mask in a gas-filled chamber in less than five seconds without getting even a whiff of gas. In a letter written to Estelle on February 12, Byron observed: "Oh yes, this morning we went into the gas room to test our masks. While the gas was four times the density of the cloud gas at the front, there was not the least odor thru' either of the masks. That gave us a lot more confidence than we had had."

American Expeditionary Force medics wearing gas masks, February 7, 1918. (Photograph by Army Signal Corps.)

On other matters, Byron was not nearly as confident. As the gruesome reality of the war drew closer, Byron's letters to Estelle assumed a more cautious tone. In a January 3 letter, after telling Estelle about the immediate task of training for the front, Byron talked reflectively and more tentatively about the future: "Last night I was on guard duty for four hours with lots and lots of time to think. And lots to think of. So much of the time I plan things for the time when I <u>may</u> get back." Then, in a January 4 letter, Byron followed up by imploring Estelle to enjoy herself in an almost live-for-today flourish that was highly unusual for a Methodist: "Everything is getting more and more business-like as the weeks slip away that separate us from the real action. But I'll bet you get tired of reading—war—war—war—and so do we. I hope things aren't all balled up, and the fun prevented by the war. Have all the fun you can—and you can have lots. Love to you—my dear Jimmy."

In yet another letter on January 6, Byron conveyed his anxiety by resorting to a prearranged code with Estelle, which consisted of employing obvious misspellings, grammatical mistakes, postscripts, or added emphasis to convey an opposite meaning, so as not to draw the scrutiny of censors: "No, it don't exactly seem a dream—this war—over here. We've begun our classes on gassing now. And our helmets and hip boots are all ordered. But, 'everything <u>is</u> fine with me.'"

That Byron would be anxious about the uncertain fate that awaited him at the front was only human. That he would also want to hide that anxiety from the superior officers who censored his letters was equally understandable. At this point, Byron still quietly hoped for advancement in the company. Although he was far less optimistic about his prospects than when he'd first enlisted, he almost certainly would not have wanted to jeopardize even the slimmest chance for promotion by divulging any uncertainty or fear. In a letter to Estelle on January 29, Byron lamented:

> No, my dear, advancement and promotion don't grow on trees around here. Jimmy seems as far away from the chosen jobs as ever. Not kidding myself or you in the least, I know I could handle a corporal or sergeant's job well. But, many things, some fair,

some very unfair enter into the selection. There is no open com-
petition here as in the "line" infantry, cavalry, or artillery, where
whoever does well has a trial at least as a non-com. Favoritism
enters in very strongly in choosing. I do not smoke or drink or
joke with the men who have the influence. I have stuck strictly
to the middle of the road.

One of the factors that Byron alluded to as militating against
his being promoted at this time was his age. It was a legitimate concern. At the time of his enlistment, Byron was the youngest member of the ambulance company. Whether grown men would be
willing to take orders from an untested twenty-year-old (much less "a
whipper-snapper-college man") in the heat of combat was a fair factor
for superior officers to consider. Of little or no importance in deter-
mining his fitness for promotion, however, was Byron's clean-living
lifestyle. Although his self-imposed code of conduct had likely set
him apart from less restrained members of the ambulance company,
there is no indication that he was ever self-righteous about it, or that
any of the men resented him for it. To the contrary, it seems to have
endeared him to many of his colleagues in the unit, as evidenced by
his nickname—Fraisee. In practical translation, it was the "Soda Pop
Kid" with a French twist—a good-natured reference to Byron's bever-
age of choice while stationed in France, *Fraisé*, a strawberry-flavored
nonalcoholic drink. It was a fitting tribute—at this point, as Byron was
still remarkably sweet and pure of heart.

Not only did Byron abstain from drinking and smoking, as reflected
in a letter to Estelle on January 18, he didn't usually play cards and
he most definitely didn't gamble: "We've been playing '500' this evening, and Dwight, my 'pardner' and I were beaten. Cards are our only
diversion except amusements at the Y., and we can't be over there all
the while. Under the circumstances I think their use is entirely warranted, as there is never even a thot' of gambling among any of us." In
a note to Byron's son, Fiske, fifty years later, Estelle would annotate
the margin of this paragraph, "*Methodists were strict!*" It was an under-
statement on her part. Methodists at that time frowned on a litany
of perceived corrupting influences, including card playing, saloons,

dancing, theater, cigars and tobacco, Sunday baseball, and gambling. As if to further underscore Estelle's observation about Methodist restraint, Byron mentioned later in the same letter selling to other soldiers the packages of cigarettes and tobacco he had received from the "Our Boys in France" fund and the Jackson County Board of Supervisors—although he readily acknowledged that there were "lots of times they would seem welcome."

The fact that Byron played cards and sought respite at the YMCA to relieve the tension was a good thing. A new kind of war brought new equipment—and with it, an added level of uncertainty. Gas masks, hip boots, and puttees were issued. The old campaign hat worn in previous wars had been replaced by a steel helmet that soldiers called a "Carnegie Stetson." The new tools of the trade took some getting used to, but at least they were designed for survival. The issuance of dog tags, however, was a totally different matter—the grave purpose of the round aluminum discs was a stark reminder of the grim reality of war. The sanitary train was among the first American units to receive dog tags—Byron's number was 877.

In addition to the usual stories of brutality at the front, recent accounts of German soldiers wantonly firing on litter bearers and other medical personnel prompted Byron and others to purchase clasp knives, which was no casual endeavor. Under the Geneva Convention, medical personnel were considered to be unarmed and not subject to harm by hostile forces. On occasion, when the terrain and vegetation required it, medics needed to carry a hand ax or bolo knife in the normal performance of their duties which, according to the rules of war, was permissible. The all-important distinction between those tools of the trade and a clasp knife was its pointed end, which turned a clasp knife into a stabbing implement and the person caught carrying it into a combatant.

Apparently, Byron thought that the risk of carrying one was worth it—rumor had it that German soldiers had no regard for the Geneva Convention anyway. In a letter written to Estelle on February 2, Byron explained his reasoning: "We're—a lot of us—buying some little weapons which wouldn't be allowed to be carried in the states. They are clasp knives with a six inch blade to be carried up there—for defensive measures only. And believe me, they will be for nothing else as far as I'm concerned. The thot' of slicing flesh doesn't have any appeal for me."

In late January, signs of imminent departure grew more pronounced. First, the number of men in the ambulance company was reduced to the prescribed combat strength of 122 soldiers, the excess personnel being distributed among other companies that were also headed to the front. After that, Byron and his housemates were told to vacate their room in town and take their place in the barracks with the rest of the company. On February 4, Byron finally "got some new spectacles" suitable for the front, with "rims heavy enough you couldn't break 'em if you tried." Then, on February 7, Byron and the rest of the company had their heads shaved to help prevent catching lice in the trenches.

Also on the 7th, Byron's "chummie" Herbert Jackson was finally discharged from the hospital and rejoined the unit. During his ten-week hospitalization, Jackson had seen and talked to many of the first American casualties of the war. After listening to Jackson's grim account, Byron noted in a letter to Estelle: "Even if nothing comes—, I shall be glad to have had your encouragement now. I can't live too far ahead—none of us can now."

As he often did in times of uncertainty, Byron drew inspiration and strength from his religion by reading the Bible and praying privately. News from home that he'd received his exhorter's license in the Methodist Church and would soon get his local preacher's license seemed to lift his spirits. On February 10, Byron took part in a religious service at the YMCA. It was the first Sunday service he had attended since October, when he accompanied his parents to the Methodist Episcopal Church in Hempstead. In a letter to Estelle on the evening of the 10th, Byron described the service: "As you say, 'another Sunday night.' This morning I played the piano during the singing of songs, and Mr. McDonald gave a fine talk on 'Remember Jesus Christ.'"

Invoking God's name in time of war was a righteous tradition embraced by both sides. The Germans were no less devout in the belief that their cause was a just one in the eyes of the Lord—so much so that their uniform belt buckles and tunic buttons were embossed with the imprimatur *Gott mit Uns*—"God is with us." Sermons comparing Jesus

Christ's sacrifice on the cross to the ordeal that soldiers headed into battle were about to endure was a well-worn refrain—all that mattered was that each generation of young soldiers who heard it for the first time found inspiration and comfort in those words as they began to steel themselves for combat.

As Byron's letter had so aptly put it, none of the men could afford to live outside the moment now.

11
BAPTISM BY FIRE

By the middle of February, the Rainbow Division had completed its training. Shortly before midnight on the 17th, the Michigan Ambulance Company caught the train out of Rolampont for the front. Twenty hours later, the men arrived at the village of Moyen. In a letter to Estelle written on February 27, Byron described the trip:

> We left our rest town on Sunday night—a week and a half ago. We had our barracks bags packed away for several days awaiting orders to come up. Sunday was filled with preparations for the departure. Part of the day we spent at the Y. At 10 P.M., we lined up and marched over there where they gave us hot chocolate and bread and butter. Then the other companies and ours stood around in groups and sang their various state songs and gave their yells. Shortly before twelve we marched over to the train where we piled (all except the officers) into the boxcars. There were about thirty-five of us in our little car, but we were lucky in having six inches of straw on the floor. We staid there the rest of that night and the next day, getting out in the evening and gladly too. That night we slept (?) on the board floor of a French barracks, and nearly froze to the floor. . . . The next morning we discovered we had to stay temporarily in a little country village 20 kilos away—so we hiked over there during the day.

At the time of writing this letter, Byron was apparently unaware of the reason for the twelve-mile hike. He was not alone. Initially, the men assumed it was part of normal troop movement at the front or possibly even a training exercise to toughen them up. Later they would learn the truth—it was simply another administrative blunder. The sanitary train had been dropped off in the wrong town. The village of Moyen was not their intended destination.

At this point in the war, the American Expeditionary Force (AEF) was still a work in progress—an experiment, in the view of some. The logistics of expeditiously moving large numbers of men and equipment in a foreign country was still a new and vexing problem for the American army. As Byron would later lament in a diary entry concerning this incident: "Too often it has seemed as tho' our whole division were a plaything knocked and ordered about here and there to no purpose." In reality, the misadventures of maintaining an army in the field were not unique to the AEF. They were endemic to all armies in all wars—from Hannibal crossing the Alps to Napoleon's long retreat from Moscow. In World War II, American GIs would become so accustomed to the misdirection, miscommunication, and misapplication of men and resources that the acronym SNAFU was coined to describe the usual state of affairs in the army: situation normal—all fucked up.

In this war, the units that eventually followed in the footsteps of the Rainbow Division found that many of these snafus were straightened out long before they headed into battle. At this particular moment, however, as the Rainbow Division continued on its march toward the front, it took each unexpected obstacle in stride—fending for itself whenever necessary. That night, a group of enterprising officers walked into Moyen determined to find quarters for the men. While the officers were trying to arrange for billets in the village, men lit fires by the side of the railroad tracks in an attempt to stay warm. Fearing that the fires would attract the attention of German airplanes and artillery, French soldiers immediately rushed out to douse the flames. As temperatures continued to drop, men resorted to huddling by the locomotive or curling up next to smoldering cinders for warmth. By midnight, officers were finally able to find shelter for the exhausted men in unheated barracks and barn lofts.

The next day broke cold and clear. In the early morning light, long, dark observation balloons hung like storm clouds on the horizon. As the sky lightened, airplanes could be seen dueling in the distance as they dodged bursts of anti-aircraft fire. German *Drachen* (Dragon), or "Archy," as the Americans called the highly flammable hydrogen balloons, were tethered by cable to a communication post on the ground. At a height of fifteen hundred feet, observers hung from a basket just below the balloon, where they were able to help artillery batteries zero in on targets located miles behind enemy lines.

Both sides used observation balloons to great advantage, and in the early morning, the first order of business for aviators was to knock the enemy's balloons from the sky. Strafing and flaming an observation balloon was no easy matter, as nearby anti-aircraft gunners were able to fix the precise height at which their deadly shells should explode for maximum effect. To make things even more perilous, supporting airplanes often hovered above the balloons looking to pick off attacking pilots. As related by ace American aviator Eddie Rickenbacker:

> German "Archy" is terrifying at first acquaintance. Pilots affect a scorn for it, and indeed at high altitudes the probability of a hit are small. But when attacking a balloon which hangs only 1,500 feet above the guns (and this altitude is of course known precisely to the anti-aircraft gunner) Archy becomes far more dangerous. So when a pilot begins his first balloon attacking expeditions, he knows that he runs a gauntlet of fire that may be very deadly. . . . The experienced balloon strafers . . . do not consider the risks or terrors about them. They proceed in the attack as calmly as though they were sailing through a stormless sky. Regardless of flaming missiles from the ground, they pass through the defensive barrage of fire, and often return again and again, to attack the target, until it finally bursts into flame from their incendiary bullets.

That same morning, the men were served a breakfast of black coffee and raw bacon before setting out on the twelve-mile march. By the time the men had finished eating and slung on their haversacks, the sun was up fully. The road to Loromontzey crossed over the first battle-scarred terrain the men had encountered. After they had been hiking two hours, the town of Gerbéviller came into view. In his letter to Estelle, Byron described the hike: "All of this region was held by the Boche during the early weeks of the war, and evidence of this was everywhere. All along—by the roadside, in the woods, in the fields were graves where brave Frenchmen had fallen. The towns, one in particular, had been shelled until there was barely a building left intact."

Gerbéviller was a ghost town. In 1914, German artillery had reduced the once thriving village to a pile of rubble. Accounts differed as to how the "Martyr City" of France met its fate. Some said that an enraged German general had ordered its destruction after his horse had been shot out from under him while the Germans lay siege to the town. Others claimed it was the inevitable result of the prolonged and fierce resistance the city had offered during the failed German offensive. Regardless of the cause, the result was the same. Long after the Germans had retreated, the town ceased to exist. And three years later, as Byron marched in, other than a convent and small hospital, all that remained were the charred and jagged walls of bombed-out buildings and the shanties of a few desperate souls who managed to live nearby.

Grande Guerre 1914 1917
GERBÉVILLER la MARTYRE. - Rue de la Poste - Au fond : le Château et la Chapelle en ruines

Postcard of war-damaged Gerbéviller, France. Byron collected over two hundred postcards during the war (often in booklets containing twenty or more depictions of a particular location). He periodically sent these home in packages also containing French coins, stamps, and other paraphernalia.

While the company stopped to rest among the ruins, a group of French soldiers, on leave from the front, were at work rebuilding a block of storefronts from the pieces of brick and other debris they had been able to salvage from the rubble. It was a small but significant start. Men from the sanitary train walked over and shared cigarettes and small talk with the grateful French soldiers. The eager Americans were told that the front lines were still ten miles away, although the rumble of guns made it seem much closer. After a lunch of corn willie (slang for the corned beef often served to soldiers), hardtack, and coffee, the company marched the rest of the way to Loromontzey, arriving by nightfall.

Loromontzey was actually two small villages, Loro and Montzey, separated by a field of hops. For the five hundred residents who lived in the heart of this rolling farmland, growing hops was a way of life. Other than two wine shops, there wasn't a store in either village—much less anything for the men to do while they waited three days for orders to continue their march to more permanent quarters. In the interim, men slept in barns, sheds, and haylofts. Byron kept himself busy by volunteering to work on the wood-chopping detail. Although winter was beginning to fade, fuel was still needed to heat sleeping quarters at night. During the day, conditions were consistently miserable—vacillating between cold rain and slushy snow. At night, when the men weren't gathered inside around a warm stove, they were huddled outside in the dark, watching flashes of cannon fire, like lightning strikes in a distant storm, at the front.

The highlight of the company's stay in Loromontzey was the day that a detail of men who'd been sent to Saint-Nazaire, returned, driving thirty-six new GMC ambulances and two Pierce Arrow trucks. On February 24, the Michigan Ambulance Company broke camp, loading the vehicles with everything but the kitchen sink (which actually was carried in the mess wagon). Then, piling in too, the men rode out for Baccarat.

The village of Baccarat was home to the finest crystal ware in the world, known as the Crystal of Kings. Founded in 1765 by the royal decree of Louis XV, the Compagnie des Cristalleries de Baccarat had taken root in the hardwood forests of the Vosges Mountains along the banks of the Meurthe River. To nurture and support the families of the seventy artisans who worked in the factory there, the utopian

"Comrades in Arms." Front cover of *Leslie's Weekly*, February 16, 1918, illustrated by C. Leroy Baldridge.

community of Baccarat was born. By 1918, when the Michigan Ambulance Company rolled into town, the city had grown to nearly fifteen thousand residents. Although German guns had left much of the idyllic village in ruins, the factory was still intact. Out of necessity, the manufacture of fine glass had been converted to the coarse business of war.

On the campaign map, Baccarat was located fifteen miles southeast of Lunéville, in the so-called quiet sector of the front. The Michigan Ambulance Company was initially headquartered in Baccarat, with responsibility for tending to the nearby medical posts at Pexonne, Montigny, Saint-Maurice, and Gran Bois. The rest of the sanitary train and other units of the Rainbow Division were stationed in Lunéville or in various other towns in the sector. The plan was to pair units of green American soldiers with experienced *soldats* from the 128th French Infantry Division for a month of training in the trenches, then move the Rainbow Division out to a more demanding sector of the front.

By the time the Rainbow Division entered the front lines of the Baccarat sector, an intricate network of trenches stretched for nearly five hundred miles, from the North Sea to the Alpine frontier. Byron, understandably curious about this system of earthworks, took the opportunity to explore them on first entering the frontline sector, often venturing as close to German lines as possible. In some sectors of the front, the distance between opposing frontline trenches could be as narrow as a few hundred yards—or as great as one mile in other sectors. Each side's second- and third-line trenches were located well behind the front line to serve as fallback positions in the event of an enemy breakthrough. Running between these three defensive lines was a labyrinth of perpendicular and diagonal trenches that were used to carry supplies, wounded men, and messages. Trenches were generally eight feet deep and four feet wide, laid out in zigzag patterns to minimize collateral damage from an exploding artillery barrage or enfilading fire. On the front line, or firing line, sandbags were piled an additional two or three feet high for extra protection.

The materials used by the Germans and French to construct their respective system of trenches reflected an all-important difference in mindset. The Germans had invaded France to stake their claim to disputed territory and had no intention of leaving. As such, the walls of German trenches were often made of concrete to serve as permanent fixtures. To this day, they are still in relatively good condition. The French approach to constructing trenches was quite the opposite—they intended to expel the German invaders from French soil as quickly as possible. Accordingly, their trenches were designed to be temporary structures—the walls were shored up by a make-shift composite of logs, tree branches, wire mesh, and corrugated sheet metal. Not surprisingly, the only French trench works that still exist today are those maintained by historical conservators.

For the next seven days, the quiet sector lived up to its billing. As noted in Byron's diary: "We just laid around and marked time. . . . We enjoyed our time in Baccarat tho'. There is a good Y. there, a French cinematographe, and many good stores and barbershops." While marking time in Baccarat, Byron took the opportunity to attend to a few personal details before entering the trenches—like sitting for a studio portrait photograph. On March 3, Byron, Horace Sprague, and Herbert Jackson sat for a one-for-all Musketeer-like portrait in Baccarat. For one of their families, the photograph would serve as an everlasting memorial.

For the duration of the war, Byron would be a frequent visitor to YMCA huts. As ordered by General Pershing, the designated role of the YMCA was to "provide for the amusement and recreation of the troops by means of its usual programme of social, physical, educational and religious services." In addition to attending church services at a YMCA hut, Byron was able to get a drink of hot cocoa or a taste of chocolate, obtain reading and writing materials and, of course, play the piano.

Depending on their proximity to the front lines, YMCA facilities ranged from large, well-stocked canteens in villages to rudimentary dugouts at or near the trenches. Thousands of civilian volunteers worked for the YMCA in France during the war. The woman assigned to run the YMCA hut in Baccarat was Gertrude Bray from Providence, Rhode Island. Like Byron, Gertrude was an enthusiastic supporter of America's war effort and was eager to help in any way she could. At the age of thirty, Gertrude had decided to forsake the financial security of her job as a clerk in a manufacturing company in order to enlist as a

Portrait photograph of Byron (*center*), Herbert Jackson (*left*), and Horace Sprague (*right*), Baccarat, March 3, 1918.

militarized member of the YMCA war service. It was by far the boldest move of her life—compared to her having left home to attend Wheaton College in nearby Norton, Massachusetts, this was a bona fide adventure, and an especially audacious one for a single woman of that era.

In January 1918, Gertrude reported for duty in France, along with twenty or so male coworkers. She was one of five women assigned to

"Comfort." Front cover of *Leslie's Weekly*, June 1, 1918, illustrated by Charles Sarka.

YMCA dugout near the frontline trenches. (Photograph by Army Signal Corps.)

the Rainbow Division. For the duration of the war, Gertrude and other YMCA workers would travel in close proximity to the division as it moved from sector to sector. Male workers were assigned to huts at or near the trenches, while the women were responsible for managing the more elaborate huts located in villages well behind the lines. All were exposed to danger, however, as German artillery and planes were capable of raining death and destruction on areas far removed from the front lines. During the war 135 Y workers would be killed, wounded, or gassed.

Although Gertrude and Byron never mentioned each other by name in their diaries and many letters home, their paths had undoubtedly crossed, as Byron frequently played the piano and led the singing at YMCA church services, in addition to entertaining himself and others at Y huts whenever time permitted. As evidenced by Gertrude's letter of March 4, apparently Byron's musical skill did not go unnoticed: "The bad weather brings the men inside and our canteen is a very popular place. Two men from the Sanitary Train who usually come in together are an entertainment in themselves: one plays well and the other sings, and they have their own music."

Other than ferrying a few wounded men back from the third-line trenches to one of three hospitals in Baccarat, Byron found the situation generally uneventful. Which was the way both sides wanted it. After the German offensive in Lorraine had collapsed in a stalemate in 1914, the front lines around Lunéville were treated as a de facto no-fire zone. With the exception of an occasional artillery salvo, which rarely came as a surprise to the other side, the French and Germans adopted a live and let live philosophy—using the quiet sector as an unofficial R&R station for battle-weary soldiers on break from the killing fields in the other sectors of the front. Now that the Americans were added to the mix, that peaceful accord would soon dissolve.

According to most accounts, the catalyst for this change was provided by sharpshooters from the 167th Alabama Infantry Regiment. On entering the trenches, the Alabamans immediately began to pick off German soldiers who were accustomed to strolling unmolested into no-man's-land to wash their clothes in rainwater that had collected in the shell holes. When confronted by irate French soldiers for jeopardizing their peaceful coexistence with the Germans, the incredulous southerners replied that they had come there to kill Huns, not watch them do laundry.

The German response was predictable. In the early morning of March 4, all hell broke loose when German artillery welcomed the American troops to the trenches of France. The 168th Iowa Infantry Regiment was the recipient of this particular German calling card. It was delivered in the form of a box barrage, beginning with a storm of high-explosive shells that rained down on the American positions, collapsing dugouts and caving in trenches, while a second line of fire landed behind the front lines to prevent any possible retreat. Then, hoping to capitalize on the confusion and fear in the American ranks, battle-hardened German infantry stormed across no-man's-land with bayonets fixed.

The untested Iowans were rattled but stood fast—giving as good as they got over the next few hours. Later that morning, when the smoke had finally cleared, it was grimly apparent that the Iowans had managed to repulse the German attack. No-man's-land was strewn with dozens of German dead. Among the Americans, one captain and eighteen doughboys had died; another twenty-two were wounded.

Compared to the scale of things to come, it was a small battle, but nevertheless an important one. Notice had been served—the Americans would not run.

During all of this, some members of the Michigan Ambulance Company carried wounded back from the front line. Byron and others worked at a dressing station between the second and third lines in Montigny. As reflected in a diary entry for March 5, Byron was delighted: "At last we were at it! We were mighty pleased to be told to roll our rolls for an indefinite stay at Montigny. There are about twenty of us, Sarg. Abbott and Lieut. Hanna. We were billeted in the only wooden barracks anywhere around. Most of the town was ruins. No civilians left. There were French soldiers and Italian laborers there.

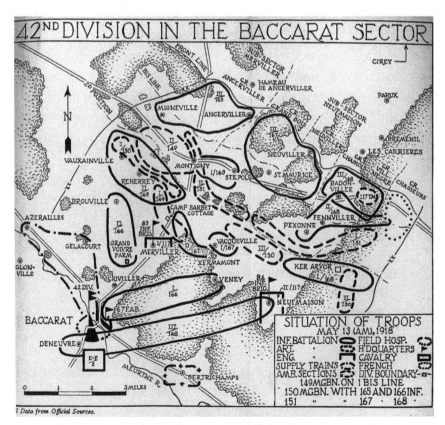

Sector map of Baccarat. (From Henry J. Reilly, *Americans All: The Rainbow Division at War* [Columbus, OH: F. J. Heer, 1936], 228A.)

For two days we worked in the clay, made mud by recent rains, laying a road thru' the orchard to the dugout, with no special excitement."

As expressed in a March 5 letter to Estelle, Byron was apparently unaware that the Iowa Infantry had just experienced all of the "excitement" they could possibly endure and more. Based on his limited perspective behind the second line in Montigny, Byron wrote: "Yesterday our men carried back a bunch of American wounded. The Boche started a barrage intending to make a raid, but the French and American batteries made such an effective counter-barrage that the Boche were barely able to get out of their trenches."

Byron's assessment that the American and French batteries had managed to launch an effective counter-barrage may have been an accurate account of what had occurred in his section of the line—the reality of the overall situation, however, was that the Germans had shelled the entire American line generally in order to conceal the focus of their infantry assault on the Iowa position specifically. After this the Germans not only managed to get out of their trenches but actually succeeded in inflicting great harm on the Iowans stationed there.

By this point, it was apparent that the quiet sector of the front was beginning to heat up. In a letter to Estelle on March 7, Byron noted:

> While the front has been considered a quiet one, there is every indication that it will not long continue so. . . . The Boche and French artillery have been very active during the last two days. . . . There is a terrific bombardment on tonight. We can hear the shells come for three or four seconds—whistling thru' the air—then they burst with a mammoth explosion. Last night a gas attack was pulled off near us, and had our masks at "alert" ready to pull over our faces for an hour. We simply have faith and trust that all will be well.

In a diary entry for the 7th, Byron described the gas attack in greater detail:

> The evening of the seventh we witnessed our first bombardment. Just at dusk we were hearing shells scream over and burst in a

field a quarter kilo away. Suddenly we saw a string of five green lights over the trenches—and wondered what the big idea was. We soon knew, for the Frenchman on our telephone exchange nearby came rushing out yelling "gas," "gas." We didn't waste a second getting our masks on either. Then I ran into the Y. and yelling it there, saw the French and Americans dive into their masks. The French have learned and we are learning that gas is our deadliest enemy.

In the face of such a withering attack, Byron simply chose to place his faith and trust in God that all would be well—that others in the trenches nearby weren't nearly as fortunate or blessed underscored the utter randomness and cruelty of war. In a section of the line called Rouge Boquet Chausailles, the accuracy of German gunners had left its deadly mark on the ranks of New York's Fighting 69th Infantry Regiment, killing twenty-one men. The poet Joyce Kilmer, a sergeant in the 69th, lived through the attack, later memorializing the death of his fallen comrades in the poem "Rouge Bouquet."

On March 9, Byron and other members of the Michigan Ambulance Company were chosen to take part in the first American offensive action of the campaign. The coup de main went off without a hitch; the American and French soldiers stormed the German trenches and captured a few German prisoners—one by the young Colonel Douglas MacArthur at the point of a revolver, for which he received a Distinguished Service Cross. Throughout the war, MacArthur always seemed to be in the thick of the action, leading by example and not from the rear, earning an extraordinary six Distinguished Service Crosses in the process. Years later, accusations that MacArthur had been vainglorious with regard to his exploits in battle did not detract from the fact that he was without doubt courageous. Whether his gallantry was especially noteworthy, however, when compared to the everyday sacrifice of the average doughboy is an issue that haunts his legacy to this day.

In newspapers back home, the coup de main was heralded as a great success—the American public needed heroes and good news from the front. As reflected in Byron's diary entry for March 9, though, the truth was somewhat less flattering:

Capt. Baskerville said, "I want volunteers for a very dangerous job but a fine one." Every man raised his hand. Eight of us were picked, then twelve more added to go up for litter bearing. Sar. Baughman was sent up to take charge of the detail. He was simply scared silly. First he got things all balled up and landed us in Aucerviller within 600 yards of the Boche. Then he got more excited, ordered the ambulances to tear back over the road, which the Boche had full view of. Next we dashed off towards Germany in the direction of St. Maurice. Finally we landed in a sawmill in the woods, which was to be our station. There was a "coup de main" by the French and Americans with 5 PM as zero hour. About two, the intermittent barrage began, and the aeroplanes came out. There were lots of 'em—Boche and French going here and there—occasionally firing a few shots at each other and then veering away. They didn't seem to want to mix. About six, when the guns all about us were tearing things to pieces, eight of us started up the narrow gauge with some Frenchmen. We walked up three kilometers thru the air heavy with powder and smoke, to a small French dugout. Here in the woods, we waited for the wounded to be brought to us, or the Boche to send over a counter barrage. Neither thing happened. Only one man was injured in the whole "coup" and the other litter carried him back. The simple fact was that there was a leak. Every German had left his trench the day before carrying everything with him. So, when our boys got over, while every trench and dugout was torn up by the barrage, no prisoners or materials could be found anywhere. The boys went forward three kilos then came back in disgust. We got back to the sawmill late, and nearly froze to death that night. Had no overcoat or blanket and I thought I would be stuck to the chickenwire mattress in the morning.

The fact that he'd thus far led a relatively charmed life was not lost on Byron. In a diary entry for March 16, he noted: "We had a shell land within twenty feet of us, when we were working by the dugout. Two duds had come over before so we headed for the doors and luck was further with us on this one—a shrapnel at that—it didn't explode till three feet in the ground—hurting no one."

As deadly German shells continued to fall around him, Byron's good fortune held in the days to come. In diary entries concerning the week of March 17, Byron noted:

> This week was fuller than any before. It started in the morning, Monday with a terrific bombardment at the old 90 battery. We stood out in a field fully a half kilo away but the pieces of shrapnel landed all around us there. Tho' the bombardment lasted fully two hours, when I walked over the ground at noon, I found very little injury done—none to guns or ammunition. The next day, the 19th, the Boche turned their guns toward the battery of two 1918 75s about 200 yards beyond our eggshell billet. This bombardment too, began about ten in the morning when, for some reason, all of us were there. We heard the first shell coming and sail overhead, and beat it for the dugout. While I was the first into the dugout, I was among the first coming out, as we soon discovered that the battery and not we were the target. If a shell had fallen 200 yards short, or a 100 yards shorter than the nearest one, it would have got a lot of us. . . . The next day they tried at the 90 battery with no more success than the first day. We had had several gas attacks during our stay but the longest was in the wee morning hours of the 21st when we laid in bed for an hour while the shells exploded nearby.

The "75s" and "90s" and "150s and 320s," mentioned in Byron's diary entries of March 4 and 17 referred to the caliber in millimeters of medium and heavy French artillery pieces. The 320s were enormous railway guns capable of firing accurately for a distance of nineteen miles. The Germans countered with an array of heavy artillery of their own, notably the forty-two-centimeter super-howitzer "Big Bertha" and the ultra-long-range railway gun "Langer Max." The most notorious German artillery piece was the "Paris Gun," which rained two-hundred-pound shells on Paris from a distance of sixty miles. By the end of the war, the unremitting barrage from these artillery pieces reduced the villages and terrain at the front to virtual moonscapes.

French railway gun. (Photograph by Army Signal Corps.)

Remnants of German artillery piece with seventy-six-foot barrel. (Photograph by Army Signal Corps.)

At the time of making his diary entry on the 17th, Byron made no mention of the severity of the damage that German artillery had actually inflicted on other units stationed nearby. Once again, it was New York's Fighting 69th that would bear the brunt of the blow, sustaining over four hundred casualties in the gas attack. On March 20 and 21, the New Jersey and Oregon Field Hospitals treated over five hundred gas victims from the Rainbow Division. After sustaining such debilitating losses, the New York unit was taken out of the line of fire and placed in a reserve position to recuperate for the next several weeks.

One possible explanation for Byron's failure to mention the severity of the gas attacks in his diary was that until April 6 he was simply too busy attending to his duties at the front to begin a new diary to replace the one he'd left in his barracks bag at Rolampont. When he finally got the time to recommence his diary, he'd been forced to quickly recount the prior six weeks' events from memory, often lumping days together in cursory entries. Even from these entries, however, it is readily apparent that there was a marked difference between the contents of his diary and the war-related information, if any, he included in his many letters to Estelle and his parents. Throughout the war, Byron would make a habit of sparing them any worrisome details about what he was actually experiencing in the trenches. For example, on March 20, Byron made an artful dodge to evade specific questions from Estelle about "his adventures," as she had once naively phrased it. "What shall I write of? I often think my letters must be the same old stuff. I can't help but see how awful tired you people back home must be getting of war. . . . The newspapers, the preachers, the public speakers—all are full of war—war—war. . . . Now—along I come with a letter or two a week, and these too are full of the 's.o.s.'"

In fact, Byron's letters were anything but the same old stuff. They were full of the stuff that soldiers dream of—loved ones, and the peace and quiet of home. In that vein, Byron's letter to Estelle on March 22 described his first stint in the trenches summarily and simply: "Well we walked back five miles yesterday to our company headquarters, where we will stay for a couple of days before going on a ten day hike back to our rest camp. I guess we'll need a rest alright after the hike. So I won't be able to write again till then—possibly two weeks in all. Now, our first month at the front is over, and we'll have a month of something else before coming back. Our baptism of fire has been given, and we're all safe." Then, after discussing at length the opening of delayed Christmas packages and letters from friends and relatives at home as well as other lighthearted matters, Byron affectionately closed: "And I might sit around the kitchen and laugh at you while you washed dishes. Oh, there's a hundred ways I might bother you. But I love you—does this little, Jimmy."

Byron was not alone in his escapist reverie. For men who had just gotten their first taste of battle, thoughts of loved ones and home provided a refuge from the bitter reality of war. For the moment, a baptism of fire had been endured and all was well. But every man knew that far greater challenges lay ahead. It was the crucible of sacrifice, as the men later called it, that would truly test their mettle.

12
THERE MUST BE A KIND GOD ABOVE

The Rainbow Division's ten-day march to the rear lasted all of three hours. By noon on March 23, Byron and the rest of the Michigan Ambulance Company found themselves in the village of Domptail, frustrated and more than slightly confused. As reflected in a diary entry beginning on March 22:

> We spent that [day] in Baccarat, dismayed with the thoughts of the prospective ten-day hike to Rolampont. All of us preferred staying "up" to hiking back even if to rest camp. Early on the morning of the 23rd we rolled our rolls, put our extra stuff on the trucks, and left for Domptail on our way south. The hike lasted but three hours, and we stopped in some barracks just outside the partially destroyed town of Domptail. It was sure a dead place and we were anxious to get on. The next day Oklahoma and Tennessee joined us there. We thought certainly we would start on south then, but no—for some reason we didn't continue.

After a week of marking time in Domptail, Byron wrote: "All the plans of going south were thrown over. Some day will know the strategic reason why. Probably it was that we could come back to release French veterans who could better serve in the Somme." Byron's supposition was in fact correct. On March 21, Germany had launched the *Kaiserschlacht*—a spring offensive intended to bring the war to an end. Plans for the attack had been formulated in the fall of 1917, shortly after the surrender of Russia, making it possible for Germany to move nearly fifty divisions of battle-hardened soldiers, artillery, and materiel from the eastern front to the western front. At this point in the war, only two hundred thousand American troops had set foot in France, and the German high command was hoping to take advantage of its numerical superiority before an additional 1 million doughboys could arrive later in the year.

The spring offensive consisted of a series of attacks, the most important of which was directed at the weakest link in the Allied line of defense—the beleaguered British troops stationed at the Somme. Using all the manpower now at its disposal, the German attack was designed to overwhelm the outnumbered British forces, driving a wedge between the British and French Armies. According to the plan, after German forces initially broke through the Allied lines at the Somme and encircled the British Army, another German attack force would drive north to capture the all-important port cities of supply and reinforcement, while yet another German force advanced toward Paris, drawing French troops in that direction to prevent them from reinforcing the besieged British. If everything went according to plan, the Germans believed that the British would have no choice but to surrender after finding themselves surrounded and without hope of reinforcement. As it turned out, however, now that the Rainbow Division had entered the trenches, it was the Germans who would suddenly find themselves on the brink of disaster.

The attack began at 4:00 on the morning of the 21st. For two hours, German artillery batteries bludgeoned British forces in the trenches of the Somme with deadly accuracy. Shrouded in a dense morning fog that didn't lift until noon, waves of German troops stormed across no-man's-land. The British had been expecting the attack but were unprepared for its intensity. Enemy forces advanced over battle-scarred terrain at an alarming rate. The pressure of the German onslaught was relentless.

In the initial phase of the attack, the Kaiser's gambit came dangerously close to succeeding. British soldiers fought tenaciously, forcing the Germans to pay dearly for every yard of blood-soaked terrain they gained. Only grudgingly did British troops fall back—repeatedly regrouping to dig in again and again. Casualties on both sides were horrific. For the first time since 1914, Allied lines bent back toward Paris. Before German troops could break through Allied defenses completely, the 128th French Division was abruptly pulled from the Baccarat sector and sent to the Somme to reinforce the dauntless but faltering British. And just as suddenly, the men of the Rainbow Division found themselves holding the line in Baccarat—alone.

By March 31, Easter Sunday, the entire Rainbow Division was back in the trenches. For the ambulance companies assigned to the sanitary train, a field headquarters had been set up in Bertrichamps, a small village between Baccarat and Raon-l'Étape. Byron didn't report there initially, however. He'd been selected as part of the first detail of men to be stationed at dressing stations at the front line. Each ambulance company was responsible for detailing thirty-two men to the four dressing stations on a weekly rotation. After an uneventful week at the dressing station in Pexonne, Byron rejoined the rest of the company at Bertrichamps.

The men who remained in reserve at Bertrichamps were put to work cleaning the town. After nearly four years of war, Bertrichamps was like most other French villages close to the front—haggard, dirty, and gray. Residents were focused on simply surviving. Public sanitation wasn't even an afterthought. For the 117th Sanitary Train, getting the refuse- and manure-infested streets swept and cleansed was medically necessary in order to control the spread of pestilence and disease. It was also an odious chore—when it was coupled with twenty-four-hour guard duty and drills, most of the men preferred being back at the front. Byron was no exception.

After only five days in Bertrichamps, Byron returned to the front. As reflected in his diary entry of April 12, he did not seem the least bit disappointed:

> I got picked on detail for work at the front. Incidentally, I had my first bath (shower) in two months in the army bathhouse. After a lot of fool inspections by our own and higher officers, we got away in the ambulances for our posts. We rode to St. Pole, walked over to the saw mill, stayed till dark, then carried on through

THE WAR IN PICTURES

MAR 30TH 1918

Leslie's
Illustrated Weekly Newspaper

PRICE 10 CENTS

EASTER

"Easter." Front cover of *Leslie's Weekly*, March 30, 1918, illustrated by Norman Rockwell.

St. Maurice and on around the camouflaged road to Grand Bois. Here was our station with an Alabama infirmary. There were four of us in our dugout—a litter squad. We had a fine dugout too—27 steps down—well protected from gas.

In a letter to Estelle on April 19, Byron included a diagram showing the layout of the dugout, which he described as "real homey." Depicted in his diagram of the underground lair were the log-reinforced dirt walls, two small benches, a table and stools, and crude wooden bunks used for sleeping. As in a rabbit warren, an underground passageway led to another dugout. One of the less homey aspects of dugout life not mentioned by Byron was the gas that could waft into the dugouts or get tracked into the confined quarters on contaminated boots and clothing. To reduce the threat of gas inhalation, anti-gas blankets were draped over the entranceway of dugouts. The blankets, soaked in an absorbent alkaline-like solution, were spaced about eight feet apart to create an anteroom that helped prevent chlorine and phosgene gases from poisoning the air supply whenever men entered or left.

Another discomfort of dugout living not depicted by Byron was the filthy water and ankle-deep mud that men often had to stand in at the bottom of trenches and dugouts. Although some of the dugouts, like Byron's, were burrowed more than twenty feet deep to withstand large-caliber artillery barrages, rainwater still managed to seep into the underground rooms whenever it poured, at times enough to submerge the duckboards that covered the dirt floors. Predictably, trenchfoot often resulted from continuous exposure to such squalid conditions, not to mention the rats that ran amok in the trenches and dugouts, eating everything and spreading lice. Despite Byron's depiction of his dugout accommodations as "homey," for the most part, trench duty was a troglodyte existence.

Considering these unsanitary conditions, it was only fitting that Byron would choose to mention something as incidental as a shower in his diary. It was indeed a memorable event. To combat the spread of lice and scabies among the men detailed to the trenches, the army instituted an exacting cleansing ritual that was more than just a little soap and water behind the ears. In *Iodine and Gasoline*, one of the books that Byron later coauthored, the elaborate process was described as follows:

> The first bath was an experience that will remain long in the mind of the Doughboys who went to Scratchville. Every bit of equipment that could possibly furnish a hiding place for the hated cootie was checked in at the bath-house where it was run through a sterilizer. Every cootie and egg was cooked to a crisp by the intense steam. While sterilizing the equipment was going on, the patient also passed through a cleansing process. In the undressing room was a barber. As each human entered he was relieved of his clothing and given a haircut. To be more exact, his hair was clipped close to the head, as short as a pair of close clippers would do the job. It mattered not if he had long hair, short hair, light or dark, off it came. As the weather was warm, there were very few complaints from the "sheering pen." However, some were not willing to part with the pompadours that had taken years of training and labor on the part of the hometown barber. But the bath-house sergeant was firm. He had his orders to cut every head of hair, and every head was clipped before it entered the bathroom. Passing down a short narrow hall, the victim dressed a la Garden of Eden, found himself in a small room. The floor covered with rubberoid roofing slanted to a depression in the center to furnish drainage. Overhead were twenty-one showerheads, connected with a heater outside. The Meurthe supplied the heater with clean mountain water. When there was a man under each showerhead, the bath attendant uttered a phrase which eventually became camp slang throughout the division, "Let 'er go, Andy," and the warm water began to spurt. Every man had been given a small amount of green soap, with which he thoroughly scrubbed himself, aided with a stiff bristle brush. When not in use these brushes were kept submerged in a disinfectant solution. After ten minutes of lathering, each man scrubbing the back of the patient in front of him, the water was turned off, and for ten minutes the men rubbed themselves and each other until their bodies became rosy. Then the water was turned on for five minutes, the men washed off the soap they had so thoroughly applied and proceeded into a drying room

receiving there a large bath towel. After drying themselves they were introduced to a bucket containing a mixture of lard and sulphur having the appearance of tub butter. This sulphur ointment, the patient rubbed on himself except those portions of his anatomy he could not reach. The ring method overcame this difficulty. To gain the cooperation of the patient, it was explained to him why this was done. How the female germ which caused scabies, buried herself under the skin to lay her eggs, coming out only at night to meet her gentlemen friends who were loath to adopt such tactics as hiding in a dugout. The bath washed off these Romeos and the sulphur made it mighty unpleasant for the weaker sex. So upon perseverance, soap, sulphur, frequent changing of clothes and absolute cleanliness, depended speedy recovery. A portable power laundry arrived, borrowed from the French and was set up on the bank of the river with the aid of several Frenchmen. It was a very efficient apparatus, having boilers, washers, extractor and drying room all mounted on two large wagons. Had it not been for this laundry and its rapid work, it would have been an impossibility to furnish clean clothes to the patients as often as they needed them.

Compared to the life-and-death struggle that was playing out in the trenches of the Somme, the Baccarat sector was relatively calm. With neither side looking to make a major push in this sector, maintaining the status quo was the order of the day. Activities for the most part were confined to keeping night vigil against enemy raiding parties and hunkering down during artillery barrages. Still, Byron was quickly becoming accustomed to the tragic consequences of war, being called upon to carry his share of wounded and dead back from the front. In an April 19 letter to Estelle, Bryon wrote:

We've been pretty busy here the last three days—carrying back wounded on our *petit chemin de fer*, and working around our dugout....

But we like it, even when it's like it was a few days ago when we were rousted out at one A.M., and had to go up in front and bring our men back to the ambulance five kilos away....

How sweet is life, if there are those who care. We had a boy the other day who'd paid his last debt. He may have erred, but those who care forgive. When his mother gets the aluminum disc, the one he wore beside the other buried with him—she will also get the old envelope on which he had written—"my last thots were of you, my mother." And she will smile through her tears and be glad to have given him.

It is unknown whether Byron actually helped this particular dying soldier pen a brief farewell to his mother, although doing so certainly would have been in keeping with Byron's sensibility and love of family. And, in the relative calm of the dressing station, it is likely that he would have had the opportunity to ensure that a final note was written.

As to his mention of being "rousted out" in the early morning to go up to the frontline trenches, Byron explained the incident more fully in an April 16 diary entry: "At one o'clock in the morning, to carry some wounded. The daw-gone Alabama infirmary men wouldn't carry down the wounded—their own men wounded by their own men at that. We went up to the front line—carried them back—two to a litter—nearly pulling our arms out of joint." From Byron's diary entry, it is unclear exactly what circumstances led to the Alabama soldiers being shot by their own men. What was generally observed in other firsthand accounts, however, was that upon their arrival in the trenches in February, soldiers from the 167th Alabama Infantry Regiment had been so eager to mix it up with German forces that they immediately began to snipe at enemy soldiers whenever the opportunity presented itself. And when those opportunities weren't readily available, the Alabamans went in search of them—often making impromptu incursions behind German lines to wreak havoc. That such precipitous action could have resulted in friendly-fire casualties is a distinct possibility; that it could have engendered retaliatory attacks by the Germans is an equally likely scenario. That such reckless abandon would to this day brand them with the inimitable nom de guerre Alabama Wildmen is the stuff of legend.

Motorized ambulance. (Photograph by Army Signal Corps.)

Medics carrying a wounded soldier to dressing station, Bertrichamps, April 1918. (Photograph by Army Signal Corps.)

Regardless of the circumstances that led to these particular men being wounded, throughout April and May raids and counter-raids by both sides continued to grow more frequent and hostile. On May 12, an American incursion behind enemy lines was especially noteworthy for its wanton abandon—led by Lieutenant Breeding, an Alabama infantry officer reputedly of Native American descent, a rescue party set out to retrieve two Alabama snipers who had recently been captured by the Germans. After successfully sneaking through no-man's-land undetected, Breeding and his men fell upon the German position with bayonets and bowie knives, killing seven Germans and wounding several others. On finding only one of the captured snipers still alive (the body of the other rifleman was never found), the angry Alabamans decided to exact some measure of revenge by desecrating the body of a German soldier they had just killed—stringing the corpse over the barbed wire of no-man's-land, where it was left to rot. By this point in a long and brutal war, the Germans weren't the least bit intimidated by what was in essence an Alabama scarecrow, even if it was the body of a fallen comrade. If nothing else, though, the carcass served as a grim reminder to both sides that any pretense of adhering to the civilized conventions of war had eroded long ago.

For their part, the Germans were hardly above such barbarous conduct, at times not even confining their aggression to combatants which, according to the Geneva Convention, should not have included medical personnel. Byron and other medical personnel had been issued Red Cross brassards to signify their status as noncombatants, but they often felt that wearing the armband was tantamount to having a bull's-eye painted on their backs. As hostilities continued to intensify, ambulances, litter bearers, and hospitals often found themselves the recipient of German sniper fire, artillery barrage, or airplane attack. On one such occasion, a hospital clearly marked with a large red cross was strafed by a German airplane, the pilot also managing to shoot a tin cup out of the hands of an orderly from the Michigan Ambulance Company who was standing just outside the door.

Finally, on the evening of May 26, hostilities in the quiet sector escalated beyond isolated skirmishes, erupting in one of the worst gas attacks of the war. The epicenter of the attack was Village Negre.

Village Negre was not a village per se. It was a defensive position in the Allied front lines situated in a small depression between two hills, having derived its name from the unit of black French soldiers first stationed there in 1914. In an effort to escape the incessant German artillery bombardment in that sector of the line, the French soldiers had tunneled into the nearby hillside, where they built an elaborate system of passageways, rooms, and a dressing station capable of sheltering hundreds of men. As recounted in Byron's diary:

> This was the night of the big gas attack around Village Negre. All the ambulances were busy, and a lot of men were up at Pexonne busy as beavers. It was surely the biggest thing the Boche had tried. We lost several men dead and had at least 300 sent to the hospital for treatment. I was around the company doing the ordinary things wishing I was at the front helping out when Tuesday tales began coming in that our drivers and orderlies were being overcome by gas and fatigue. Tuesday afternoon I went out with Gates' car and worked with it till the middle of Wednesday—hauling men from Village Negre through to the base hospital. During the night of the 28th, Panic, Cleveland and I slept in gassed blankets in the dugout in Village Negre. I subsequently found that I received a little gas from this. I was surely pleased at getting out on the car—my first such experience at the front. The most novel thing was driving with a mask on at night—a strange experience. I had my first good odor of gas, too, just like new mown hay. . . .
>
> At 1:30 AM Thursday morning, Bottomly woke me up and said I was to get out and drive Rowston's car—as Rowston had been sent to the hospital. I got out in a hurry and spent all that day evacuating sick men to the hospital.

The odor of "new mown hay" referred to by Byron came from phosgene gas, one of three poison gasses used by both sides with deadly effect. The other two gasses were mustard and chlorine. Inhaling a lethal dose of these gasses resulted in a ghastly death that the men referred to as "drowning on land," in which the victims ended up suffocating on their own blood and pulmonary fluid. The blistering effect of mustard gas left many of its victims blind, as members of New York's Fighting 69th had discovered two months earlier.

In responding to help victims of the Village Negre attack, fifteen members of the Michigan Ambulance Company suffered from gas inhalation, four of them seriously enough to require hospitalization. Apparently, Rowston, the driver Byron had been called on to replace, was one of them. In accordance with his effort to keep Estelle from worrying about the danger he was constantly exposed to, Byron never mentioned the Village Negre gas attack specifically. In a May 28 letter, Byron merely noted that he "got called to take another fellow's place driving an ambulance" that night, without making any reference to a particular incident. Byron's most explicit description of the devastation caused by a gas attack was a brief and apparently inadvertent one, slipping out in a letter to Estelle on June 8: "But if you ever saw a dead place, it wouldn't beat a region which has been recently gassed. Every louse, rat, bird, or animal of any sort, every flower, shrub, piece of grass and tree is dead. Happy will be the day when such destruction is at an end."

Other than that brief description, however, Byron didn't dwell (at least not in writing) on the ever-present danger of being gassed, choosing instead to focus on more pleasant things. In this particular letter, it was the arrival of spring and Estelle's summer job working in a greenhouse that occupied his thoughts, as well as reporting on the flowers that were presently in bloom in France. Then, in a romantic closing flourish, Byron made special mention of the one flower that he was never without, regardless of season or circumstance: "I wear a little sack... there are a lot of old brown rose leaves in it, which you gave me at one time or another—and there's still the faintest odor—and—I love them and carry them always near my heart, as you are always in my heart. Lovingly."

Byron was not the only doughboy consumed by amorous thoughts. Spring fever afflicted the ranks. Gertrude Bray and the other female YMCA and Salvation Army workers frequently found themselves the objects of men's attention, having to politely turn down invitations to go to movies or walks about town. Attendance at some social events, however, was mandatory, like formal dinners and dances with officers.

Despite all the attention, Gertrude maintained a sisterly relationship with all of the men except one—"my Harry," as Gertrude referred to him. Harry Scott Lane had literally ridden into Gertrude's life on a horse. As a mounted military police officer, Harry didn't have the swaggering ego or the impressive rank of General Douglas MacArthur, Major Bill Donovan, or the other larger-than-life personalities that populated the pages of Gertrude's diary, but Harry was a steady presence, and over the months Gertrude had come to rely on his companionship. When Harry was on patrol or otherwise away, Gertrude missed him terribly—on one occasion using a courier to convey a hastily written message to Harry, who, on receiving it, walked miles through the mud, rain, and windblown conditions to meet her for a few precious hours. In the cruel and uncertain world of war, however, any thought of a more lasting relationship was just tempting fate, and for the time being, Harry's special status was not something Gertrude was willing to share with others. As Byron did his little sack of rose petals, she held her affection close to the heart.

On June 3, Byron celebrated his twenty-first birthday on guard duty, alone, where he had "lots of time for reflection." As set forth in his diary, Byron was: "21 years of age—a voter and a man. I resolved to be more a man than ever before, worthy of what my parents and girl think I am and should be. The officers don't seem to understand but I can't help that. They always seem to depend on me in a time of need—such as this one where I went with the ambulance, which gives me some satisfaction." Under the circumstances, Byron's apparent struggles with assuming the mantle of manhood were totally understandable. Learning to shoulder the burden of being a responsible adult is a difficult enough process for any twenty-one-year-old in the best of times—in the throes of war, the learning curve is extreme, and the growing pains excruciatingly intense. Boys who are barely old enough to shave are thrown into battle. Some manage to become men overnight. Others don't make it that far. In letters to Estelle during his first few weeks at the front, Byron alluded to "combats with himself" and his "hope to be kinder, and purer, and braver, and more self-sacrificing—if I can be these on my return, then this will not have been in vain. My guiding star will be higher because I have learned much."

Although the exact nature of these struggles is not known, the nerve-racking stress and nagging self-doubt men at the front were subject to are not hard to imagine. Reminders of their own mortality were ever present. On June 12, cohorts of Byron's from the Michigan Ambulance Company, brothers Frank and Clifford Mills, were severely wounded by an artillery barrage that destroyed the dressing station where they were working, killing several of the men inside. To break the tension of living on the edge, soldiers resorted to any number of distractions. Some men played cards or engaged in other games. The YMCA in Baccarat provided a variety of social events to entertain the men during their idle hours. In addition to playing the piano at church services, Byron played at social affairs as needed. He also attended movies at the YMCA, saw vaudeville acts, and even enjoyed a lyric opera production from Paris, *Drama lyrique*, complete with orchestra.

One type of YMCA show in particular was always a big hit with the men. As noted by YMCA worker Gertrude Bray:

> Two lady entertainers and a man accompanyist are in town, and they gave a show here with the Saxophone Sextette. Of course, a show of any kind will attract the men, but one with a girl in it, even if she is as graceful as a stick or has a voice like a factory whistle will draw the men like sugar will flies. This night there wasn't an inch of ground vacant, up to the foot of the platform, over the counter, on the shelves, in the windows, up the trees and over the abri, was the audience. What they did was pretty fair, but as long as it entertained the boys, I was glad; the saxophone sextette is always good and always popular.

During one of Byron's breaks from duty at a medical post in the front line, he got to participate in another unexpected diversion—the making of a silent moving picture for public consumption back home. He noted in a April 29 letter to Estelle:

> Yesterday we performed for the "movies." As many of the ambulance section of the Sanitary Train as could be gotten together were lined up in a column of fours and paraded by the camera.

While we weren't told anything definite, we understand that they are to be of a general film of the whole division. It may be called the "Rainbow," or pretty near anything. If by any chance you should be where you could see it, Sprague and I are both marching in the front set of fours in the last ambulance company. I am second from the camera, and he is third.

As entertaining and distracting as some of these activities may have been, the war was never completely out of mind. As reflected in Byron's diary entry for June 19, even a seemingly harmless YMCA gathering was not immune from attack: "We had a band concert on the main corner every night, and were having the usual one Wednesday night. Nelson of the New Jersey Ambulance started a solo 'One, two, three, boys and over we go.' That was one too many for the Boche. Right in the middle of the song the H.E.s [high-explosives] and shrapnel began tearing in pell-mell. We didn't waste any time breaking up the meeting and tearing for cover. Several Americans were killed and wounded during the bombardment."

Whenever time and duties permitted, Byron attended church services at the YMCA, where he heard sermons and speeches from a variety of speakers and chaplains, all with differing war-related themes. According to his diary and letters, the subject matter of some of those sermons were "Jacobs character as it relates to army life"; "The Spiritual Significance of the Flag"; and "Duty, Devotion and Discipline in Religion." There were also passages from the Gospels of Luke and Matthew. As with most things spiritual, whether Byron or any of the other churchgoing men were able to find guidance or solace in any of those themes was a matter of personal preference.

According to Father Francis Duffy, the storied chaplain of New York's Fighting 69th who also served as the divisional chaplain of the Rainbow Division, the chaplains who connected best with the men were those who kept their sermons simple and direct: "[s]traight talk on religion that were free from speculation and over refinement of thought, sermons belonging to their condition on life." Duffy had small regard for "high brows"—ministers whose erudite sermons and lectures did little to comfort men who were about to confront death in battle. It would appear from Byron's diary and letters that he generally found the speeches and sermons that he listened to uplifting.

What Byron did find a bit unsettling, however, was the replacement of the regimental chaplain with a Roman Catholic priest. Although Byron never indicated that he was averse to attending religious services led by a priest, at this point in time, the Rainbow Division was manned mostly by Protestant soldiers, and apparently Byron was not alone in his displeasure. Following up on a June 3 letter to Estelle in which he made mention of having a priest as their chaplain, Bryon wrote in his diary on June 9: "Sunday we went down to Baccarat again. Our chaplain did not appeal to us at all—in fact he seemed to consider it a concession to talk to us. So we try to go to other services whenever possible."

AEF records indicate that the chaplain assigned to the 117th Sanitary Train at that time was Father George Carpentier, a Roman Catholic priest from Ohio. Carpentier was well regarded by Father Duffy, having been selected by Duffy to replace him as divisional chaplain during Duffy's brief incapacitation due to exhaustion, after which Carpentier returned to being regimental chaplain of the 165th and 167th Infantry Regiments as well as the 117th Sanitary Train. As amply demonstrated by Duffy's exhaustion, tending to the spiritual needs of thousands of men in a war zone was no small matter. Under such demanding conditions, it is likely that Byron's perception of Carpentier's alleged deficiencies as a chaplain may simply have been the result of the priest being stretched too thin. There is also the unflattering possibility, however, that Byron's displeasure with Carpentier stemmed from the prejudice and distrust that commonly existed between religious denominations in America at that time. Regardless of the cause, it would soon become apparent to all the men that Father Carpentier was prepared to sacrifice his own life for any soldier no matter what his religious background—by the end of the war George Carpentier would be awarded the Distinguished Service Cross and several other citations for extraordinary heroism and courage in battle.

In a March 27 letter to Estelle, Byron highlighted the unique selflessness of men like Carpentier in battle: "Our division had made a name known all over France, as it is known in the States. Forty-eight men from one regiment alone were awarded the Croix de Guerre by the French. Every branch did its duty. Secretary of War Baker who received us at Camp Mills, and who saw our work here signally praised us. So, well may we be proud of our chance to be in this premier volunteer division."

Of the forty-eight men from the Rainbow Division who received the Croix de Guerre on March 22, two of them couldn't have been more different, though they were similar in courage. One was William "Wild Bill" Donovan, the legendary major of New York's Fighting 69th Infantry Regiment. Donovan was a Columbia University–educated Wall Street lawyer, former football star, and all-around man of action whose strength of character drew others to him like steel to a magnet. The other was Sergeant Abram Blaustein, a working-class Jew from Brooklyn, whose quiet demeanor and steady resolve went largely unnoticed except in time of crisis.

For both men that crisis presented itself on March 7 during a German artillery barrage of the Rouge Bouquet Forest, where soldiers from the 69th Infantry Regiment were stationed in the frontline trenches. As later related by both Donovan and Blaustein, that section of the line was devastated by a ferocious barrage of high-explosive, shrapnel, and mortar shells that destroyed trench works and collapsed dugouts—one dugout becoming a tomb for twenty men trapped forty feet underground. As the relentless barrage continued into the night, Donovan left his post of command in the rear and went forward in an attempt to restore some semblance of order to the badly traumatized survivors of Company E, whose morale "was shot to pieces." Also responding to the scene of the disaster was Sergeant Blaustein, who found the soldiers so "dumbfounded" they hadn't as yet begun to attempt to rescue the men who had been buried alive.

At first blush, Blaustein's observation of having found the men dumbfounded appears to be at odds with Donovan's account of encountering pandemonium at the scene, requiring him to "hit" one hysterical man "on the jaw" to "quiet" the "others." On further reflection, however, both versions are remarkably consistent in that they encompass the wide range of reactions displayed by soldiers who were suffering from what was then called "shell shock" or "war hysteria."

As later explained in a review of the medical case files of soldiers who were treated for psychological trauma at the National Hospital of London during the war, the individual tolerances and responses of traumatized soldiers varied greatly. The presentation of symptoms included but were not limited to paralyses of arms and legs, involuntary tics, tremors, spasms, and shakes, irregular gait, dizziness, blindness, deafness, heart palpitations, difficulty breathing, speech and sleep disorders, depression, anxiety, and dissociation. That this disabling condition was so little understood at the beginning of the war is evidenced by the fact that commanders in the British, French, and German armies often misinterpreted the appearance of these symptoms in traumatized soldiers as acts of insubordination or cowardice: hundreds of afflicted men were court-martialed, some even executed.

By the time the Rainbow Division had entered the trenches of France in the spring of 1918, the psychological traumatization of battle-weary and artillery-bludgeoned soldiers was recognized as an injury of modern warfare—no less debilitating in its impact than a bullet to the torso or a piece of shrapnel to the head. As later explained by General George C. Marshall in his memoir: "In addition to those who were actually wounded, many of those untouched became in effect casualties from the hostile artillery. . . . A 3-inch shell will temporarily scare or deter a man; a 6-inch shell will shock him; but an 8-inch shell, such as these 210 mm. ones, rips up the nervous system of everyone within a hundred yards of the explosion."

On arriving at the scene of the disaster that night, Sergeant Blaustein, less concerned with the psychological well-being of the men from the Fighting 69th who were still standing than he was with the fate of those who had been buried alive, lost no time in organizing a rescue party. Recently trained as a Pioneer unit engineer, Blaustein slid into a chasm in the ground that had been hollowed out by an enormous delayed-fuse *minewerfer* (mortar). For eight nonstop hours, Blaustein led the way, wriggling himself into the most precarious spaces as he lay on his back, at times upside down, digging with a trenching tool. During it all, German artillery continued to come in "thick and fast," often burying him under avalanches of dirt and debris as broken timbers and rock shifted and collapsed with each new salvo.

Without regard for his own safety, Blaustein was able to save several men. By the time he had finally dug down to the dugout itself, however, most of the men had already perished.

Private Alf Helmer, one of the survivors whom Blaustein had managed to rescue, later confided that as he lay there in the dark waiting to die, he could hear the other men as they slowly expired from suffocation and saw a faint purple light escape their bodies, rising to the ceiling before finally disappearing from sight.

As mystifying as Helmer's claim may have been, an equally incomprehensible turn of events related to this incident was about to unfold. Several days later, the Allied high command singled out Major William Donovan for his extraordinary courage that night, informing him that he was to receive the Croix de Guerre. In choosing to recognize Donovan alone, the high command had in essence ignored the heroic action of Sergeant Blaustein and others of lesser rank who had also risked their lives. Donovan, who was not in the habit of mincing words or suffering fools gladly, called it for what it was: discrimination based on rank—or worse, anti-Semitism. He refused to accept his medal if Blaustein and other deserving soldiers didn't receive theirs as well. Confronted with what threatened to be an awkward if not utterly embarrassing situation, the high command decided to reconsider the overall merits of the situation. Sergeant Blaustein and others were rightfully awarded the Croix de Guerre for their heroic action that night.

It was a graceless blunder that would not be repeated. The fact that it had occurred in the first place was actually not all that surprising—the issuance of medals for valor was not something with which the U.S. Army had a great deal of experience. The precedent for rewarding acts of gallantry by soldiers in the service of their country was established in 1782 when General George Washington bestowed the first "purple cloths of heart" to three sergeants in the Continental army. The Badge of Merit, as the medal was then called, was awarded only sparingly, however. Old-guard generals like Winfield Scott eschewed the issuance of medals for meritorious action, claiming that it smacked of European affectation. President Wilson felt otherwise—on April 6, 1917, the Distinguished Service Cross was established by order of the president. Over the course of the war, 6,309 Distinguished Service Crosses would be awarded to deserving recipients for individual acts of bravery. That these awards had a positive effect on morale is evidenced by the numerous prideful references contained in Byron's letters and diary.

After manning the trenches for more than one hundred days, the Rainbow Division was finally taken out of the line at Baccarat. According to Byron's diary, the Michigan Ambulance Company was "among the last units to leave," the men staying on with their ambulances to help the unit that would replace them: "Our place was being taken by the men from the 'Metropolitan New York'—77th Division. They treated us very rudely, refusing to stand gas guard when they had twenty men and we but two—refused to give us breakfast and stole part of our rations. But there are men of every type in the army and we're fast learning to know them."

Although the street-tough ways of the 77th may have offended Byron's small-town sense of civility and cooperation, the New Yorkers' us-against-the-world mentality later served them well. Four months later, the Lost Battalion, as the New York 77th would forever be remembered, suddenly found itself surrounded and greatly outnumbered during the battle of the Argonne Forest. For six days, the New York 77th managed to repel repeated German attacks, all the while going without food and water. Despite sustaining heavy losses, the 77th refused to surrender, relying on guile and New York moxie to hang on. Of the 550 New Yorkers who entered the battle, only 194 were able to hold out to the end—the rest were either killed or captured before Allied forces could break through German lines and rescue them.

But that lay in the future. At the present time, the surly New Yorkers were still comfortably encamped in Baccarat, where Byron and other members of the ambulance company were trying to help them. As a parting gift from the Germans, Byron got to share one last bombardment with the New Yorkers: "Thursday evening. I had taken the last load in Art Miller's ambulance and when I came back ran into a bombardment. Altho' the shells fell all around we were safe. So we finally left the front for Bertrichamps in the afternoon June 21. The French gave us a dandy little feed and send off."

After two weeks of being incommunicado, on June 24 Byron finally got an opportunity to write a letter to Estelle, summarizing his stay at the front simply, if not gratefully:

> I couldn't write before tonight, and I suppose this letter won't leave for a few more days. However, I think you are always anxious to get some word as often as possible. I know I am. Work has been more or less varied lately but there is no chance to describe it. Sometimes it is litter bearing, at others work in a dressing station, and sometimes a chance at driving. Of course we're seeing things—but there must be a kind God above us. I don't see how men can help but love God and be thankful when they are lost by the shell on which their name is written. When the shells fall all around us and we don't even get a shrapnel scratch, I can't help but think how good God is. They've been popped off, millions of boys fighting God's battle on earth, and right must come of such sacrifice.

After much loss of life, right did finally come from such sacrifice—at least for the time being. The British had succeeded in holding the line in the Somme. By the end of April, the German offensive had collapsed totally. The fact that the Michigan Ambulance Company had barely sustained a scratch during its time in the trenches was truly a godsend.

13

A SCENE THAT WOULD SHOCK
THE WORLD FOR ALL ETERNITY

After the Rainbow Division left Bertrichamps, rumor had it the men were headed for an Arcadian rest camp, or they would be sent to Paris to march in a Fourth of July parade, or perhaps they would be assigned to another hot spot in the front line. None of these rumors proved correct, for the moment anyway. Instead, on June 22, Byron found himself billeted in a barn in the village of Girecourt-sur-Durbion.

Girecourt was a manor town typical of its time. An old château owned by the comte de Bourcier anchored the center of the village. The sanitary train was temporarily headquartered at the château, which gave Byron and some of the other men an opportunity to get acquainted with the ruling class. As reflected in his letter to Estelle on June 24, Byron's exposure to the comte and his family gave him pause to reconsider his dim view of all things aristocratic:

> The count owns everything the same as in olden times, and the people love him and his wife to excess. I had a lot of long talks with our old land-lady while we were billeted in her barn. It seems she was a special friend of the Comtesse. She showed me several pictures of the family and a lot of letters from both she and the Comte. They must be very kind. Incidentally, I stood guard for four hours in the rain over this same chateau. It seemed strange to us but the Comte is a private, driving a truck in Paris, while his wife also lives there working in the hospitals. Certainly that

is a sacrifice. In the French army there is no Comte—no gentle names, or other reminders of Napoleon's regime.

Although Byron's diary and letters made frequent mention of his disdain for an Old World order based on the rule of monarchs and an aristocratic elite, in a somewhat ironic twist of fate, Byron would later learn that he was in fact descended from both French and English aristocracy. In 1934, Byron's father, James Bird Field, wrote a detailed genealogical treatise, *Progenitors and Descendants of Our Grandfather Seldon Field*, tracing the Field family line of descent back to Count Roger de la Feld of Alsace-Lorraine. Unknown to Byron during his service in the war, the ruins of de la Feld's château were located in a pass of the Vosges Mountains, only a few days march from Girecourt, where he was encamped in the spring of 1918. As set forth in the treatise, in 1066 one of Count de la Feld's sons, Hubertus, invaded England as a soldier in the army of William the Conqueror. At the conclusion of the Norman invasion, Hubertus was rewarded for his loyal service to William with a grant of land in England, thereby establishing the Field line of descent in that country. That Byron was to some extent proud of his family heritage is evidenced by a copy of the Field family coat of arms found among his personal effects. Appropriate to Byron's devout nature, the motto on the crest reads *Sans Dieu Rien* (Without God Nothing).

After spending three nights in Girecourt, the ambulance company stayed in Toul for one day before moving on to the small village of Cheppy just south of Châlons-sur-Marne. Cheppy was in the heart of the Champagne region of France. When the company arrived there, it soon became apparent that the land of Champagne would belie the refreshing image normally associated with its name—nothing but a flat expanse of chalky arid ground stretched between the Rainbow Division and the German front lines. Without the benefit of natural cover, troops had to avoid congregating in large groups in the open. To do otherwise ran the considerable risk of being seen by German spotters aloft in observation balloons and airplanes. Most of the men hung around the barracks waiting for word of their next assignment. Byron used the time to answer letters from home.

In a July 2 letter to Estelle, after bringing her up to date on innocuous activities concerning the war, Byron steered clear of engaging in a more detailed discussion, explaining, "Some of your questions I can't answer. I'm mighty sorry but my letters will have to be fewer and shorter." Then, as always, he turned his attention to Estelle's affairs, saying that he hoped that she'd changed some of her "old notions" about the war after having read *Over the Top*, a firsthand account of life in the trenches. This was followed immediately by a fanciful but heartfelt wish that he could be with her at Bay View, a Methodist summer camp meeting, pursuing his religious studies. Then he addressed one of Estelle's most important social causes—women's rights—reluctantly but by no means completely conceding: "Yes, it certainly seems some organization of factory girls is necessary—particularly now, when all the natural order of things is upset." Before ending his letter he attempted to assuage Estelle's apparent fear that her studious and assertive manner might be off-putting: "I won't let you be an old maid or teacher all your life, if I can help it. And I think—."

When Byron wasn't writing letters home, he was busy exploring the surrounding area, dropping in on the small YMCA hut in Cheppy or hiking with Herbert Jackson and Horace Sprague into Châlons, where they visited the Red Cross canteen, the YMCA hut, and the city's impressive cathedral. On one of their excursions, Byron and Jackson hiked three miles down the road to a large French aviation center where squadrons of planes took off on bombing runs over German lines. Byron was fascinated by airplanes and lingered at the airfield one night, studying the different machines and talking with the pilots. To Byron, airplanes represented both the best and worst of modern warfare. Much like the other engines of mass destruction that had been introduced by this war—artillery, poison gas, machine guns, and tanks—bombers were "huge affairs carrying three men and ten hundred pound bombs" capable of killing large numbers of people from afar. Yet airplanes could also be small enough to lend themselves to the air duels that Byron described as "wonderful" and "heroic" reminders of the honor and bravery associated with the individual combat of yesteryear. It was hardly unexpected, then, that while camped nearby, Byron and Jackson made plans to see what the new face of warfare looked like from high above the ground. As he set forth in his diary: "For a little consideration, we fixed it up for a flight for the next night. Unfortunately, some of the fellows raised Cain in the billet that night, so we were confined for the remaining evenings, and could not get our much desired ride."

Before Byron and Jackson could get back to the French aerodrome and cash in on their tickets to ride, the ambulance company was on the move again—this time courtesy of French general Henri Gourard. General Gourard was aware of the Rainbow Division's exemplary performance in the Baccarat sector, where it had been lauded for its offensive ardor, spirit, and discipline. Gourard also recognized another important trait—one that he happened to share with the men of the Rainbow. Both were grossly underestimated by the German high command.

The Germans were well acquainted with Gourard. In the Dardanelles campaign two years earlier, he'd come out on the short end of the battle of Gallipoli, losing his right arm and breaking both legs. After willing himself through a hasty period of recovery, Gourard was back in the war only six months later, this time taking charge of France's 4th Armée in the Lorraine sector.

"The Lion of Champagne," as Gourard would later be called, was a resourceful and determined adversary. As a commander, Gourard was as devoted to his men as they were to him. As a combat soldier, he wore his war wounds as if they were medals—never attempting to disguise his armless right sleeve or considerable limp. Not a physically imposing figure, Gourard was nevertheless a compelling one. With a glistening red beard, gleaming eyes, and resonant voice, he exuded an aura of supreme confidence that was utterly contagious. In the words of General Douglas MacArthur, "Gourard was magnificent, of all the leaders I have known anyplace, anywhere." Gourard in turn, deemed MacArthur one of the bravest and finest officers he had ever served with. Together they would prove the German high command incompetent, ill informed, and arrogant.

Gourard moved the Rainbow Division into the line between the 170th French Infantry Division on the left and the French 13th Infantry Division on the right. Gourard was confident that with two divisions of elite French *chasseurs á pied*—the "Blue Devils," as the Germans called them—on either flank, the doughboys would be more than ready for whatever they might face. What came next for Byron was an abbreviated Fourth of July celebration. He wrote in his diary:

> We had planned to have a celebration on the glorious Fourth, but orders for movement prevented it. The other companies and officers celebrated with special messes but we with our untouched $2,000 mess fund had hamburgers for dinner, and white beans for supper. That afternoon the French put on a fine program in a small theater in honor of our great day. There were song, violin and piano solos, monologues and comedy—very good, particularly in the spirit it was given. After dark, we were taken to Camp de Chalons near Suippes. It was nothing less than a planted woods of firs among which we pitched our tents. The first night we slept under the sky. Here we were closer than ever and every precaution possible was taken to prevent the Boche knowing we were anywhere around. As a matter of fact the presence of the division was a secret. A Boche drive here was contemplated and we were here to stem the tide if necessary. Day and night we heard planes overhead—our ceaseless, tireless guardians. Our camp was between two railroads—a narrow gauge over which munitions were going up day and night. The other was a main line, on which troops and armored cannons went up and back every day.

Over the next few days, all of the Rainbow Division's movements were made under the cover of darkness. The Germans weren't nearly as secretive about their intentions, however; it was readily apparent to French spotters aloft in surveillance planes and observation balloons that German forces were preparing to launch a major attack on Allied positions somewhere between Verdun and Soissons, east of Reims and north of Château-Thierry. Gourard had been expecting it. He understood how the enemy thought. After their stinging defeat at the Somme, it would have made more tactical sense for the Germans to regroup and begin preparations to defend against an almost certain French counteroffensive. Gourard knew, however, that for the German high command, and the Kaiser in particular, Prussian pride usually trumped better sense. Tactical retreat was not an option—not at this point, at least.

The German high command still clung to the belief that German forces could break through the Allied lines at Suippes and be in Châlons in twenty-four hours, after which they would be able to cut off the Reims salient and control the Meuse, and with it the plains of Châlons. To prevent that from happening, Gourard put the Rainbow Division and French Blue Devils in the path of the coming storm. What he didn't know at the moment, though, was when the onslaught would begin.

On Sunday July 7, while Byron waited "for the big show" to start, he attended a church service at the YMCA, where "Mr. Wycof gave a fine talk about 'keeping the faith' in the evening." Earlier that day, General Gourard had also urged his troops not to break faith, albeit in an entirely different way. It became known as Gourard's "stand or die" speech. Translated for the American soldiers by their French counterparts, the message read:

> To the French and American Soldiers of the Army:
> We may be attacked from one moment to another. You all feel that a defensive battle was never engaged in under more favorable conditions.
> We are warned and we are on guard. We have received strong reinforcements of infantry and artillery. You will fight on ground which by your assiduous labor you have transformed into a formidable fortress, into a fortress which is invincible if the passages are well guarded.
> The bombardment will be terrible. You will endure it without weakness. The attack in a cloud of dust and gas will be fierce, but your positions and your armament are formidable.
> The strong and brave hearts of free men beat in your breasts. None will look behind, none will give way. Every man will have but one thought—"Kill them, kill them in abundance, until they have had enough."
> And therefore your General tells you it will be a glorious day.

Gourard's stand or die speech was not just another piece of rhetorical hyperbole meant to inspire troops on the eve of battle. Gourard hoped that the unyielding tenor of his message would help set the stage for a carefully laid trap—an artifice that the French called an "elastic defense." This was but the latest version of a two-thousand-year-old stratagem first used by the greatest general of them all, Hannibal Barca of Carthage, to slaughter fifty thousand Roman soldiers on the fields of Cannae. Gourard was planning to employ a variation of this artifice to thwart a new battle tactic that the Germans had recently used to great effect. Only months earlier, at the battle of the Somme, the Germans had successfully unleashed specially trained *Sturmtruppen* to penetrate entrenched Allied positions. Gourard had every reason to believe they would try to use the same tactic again to break through French lines in Lorraine.

Gourard's plan was, essentially, to vacate the frontline trenches, keeping only a token force in place to impede the advance of oncoming German troops just long enough for a withering artillery barrage to deplete their ranks. Gourard believed that after breaching the frontline trenches, the Germans would be so eager to press their apparent advantage that they would rush headlong into the great void that stretched between the first- and second-line trenches, where a murderous maze of barbed wire, land mines, artillery, and machine-gun fire would slow the exhausted storm troopers to a crawl. At that point, they would be enveloped and destroyed by French and American troops lying in wait.

In addition to secrecy, the key to springing the trap was to keep just enough troops in the frontline trenches so their "stand or die" resistance would fool the Germans into thinking that they were fully occupied, causing the main thrust of the German artillery barrage and infantry assault to be concentrated on the sacrificial defenders who were stationed there, instead of on the real strength of Gourard's army which was positioned in the rear. It was a great deal to ask of the men who were to be stationed in the forward-most positions. In the sector of the line assigned to the all-black 369th Infantry Regiment (formerly Harlem's New York 15th, now fighting under

Gourard's 4th Armée), the honor of manning those frontline positions fell to Company K, commanded by Captain Hamilton Fish. That Fish fully understood the great sacrifice and almost certain death that awaited his men is apparent in a letter he wrote to his father on the eve of battle:

> I am writing you a few lines to say that I am assigned with my company to two French companies to defend an important position against the expected German offensive. My company will be in the first position to resist the tremendous concentration against us and I do not believe there is any chance of any of us surviving the first push. I am proud to be trusted with such a post of honor and have the greatest confidence in my own men to do their duty to the end. The rest of our regiment is dug in far to the rear. . . . In war some units have to be sacrificed for the safety of the rest and this part has fallen to us and will be executed gladly as our contribution to final victory. How fond I am of you, and thank you for all your care and devotion—words utterly fail me. I want you in case I am killed to be brave and remember that one could not wish a better way to die than for a righteous cause and one's country.

In anticipation of the carnage that would take place there, on July 12, Byron and Jackson were sent forward to Camp de Echelon to work as litter bearers. After arriving there, they hunkered down with other soldiers in the second-line trenches, wondering if the Germans would take the bait. Until the battle began in earnest, no one would know for sure. Gourard had never been one to leave anything to chance, though, and in the intervening days he had been sending nightly patrols behind German lines in search of intelligence. On the night of July 14, Bastille Day, a French patrol brought back a German prisoner who divulged the precise time of the attack—fifteen minutes after midnight, scant hours away. A prearranged code, "François 570," was quickly spread down the Allied line to warn of the attack, followed by a heartfelt *Bon chance*. Shortly before midnight, Gourard beat the Germans to the punch by sending over a preliminary barrage to soften up the storm troops that were massing for the attack.

At 12:15, the Germans countered with an artillery barrage of their own—one of the greatest in military history. It was later estimated that over three thousand artillery pieces pummeled French and American positions for four hours. The "symphony of hate," as it would later be described in *The History of Ambulance Company 168*, was so deafening that Parisians could hear it almost one hundred miles away. So blazing was the ensuing conflagration that men in Châlons, five miles away, claimed they were able to sit outside and read newspapers as if it were daytime.

Byron was among the first to suffer the bombardment's devastating impact. As recounted in his diary:

> Shortly after midnight the first Boche shell screamed over our heads. We tore—believe me, we tore out of bed, got into our clothes and rushed for the dugout "so-called." The second shell

Medics administering first aid in shell hole, July 5, 1918. (Photograph by Army Signal Corps.)

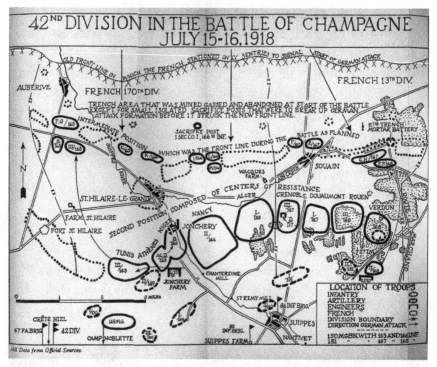

Sector map of the battle of Champagne. (From Henry J. Reilly, *Americans All: The Rainbow Division at War* [Columbus, OH: F. J. Heer, 1936], 304A.)

went over on our way there, and the third exploded just as the last of us—Jackson and a Supply Train man were getting into the low entrance. The shell must have burst within five feet of the entrance, and none of us knew a thing for several seconds. The exploding powder seemed to envelop everything as with liquid fire. Instinctively we all put our masks on. They were of no use against burning powder in our lungs, which seemed to be burning everything away. We had heard moaning and knew some were hurt. As soon as possible, we found the two men out. They were Jackson and the Supply Train man. We paid no attention to the shells then, but got them into the ambulance in a hurry and rushed them on. We decided afterwards that they both must have been dead before we got them away. I was very groggy and almost under, but thot' of my ammonia tube which

I stuck into my mouth and poured down regardless of the pain. The relief was instant. Then Wiota and I rushed around hunting for more wounded, but none were found, but one wagoner slightly wounded in the leg. We thot' best to keep him. The dugout was so full of powder we couldn't use it, so we had to stay in the open for two hours—as Lieut. Drake did not want us to leave our post. The shells cried overhead incessantly and a score of times we thot' all was over. I think we were all praying as never before. We learned afterward that it was one of the most furious bombardments of the war, but our side was better.

Just before the break of day, the German infantry assault began. By the time the sun was up, Byron had made his way to Camp Lyre, where most of the other ambulance men were assembled, awaiting assignment. All morning long the battle raged, with wave after wave of German troops dashing across no-man's-land in a desperate attempt to break through Allied lines. And time and again, American and French forces beat them back.

By early afternoon, Byron was driving an ambulance loaded with casualties from the frontline dressing stations to the hospitals at Bussy-le-Château and Châlons. It was an assignment fraught with extreme peril. German artillery had destroyed the French airfield nearby, making it possible for German planes to completely control the skies above the battlefield. In addition to strafing Allied troops in the trenches, German pilots targeted ambulances and litter bearers tending to the wounded, even acting as spotters for German artillery to bomb the hospital at Bussy-le-Château. As set forth by Byron in the "Champagne" chapter of *Iodine and Gasoline*:

> The assumption that the hospital was immune from Boche bombardment was false. For daylight brought more shells to Bussy le Chateau. Just as soon as the sun made aerial observation possible, a Boche plane started circling in the sky over the hospital directing fire, and the bombardment began in earnest. The first whining 210 m.m. projectile took the roof off of the railway station; the second knocked the tank off the water tower on the

opposite corner of the hospital ground; and the third crashed through the roof of the surgical ward killing two patients in their beds and another outside. The big red cross of chalk and brick dust on the lawn was laid wide open with a shell crater and still the shelling continued.

By midafternoon the hospital at Bussy-le-Château had to be evacuated, forcing the sanitary train to move wounded men to a hospital in Châlons. Later in the day, that hospital would have to be evacuated as well when it became the target of long-range German artillery.

In the interim, Byron continued to ferry wounded soldiers from the frontline dressing stations past Saint-Hilaire to the base hospitals, without regard to distance or attendant danger. In the "Champagne Front" chapter of *The History of Ambulance Company 168*, one of Byron's many trips that day was mentioned for its exceptional daring:

> One crew had to cross a field about half a mile long to get to the road from a battalion aid station. This particular piece of ground was in plain view of the German observation balloons. Planes circled around watching, and shells dropped in, potting up the field like holes in Swiss cheese. This driver, with his orderly, had been told by a Captain that he could never make it across the field; but nevertheless, undaunted by this he started. The orderly tells the story like this: *"We started and I told the driver to give her all he had, and watch the intervals between shells, then step on her tail and take her through. We could see big shells drop in ahead of us and burst in clouds of dirt and smoke. Suddenly, directly ahead of us some twenty yards or so the road just seemed to disappear in a terrific burst of black smoke, dirt, stones and flying shell fragments. We swerved just in time to dash past a shell hole big enough to bury a freight car. We had just pulled into the road when another burst landed just in front and a little ahead nearly burying the ambulance. Before we could adjust ourselves to this, another big one shook the car as it hit directly in back of us."* They made it, but the men at the dressing station held their breaths as the car seemed to disappear in clouds of dirt and smoke as each shell burst so near.

Other cases were deliberately fired upon by German planes. The planes would follow a car along a road with machine guns spitting a hail of fire at the ambulance, disregarding the fact that a G.M.C. Ambulance cannot be mistaken for any other kind of car, and that the top is plainly marked with a large red cross. Many instances of this outrageous and shameful work can be told and testified to by our ambulance men here and on other fronts.

Other instances of German ruthlessness were recounted by members of New York's Fighting 69th, where combat in the trenches of that sector of the line was often hand to hand and no holds barred. Such unsparing tactics highlighted the desperate straits that German troops found themselves in as their attack began to stall, and the lengths they would go to in order to infiltrate enemy lines. The New Yorkers reported encounters with German soldiers who had donned French helmets and uniforms to be able to work their way close enough to Allied lines to toss stick grenades at the unsuspecting American soldiers. On one occasion, as related by a disgusted doughboy, "[T]hey came over in French uniforms, some with Red Cross bands on their arms and stretchers, and on the stretchers they had machine guns. They received the same deal the rest of them got, they didn't get away with their trick."

For their part, the American troops weren't necessarily above reproach either, especially the Alabama Wildmen. It was widely known that the men of the 167th Infantry were not in the habit of taking prisoners—some independent sources even claimed to have witnessed Alabama soldiers killing wounded and defenseless German soldiers during the battle. Although a subsequent investigation by AEF headquarters would ultimately clear the 167th Infantry of any wrongdoing, long after the war was over, rumors of atrocities committed by the Alabamans continued to linger.

According to Byron's diary, while the battle raged he worked as a driver "all that night until the next morning," and after being "relieved went back to the hospital" in Miomandre, where he "worked and drove some more that day, Tuesday, and the same that night." Throughout the ordeal, the ancient ruins of Attila the Hun's camp loomed like an augury on the outskirts of Miomandre, where Roman legions had stopped the barbarian horde two thousand years earlier. As later related by Byron in the "Champagne" chapter of *Iodine and Gasoline*, the ferocity of the ongoing battle was evident from its unprecedented carnage: "No picture of the shambles wrought by this battle can portray its gruesome actuality. In the wildest of Dante's dreams of Inferno, he did not picture such a scene; men piled in great heaps, the dying with dead,—legs, arms, heads and torsos; gray and blue, and khaki intermingled; blood, red and clotted black; torn, seared, crying flesh,— all in a labyrinth of mutilated trenches as though old Mars himself had planned a scene that would shock the world for all eternity."

Fourteen years later, Byron would take particular note of a similar description contained in a book written by fellow Rainbow man Leslie Langille of the 149th Illinois Field Artillery—the unit to which Byron and Herbert Jackson had been temporarily assigned on July 15, and where Jackson was among the first to fall mortally wounded. There is no indication that Byron knew Langille personally, but that he found a certain passage written by Langille especially poignant and reminiscent of his own writing years earlier is evidenced by his having turned down the corner of that page. In writing *Men of the Rainbow*, Langille said it was his intention to give the youth of 1933 an honest depiction of the incredible sacrifice and suffering wrought by war. The passage written by Langille that Byron earmarked reads as follows:

> Again, it becomes absolutely impossible to describe the terrific struggle that the past ten hours have witnessed. The greatest stretch of imagination possible could not, even in a small measure, conceive the horrible scene that has taken place. Solid formations of thousands of men have been walking into sure destruction. After the first few minutes they have had to literally climb over their own dead in order to make progress—only to meet their fate a few steps further forward. I call upon Deity, in whatever form you may see fit to worship it, to look down on these bleeding, mangled, dying and dead heaps of humanity. Ten, hundreds, thousands of souls, have through no act on their own part, but as pawns, dupes, patriots, heroes—call them what you will, been led to slaughter,

as sacrifices to the hideous creature we are disposed to call "Mars." Oh, the irony contained in that word! It is given as the answer to our query. "Why?" It hides the real motive of jealousy, hate, commercial advantage, money, diplomacy, statesmanship. It is the rock behind which those responsible hide their guilt. . . . A more glib pen than mine could write volumes on the data these last few pages have contained; but in the end the results will be the same, namely, dead men, hundreds of dead men, thousands of dead men; wounded men, bloody men, bleeding men, broken men, men who will never again be able to see, having lost their sight; men who will never be able to walk again, having lost their legs; men whose bodies will never again be the perfect mechanism that this morning's sun found them to be. Years of hospitalization await many of these men who last night had youth—and health and hope for the future. "But this is War!" This is the thing that we, in our effort to picture what confronted us, might have partially pictured; but in our wildest stretch of imagination we could not have pictured these scenes without experiencing them. Those pleasant days at Domjevan and Merviller belied our mental pictures at one extreme—they were too tame. This pendulum swings the picture to the other extreme. Never before, at any time or at any place in the entire world's history, have men faced each other in mortal combat on such a tremendous scale as this battle presents. We wonder if our future battles will be as severe. If so, how can any of us endure?

After three days, the German offensive had burned itself out like a great wildfire, leaving only scorched earth and battered men. Somehow, Byron had been able to withstand its fury—whether his once unquestioning faith in a kind and loving God had managed to survive as well remained to be seen.

14
THE RIVER OF BLOOD

The smoke had no sooner cleared from the battlefields of Champagne than the Michigan Ambulance Company was on the move again, encamping this time on the outskirts of Châlons-sur-Marne. Although the German army had just taken a severe beating, it was far from defeated—in grudging retreat, German artillery and airplanes continued to lash out at Allied positions from afar. Byron and other soldiers from the Rainbow Division soon discovered that they would be on the receiving end of that wrath—on many of their nighttime visits to the YMCA hut in Châlons, they had been forced to seek shelter in the great limestone wine cellars used by villagers to escape the recurring air raids by German bombers.

The bombing campaign directed at Châlons had left much of the city in ruins. As noted by Byron, "At the opening of the Mar. 21st drive on Paris, the city was bombed by night raiders for a week. Considerable material damage was inflicted including a large hole in the cathedral roof. Thousands of people left town, making the city seem quite deserted in the resident part, tho' most of the stores are open." Much of the terrain in Champagne was laced with a labyrinth of tunnels and caves, some stretching for thousands of yards, dating as far back as the Roman legions, which had extracted chalk and salt from them. Over the last three years, the immense caverns had provided emergency shelter for thousands of residents who took refuge there. What remained of Châlons above ground became a virtual ghost town at night. In an attempt to minimize the destruction to Châlons by the German night raiders, each evening twelve barrage balloons were deployed in a defensive array. According to Major William Donovan of New York's Fighting 69th, despite this effort, German bombers still managed to penetrate the protective shield:

> While at our old station, two of the officers went to Chalons and were caught in a raid. Everyone was obliged to go underground. They went into a cellar on the side of the hill. This was divided into huge compartments. The place contained thousands. Tents were placed and small shacks were thrown up. It was much like you read of the early Christians dwelling underground. The night we left, our town and station were bombed just as we pulled out. The succeeding troops were roughly dealt with. We were forced to wait outside the big town.... You could hear the "whirr" of the machines, the shrapnel of the anti-air guns was breaking directly overhead and the shell cases dropping all about us, the machine gun tracer bullets dotted the sky with vari-colored flames. To our rear we could see the flames of buildings that were struck.

Châlons was no means the sole focus of raids by German night bombers. At this point in the war, both sides engaged in the strategic bombing of various cities far removed from the front lines, as much for the purpose of wreaking havoc, fear, and dissent among the civilian population as to inflict damage on purportedly legitimate military targets. The infamous "Paris Gun," capable of raining death and destruction on innocent Parisians from a distance of over sixty miles, highlighted the far-flung lengths to which each side was willing to go in order to win the war. By now, it was abundantly clear even to true believers like Byron that the pretense that they were fighting a just war had deteriorated. Still, Byron soldiered on.

On July 18, Byron began to write to Estelle: "My dear: We've been mighty busy these last few days—mighty busy." That was as far as he got. Byron had more immediate concerns to attend to. With the Germans set back on their heels, the Rainbow Division was suddenly on the march. On July 24, the Michigan Ambulance Company left the

The Crowning Atrocity

While the churches of Paris were crowded with worshipers on Good Friday, the Germans opened fire on the city with their mystery gun from the roof and pillars killed upward of a hundred worshipers

Drawn for Leslie's by L. F. Grant

"The Crowning Atrocity," *Leslie's Weekly*, April 20, 1918, 538, depicting Parisian churchgoers killed by the Paris Gun.

pockmarked and trench-scarred terrain of Lorraine for the lush farm-land surrounding the city of Château-Thierry.

In order to reach Château-Thierry, the sanitary train had to first pass through the picturesque city of Luzancy. Nestled in a valley on the western bank of the Marne River, Luzancy was only twenty miles downstream from the blood-soaked streets of Château-Thierry. Despite its proximity to the front lines, the countryside surrounding Luzancy had somehow managed to escape the ravages of war. It was an idyllic setting worthy of a painting *en plein air*. Here, the waters of the Marne ran clear and smooth. Sun-splashed fields of red poppies and golden wheat stretched across the gentle rolling hills, rippling in lan-guorous waves with each blush of wind. The all-consuming focus on the war notwithstanding, late July was still harvest time. Women, and men on leave from the front, tended the fields. In a country starved for food, grains of wheat were more precious than bullets.

When the Rainbow Division finally reached Luzancy, the atmo-sphere grew heavy with dread. Under the great weight of the war machine that rumbled through the village streets, the picture of peace and tranquility that had existed in the valley only moments before was now a kaleidoscopic jumble of discordant pieces. Off in the distance, gray observation balloons hung like thunderclouds in the summer sky. At Château-Thierry, the Marne was called "the River of Blood." During the recent spring offensive, German storm troops had succeeded in penetrating Allied defenses in this sector of the front. In just three days' time, the Germans had advanced as far west as the village of Château-Thierry before being stopped by American troops from the 3rd Army Division and the 4th Marine Brigade. After twenty days of bitter fighting, the Marines had finally managed to drive the Germans from Belleau Wood. At the same time, 3rd Divi-sion was dug in on the western bank of the Marne at Château-Thierry, where it had repeatedly denied the Germans passage across the river and a clear road to Paris only thirty-seven miles away. Although the German offensive had not been able to break through Allied defenses completely, Parisians still girded themselves for the worst. For most French citizens, the presence of a division of the Kaiser's elite Impe-rial Guard this close to Paris was the nerve-wracking equivalent of being asked to stand blindfolded before a firing squad while waiting for a sentence of execution to be carried out. Those Parisians who could afford to fled.

The first objective of the Allied counteroffensive was to eliminate the threat to Paris by displacing the German Army from the Château-Thierry salient. In order to accomplish that, on July 19, Allied troops launched the first strike in a series of attacks called the Aisne-Marne Offensive. Not only would the attacks succeed in rolling the Germans back from the salient, they wouldn't end until the enemy was nearly driven from French soil, and the Armistice was declared on November 11.

With National Guard units from New England's 26th Yankee Division leading the charge, Allied forces crossed the Marne, and after five days of fierce combat managed to dislodge German troops from Château-Thierry. By July 24, in the face of stiff resistance, the New Englanders had succeeded in advancing as far as the village of Épieds, suffering over four thousand casualties in doing so.

In the early morning hours of July 25, the Rainbow Division arrived at Château-Thierry to relieve the exhausted New Englanders. Having demonstrated its tenacity on the Champagne front, the Rainbow Division would be used as shock troops for the remainder of the war—which meant that it would be held in reserve until the appropriate moment, and then unleashed to deliver knockout punch after knockout punch to the enemy. Although the ranks of the division would eventually be decimated from being deployed in this manner, the spirit and resolve of the men never diminished. To the contrary, their great sacrifice would become a badge of honor. As noted by Byron in a diary entry: "Our men are filled with nothing but fight. The Hell at Champagne had given them the thirst for Boche blood. And they got their fill here. This—the Second Battle of the Marne. How proud we can be to have been some of the crack troops picked for the job. All of us were anxious to get up there." Despite the unbridled enthusiasm and confidence of the men, the ensuing battle was an unprecedented bloodletting. As later related by General Douglas MacArthur, the series of battles at Château-Thierry were "six of the bitterest days and nights of the war for the Rainbow." Waiting for them on the other side of the Marne was

"Doing His Bit." Front cover of *Leslie's Weekly*, April 13, 1918, showing the adverse impact of German menace on the French psyche.

Sector map of Château-Thierry. (From *The Medical Department of the United States Army in the World War*, vol. 8, *Field Operations* [Washington, DC: Government Printing Office, 1925], plate 10.)

the deadly embrace of the elite 4th Prussian Guards, led by the Kaiser's son, Crown Prince Friedrich.

As the men would soon discover, the gentle rolling terrain that surrounded Château-Thierry lent itself to a different kind of warfare from the trench tactics of the previous three years. There were no fixed lines of engagement or permanent defensive fixtures like the trenches and dugouts of Lorraine. On this front, the men were deployed in a wide-open and relatively freewheeling attack that was often so fast moving that it was difficult to provide artillery fire in support of advancing troops for fear of killing friendly forces. To compound matters, the Germans didn't simply retreat in a customary rearguard action. Instead they fell back in a stop-and-go fashion, looking to disrupt the Allied attack by constructing successive lines of defense, which essentially served as speed bumps to an onrushing army. By lying in wait behind whatever protective shelter the terrain had to offer—stone walls, rock outcroppings, copses of trees, and farm buildings—the Germans were poised with mortars, artillery, and machine guns ready to slaughter the American and French troops that were forced to advance across the open fields with barely the width of a bayonet for cover.

In pursuing the Germans, the Allied pressure was relentless. The cost in American and French lives was staggering. By the time the Rainbow Division relieved the Yankee Division, the Germans had already been driven from the village of Épieds, six miles past Château-Thierry. Byron and several other men from the ambulance company were immediately detailed to the front to set up a dressing station at Épieds. Getting there in a timely fashion, however, was difficult. As reflected in Byron's diary, the devastation he witnessed en route to Épieds was overwhelming:

> Our road was through Chateau Thierry and from there on all we saw was debris—walls of buildings tumbled down, personal stuff everywhere—the road potted with shell holes, bridges blown up, thousands of Boche shells of all caliber lying everywhere, machine guns and dead Boche and horses littered everywhere—all evidence of their precipitate flight. Still our men pushed on, often in the face of grueling machine-gun fire

and intermittent artillery fire. The Boche retreat was so rapid that our artillery couldn't keep up so as to throw a protective barrage ahead of the men.

The going was as odious as it was onerous. In the heat of the July sun, the smell of decaying flesh was stifling. Bloated and blackened corpses were strewn grotesquely by the side of the road and across fields. It was hard to breathe without inhaling the black flies and gnats that swarmed in the air. Some men wore gas masks in an attempt to filter out the stench of death. Here and there, a few makeshift graves were marked by sticks and upended rifles, but mostly the dead were left to fester where they had fallen. Until there was time to safely bury the remains, corpses would serve as a grim reminder that the outcome of the war still hung in the balance.

What was left of the shell-pocked road to Épieds was choked with everything necessary to keep an army on the march in motion. Ammunition trucks, artillery canon of every caliber, caissons, tanks, kitchen and food wagons, ambulances, and thousands upon thousands of troops on foot and in trucks stretched out for miles like a great khaki-colored snake inching ever closer to its prey. The going was excruciatingly slow, especially under the constant strafing from German airplanes. When the men weren't hitting the mud, they were getting stuck in it. At the risk of sinking up to the axles, a few impatient drivers attempted to make end runs through the sodden fields—some made it; most didn't. It took Byron's ambulance the better part of the night to reach Épieds.

Lieutenant Lecklider's detail was the first unit of the sanitary train to reach the ruins of Épieds. The Germans had evacuated only hours before, leaving wounded American and French soldiers among the dead and dying. Utter devastation awaited Lieutenant Lecklider on his arrival. Whole blocks of houses had been leveled. Evidence of the desperate hand-to-hand battle that had just played out there was strewn wildly about the streets, courtyards, and fields. In the center of town, an artillery round had decapitated the steeple of an old Gothic church; others had punched gaping holes in its roof. Just around the corner from the church, there was a great deal of activity as medics at a dressing station worked frantically to save the lives of wounded soldiers. Lieutenant Lecklider quickly converted the dressing station into a triage unit. By the time Byron and other ambulance drivers had arrived, there was no shortage of wounded men in need of immediate treatment. Within hours, over four hundred patients were waiting to be evacuated to hospitals.

The sudden influx of wounded was the unfortunate but not unanticipated result of the attack by the 167th Alabama Infantry Regiment on German troops hunkered down at Croix Rouge Farm. Situated in the middle of an open field measuring a mile square, the large stone farmhouse sat at the top of a small rise on the south side of the Ourcq River. The farmhouse was the key to controlling the approach to the river and the heights beyond. The Germans had fortified the position accordingly. Over two dozen water-cooled machine guns manned by five-man crews were situated at strategic locations so that interlocking

42nd Division dressing station, Épieds, July 27, 1918. (Photograph by Army Signal Corps.)

fields of fire covered all approaches to the farm. Red marks had been painted on trees, allowing German gunners to sight accurately for up to one thousand yards—although the combined machine-gun firepower of ten thousand rounds per minute made a keen eye less important for the gunners than laying down a steady stream of lead. It was this virtual scythe of hurtling metal that had cut the New Englanders down in driving the Germans from Château-Thierry. Now it was the Rainbow's turn.

On the afternoon of July 26, a battalion of Alabamans from 167th Infantry Regiment stepped out from the protective cover of the woods located just south of the farm into the hot French sun. With a battalion of soldiers from the 168th Iowa Infantry Regiment in support, they had been ordered to make a bayonet charge without the benefit of artillery support. Colonel William Screws of the Alabama infantry, after surveying the well-entrenched German position for the first time, attempted to get the hastily conceived attack postponed. Screws protested so vociferously, in fact, that he was almost relieved of command. Whether the plan was ill conceived or not, French general Jean Degoutte and AEF corps commander Hunter Liggett would have their bayonet charge. With bayonets fixed, the Alabamans obeyed orders and the charge began. It did not go well.

The 1st Battalion of the Alabama infantry was cut to ribbons by enfilading German machine-gun fire. With the soldiers pinned down for more than an hour in an open field, the day appeared to be lost until a second assault was launched that evening. Successive waves of Alabama infantrymen poured out of the surrounding woods, attacking from different angles and sweeping across the fields. As the battle wore on, Rebel yells filled the night air. Eventually, the Alabamans gained traction and closed on the farmhouse. At this point, the fighting was hand to hand, with no quarter asked and none given. After four long hours the Alabamans prevailed. Fully 283 Germans lay dead, killed by bayonet. The impact of the battle was immense, the carnage unforgettable. Lieutenant Colonel Walter Bare of the 167th Alabama Infantry described the ground leading up to the farm as "literally covered with killed and wounded, both American and German. For some distance you could actually walk on dead men. The two Battalions in the attack suffered so heavily that it took a large proportion of those not killed and wounded to move the wounded back to the first aid station, which was established by the side of Lake de la Logette, some two and a half miles to our rear."

In his memoir, MacArthur romantically remembered the charge as being unsurpassed in military history for its gallantry. For Colonels Screws and Bare, however, and the Alabama infantrymen who had actually had to make the charge, it would never be forgotten as an unparalleled loss of life.

By daybreak on July 27, the Germans had been driven from the area that surrounded Croix Rouge Farm and had fallen back to their next line of defense on the north bank of the Ourcq River. The Alabamans were in no condition to continue pursuing the Germans—two of their three battalions had suffered over 50 percent casualties. The next phase of the battle would unfold with other elements of the Rainbow Division taking the lead as the Germans lay in wait on the north side of the river. Although the Ourcq was barely knee deep and only several yards wide, the land sloping down to the river greatly favored the defender. In order to ford the river, soldiers would have to first make it across a stretch of open terrain approximately one-quarter of a mile wide, and then make it up another barren stretch of sloping ground before reaching the enemy. With the exception of an occasional gully or depression, both slopes were absolutely devoid of cover. It was a perfect killing field for German gunners.

During this phase of the attack, the 168th Iowa and the 166th Ohio Infantry Regiments were assigned the task of driving the Germans from the villages of Sergy and Seringes-et-Nesles on the opposite side of the Ourcq. In three days of continual fighting, the Iowa and Ohio Infantry Regiments succeeded in crossing the river and capturing the much-contested village of Sergy. In the back-and-forth battle for control of the village, Sergy would change hands seven times. The capture of Seringes was an equally tough objective, as described by Douglas MacArthur in his memoir, *Reminiscences*:

> It looked like a small Gibraltar, with its flanking guns and its barricaded streets and houses swarming with troops. I formed our infantry on the south side of the stream and rushed the town.

Their artillery concentrated, their machine guns east and west of the town raked us fore and aft, but nothing could stop the impetus of that mad charge. We forded the river. We ascended the slopes. We seized Hill 184. We killed the garrison in the town to a man. At dusk on July 29th we were in sole possession.

While this was occurring, New York's Fighting 69th and what was left of Alabama's 167th were also being sent in harm's way. Their objective was to cross the river and fight their way up the utterly barren slopes of the valley, and then traverse the open fields of Meurcy Farm, where German troops were ensconced on the heights. Once again, the men of the Rainbow were being asked to attack without artillery support. According to Father Francis Duffy, Major Bill Donovan and the other battalion commanders were less than confident of their prospects for success. Nevertheless, in keeping with the Fighting 69th's time-honored motto, "Never disobeyed an order, never lost a flag," at 5:00 that morning the men stepped off as ordered. As always, just before battle Father Duffy hurriedly heard confessions or gave a word of comfort to any soldier who asked for it, Catholic or not. It was no small gesture—as Duffy later recalled, many of the men "would be dead or wounded up that pleasant little valley and along its eastern slopes before the sun rode at mid-heavens."

In all the engagements at Château-Thierry, the Germans had had ample time to carefully prepare their defenses, and the number of American casualties was appalling. Still, the Americans continued to advance in the face of almost certain death. As Byron wrote in his diary:

I carried litters, loading and unloading dozens of ambulances— the same all that night. The next day I drove an ambulance and most of that night. The next day encore. Most of the driving was Epieds up to the front at Villers sur Fere. Our first trip—Tracy and I—was six hours after the Boche had been driven from the town for the last time. These were real trips, as much of the road was exposed and we were frequently the objects of fire. At one time, we had to change a tire by the chateau which was being shelled at the time. It never seemed as tho' my hands were so clumsy. But we made it! About noon we got back, and turned the ambulance over to the regular driver. Then we layed down till about four when we were sent up to Beauvardes, where we had another receiving and forwarding station.

As Allied troops continued to push the Germans back, the distance between the triage unit and the front lines lengthened, making it more difficult for litter bearers to reach wounded men and bring them back for timely treatment. In the midst of combat, retrieving a wounded man from the field of battle was not a simple matter. Litter bearers were often subject to many of the same perils as their comrades in infantry units—having to struggle across miles of open field and through tangled underbrush, all the while under a hail of enemy fire. Moreover, in the ebb and flow of combat, as units attacked, fell back, and then counterattacked, the shifting lines of demarcation between opposing armies was ill defined at best, and at times subject to being fatally misread. With no fixed points of shelter to tend to the wounded men, litter bearers were forced to huddle in ditches or shell craters or hide behind stone walls while they applied field dressings or whatever it took to stem the bleeding before starting out on the long trek back to a dressing station with a wounded man. At night, medics often resorted to using a pocket lamp for illumination, at the risk of attracting a sniper's bullet, an airplane's bomb, or a mortar round.

No doubt the delay in retrieving the wounded contributed to the loss of countless lives. Indeed, fifty years later, in a letter remarking on a speech given by General William Westmoreland concerning the U.S. Army's ability to effectively treat wounded soldiers in Vietnam, Doctor Arlington Lecklider, the sanitary train lieutenant in charge of the triage unit at Épieds, put the battlefield and medical conditions of 1918 in proper historical perspective:

> The evacuation of wounded in 1918 were those of our Civil War of 1865—using litter bearers from trenches to the immediate rear, then mule drawn ambulances to collecting station from which, after a period, motorized ambulances became available for transport to field hospital or evacuation or base hospitals.

These vehicles could use the roads and sometimes the open country when the roads were taken over by ammunition trucks.

In a way the primitive equipment met the needs of static trench warfare since the shell-pocked roads were more negotiable for the mule drawn ambulances. However, mules may be perverse, they die, lose their shoes, slip on icy hills and must be shot.

Medical treatment for the Army has advanced 1,000 years since 1918. As General Westmoreland points out, the medical aid man in the unit has effective means of help today that were not at all available in 1918—blood transfusion for one. Today there are plenty of communication facilities upon call for transportation—often within a few minutes.

As for a comparison, at Epieds, north of Chateau Thierry in 1918, some of our wounded were brought in with maggots in the wound, indicating long delays in being able to retrieve the wounded. In the area at our collecting station several score litter cases were often spread around—awaiting transportation to the rear—to Coulommiers—60 kilometers—possibly by motor ambulance and often by empty ammunition wagon. Some would be sent to the railroad station at Chateau Thierry after traversing the main highway, which was under fire for nearly a week. Such delays created unforgettable incidents. At Epieds my sergeant informed me that the next patient in line for transport to Coulommiers (60 K.) had asked that others be sent in his place. I removed his head bandage and found no top to his skull. His judgment was good—he did not need the long ride. He died right there at Epieds within an hour.

In an attempt to alleviate the problem of delay, Lieutenant Roy Bryson was sent to Beauvardes with a detail of men to set up a dressing station closer to the front line. As noted in Byron's diary, on arriving at Beauvardes with Bryson, Byron immediately went to work:

Here I was put in charge of a litter squad who in the fourteen hours following loaded and unloaded at least five hundred patients besides giving them all sorts of assistance. In the morning, we went to bed for some much needed rest. However, when

Sgt. Gallagher came around about ten thirty hunting for men for litter work at the post, Livy and I volunteered again, while Gallagher got six more to go with us. We were taken up to the 168th Infirmary in charge of Capt. Bunch, and then sent out to the field dressing station under Lieutenant Davis. We had an accompaniment of Boche shelling all the way over, and from then on until our twenty-four hours was over. We carried the litters about two kilos and it surely was a man-killing job. The Boche seemed to want to get our place, as there were no other targets anywhere thereabouts. Our station was a little abandoned stone house. When it seemed sure it would be struck we moved out in a sunken road nearby. There were so many wounded, that Harry and I pitched in helping the infirmary men (the other boys were laying in their holes). Well, there were a lot of close calls but we kept it up, in spite of the fact that the other six men quit us cold and we had to make shift "drafting" passersby into helping us.

In a passage from *Rainbow Bright*, Lawrence Stewart of the 168th Infantry Regiment wrote a similar account of the "man-killing" nature of the work at Château-Thierry:

Many stretcher bearers were wounded or killed in the performance of their duty as they were forced to move slowly with their heavy suffering burdens, plunging up to their knees in the mud, fighting their way through the almost impenetrable thickets, all the time directly in line of the shells from both sides. Sometimes the Yanks, mistaking the grimy figures moving toward them from the opposite direction, shot at their own men; litter bearers were always prey to German snipers. Yet never once did they stumble or drop their wounded comrades. While I was on duty at an advance first-aid post I witnessed the tragic and heroic act of one of the men. Four stretcher-bearers were bringing in their burden and had reached the courtyard of the farmhouse, when a shell landed in our midst.... A moment later, . . . there on the ground lay three stretcher-bearers and their patient. Two stretcher-bearers and the patient had been killed, the third stretcher-bearer had received only a slight cut and was a little stunned by the concussion. When he saw that nothing more could be done for his buddies, he turned and started back up the line for more wounded. The last I saw of him he was disappearing over the top of the hill to resume his work, as though nothing had happened.

On the night of July 31, an exhausted Byron and Harry Livingstone were finally able to get some rest. Exactly where they slept is unknown. The fact that they had been able to sleep through a gas attack substantial enough to leave them "groggy for ten days" without having been awakened by others suggests that they had most likely pitched their pup tent on an out-of-the-way patch of ground. They were not alone in their ability to sleep through the smell of war. The stench of cordite, mustard gas, and decaying flesh seemed to permeate everything: hair, clothing, and the pores of skin. In the midst of the Château-Thierry offensive, exhausted troops slept wherever they could—some curled up in the back of empty trucks, others in ditches, foxholes, and the corners of ruined buildings. On one occasion, in the dead of night, a company of artillerymen stumbled into a glen of splintered and gas-withered trees searching for a place to sleep before finally flopping down on the first open patch of ground the men could find. On awakening the next morning, they were shocked to discover that the objects they had stumbled over in the dark had been their unwitting bed partners—scores of decaying corpses.

During twelve days of battle, the dead piled up everywhere, including triage units and hospitals. The first big wave of casualties to arrive at medical units was on July 26, shortly after the attack on Croix Rouge Farm commenced. As the Allied offensive continued, the deluge of wounded did not relent, quickly overwhelming field hospitals and triage units. Litter bearers soon found themselves exhausted. Ambulances crews were stretched to their geographical and physiological limits—weary drivers clutched steering wheels as much for support as for guidance as they made long trips in search of hospitals capable of handling the staggering number of wounded. One ambulance company somehow managed to log an astounding fifteen thousand miles over artillery-ravaged roads in eleven days of battle. Surgeons were far too few and essentials in woefully short supply. When one field hospital ran out of sterile wraps and bandages, the staff resorted to using paper bandages that had been left behind by the Germans. Hungry orderlies and doctors, who couldn't leave their post at triage units, ate the rations of dead soldiers who never made it that far. Everyone pitched in to help stem the bleeding—medical personnel were drafted from units as far away as Paris. A team of navy surgeons was even sent to relieve exhausted doctors who had been working nonstop for days.

More men from the Rainbow Division were wounded or killed in this series of battles than in any other engagement in the war. The sanitary train treated over fifty-four hundred patients, although accurate record keeping at the time of the encounter was more an afterthought than a priority. As set forth in *Iodine & Gasoline* by Colonel Wilbur Conkling, in charge of the sanitary train, "[T]here was no way of having the accurate number of patients handled during this engagement. Ambulances transported many patients which passed through the field hospitals without any record taken of them." Douglas MacArthur estimated that the Rainbow Division "had lost nearly half of its effective combat personnel."

Of the wounded men who would ultimately receive treatment from medical personnel, Major William Donovan of New York's Fighting 69th was particularly noteworthy. Like many others, Wild Bill had refused to leave the field of battle for treatment until the fighting was over. For eight grueling days, Donovan had been in the lead as his battalion fought its way out of Villers-sur-Fère, across the Ourcq River, and up the unsheltered slopes to the heights of Meurcy Farm, where the Americans finally vanquished the Germans in brutal hand-to-hand combat. During the battle, Donovan was wounded twice. Several additional close calls prompted him to remark sardonically that he had been "born to be hanged." Many of the others in Donovan's battalion weren't nearly as fortunate. For them, the imposition of sentence had been immediate and severe—nearly 50 percent of Donovan's men were killed or wounded. Among the dead were Sergeant Joyce Kilmer, the poet, and Lieutenant Oliver Ames, Donovan's loyal adjutant who was fatally shot while trying to shelter Donovan from enemy sniper fire. For his extraordinary courage in battle, Donovan was awarded the Distinguished Service Cross—an accolade that he described in a letter to his wife as being "too exaggerated," and one that he would have gladly traded for the lives of his men.

Among others cited for bravery in the battle was Father George Carpentier, the Roman Catholic priest whom Byron had previously mentioned in a letter as being indifferent to their needs. As noted in a subsequent citation from the grateful men of the 167th Alabama Infantry Regiment, Carpentier's ability to reach out to his fellow man in time of crisis was totally selfless and never in doubt:

> At great danger to himself, he searched for and found many wounded soldiers. By his unselfish devotion to duty and disregard for dangers and hardships he not only set an inspiring example to the men but saved the lives of many American soldiers. Under terrific artillery and machine gun fire he worked his way along our front lines, in addition to dressing wounded men and locating our own and the enemy's front lines, he later crossed shell swept ground conveying important information to the battalion commander.

When it came to bravery, the "Wildmen" of Alabama were not a group to be easily impressed. Given Byron's duties as a litter bearer and ambulance driver, it is likely that he had witnessed Carpentier's courage firsthand—perhaps even causing him to reconsider his opinion of the man.

The war had a way of doing that.

15
THE DEVIL'S BUSINESS

After seven days of bitter fighting, the Rainbow Division had managed to push the German Army back as far as the Vesle River. At that point, the men were too exhausted, bloodied, and wracked by dysentery to continue the pursuit. The 32nd and 4th Divisions were brought in to relieve them, which allowed Byron and other members of the Michigan Ambulance Company to retire to the village of Épieds, where they spent the next ten days recuperating. In an August 1 letter to his parents, Byron wrote: "Sunday evening, I played the organ in a Y. service in a partly ruined church which the Boche had held a scarce ten days before. The text was, 'And He Gave Thanks and Took Courage.' And so must all of us after the long string of victories."

No sooner had the men finished giving thanks than their minds turned to less spiritual thoughts. "Where were the spoils?" men wondered, like passes to visit Paris or other much-desired areas of furlough. After having gotten the better of an elite division of the Kaiser's army, one of the best combat units in the world, more glory was bestowed on the division—the coveted French *fourragère*. Still, the men wanted something more tangible. Nothing but uncertainty followed.

Rumors ran rampant again. It was the usual state of affairs for an army at rest—R&R was the fertile breeding ground for rank speculation as enlisted men tried to make sense of their predicament. At this particular moment, however, the unenviable position the Rainbow Division found itself in was one of having to sit back and lick its wounds. For a victorious army, it was not an uncommon occurrence. Caught in the clutches of war, the men had become the victim of their own success.

Collectively, they were proud of themselves; they had persevered in the face of seemingly insurmountable odds. Individually, though, they wondered if their victory had been a Pyrrhic one. One more victory like this and the division would cease to exist at all.

The core of Alabama's 167th, Iowa's 168th, and New York's Fighting 69th Infantry Regiments had been eviscerated in the fighting. Raw recruits had been brought in to fill the ranks. But for those who were left standing, nothing could ever replace the esprit de corps, training, and courage of the departed. A soldier's lament for fallen comrades is one of war's eternal refrains. Unfortunately, it was one that the men would hear repeatedly in the months to come.

On Sunday, August 18, the Michigan Ambulance Company moved back to Luzancy, where Byron played the piano at two YMCA church services. On the 20th, the company packed everything back in the ambulances and was on the move again, landing in Rosières on the 21st. Men wondered what awaited them there. As noted in Byron's diary: "We had all been led to believe that we were to have a month's rest now—and that at last our furloughs were to materialize. Surely we deserved them. Such was not to be."

What awaited Byron next was an attack of a totally unexpected sort. As he wrote in a diary entry of August 21: "We laid on a stone floor where I nearly got stricken with rheumatism. I did get a little touch, which I rode out in a long bicycle ride a few days later." Rheumatism is not a medically recognized disease or diagnosis. In Byron's time, it was a layman's term generally used to describe various aches and pains of a musculoskeletal nature that were in fact the symptoms of other diseases, such as rheumatoid arthritis, bursitis, tendinitis, or another inflammatory condition. Given Byron's age, twenty-one, and relative good health, it is highly unlikely that he suffered from rheumatoid arthritis, and there is nothing in his subsequent medical history to indicate any other muscular or skeletal debility. It also seems equally unlikely that after having slept outdoors in the cold, damp, and windblown conditions of France for months on end, symptoms of arthritis or another rheumatic-like disorder would suddenly manifest itself in the relative warmth of August, stone floor for a mattress notwithstanding. A more plausible explanation is that Byron had contracted a mild case of influenza—the timing of the attack makes this conclusion more than mere conjecture.

In August 1918, the second wave of the great influenza epidemic was just beginning to sweep across Europe. Earlier in the year, outbreaks of influenza had occurred in training camps in the United States. The flu was particularly prevalent on the eastern seaboard, where troopships were loaded with soldiers departing for France, and in Brest, the largest port of entry for American troops. On reaching France, as infected soldiers moved inland, some of them as replacements for exhausted and war-depleted units like the Rainbow Division, the flu traveled with them. Like a stowaway, however, the disease didn't make itself known at first.

According to observations made by Captain Alan Chesney, a medical officer stationed at an AEF hospital in Valdahon, France, who would later become the dean of Johns Hopkins Medical School, with each new wave of soldiers landing in France a more virulent strain of influenza came ashore with them. In June, only a few mild cases of flu were documented by Chesney in the first group of men at an artillery training camp in Valdahon. In August, a more serious strain appeared in the next group of trainees, incapacitating a significant number of men. By September, Chesney noted that the virus had grown in lethality, infecting over a third of the men in the training camp, killing 151.

In an attempt to control the spread of the virus in military camps, Surgeon General William Gorgas recommended that the army provide sixty square feet of housing per man—which was practically impossible given the urgent need to train and transport thousands of men on short notice. Byron had inadvertently highlighted this dilemma in his letter to Estelle dated August 19, 1917. As depicted in a diagram included therein, his tent at Grayling, Michigan, measured only fifteen feet square, yet it was still used to accommodate ten men at a mere twenty-two and a half square feet per man—which was relatively spacious when compared to the hold of ships, cattle cars, trenches, and dugouts, where men were crammed together in virtual incubators of disease.

Although the flu, and the pneumonia that often accompanied it, would end up killing more American soldiers than the war itself, not every person exposed to the virus was severely afflicted by it. Some men were simply carriers of the disease, exhibiting no symptoms at all, or only vague symptoms like the muscle aches and joint pain normally associated with a perceived case of rheumatism, or the coughs, sniffles, and mild fever typical of a common cold. Byron was one of the lucky ones. According to his diary, by the end of August he was able to finally peddle and sweat the "rheumatism" from his system on a bicycle ride to Vittel.

YMCA worker Gertrude Bray's boyfriend, military police officer Harry Lane, was another soldier who was lucky to have contracted only a mild case of flu. In writing to Gertrude that fall, Harry said that after being laid low for several days with a bout of "rheumatism," he finally sought treatment. But when the doctor mentioned wanting to admit Harry to the hospital, he left as soon as the doctor turned his back to tend to another patient. At that point in time, Harry and Gertrude were communicating by letter. For several weeks in the late summer and early fall of 1918, Gertrude had been separated from the Rainbow Division, having been selected to represent the YMCA at the Women in War Work Congress held in Paris that August. After attending the conference, Gertrude didn't catch up with the Rainbow Division until mid-September, and she didn't see Harry again until even later. Had she been present during Harry's rheumatic blues, she most likely would have insisted that he submit to a doctor's care. Although Harry and Byron would both manage to survive the influenza epidemic without receiving proper medical attention, others would suffer the consequences of their decisions. As carriers of the deadly virus, Byron and Harry almost certainly infected others.

Besides influenza, September ushered in two additional concerns. One was a natural occurrence, the other man-made—and the two were inextricably linked. The first was the rainy season. Every September, rain drenched the Alsace-Lorraine region of France. It lasted for weeks. The fall of 1918 was no exception. For men camped in pup tents, the conditions were unrelentingly miserable. According to Father Francis Duffy of New York's Fighting 69th, "We were living like Paleozoic monsters in a world of muck and slime."

The second condition was far more troubling. Rumors persisted that the Rainbow Division was about to engage in yet another major battle. Men quietly speculated that the reduction of the Saint-Mihiel salient would be their next objective. Like a drum roll preceding a momentous event, the rain continued to fall while men waited for word to come down from on high. Soon the air grew thick with a mixture of uncertainty and dread. New recruits arrived and were quickly put through a vigorous training regimen. Finally, men stopped wondering. As far as they were concerned, rumor had hardened into fact. As Father Duffy observed, "If it is a secret, all the world seems to know it."

Even the Germans knew—how could they not? It was the next logical step in the Allied counteroffensive. Reducing the Saint-Mihiel salient was essential to driving the Germans out of Metz and regaining control of the all-important railroad lines that connected the French military-industrial complex to the iron and coal mines of the Saar region. The immediate problem for the Allies was being able to launch the attack before the Germans could regroup and sink their plans in a sea of mud.

The prospect of locking horns with the Germans again was greeted by the men with a combination of enthusiasm and dread. The new recruits were too inexperienced to understand what awaited them, and the veterans of the carnage at Château-Thierry were too hardened to let their emotions show. Some men wrote letters home; others looked to get right with the Lord.

On Sunday, September 1, Byron's pup-tent mate, Harry Livingstone, a Jew, accompanied him to a YMCA church service. This was not an unusual occurrence—for men caught in the throes of war, any preexisting notion concerning the sanctity of one particular religious service over another quickly became a theological distinction without relevance. The only religious practice universally observed by men about to confront death in battle was finding some measure of solace, regardless of the source of inspiration. As set forth by Father Francis P. Duffy, chaplain of New York's Fighting 69th:

> I never hear confessions in a church, but always in a public square of a village, with the bustle of army life and traffic going on around us. There is always a line of fifty or sixty soldiers, continuously renewed throughout the afternoon, until I have

heard perhaps as many as five hundred confessions in the battalion. . . . Non-Catholics also frequently fall into line, not of course to make their confession, but to get a private word of religious comfort and to share in the happiness they see in the faces of others.

Officers who are not Catholic are anxious for their men to go to confession; not only through anxiety to help them practice their religion, but also for its distinct military value. Captain Merle-Smith told me that when I was hearing confessions before we took over our first trenches, he heard different of his men saying to his first sergeant, Eugene Gannon, "You can put my name down for any kind of job out there. I'm all cleaned up and I don't give a damn what happens now." That is the only spirit to have going into battle—to be without worry for body or soul. If battles are to be won, men have to be killed; and they must be ready, even willing, to be killed for the cause and the country they are fighting for.

As reflected in a letter from Byron to Estelle on September 1, the subject matter of that evening's sermon couldn't have been more timely: "The Y. service was held in a barn tonight. We sat around on the farm instruments. From my seat on the hay mower, I led the singing in lieu of there being no one else to do so. The talk was on—'When Christians fight are they Christians?' The opinion we reached was that one was not a Christian who would <u>not</u> fight for <u>right</u> against wrong + <u>was</u> a Christian who <u>would</u> fight for right against wrong."

It is unclear if Byron was actually attempting to disguise his true feelings on the matter from censors by employing a prearranged code with Estelle in which certain words were emphasized to convey an opposite meaning. Nevertheless, based on his prior letters to Estelle, in which he discussed the righteousness of the war in no uncertain terms, it is apparent that Byron's current response was more measured, perhaps indicating that there had been a frank and open discussion among the men about the issue of killing. Considering what they had just been through, it would not have been unexpected.

For most of the men, the utter savagery of war was a disturbing revelation—wholesale killing was no longer an abstract concept.

Men had seen and done things in battle they never thought imaginable. Beyond all doubt, they now knew that war was a mean-spirited business—rarely given to acts of Christian kindness or forgiveness. They also understood that in order to survive its wrath, the best they could do under the circumstances was to soldier on—without reserve and with no remorse. There would be time for reflection and repentance later.

In 1969, Estelle would highlight the seemingly eternal dilemma that war posed for Christian soldiers, writing in the margin of Byron's letter, "[S]till a question 50 years later." Others would be confronted with this question later in life as well. Among them was Major William Donovan, the man President Dwight D. Eisenhower would call "the Last Hero." In a letter written to his wife shortly after the battle of Château-Thierry, Donovan lamented the needless slaughter of unarmed German soldiers by men under his command. Out of twenty-five prisoners who had been captured by his men, Donovan was able to save only two from being killed in an apparent act of vengeance. "The men when they saw the Germans with red crosses on one sleeve and serving machine guns against us, firing until the last minute, then cowardly throwing up their hands and crying 'Kamerad,' became just lustful for German blood. I do not blame them."

In essence, Donovan was taking the position that in certain instances the psychological duress of war was sufficient cause to absolve men of their wanton conduct. Although somewhat understandable, it was a proposition fraught with ethical peril. It also ran contrary to the law of war. Beginning with George Washington's edict to his troops in the Continental army, the long-standing policy of the Armed Forces of the United States has been that quarter should be given to any enemy combatant who seeks it. This policy was reaffirmed by Abraham Lincoln during the Civil War in the so-called Lieber Code, and later codified as international law in Article 23(d) of The Hague Convention in 1907. Simply put, once an enemy combatant throws down his gun and raises his hands in surrender, he should not be killed.

Implementing that policy in the heat of battle, however, was a complicated matter. Reprisal killings for bloodlust and vengeance

Copyright, 1918, by Leslie's

Drawn by Chas. Sarka

Kamerad

One of the simplest of the Huns' treacherous murder traps. In towns from which the Hun has been driven all manner of devilish contrivances have been found such as gas-filled bulbs and loaves of bread loaded with bombs.

"Kamerad." Front cover of *Leslie's Weekly*, September 21, 1918, illustrated by Charles Sarka.

were the inexcusable but inevitable by-product of war. For commanders in World War I, preventing their occurrence was like trying to tamp out brush fires in the middle of a raging inferno. Men were focused on killing and staying alive, not sparing the lives of enemy combatants. Officers could not be everywhere. The best they could do was to lead by example.

A more vexing and personal problem for frontline commanders was what to do with prisoners when they had in fact been captured but the outcome of a battle still hung in the balance. In circumstances where manpower could not be spared to safely escort them to the rear, execution was viewed by some officers as a necessary but regrettable action. In certain cases, it was a decision that would haunt them for the rest of their days.

Donovan was a moral man and undoubtedly understood the necessity for the rule protecting prisoners. But he was also a realist who understood that unloosing the savage in man was the devil's business, but that this unpleasant truth was exactly what war demanded of the men who were compelled to fight it. In choosing not to blame his men, Donovan was acknowledging that ultimately it was society, and by extension himself as a commander, who bore the shame and responsibility for having put otherwise peaceful men in such a god-awful position. Like a good shepherd, Donovan was prepared to shoulder that burden for his men, taking the regret for their transgressions to the grave with him.

Later in life, Donovan would again be presented with this difficult issue when President Harry Truman appointed him to assist the chief U.S. prosecutor at the international military tribunal at Nuremberg. As a member of Supreme Court Justice Robert H. Jackson's staff, Donovan was wholeheartedly in favor of prosecuting Nazi officials and members of other nefarious government entities, like the Gestapo, for the heinous crimes they had committed against humanity. But when it came to prosecuting the German General Staff and corps of regular army officers as war criminals, Donovan balked at recommending charges for offenses that did not amount to direct violations of the Geneva Convention.

Donovan felt that for commanders whose troops were caught in the throes of battle, strict compliance with the rules of war was at times an unattainable ideal—not easily understood by those who had never been subjected to the chaos of combat, much less fairly judged in the sterile vacuum of a courtroom years later—and he made his feelings known. Justice Jackson, however, was unconvinced, and insisted that the German General Staff and officer corps would have to be charged as war criminals. At that point, Donovan resigned from Jackson's staff. Donovan later explained that in good conscience he could not recommend charges against German officers who were simply following orders—knowing that if World War I had gone the other way, he, Pershing, MacArthur, and others could have been charged as war criminals as well. For Donovan, Byron, and other Christian soldiers who had been baptized in the hellfire of war, the realization that the devil was not so black as he is painted was as much a sobering depiction of self as it was of foe.

At the moment, however, Donovan was still decades removed from the courtrooms of Nuremberg, mired instead in the mud and gloom of September 1918, trying to get his battalion ready for its next showdown with death. Two-thirds of Donovan's men were raw recruits. The rest were familiar faces, now hardened nearly beyond recognition. On her return from Paris in mid-September, Gertrude Bray had noticed a disturbing change among the men of the Rainbow Division as well. Many of the soldiers she'd gotten to know had been killed or wounded at Château-Thierry. In a letter home, Gertrude remarked:

> The men all act as if they were living under a strain: some look from five to ten years older than they did when I saw them last. They have grown thinner and harder looking, and there is a far-away look in their eyes—as tho' they are re-living the things they had gone thru. They have become fatalist in a measure. I have heard so many say, "Well, if there is a shell with your number on it, you'll get it anyway, whether you're in a dugout or not." A lot of the boys I haven't been able to find out about yet, and every time I ask I'm afraid what the answer will be.... Don't think from what I've said, that the boys have lost their nerve, they haven't, they are hardened fighters now, but they are worn out from fighting, little food, drilling when they had that week in

Baby-faced killers. Soldiers of the Yankee Division line up to take a delousing shower, August 10, 1918, only days after the deadly battle of Château-Thierry. (Photograph by Army Signal Corps.)

> Bourmount, receiving replacements, then hiking day and night
> to this sector in bad weather.

Gertrude's description of the dissociative condition in which she found the men in the Rainbow Division was in essence a layman's diagnosis of what was then referred to as war neuroses. In World War II, the catchphrase *two-thousand-yard stare* would be used to the describe the faraway look in the eyes of traumatized soldiers who were suffering from what was then called "battle fatigue." In later conflicts, the stuporous-looking mask worn by battle-weary soldiers would be recognized as a telltale sign of post-traumatic stress disorder.

As always, Byron made no mention of this dispiriting development in his letter to Estelle, choosing instead to close with his customary upbeat flourish: "Yes, the way things are constantly continuing to come our way, I confidently expect 'deo volente' that the guerre will be over and we'll be back in school next fall. Then—for the happy days again—the crammed-in busy—happy days of college life. More anon.—" For those back home in need of reassurance from the front, Byron's words were well received indeed.

16
THE FIRST ALL-AMERICAN AFFAIR

On September 2, Labor Day was celebrated in the United States with an added sense of purpose. Heeding President Wilson's call to embrace the occasion as "a day of fresh comprehension" and "consecration," the American army of labor rallied in support of "everything the laborer has striven for and held dear since freedom first had its dawn and its struggle for justice began." Across the country, displays of American resolve were legion. In France, legions of American troops were gathering and strengthening as well. As the expeditionary force readied itself for the first all-American action of the war, parades of a different sort were occurring. Long lines of troops and equipment were being quietly maneuvered into position—it was the largest concentration of American military might since the Civil War.

Although the Germans knew that a major assault was imminent, the Allies hoped that by moving men and equipment under the cover of darkness, the scope of the attack would remain a secret, at least for the time being. As noted in Byron's diary, American troops were beginning to pour into staging areas near Saint-Mihiel from all over France: "On the 7th, we left for Bicquely, six kms. out of Toul. We got there early Sunday morning. As there was nothing else to do, I went over to Toul with Ed Berndt. The places seemed familiar after our two months previous visit there. The city seemed alive with Americans, nurses, aviators, and every branch."

For Byron, the opportunity to mix with so many aviators must have been heady stuff. An unprecedented fourteen hundred aircraft were being amassed to fly in the offensive. During the war, it had become increasingly clear that the power, speed, and range of air-planes rendered them a force whose full potential was just beginning to be realized. Byron was among those who were enthralled by them. On the outskirts of Toul lay the Gengault Aerodrome—a large airfield that served as home to both French and American aviators. Among those stationed there in the summer of 1918 were Eddie Rickenback-er's *Hat in the Ring Squadron* and Lieutenant Colonel Billy Mitchell, who would later be promoted to chief of the Army Air Service. As had previously occurred on the eve of battle in Champagne, however, Byron would not get the chance to arrange for his much-desired ride with any of the aviators. Later that night the Michigan Ambulance Company broke camp and moved on.

As further reflected in his diary, for the next few days the company continued to pick up stakes and relocate:

> That night we left again, running around the corner of Toul, landing in an orchard at Lagney. It was wet and rainy—and we were hungry, but no kitchen. So I hunted up a meal, then found a Salvation Army hut, where there were two smiling American girls, who laughed and joked—and a good library. I settled to "K" by M. R. Rhinehart, and spent most of the day in solid enjoyment reading it.
>
> Of course it was no secret by now that a great drive was imminent. We had expected it for a long time. I had predicted that it would be our next drive as soon as our drive at Chateau-Thierry salient was over. So as we stood on the hill at Lagney, we looked over with a bit of spirit at the long row of Boche hills in the distance—the backbone of the St. Mihiel salient, the "her-nia," and to Mont Sec, the key to all of them, which the French and English had lost tens of thousands trying to hold in '14. And we were expected to retake these and more.
>
> That night again—the night of Sept. 9th—Monday, we packed and went over to Ansauville, where we pitched tents over night in rain again. This town is crowded with soldiers eager and expect-ant. We got some good stuff to eat from the Salvation Army and the Y., God bless 'em. During the day of the 10th, we were moved over to Hamonville, where I slept on the floor that night.

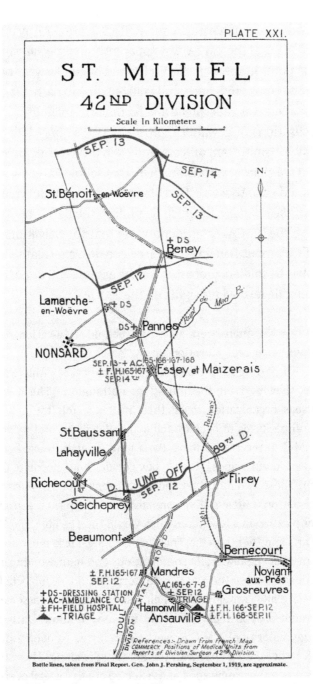

Sector map of Saint-Mihiel. (From *The Medical Department of the United States Army in the World War*, vol. 8, *Field Operations* [Washington, DC: Government Printing Office, 1925], plate 21.)

Byron's mention of having frequented a Salvation Army hut, in addition to or in place of the YMCA, was apparently an especially noteworthy one. At this point in the war, the YMCA had begun to wear out its welcome with the troops in France, and enlisted men in particular. Criticism of YMCA workers was widespread and far ranging, including but not limited to accusations of cowardice, proselytizing, selling donated goods, showing favoritism toward officers, and even profiteering by some of its members. It was hardly surprising, then, that fellow Rainbow man Leslie Langille would echo those sentiments in the Saint-Mihiel chapter of his book *Men of the Rainbow*, in which he praised the Salvation Army while condemning the YMCA. After mentioning that the Salvation Army and Knights of Columbus had given out free cookies, chocolate, doughnuts, and pancakes to soldiers preparing for the assault at Saint-Mihiel, artilleryman Langille leveled his sights on the YMCA:

> There in the shell-swept town, we behold a Salvation Army kitchen, with real Salvation Army lasses, passing out those never-to-be-forgotten doughnuts and pancakes. And what's more, they're giving them away for nothing! . . . The K. of C. overseas organization make their presence felt by donating several packages of cookies and some chocolate, and a couple of Y.M.C.A. secretaries leave Paris long enough to establish a canteen in our woods. You can buy cookies and chocolate from them. Those two birds had apparently gone broke in Paris and were out on a little selling campaign to recoup their fortunes. After picking up a few francs, they would then be able to return to Paris and their harems, and live like kings. It is most unfortunate that the few really conscientious and hard-working secretaries that wore the Y.M.C.A. uniform should be subjected to the scorn and contempt that their less conscientious associates bring down upon their heads, but it is a well-known fact that a large majority of Y.M.C.A. workers preferred to hang around Paris rather than go out with the fighting divisions, where they could have done some good and reflected credit instead of scorn upon that organization. I personally do not remember ever having been given anything free by anyone wearing a Y.M.C.A. uniform. You paid for everything you got.

To some extent, Byron seemed to confirm this less than charitable view of the YMCA mission in France by noting in his diary three weeks later that he and Horace Sprague "bought what we could" from a YMCA hut in Souilly. Not everything that the Y had to offer, however, came with a price tag attached, and not all of its workers were as mercenary as those depicted by Langille. Among those who toiled tirelessly for the benefit of the men while staying perilously close to the front lines was Gertrude Bray. On September 12 and 13, in the midst of the Saint-Mihiel offensive, Gertrude and fellow Y workers Edith Knowles and Mary Holiday cooked ten thousand doughnuts each day for soldiers, later receiving well-deserved commendations for their extraordinary effort. As if to underscore the enormity of that enterprise for posterity, Gertrude left among her personal papers the recipe for an army-sized ration of doughnuts.

On September 11, men waited anxiously in wet and miserable conditions for the drive to start. Byron stood gas guard until midnight and had just fallen asleep when he was awakened with a start: "particularly loud after the almost complete silence of several preceding days. It was a good bombardment all-night, tho' not to be compared with the Champagne affair. Everyone expected a violent Boche counter bombardment. The absolute silence of the Boche batteries all night was the first of many surprises we had in the next few days."

The American artillery barrage was withering. Commencing at 1:00, it lasted until H-hour (start time of attack) at 5 in the morning. To everyone's surprise there was no significant German counter-barrage. "Wild Bill" Donovan, who'd recently been promoted to lieutenant colonel, immediately surmised that the Germans were withdrawing. After his promotion, Donovan had declined overall command of the Fighting 69th, choosing instead to remain on the front lines with his old battalion, which included an inordinate number of raw recruits who would need his cool head and steady hand as they headed into battle for the first time. Donovan viewed the absence of a German counter-barrage as a cautious but hopeful sign that the enemy would offer little resistance. Still, as he stepped off at the appointed hour, leading his men out of the protective cover of the woods into no-man's-land, Donovan worried.

Advancing just ahead of Donovan's regiment was a battalion of tanks under the command of Lieutenant Colonel George S. Patton Jr. Following closely behind Patton's tanks were ambulances and litter bearers from the sanitary train—and with good cause. Patton's as yet untested Tank Corps was derisively referred to in some quarters as "the Suicide Club," which was actually in perfect accord with Patton's expectations of his men. Patton's tank men had been repeatedly told that under no circumstances were they to relent in combat. On the eve of battle, Patton reinforced that edict once more when he issued the following instructions: "No tank is to be surrendered or abandoned to the enemy. If you are left alone in the midst of the enemy keep shooting. If your gun is disabled use your pistols and squash the enemy with your tracks. . . . You must establish that AMERICAN TANKS DO NOT SURRENDER. . . . This is our BIG CHANCE; WHAT WE HAVE WORKED FOR . . . MAKE IT WORTHWHILE."

As the tanks started out that morning, surrender was the least of Patton's worries—just making it into battle was his immediate concern. It had rained for days. The great unknown was whether Patton's tanks would be able to traverse the crater-riddled mud fields of no-man's-land, and then breach the labyrinth of wide and deep trench works without getting bogged down. Although the British Army had successfully used larger Mark IV tanks in November to break through entrenched German defenses at Cambrai, the American high command was anxious to see how Patton's smaller Renault tanks would perform in battle.

Patton had assiduously prepared for this day. In November 1917, Pershing had tasked Patton with assembling and training the first Light Tank Brigade in the army's fledgling Tank Corps. It was an assignment that lent itself to Patton's unique temperament and organizational skills, and was especially suited to his tactical background as a former cavalry officer. Patton believed that tanks could be more than just lumbering pillboxes, recognizing that the mobility and range of light tanks made them an ideal complement to support infantry in the field. Patton also saw this assignment as a unique opportunity in which to forge the sword that he would ultimately wield to attain his destiny.

In forming the brigade, Patton left nothing to chance. He established a tank school in Bourg, where the training was rigorous and the discipline tight. He consulted with British tank corps officers on the tactics and performance of their tanks at Cambrai. He also visited a factory in France in order to better understand the construction and capabilities of tanks, during which he suggested a few design changes to improve the overall performance and safety of light tanks.

Although Patton had painstakingly assembled and prepared his Tank Corps, on the eve of battle he was worried about the fate of his untested troops. The use of tanks was an entirely new endeavor for the U.S. Army, and Patton realized that much could, and undoubtedly would, go wrong. Moreover, he also knew that in the heat of battle he couldn't be everywhere to attend to each problem as it arose. So he decided to give more leeway to the most experienced of his battalion commanders, Captain Sereno E. Brett. Brett was a battle-tested veteran whose tanks were assigned to support infantrymen from the 1st Division. In addition to being experienced in battle, the men of the 1st had prior experience working with French tanks—having fought alongside them at the battle of Cantigny in May. It seemed like a safe choice.

Patton was more concerned with the performance of the less experienced of his tank commanders, Captain Ranulf Compton, whose battalion was assigned to support the Rainbow Division. Compton had limited combat experience, and although the Rainbow Division was thoroughly battle tested, it was totally inexperienced when it came to working with tanks. Out of necessity, Patton chose to place himself in close proximity to Compton and the men of the Rainbow—which put him in the thick of the action with Byron.

For the battle, Byron had been temporarily assigned to Donovan's Fighting 69th as a litter bearer working under Dr. (Major) George Lawrence, close behind the advancing front line. As noted in Byron's diary:

> Well, we knew the horses were off. Right after breakfast, a batch
> of Boche prisoners came by, forerunners of thousands. . . . All
> the way up thru Beaumont and on into the woods were prisoners,

prisoners and disabled tanks and artillery. We worked in the mud at the edge of the woods till after dinner. What impressed us right away was the easiness of the whole thing, very very few wounded and killed. Word kept coming back that our boys could hardly keep up with the Boche. In the afternoon we packed the stuff on some ambulances, and hiked with Major Lawrence over to St. Baussant. Here we cleaned up a couple of dug-outs the Boche had left earlier in the day—fixed it for a station. On our way across No Man's Land we followed in the path of our tanks. This was the first American manned affair. . . . The engineers were already busy building bridging over the trenches. Autos were in the ditch everywhere. Ahead the village and woods were aflame, and smoking a hundred feet in the air. Everyone was hurrying on. There was nothing for us to do. By daylight the next morning we were off hiking again—through Maizerais and Essey on to Pannes. In Pannes we ran a-muck in a great storehouse of a Divisional Quarter-master. The night before the men had found all sorts of things to eat and drink. We had honey, sugar, bread and butter and jam, fish and other stuff left in the officer's quarters. And all of us got lots of souvenirs—all kinds and descriptions.

Although Byron made mention of American soldiers running amok and feasting on foodstuffs and other delicacies stored in a German quartermaster's warehouse in Pannes, it should be pointed out that the German Army was not well provisioned at this time—and that none of these items were reserved for, or normally consumed by, the average German foot soldier. To the contrary, as reflected in letters written by German soldiers that were intercepted when the Rainbow Division captured a German mail depository during the Saint-Mihiel offensive, morale, food, and basic living conditions in the German Army were at an all-time low. In later emphasizing this point in a letter to his wife, Lieutenant Colonel William Donovan of the Fighting 69th included a series of excerpts from the captured letters. According to a letter written by German NCO Fritz Pieper, 47th Infantry Regiment, 10th Division: "The men are so embittered that they have no interest in anything and they only want the war to end, no matter how.

We are certainly only the slaves of our Government." That this sentiment was shared by other beleaguered German soldiers is evidenced
by Army Signal Corps film footage taken of prisoners captured during
the Saint-Mihiel offensive. After four years of unremitting warfare, the
prisoners appear to be haggard and battle weary. A great number also
look relieved—some even glad that for them, at least, the war was over.

Of these captured prisoners, many were wounded. As further
noted in Byron's diary entry for this date: "Here I helped to handle a
lot of Boche wounded—tried to treat them same as our own men tho'
God knows they don't deserve it." This was not an insignificant statement on Byron's part. Although his actions may have been laudable,
the sentiment underlying them was nevertheless a disconcerting one:
apparently, Byron's heart had hardened since first enlisting. Unfortunately, this was not an uncommon occurrence—one of the great perils
of warfare is its ability to dehumanize its participants. Byron's statement that wounded German soldiers were somehow less deserving of
God's mercy and his medical attention appears to be a regrettable but
inevitable result of his prolonged exposure to the ravages of war.

Ironically, it was a young German soldier, Franz Blumenfeld, a former student not unlike Byron in his unbridled patriotism and idealism at the beginning of the war, who perhaps best articulated the loss
of human kindness in war. In a letter written to his mother on October 14, 1914, Blumenfeld worried:

> One thing weighs upon me from day to day—the fear of getting
> brutalized. Your wishing you could provide me with a bullet-
> proof net is very sweet, but strange to say I have no fear, none
> at all, of bullets and shells, but only of this great spiritual lone-
> liness. I am afraid of losing my faith in human nature, in myself,
> in all that is good in the world! Oh, that is horrible. Much, much
> harder for me to endure is the incredibly coarse tone that pre-
> vails among the men here. The sight of the slightly and danger-
> ously wounded, the dead men and horses lying about, hurts of
> course, but the pain of that is not nearly so keen or lasting as
> one imagined it would be. Of course that is partly due to the fact
> that one knows one can't do anything to prevent it. But may it

not at the same time be a beginning of a deplorable callousness, almost brutality, or how is it possible that it gives me more pain to bear my own loneliness than to witness the suffering of others. What is the good of escaping all the bullets and shells, if my soul is injured?

Two months after writing this letter, Franz Blumenthal was killed by a French artillery shell.

For Byron, after grudgingly treating German prisoners at Pannes, the assault would continue—but not without incident. As reflected in his diary: "After dinner we started on again, hiked on up through Beney, where our whole party had a close call, and on out to St. Benoit. Our division had long since reached its objective—went beyond in fact and had to be drawn back. By ten in the morning of the 13th the drive was over as far as we were concerned, and the boys had been given several days to accomplish it."

The "close call" at Beney referred to was apparently noteworthy to other commentators as well, not for the ferocity of the encounter per se, but for the display of temerity involved. It was a moment that for better or worse captured the very essence of George Patton, the ever-forward-thinking adversary that the German high command would have to contend with in yet another war to come. Never one to lead from the rear, Patton had always preferred to be in the vanguard, not only accepting the futility of trying to dodge fate in battle but to some extent relishing the opportunity to confront it. Unlike most other officers, Patton marched into combat openly displaying his officer's insignia on the shoulder straps of his uniform, believing that it was a source of inspiration for his men, even if it meant becoming a prime target for enemy sharpshooters.

As recounted by various sources, during the attack at Saint-Mihiel, after personally leading his tanks, on foot, across a bridge at Essey that infantrymen suspected of being mined, Patton proceeded on to the village of Pannes, where he effectuated the surrender of thirty German soldiers. Later that day Patton continued to press his advantage by driving on toward Beney. At this point in the attack, the number of serviceable tanks left at Patton's disposal had all but disappeared due to a variety of causes—mechanical failure, boggy terrain, impassable trench works, and a chronic shortage of fuel. Undaunted, Patton pushed on. Like Hannibal riding astride an elephant, Patton spearheaded the attack perched atop one of the few tanks that was still running. Until Beney, that is—when German machine-gunners finally took aim. With bullets ricocheting and paint chips flying off the tank's turret, Patton leapt from his perch, diving headlong into a shell hole nearby.

On resurfacing, Patton discovered that he was truly in no-man's-land. According to Patton, whenever he tried to poke his head up to take stock of the situation, "the Boche shot at me." To his dismay, Patton discovered that the nearest Allied infantrymen were over two hundred yards to the rear, having chosen not to advance without a full complement of tanks to support them, while the lone tank on which he had been riding continued to roll forward, its driver still totally unaware of what had just transpired. At that point, Patton ran back through a hail of enemy fire in a failed attempt to persuade the infantry commander to follow him into battle. Realizing that the attack was now stalled, Patton ran forward again through another torrent of machine-gun fire. On finally catching up with the tank, Patton rapped on the rear door and informed the incredulous driver that it was necessary to turn around. It was one of the few times in Patton's military career that he was forced to retreat. Using the protective cover of the tank, Patton retraced his steps back to the waiting infantry. Patton's setback was only momentary, however. After regrouping, Patton used five fully fueled tanks and willing elements of the 42nd Division to drive the Germans from Beney, then capturing sixteen machine guns and four artillery pieces.

Although the performance of Patton's Tank Corps at Saint-Mihiel was hardly an unqualified success, it was nevertheless apparent to most observers that many of the shortcomings that they had experienced in battle could be easily remedied. From Patton's perspective, he had achieved his objective—having served notice that the new arsenal of war included tanks, which for the moment left him in the driver's seat.

By the 14th of September, the drive at Saint-Mihiel was over. After being relieved of his duties with the Fighting 69th, Byron returned to the body of the ambulance company at Essey. In just two days of combat, American troops had killed or wounded over five thousand German soldiers in addition to capturing fifteen thousand prisoners. In the press back home, the attack was heralded as a great victory. Bill Donovan of the Fighting 69th described the offensive as "a prome-nade" compared to the carnage at Château-Thierry. The relative ease with which the victory was achieved, however, was more qualified than that. The Germans had already started to withdraw from the salient before the assault began. Still, they had managed to inflict seven thou-sand casualties on American troops. It was an ominous sign of things to come.

After driving German forces from the Saint-Mihiel Salient, the Americans did not continue on to Metz, where the enemy had hoped to slow down the Allied advance by luring them into a prolonged siege of that city. Instead, the Allies pulled up and consolidated their lines. With the exception of the Kaiser, the German high command now realized that winning the war was no longer a realistic possibility. At this point, Germany's best course of action was to fall back and take a stand at the Hindenburg Line in order to retain as much of Belgium and France as possible for later use as a bargaining chip in any future armistice negotiation.

The Allies were not interested in considering any half measures, however. After four years of being on the defensive, they fully intended to press their advantage by redirecting the attack on a field of their own choosing. For the Rainbow Division, that ground would be the depths of the Argonne Forest.

17
DEATH VALLEY

As easily as chaff from wheat, it seemed the German Army had been thrashed from the fields of Saint-Mihiel. Yet after the dust had settled, the fog of war hung in the air—obscuring as always the true measure of victory.

For most of the soldiers who had actually risked life and limb in the fighting, the fact that the pivotal battle of that campaign had been waged long before the first shots were ever fired would have come as a great surprise. Equally confounding would have been the discovery that during this earlier exchange, the much-heralded all-American offensive came within an eyeblink of not occurring at all. In a nose-to-nose confrontation that was later described as a screaming match, it was the supreme commander of Allied troops in France, Marshal Ferdinand Foch, who would blink in a contentious showdown with the commander of the American Expeditionary Force, General John "Black Jack" Pershing. The confrontation had been a long time in the making—the groundwork had been laid months earlier when Pershing and his staff first looked at a map of France, searching for a sector of the western front for which the American Expeditionary Force could take sole responsibility. To Pershing's eye, the salient at Saint-Mihiel looked to be the ideal spot, and reduction of the salient the perfect assignment for the inexperienced but eager AEF. Foch, however, had other plans.

In the summer of 1917, soon after American troops first set foot in France, Foch began to pressure Pershing to permit various divisions of the AEF to be dispersed among established British and French units to fight under their command. Pershing was equally insistent about keeping his army intact, however, and not only resisted Foch's attempts to disperse American troops but eventually even persuaded him to approve a plan for an American offensive at Saint-Mihiel. That Foch had agreed to the plan only reluctantly, however, soon became apparent—his lack of enthusiasm evidenced by his having placed it last on a list of four counteroffensives to be conducted by Allied troops in the summer and fall of 1918. It was not totally unexpected, then, that after French and British successes in battles at Ainse-Marne and Amiens earlier that summer, Foch suddenly changed his mind—looking to postpone the attack at Saint-Mihiel in favor of distributing elements of Pershing's 1st Army to support a British offensive to the north.

Pershing was adamantly opposed to the idea, and said so in no uncertain terms. Foch, equally determined to get his way, attempted to bully Pershing into submission in the weeks leading up to September. Undaunted, Pershing stood his ground. He'd endured far worse contempt than Foch could muster—and for much longer. For most of Pershing's career, he had lived with the cognomen "Black Jack"—originally "Nigger Jack," an unkind epithet hung on him by racist officers for his willing service as a young lieutenant with the "Buffalo Soldiers" of the 10th Cavalry Regiment. Pershing's association with blacks and recognition of the right of all men to realize their God-given potential predated his admission to West Point and subsequent military career. He had learned to appreciate both as a young teacher of African American schoolchildren in Missouri and later as a graduate of law school.

Undeterred by the scorn of fellow officers, years later, Pershing left a desirable teaching position at West Point during the Spanish-American War to serve a second tour of duty with the all-black unit, earning a Silver Star for bravery at San Juan Hill. It was in the aftermath of the charge up San Juan Hill that Pershing witnessed an act of gallantry he would remember for the rest of his career. After the 10th Cavalry had lost half of its officers and one-fifth of its enlisted men in a long and bitter battle to capture the hill, one soldier was still possessed of enough human kindness to tend to the suffering of the enemy. As related by Pershing: "[A] colored trooper stopped at a trench filled with Spanish dead and wounded and gently raised the head of a wounded Spanish Lieutenant and gave him the last drop of water from his own canteen." In conditions where clean water was in short supply and the scourge of typhoid, malaria, and dysentery ran rampant, it was no small gesture on this soldier's part. Indeed, it was experiences like this that made Pershing as proud of his service with the 10th Cavalry as he was protective of its men, often advocating on their behalf. Protecting the AEF from Foch was just the latest stand that Pershing had had to take on behalf of his men.

Throughout his career, Pershing had never been interested in currying favor with the men under his command or fellow officers. And as a strict disciplinarian, he was often misjudged by both as being unnecessarily cold and aloof. Still, he was acknowledged by all to be intelligent, industrious, and scrupulously fair. Most important, though, he was steadfastly dedicated to the welfare of his men and the mission of the army. To the day he died, Pershing remained true to those ideals. Although he is the only commander other than George Washington to be accorded the title "General of the Armies," he considered his long and distinguished service no more important than that of any other soldier. In keeping with that sentiment, he left instructions that when he died his remains were to be buried simply—alone on a small hill in Arlington National Cemetery marked by a plain headstone, overlooking the graves of many of the men he had commanded and ultimately sent to death in World War I.

Among those who valued Pershing's unassuming nature and great strength of character was President Theodore Roosevelt, who personally appointed Pershing to the rank of brigadier general in 1906, bypassing eight hundred other officers in the process. In later picking Pershing to lead the American Expeditionary Force in Europe, President Woodrow Wilson also recognized Pershing's unique talents and indomitable will—realizing that American forces would need a commander who could not be intimidated by the oversized egos that populated the French and British high command. Pershing proved more than equal to the task.

On August 30, during a meeting in Pershing's headquarters at Ligny-en-Barrois, the simmering friction between Pershing and Foch over the fate of the AEF finally boiled over. In a clash of wills that erupted into a full-throated argument, it was Foch who backed down. Not without imposing conditions, however. Foch would allow Pershing to keep his army intact and launch an all-American attack at Saint-Mihiel, but only if he could do so by September 12, and then with the explicit understanding that the scope of the offensive would have to be scaled back. The city of Metz was no longer considered an objective.

Second, and far more important to Foch, was the caveat that Pershing's troops would have to be in position and ready to commence the Meuse-Argonne offensive on September 26. In any rational discussion of the matter, after a brief moment of reflection, Foch's second condition should have been considered a deal breaker. In the heat of argument, however, Pershing barked back his acceptance of Foch's onerous terms of engagement. It would be up to the young but very talented George C. Marshall Jr., a lieutenant colonel on Pershing's staff, to see to it that Pershing hadn't promised more than he could deliver. Failure was not an option—the independence of the American Expeditionary Force was at stake.

Marshall did not disappoint. At the conclusion of the Saint-Mihiel offensive, "the Wizard," as Marshall would later be called, managed to pull a combat-ready rabbit out of his logistical hat. In a matter of days, Marshall's staff moved four hundred thousand soldiers, four thousand artillery pieces, ninety thousand horses, and nearly 1 million tons of supplies over sixty miles of difficult terrain to reach a new front that stretched from the distant heights of the Meuse River on the east to the depths of the Argonne Forest on the west. For years to come, Marshall's brilliant handiwork would be hailed as the largest and most impressive logistical operation in U.S. military history. Even Byron was impressed: "The division was by now already to move out of this sector, and during the night of Oct. 1, it was moved—bag and baggage, infantry and all—by carrier—over to the Argonne-Meuse front. This was surely as clever a move as we ever saw—transplanting a division overnight."

The Rainbow Division was one of the last units to be moved from Saint-Mihiel to the new front, having been held back as shock troops once again. The battle at the Meuse-Argonne front began as scheduled on September 26, but the going was extremely tough. By early October, American forces had made only modest headway at very great cost. For anyone with a working knowledge of the terrain, this disheartening news came as no surprise—simply put, the Argonne Forest was a death trap. Pershing had harbored wildly optimistic expectations that his troops would be able to attain their objective in just a matter of days. In reality, it would take six grueling weeks and 117,000 American casualties to drive the Germans from the field of battle. It would also nearly cost Pershing his command.

For four years, this section of the front had been stationary, which meant that the Germans had had ample time to fortify their position greatly. In the winter of 1916–17, the Germans had even used Allied prisoners as impress gangs to help strengthen their defenses along the Hindenburg Line. Believing these defenses to be impregnable, the Germans confidently named each sector of the line after a Norse god or hero from Wagner's *Ring* operas. The sector securing the Argonne Forest was designated Kriemhilde, the avenging wife of Siegfried. In launching an attack there, it was the American Expeditionary Force that would incur the full fury of her wrath.

The objective of the Allied offensive in the Meuse-Argonne sector was to sever the main railroad line of supply that ran between German positions at Carignan in the southeast and Mézières in the northwest. The city of Sedan was situated in the middle. If the Allies were able to capture the railhead at Sedan, then the German positions in the west and northwest would be rendered untenable. The Germans, of course, were fully aware of this, and the Kriemhilde Stellung had been painstakingly designed to prevent that from occurring—the daunting defenses in the Argonne Forest were overwhelming evidence of that grim determination.

To the American soldiers who fought there, the Argonne Forest was known as "Death Valley." Instead of the usual configuration of trench works, the Germans had built a series of defensive zones into the deep defile. A labyrinth of defensive lines traversed the valley, the first just behind the front line. A second line of defense stretched across the Argonne Forest from Montfaucon to Apremont. The third and most formidable line of defense, Kriemhilde, was imbedded in the

Sector map of the Meuse-Argonne Offensive. (From *The Medical Department of the United States Army in the World War*, vol. 8, *Field Operations* [Washington, DC: Government Printing Office, 1925], plate 37.)

forbidding terrain from Bois-de-Forêt across the heights of Cunel and Romagne to Grandpré. Impenetrable thickets of barbed wire, concrete bunkers, and observation posts were situated to maximum advantage throughout. In order merely to reach Kriemhilde, an advancing army would have to fight through thirteen miles of stiff German resistance in the valley, constantly exposed to enfilading fire from a network of overlapping machine-gun and mortar emplacements, as well as deadly artillery fire from German batteries located on the high ground east of the Meuse River. And even if that army were fortunate enough to make it as far as Kriemhilde, it would still have to breach nearly impregnable defenses. The key was claiming the high ground. For the Rainbow Division, it would truly be an uphill battle the entire way.

One of the first American units to venture into the defile and feel the force of Kriemhilde's fury was Patton's tank brigade. In a letter to his wife before battle, Patton wrote that the valley was "a haunted forest." General Hunter Liggett, in charge of Pershing's 1st Army, described the terrain as "a natural fortress beside which the Virginia wilderness in which Grant and Lee fought was a park."

At 5:30 on the morning of September 26, Patton's tanks rolled forward in support of infantry from the 28th and 35th Divisions. Patton's plan of attack was simple: the first day, Captain Brett's brigade of tanks would lead the way; the second day, Captain Compton's brigade would leapfrog Brett's men to spearhead the attack. They never made it that far.

On the morning of the 26th, dense fog covered much of the valley and obscured Patton's view of the battlefield. Impatient for news of the attack, Patton went forward and discovered that his tanks were sitting idle while infantrymen were hunkered down in trenches or behind whatever protective cover they could find. At that point, the cause of the delay was not stiff German resistance but soft French soil. A large French tank was stuck at the bottom of a crumbling trench, clogging up the most advantageous crossing point between two wide German trenches.

Patton immediately sprang into action. Grabbing a shovel from a nearby tank, he led a group of men into the breach to dismantle the walls of the trench and free the tank. After extricating the heavy tank,

Patton and his aide chained five light tanks together to gain better traction, and then directed their passage across the trenches and up over the hill. Inspired by his apparent success, Patton turned and called on the infantry to follow in the tracks of the tanks. About 150 infantrymen answered the call, charging up the hill behind Patton. At the crest of the hill, Patton and his band of followers were met by a torrent of machine-gun fire. Those with any sense dove for cover—but Patton was not among them. Undeterred, he turned and yelled, "Let's go get them. Who is with me?" Five doughboys rose to the challenge. As Patton, his aide, and five infantrymen started forward, German gunners made fast work of them. Patton and his aide were the last to fall. A bullet entered Patton's left thigh, punching a large hole through his groin before exiting his buttock. On seeing Patton crumple, his aide promptly hit the dirt too, dragging Patton into a nearby shell hole.

After an hour of fierce combat, Patton's tanks and the infantrymen who accompanied them were finally able to knock out two dozen machine-gun emplacements, allowing litter bearers to evacuate Patton. For Patton, the war was over. By October 10, it had ended for other members of the Suicide Club as well—six of Patton's seven captains had become casualties, including one killed and another blinded. Two of Patton's lieutenants had also been killed, and fifteen others wounded. It was a terrible price to pay, but Patton felt the sacrifice was worth it, later writing to his wife: "[T]he tank corps established its reputation for not giving ground. They only went forward. And they were the only troops in the attack of whom that can be said." That the same could not be said of the rest of the American forces was the subject of much discussion, and couldn't have come at a worse time for Pershing.

During the first week of battle, the exhausted and decimated 28th and 35th Divisions had managed to capture the dominating heights of Montfaucon, the famed Mount of the Falcon, from which the crown prince had commanded German troops in the battle of Verdun in 1914. Beyond that, though, little else was accomplished, and on October 1, the 1st and 32nd Infantry Divisions were brought in to relieve them. Ten deadly days later, Pershing's troops had finally succeeded in driving the Germans from Exermont and had captured several of the ridges on the Romagne heights but still found themselves short of the Kriemhilde Line and lagging far behind the advance of British and French forces in other sectors of the front. Although the resistance offered by the Germans in those other sectors was just as fierce, the terrain was far less forbidding. Still, President Georges Clemenceau of France was impatient with the progress of American forces and made his displeasure known by pressuring Marshal Foch to relieve Pershing of command, while at the same time also complaining to Secretary of War Newton Baker and politicians in Washington that Pershing was not up to the task.

Foch refused to do Clemenceau's bidding, however, knowing that any attempt to relieve Pershing of command was unenforceable, and at that point unjustified. Foch would later remark that there was "no denying the magnitude of the effort made by the American army." Instead, Foch tried to placate Clemenceau by proposing that the number of American units serving under French and British command would be increased "whenever operations... permit it." That Foch was actually supportive of Pershing, merely going through the motions with Clemenceau, was evidenced by him later confiding in his memoirs that "having a more comprehensive knowledge of the difficulties encountered by the American army, I could not acquiesce in the radical solution contemplated by M. Clemenceau."

Nevertheless, Pershing felt the heat of the political firestorm and moved the Rainbow Division into the line on October 12 to relieve the beleaguered 1st Division, which had suffered over nine thousand casualties. Just prior to this move, rumors of peace had begun to circulate again. Although Byron had found previous rumors of a peace accord disconcerting, he chalked up this latest flurry of rumors to simply more gamesmanship on the part of Germany. As noted in his diary: "It was while we were still in the woods that rumors and then papers began to come in telling of Germany's dramatic 'acceptance' of all of Wilson's terms, 'with conditions.' Then excitement did fill the air. Was this the end. No, only the beginning of a clever exchange of notes at which we excelled."

Lieutenant Colonel Bill Donovan of the Fighting 69th took the rumors more seriously, however, finding them to be not only a distraction but beguiling and dangerous to the well-being of his men.

In a letter to his wife on October 8, Donovan wrote: "Germany has made her most effective counter-attack, her peace drive. . . . It is a most insidious weapon. It slips in under your armor . . . what we must all think of now is simply 'Fight.'"

Considering the stout German defenses that the Fighting 69th was about to encounter, Donovan had good cause to worry. The third phase of the attack called for the 84th Brigade, under the command of newly promoted Brigadier General Douglas MacArthur, to proceed up the wooded side of the defile with the goal of capturing Hill 288, and then the heights of Côte de Châtillon, from which the Germans had been able to deliver devastating machine-gun and mortar fire on Allied troops in the valley. The 83rd Brigade, commanded by Donovan in the field, was ordered to advance up the center of the valley and capture the village of Landres-et-Saint-Georges. Both routes would prove to be extremely difficult, Donovan's especially so without the cover of woods or adequate artillery support. As Byron wrote in his diary: "For some reason, our division never seemed to have an adequate artillery fire. Time after time they went 'over' without artillery." Lack of artillery support turned out to be a serious miscalculation on Pershing's part, and ultimately Donovan's undoing. It would also end up costing many men their lives.

As the American army advanced in the narrow constraints of the Argonne-Meuse valley, artillery batteries and ammunition trucks were often stuck in the rear, unable to move forward in a timely manner on muddy, congested, and shell-pocked roads to a position that would enable them to provide effective support for troops attacking German positions in the Kriemhilde Stellung. Of the few artillery units that had actually made it into a position to offer fire, the support provided often proved to be either ineffectual or, worse yet, deadly inaccurate. Many of the errant rounds fell woefully short, killing Rainbow Division soldiers instead of Germans.

The AEF's inability to expeditiously move large numbers of troops and vehicles was an ongoing problem during the battle. As reflected in Byron's diary, the ambulance company had been slowed to a crawl as it made its way to the front several days earlier: "The advance was in progress now, and all the roads were jammed with traffic. The next day (Oct. 5), we edged into it, and had made the eight mile journey in perhaps eight hours." British and French critics pointed to the AEF's inability to manage the logistics of mounting a large-scale attack as another example of Pershing's purported incompetence. Although this unfortunate turn of events hardly rose to the level of incompetence, to some extent the criticism was warranted. Without substantial artillery support, Pershing would have to rely on a relentless attack that utilized a numerical superiority in manpower and the tenacity of the Rainbow Division to carry the day. It was a lot to ask of the men.

For New York's Fighting 69th, the attack commenced on the morning of the 14th. Lieutenant Colonel Bill Donovan had chosen not to stay in a command post in the rear, opting instead to take command of 3rd Battalion in the field, where every ounce of his charisma, cunning, and courage in battle would be needed in leading the scores of untested rookies who filled the depleted ranks of the Fighting 69th. At the considerable risk of attracting a sniper's bullet, Donovan marched into battle that morning with his battle ribbons and officer's insignia on full display as a means of inspiring his men. In a letter to his wife, Ruth, Donovan described the conditions that greeted the men as they moved up to the front line. On disembarking near an old farmhouse that had recently been used as a dressing station, Donovan and his men were confronted by "the cast off of the dead." The wreckage of torn and broken litters was strewn across the blood-soaked ground—shredded remnants of uniforms stripped by medics from the bodies of wounded and dying men were piled in heaps, serving as grim reminders of the desperate fight for life that had just played out there. Incongruously, "a nice fat Y.M.C.A. man in a suit of blue overalls and a sombrero" had set up shop inside the now tranquil dressing station, standing ready to serve a cup of hot chocolate, slice of bread, or slab of meat to any man who could stomach it. Not knowing when his next meal might come, Donovan wolfed some down.

> Then I went up to the position we were to occupy. The division preceding us had had a terrific fight just three days before and the ground was a stew of dead things—Boche and American. One attack had evidently been made in the morning mist and

as it cleared an entire company was caught on a little rise. The bodies were laid out in rows. It was easy to determine the formation and the plans of the different leaders. In one hole we found a wounded German who had lain there three days afraid to come out—in another, a wounded German and a wounded American who had crawled to the same hole, shared their water and cigarettes, and then, rolling into the German's blanket, had gone to sleep. If we read that in a storybook we would not have believed it.

From there, Donovan proceeded to the top of a long ridge that had been recently occupied by the Germans. Surveying the terrain, Donovan later remarked: "I went to their machine gun positions. Gun after gun was there with the gunners beside them, dead. From these positions I could look back across the valley and then it was easy to see how heavy a toll could be demanded for entrance there. It was the ridge the Germans had held commanding the valley." As Donovan would soon discover, in scaling the ridges that lay ahead, the cost in human life would be no less steep.

Once Donovan had moved his men into position, battle was joined. German resistance was fierce. High-explosive, shrapnel, and gas shells began to devastate the ranks of the 69th. American aviator Eddie Rickenbacker, who had a bird's-eye view of the intensity of the artillery barrages in the valley, "wondered how the men in the trenches did not go utterly mad with terror." Years later, his observations would prove to have been uncannily prescient. The concussive effect of these enormous shells was so unrelenting and nerve-wracking that many men would carry the invisible scars from this debilitating trauma for the rest of their lives.

At the moment, though, Donovan was less concerned with the mental state of his men than he was in preventing them from being blown to smithereens. As men were being obliterated before his eyes, Donovan clung to the hope that by continuing to press the attack, the regiment would finally be able to break free of the killing field. With little or no support from tanks or artillery, the men of the Fighting 69th had made only modest progress, one mile toward their objective.

By nightfall, they were still more than 500 yards short of the German wire—their ultimate objective, Landres-et-Saint-Georges, was still several miles away. Knowing that stout German positions awaited them on the other side of the wire entanglement, Donovan called a temporary halt to the attack in order to let his exhausted men rest. With only half of 3rd Battalion still standing, Donovan told its commander to gather up the wounded men and fall back, while Donovan moved 1st Battalion into the front line to replace them.

Donovan didn't retire with the exhausted troops, however. When 1st Battalion arrived, he stayed in the front ranks—he wasn't finished trying to breach the German defenses. Under cover of darkness, an attempt was made to slip through the barbed wire and take the enemy by surprise. It ended badly when German flares lit up the night sky. The men who had gone forward were easily killed or captured. On that somber note, Donovan finally decided to call it a day. The best that could be said of the encounter was that he had managed to achieve a stalemate without getting everyone in the regiment killed.

The next morning Donovan renewed the attack as ordered, but had gone only a short distance when a German bullet struck him below the knee, shattering his shinbone. Unable to walk, Donovan continued to command from a shell crater as German soldiers poured through the barbed wire in a ferocious counterattack. Donovan's men managed to stave off the attack but were still pinned down by withering machine-gun fire from German positions in front of Kriemhilde, and on the right flank from Côte de Châtillon. A few tanks arrived to support the infantry but were quickly disposed of by the unerring accuracy of German gunners. The situation was dire. As later related by Donovan in a letter to his wife: "Messengers I sent through were killed or wounded and messages remained undelivered. We were shelled heavily. Beside me three men were blown up and I was showered with the remnants of their bodies. No connection with the rear as the telephone was still out. Gas was thrown at us, thick and nasty. Five hours passed. I was getting groggy but managed to get a message through withdrawing the unit on the line and putting another in its place." As currently situated, Donovan worried that without adequate tank, artillery, or flanking support, the battalion would soon be cut off and surrounded, so he ordered his most advanced units to with-draw from the German barbed wire, after which he consolidated his defenses in anticipation of another German assault.

On learning that the advance had stalled, General Michael Lenihan, overall commander of the 83rd Brigade, issued orders for Donovan to renew the attack. In the throes of combat, however, communication with frontline units was anything but expeditious—German artillery had severed telephone communication with the front lines, requiring Lenihan's message to be sent by horseback, and then on foot. When runners finally reached Donovan, it was too late—he had already exer-cised his own discretion in the matter, believing that without proper support any further attempt to advance was doomed to failure. By this point in the battle, Donovan was no longer willing to throw away the lives of his men needlessly. Donovan was not the only commander in the front line to take this position. As later related by Major Lloyd D. Ross, battalion commander of the 168th Iowa Infantry:

> There also existed all through the chain of command an ever-present tendency to rush troops forward and keep pushing them against enemy machine guns, howitzers, and artillery. General officers and field officers were the guilty ones in this respect. They generally, had never commanded troops in large bodies and against a first class and well armed army. Many of them employed the same driving tactics they used in smaller com-mands in the Philippine Islands and in similar campaigns. They would not take the word of the officer in the front line as to the opposing forces and weapons but kept driving troops forward inadequately supported by artillery....
>
> The same mistake was made in the Argonne, except the infantry had become wise to the game. We officers in com-mand had determined that when stubborn resistance was met we would not sacrifice men against material but take our time and gain our ends in other ways. We moved more slowly per-haps but more surely and had more men alive at the end of the action. We attained our objective but without enough artillery in support.

As the battle continued to rage, medics were finally able to extri-
cate Donovan from the field of combat on a stretcher fashioned from a
field blanket. It was done at great peril, one of the medics falling prey
to enemy fire. After being removed from harm's way, Donovan was
relieved of command and the attack recommenced, but still no progress was made. It was not until the following day, October 16, when
MacArthur's 84th Brigade, acting under orders from General Charles
Summerall "to give me Cote de Chatillon or a list of five thousand
casualties," that the most devastating source of enfilading fire was
finally removed from the valley.

As recounted by MacArthur, the heights of Côte de Châtillon were
protected by entrenched infantry and nearly two hundred machine
guns. For MacArthur, the cost in human life in taking the hill was
unforgettable—twenty-five years later, he would remark that he had
hated Summerall ever since. As further related by MacArthur: "Officers fell and sergeants leaped to command. Companies dwindled to
platoons and corporals took over. At the end Major Ross [Lloyd Ross,
commanding an Iowa battalion] had only 300 men and six officers
out of 1,450 men and twenty-five officers. That is the way that Cote
de Chatillon fell." As a litter bearer detailed to MacArthur's 84th Brigade, Byron was witness to much of this. According to his diary:

> On Sunday the 13th, our artillery opened up a little and Mon-
> day the 14th, our infantry went forward. They did not go very
> far, a couple of kilometers, but the ground was against them—all
> woods and high hills. The Kreimhilde-Stellung, a very strong
> defense line ran through here, and more—there was arrayed
> against our men the greatest artillery concentration they
> had ever seen except at Champagne. That our men didn't get
> ahead—tho' the Boche threw in reserves after reserves and
> ordered them to hold to the last man.
>
> On Tuesday (15th), I was sent on the relief up. The path we
> had to carry the litters on was around the edge of the valley,
> where the woods bordered it. The very first time we started up
> we ran into shell fire and continued to be near or in it all the

time we were up there. The haul was man-killing—four kilometers in sticky slippery mud. But we carried 'em, and laid in our
fox holes when not busy. Three or four times in particular we
were in the heart of the shelling yet escaped uninjured. Once
we were attacked by a low flying Boche plane, who machine-
gunned and bombed us. The funny part was that some Boche
boys were helping us carry the litter at the time.

On Wed. Oct. 16th, the 84th Brid. Gen. told his men that
there was still one objective to take—a certain high hill—the key
to that part. He said "The hill must be taken or we must lose
5,000 men trying." Two battalions took it in what was later vividly described by an English correspondent as "one of the boldest cleverest most successful feats of the war."

The ravages of the battle were not confined to combatants. Medical personnel from the sanitary train sustained more casualties in
the Argonne-Meuse offensive than any other engagement of the war.
Two men were killed and ten wounded as they tended to wounded
soldiers—which was hardly a surprise, considering the six-mile trek
that the litter bearers were forced to make from the triage hospital in
Baulny to the front line, and then back, often in knee-deep mud while
exposed to enemy fire.

Reaching the hospital at Baulny was by no means any guarantee of
safety, however, as German artillery zeroed in on the compound with
uncanny accuracy, at times knocking down hospital tents and forcing medical personnel to seek shelter in dugouts. At one point, artillery and airplane attacks became so intense that Lieutenant Lecklider
ordered litter bearers and orderlies to evacuate the wounded from the
hospital by ambulance in order to escape the deadly barrage.

In the midst of the chaos and death at Baulny, an especially noteworthy volunteer from the Salvation Army was working side by side
with Lieutenant Lecklider, Byron, and other members of the medical
staff. In a letter to Estelle, Byron identified the volunteer as "Mother
Springer, . . . a missionary on sabbatical leave" from her duties in India,
where she had worked in an orphanage. Unlike most other civilian volunteers in France, Mother Springer wasn't content to work in the rear,

having chosen instead to stay close to the front lines, where she ministered to the wounded in the triage hospital. Byron and the other men of the ambulance company were so impressed with Mother Springer that they later extolled her strength of character and kindness as "one of the greatest examples of applied practical Christianity we have ever seen." For her part, Mother Springer felt that it was the hand of God that directed her in this perilous work. In a letter written home just after the battle, she explained:

> God used me to my satisfaction with the wounded and dying during the fall drive. For I did little else or have done little else all Fall save field hospital work—and that with the worse wounded cases. I can never describe those days when one after another ambulance kept bringing in the wounded boys—a leg off, an arm off, a body shot through and through, a head all wounded beyond recognition, one head the brains oozing out and the patient simply drenched in blood but yet he was partially conscious and raving. I washed clotted blood from the wounded boys faces and hands . . . during those times while I was washing those poor tired boys, I had a chance to cheer him a bit, ask him about the home folks, and about his soul, and give him some promises that were precious to the sick and dying, and again and again hear them say "I believe in you and Jesus, but I have been praying" and many such expressions then maybe in a short time later see that darling boy go out to be with God. I have heard again and again boys call me mother after I had done something for them and tell me I was so kind. I feel almost as if those days were too dark and yet too sacred to lift the veil before the public eye for fear some might think I was bragging or that there was too much I—but truly Mrs. Atwater, the service God called me to from September 12th to November 19th was the most wonderful I ever did in all my life.

After the war, Eva Alice Springer, as she was more formally known, would continue to do the Lord's work—returning to the United States to obtain her nursing degree before going back to India, where she would help to found the Christian Hospital in Mongelli. For the present time, however, Mother Springer's attention was focused on tending to the wounded and dying soldiers in the Argonne Forest.

Once Côte de Châtillon fell, the devastation in Death Valley lessened as German forces fell back—and with that, the flood of wounded soldiers into the triage unit subsided as well. By the time the battle had ended, nearly 7,000 wounded soldiers had been treated at Baulny, of which 293 required major surgical operations before they could be evacuated to hospitals in the rear. Seventy-one surgical patients never made it that far and were buried in the small graveyard nearby. Many thousands more lay dead on the field of battle.

It was a staggering loss of life. For the first time, though, it appeared that the great cost in human suffering would have a lasting impact on the outcome of the war. In taking the heights of Côte de Châtillon, the Rainbow Division had not only broken through the vaunted Kriemhilde Stellung, it had created a fault line in the German psyche as well. It was now clear to even the Kaiser's most ardent supporters that a seismic shift in the diplomatic terrain of the war had just occurred.

The Allies were finally in a position to begin dictating terms.

18
ENOUGH TO NARROW
ONE'S MIND FOREVER

On November 1, twenty-six hundred artillery pieces announced the start of the final push to Sedan. Displacing the Germans from the city of Sedan was not only strategically important to the Allies, it was a matter of national pride for France, and a long time coming.

In 1870, Sedan had been the site of one of the most humiliating defeats in French history. With the capture of Napoleon III and one hundred thousand French soldiers there during the Franco-Prussian War, the Second Republic of France had come to an abrupt and igno-minious end. In its place, an impromptu government of national defense was assembled in an attempt to thwart the advance of Otto von Bismarck's army. It was to no avail. Prussian troops soon laid siege to Paris, and four months later severe privation forced the French to finally surrender. As the spoils of war, the Treaty of Frankfurt awarded most of Alsace and part of Lorraine to the victors. In renaming the region the Imperial Territory of Alsace-Lorraine, the newly unified German Empire staked its claim to the prosperous cities of Strasbourg, Metz, and Colmar, plus the iron-rich fields of Lorraine.

The treaty wasn't just a devastating blow to the economic and political prestige of France, it was viewed by Francophiles as an unspeakable affront to French honor. As far back as the reign of Louis XIV in 1648, the provinces of Alsace and Lorraine had been under the continuous rule of French monarchs and the Republic. The sudden loss of them in 1870 to the burgeoning German Empire gave rise to a social phenomenon in France called *revanchisme*—a nation-alistic fervor that infected the collective French psyche like a fes-tering disease. With "Never speak of it, but never forget it" as their mantra, French revanchists were quietly determined to repatriate the area at the first opportunity. World War I presented that moment.

The extent to which rampant French revanchisme and aggressive German nationalism were each responsible for causing the war has been the subject of much debate over the years. That over 3 million French and German soldiers would end up dying as a result of such opportunistic thinking is, however, a well-established fact. Equally clear but no less disturbing was the unfortunate plight of the many thousands of innocent civilians who were caught in the crossfire between the dueling empires. Although Alsatians of German and French descent had managed to live peacefully together for decades, often intermarrying, at various times each group had been subjected to official oppression by the other, depending on who was in control. As the Allied army continued to advance deeper into German-held territory, evidence of this quickly made itself known.

For the duration of the drive, the Michigan Ambulance Company was detailed to MacArthur's 84th Brigade. As noted in Byron's diary, the latest phase of the Allied offensive was a surprise as much for the ease and speed of the operation as it was for the discoveries that awaited the men in the wake of the retreating Germans.

> Friday night, Nov. 1st, the terrific bombardment was begun. The second and 77th divisions moved forward ahead of us. There was no difficulty at all in the rapid advance which extended over a wide front and continued to the Meuse. Our Division was in the lead for the last five days. In fact it was mentioned in the "American Communique" as having reached the heights dominating Sedan. Our division made a total advance of nearly forty kilometers—a record. . . . We passed Flirey, St. Juvin—a big Boche railhead, and over to Buzancy, the most important town thereabouts. This had been a Boche army headquarters, and had been fixed up with all sorts of conveniences, even two electric

baths for officers. We were quartered in a splendid house, where Sprague and I slept on a spring mattress....

As we surmised, these quarters were too good to last—we were rousted out and carried on to St. Pierremont the next day.... We stayed there two nights, then on the 7th hiked over to Stonne.... In the town before Stonne we had our first glimpse of refugees, while in Stonne they were crowded in everywhere. They were overjoyed with us, and wanted to do everything possible for us.... The Frenchman and his family, who had the room next to our loft there, were certainly a pitiful sight. All his children were sick from insufficient food. And the stories he told were enough to narrow ones mind forever.

For the first time since landing in France, the 42nd Division advanced through territory that was markedly different. Beginning with the onset of hostilities in August 1914, this region of subjugated France had been under uninterrupted German control. In the intervening four years, the Germans had done their best to recast the past. Polite language had all but vanished from the land. All of the signage was in German—*Verboten*, the much-used word of prohibition during the occupation, was seemingly posted everywhere. Children, though French in appearance, were German in tongue.

As the Germans beat a hasty retreat, it seemed that a vacuum had been left in their place. Everything of value had been taken with them, even young women and boys. As the Allies stepped into the void, an uneasy calm awaited them. Inhabitants of the villages were stunned to see American soldiers march in as liberators—their captors had never bothered to tell them that the United States had entered the war. No sooner had the shock of being released from captivity worn off than the joy of liberation broke out—like flowers blossoming after a long harsh winter, makeshift American flags suddenly sprouted everywhere. Fashioned from any available scrap of red, white, and blue cloth, the flags flew festively from rooftops and windows as villagers gathered in the streets, weeping and embracing the soldiers who marched by. Not all were tears of joy, however. As related by Byron, many of the villagers told of the abuse they'd suffered at the hands of German soldiers:

"Some time ago we were in the town of Stonne, which the Americans had taken—the highest point for many miles around. There were a great many civilian refugees who told us more in the time we talked with them than we had learned in all the previous years of the war. One of the men in particular with whom I talked a great deal told us tales that'll be burned in my memory forever."

On November 8, Byron and other members of the Michigan Ambulance Company left Stonne, following on the heels of the infantry as they hiked on to the village of Chemery. Most of the sanitary train's equipment was on vehicles that were stuck in the mud and traffic on congested roads. As the Germans retreated, they had succeeded in slowing the Allied advance by destroying the bridges and culverts that connected the roads. As noted in Byron's diary: "In the road near the top of the hill, the Boche had blown an immense hole—parts of the rock being fully a half kilometer away. It took engineers forty hours to a make a road passable." On reaching Chemery, the Michigan and New Jersey Ambulance Companies set up a medical post while infantry-men from the 84th Brigade continued the push north toward Sedan, only nine miles away. Up to this point, the Germans had been fighting a rearguard action, and although the Rainbow Division had encountered pockets of resistance, casualties were relatively light. At Sedan, however, the Allies expected to find the Germans dug in, and that the ensuing siege of the city would be a hard-fought and bloody affair.

During the planning stage for the Meuse-Argonne offensive, the honor of capturing Sedan had been ceded to the French Army. And rightfully so. The Americans were relative latecomers to the war, and although their losses were not insignificant, they paled when compared to those of the French. Moreover, as later observed by Brigadier General James G. Harbord, commander of U.S. Marine Corps 4th Brigade (which was part of the advance on Sedan), the long-awaited liberation of Sedan by French soldiers was for France the emotional equivalent of George Washington's Continental army assuming the lead role in accepting the surrender of General Cornwallis and the British at Yorktown, even though the French Navy and seventeen thousand French soldiers had proved indispensable in bringing about that result. Not everyone in the American Expeditionary Force seemed to appreciate the symbolic importance of the French Army entering the city first, however, and in the ensuing push to Sedan, the French nearly got trampled in the stampede for glory.

In what would later be called "the Sedan Incident," it was General Douglas MacArthur and the men of the Rainbow Division who would inadvertently keep the American Expeditionary Force from snatching diplomatic defeat from the jaws of victory, which was ultimately a good thing. In doing so, however, the high command of the American army would be made to look ridiculous and incompetent. Fallout from the incident would affect the reputations and relationships of those involved for years to come.

Among those who seemed to lose all sense of proportion and political propriety in the matter was General Pershing. In the advance on Sedan, Pershing had become frustrated with the slow progress of the 40th Division of the 4th French Army, which was lagging behind the Rainbow Division and the 77th Division. On November 3, in a fit of impatience that was reminiscent of Foch's attempt to bully Pershing only weeks earlier, Pershing tried to pressure French general Paul Maistre, overall commander of the 40th Division, into allowing Pershing's 1st Army to capture Sedan if French troops were unable to keep pace with the Americans. Pershing was a forceful advocate and eventually Maistre agreed that if the Americans got to Sedan first, they could take it. Pershing would later describe the meeting as "a plain talk" in which Maistre "not only offered no objections but to the contrary warmly approved" of Pershing's plan. Others saw it differently, categorizing the meeting as a heated argument. Considering the symbolic importance of Sedan to France, it is hard to imagine the discussion as anything but contentious. This seems to be supported by the fact that two days later, during the Allied advance on Sedan, the French 40th Division threatened to shell American troops that had cut into their area of responsibility unless they withdrew immediately. It was a curious position indeed for an ally to assume.

In Pershing's defense, although his approach may have been heavy-handed, the prosecution of war is without doubt a pressure-filled affair. Priorities and roles change as battles unfold—to remain static in the face of opportunity is to invite folly. At that point, the

American army was clearly in the best position to capture Sedan, and from Pershing's perspective, time was of the essence. Although preliminary discussions of an armistice were in the offing, formal negotiations had not yet begun in earnest, and with German troops in serious disarray, it was important for the Allies to strike quickly while the opportunity presented itself. Having said that, however, Pershing's motivation in capturing Sedan seemed to be more than just tactical. It smacked of being personal, even ambitious. Pershing would later admit as much— "[I]it was the ambition of the First Army and mine that our troops capture Sedan."

Still, when viewed in the context of recent events, his motives, though graceless, were somewhat understandable. No doubt Pershing and his staff still felt the sting of French and British criticism over the slow progress of American forces in the Argonne Forest and Clemenceau's unseemly attempt to have Pershing removed from command. That Pershing would have viewed this latest turn of events as well-deserved comeuppance for the French Army was only natural, although whether he actually did is undocumented. What is not subject to speculation, however, was Pershing's recognition of the symbolic importance that the capture of Sedan represented for the American army. For nearly two years, Pershing had had to fend off repeated attempts by the British and French high command to disperse his army. In all likelihood, the capture of Sedan represented the last opportunity Pershing would have to silence his critics by conspicuously highlighting the AEF's contribution to the war. And in doing so, the AEF would almost certainly be described in the U.S. press as having delivered the decisive blow to end the war—casting the American forces as equal to, perhaps better than, the French and British Armies. Pershing was determined that 1st Corps would have the honor of delivering that blow.

On November 5, Pershing's staff issued an order informing the commanding generals of I and V Corps of the change in plans. "General Pershing desires the honor of entering Sedan should fall to the First American Army. He has every confidence that troops of First Corps, assisted on their right by Fifth Corps, will enable him to realize this desire. In transmitting the foregoing message, your attention is invited to the favorable opportunity now existing for pressing our advance throughout the night. Boundaries will not be considered binding."

General Charles Summerall, the much-disliked commander of V Corps, which included 1st Division, was only too eager to comply with the ill-conceived and poorly worded order. Seizing on the highly unusual last sentence, Summerall purportedly misinterpreted the order as carte blanche to disregard the well-established practice of adhering to sector boundaries in combat, which were used to keep divisions from becoming entangled and mangling each other. After receiving the order, Summerall raced to 1st Division headquarters, where he verbally instructed General Frank Parker, the new and relatively inexperienced commanding officer of 1st Division, to plot the most expeditious route to Sedan. In ordering Parker to proceed in this fashion, Summerall had put 1st Division on a collision course with the Rainbow Division, the 77th Division, and the 40th Division of the French 4th Army.

Parker took Summerall at his word. At Parker's direction, 1st Division veered abruptly to the left, tacking a perilous course in front of the other divisions. In the confusion that ensued, American troops stumbled into each other during the dark and rainy night. In some unfortunate instances, shots were exchanged. The most embarrassing incident of the entire fiasco resulted in Summerall's men capturing General Douglas MacArthur at gunpoint. On the night in question, MacArthur had gone forward in an attempt to prevent friendly-fire incidents from occurring after having been informed that 1st Division troops had suddenly appeared in the Rainbow Division's sector of responsibility.

In his official report, MacArthur would downplay the circumstances of his capture, couching it in terms of a friendly encounter. It is clear from other sources, however, that MacArthur, attired in his customary though highly unconventional uniform, had in fact been mistaken for a German officer by 1st Division troops and was detained. That MacArthur had been captured unscathed was a blessing. Others were not as fortunate. Many American soldiers fell victim to friendly fire as a result of Summerall's recklessness and Pershing's tunnel vision.

Brigadier General James G. Harbord was not nearly as diplomatic as MacArthur in describing the tragic consequences of Pershing's order. According to Harbord: "The division set out on a futile errand, in executing which, it sustained about 500 casualties and marched itself to exhaustion. Considered as a military feat, the march of the First Division was worthy of its best traditions. As an illustration of lack of team work, and as an example of undisciplined inexperience, it justified much of what our associates (British and French) think of us."

On being informed of the encounter and Summerall's order, which had ostensibly gone out under his authority, an irate General Hunter Liggett, in charge of 1st Corps, intervened with a vengeance. The order was immediately countermanded. General Charles T. Menoher, in charge of the Rainbow Division, was instructed to take charge of all troops in his sector, even 1st Division soldiers if necessary. Summerall was told in no uncertain terms to back his men out of the sector. After this, the French were accorded the honor of entering Sedan.

On November 9, the Rainbow Division was relieved by the 77th Division and withdrawn to the vicinity of Buzancy to prepare for its next assignment. That the Rainbow Division was in need of relief at that point is uncontested—what other extraneous factors may have come into play in arriving at that decision is open to speculation. In MacArthur's memoirs, he alluded to the "recriminations" that flowed from the Rainbow Division's run-in with Summerall's 1st Division, which included a frivolous investigation of MacArthur for having gone forward that night without a helmet, pistol, or gas mask. According to MacArthur, "[W]hen the matter was referred to General Pershing, he replied in typical fashion: 'Stop all the nonsense,'" apparently looking to move on from an embarrassment of his own making.

Others were not as forgiving or eager to move on. Some officers wanted Summerall and Parker court-martialed. For commanders whose men had been caught in the switches that night, the eccentric maneuver was deemed by many to be a tactical atrocity. A rift had been opened in the high command of the U.S. Army that would carry over to the next war. In MacArthur's view, regardless of the ill will that may have been directed at him personally and the Rainbow Division generally, the outcome was worth it—giving the French a clear path to Sedan "seemed to me a most proper recognition of the magnificent courage, efficiency, and devotion of the French troops throughout the entire war."

On November 11, most of the Rainbow Division had been withdrawn from the vicinity of Sedan. Byron and the rest of the Michigan Ambulance Company remained at Chemery—as the field hospital nearest the front, the 117th Sanitary Train was responsible for the medical care of all American troops in the area. By this time, rumors of a pending armistice agreement were pervasive and detailed, even confidently predicting the cease-fire hour. Still, American troops continued to press the attack. As German artillery boomed in the distance, Byron refused to get his hopes up.

Although the Armistice had been signed at 5:00 in the morning, the cease-fire would not take place until 11:00 that day. As set forth in *Iodine and Gasoline*, the fighting continued to the last possible moment:

> In the village of Chemery, where the farthest advanced hospital of the Train was stationed, was a small cemetery surrounding the church. Early on the morning of November 11, ten weary hospital men were hard at work, digging a large grave along the southern wall. On the opposite side of the same cemetery, another smaller grave stood in readiness to receive its dead. Presently a short procession came from the church headed by a priest. The soldiers ceased their labor, to stand with uncovered heads while the French civilians, so recently freed from German captivity, buried one of their own. He was an elderly man who had been killed by a stray shell a few days before. After the funeral was over, the priest, seeing no chaplain present among the soldiers, asked if his services were needed. He was assured by the men that his kindness would be appreciated, and that all would be in readiness at ten o'clock. At the appointed time, the priest returned, followed by as many, if not more, French people than attended the former funeral. A short service was held, and at its conclusion, the daughter of the civilian who had been buried only a short time before, noticed that the Yankee grave had no flowers. Unhesitatingly, she went to her father's

grave, selected the largest and most handsome wreath, brought it and laid it on the bare grave of the American soldiers. Her eyes were filled with tears as she said, "My father would have it so." Such was the bond of brotherly love the Americans had established in the hearts of their allies. The sacred silence lasted but a moment. For the screech of an alien shell, whining closely over their heads, ended in a crash of black smoke over the corner of the cemetery. It was the last shell that broke in the hearing of any member of the Sanitary Train, for at 11 o'clock the same day, the Armistice took effect.

Nearly eleven thousand soldiers were killed or wounded on the final day of the war, many having been sent in harm's way by commanders who knew that the Armistice had already been signed. The last American fatality occurred at one minute before 11:00. In a war that had already distinguished itself for unprecedented carnage, these senseless deaths were especially hard to reconcile.

As both sides would soon discover, however, being able to bury the bones of contention proved every bit as difficult.

19
THE DAWN OF PEACE

News that an armistice agreement had been signed was received by both sides with a mixture of trepidation and relief—how much of each was a matter of perspective.

For their part, the French and British armies were glad that for the moment, anyway, the fighting was over. And that they finally had the upper hand—though they were still wary of the German Army's ability to renew hostilities after a brief respite. It was going to take much more than a brief respite, however, for German troops to continue fighting. Not only had they been set back on their heels, they had been knocked clear off their feet. A combination of casualties, exhaustion, desertion, and influenza had depleted the ranks. In the final months of the war, adolescent boys and middle-aged fathers had been conscripted to fill the vacancies once occupied by stalwart soldiers. To add further worry to an already woeful situation, the German high command despaired of the untenable position the army was in tactically, and feared that any future peace negotiations would require German forces to disarm completely.

Although each side had ample cause to remain apprehensive of the other, neither was eager to resume hostilities and a tentative silence settled over the front. As set forth by Byron in the "Dawn of Peace" chapter of *The History of Ambulance Company 168*, American troops were cautiously optimistic:

> Our company was at this time, in Chemery, 14 kilometers from
> Sedan. This was so far forward that it was hard to get reliable

information as to what was going on outside. But through the haze which always surrounds the advancing troops, the light of peace kept trying to shine upon us. But the peace propaganda had come to sound as false in our ears as the shouts of the boy in the fable when his sheep really were being attacked by the wolf. We had been bantered by peace talk for five weeks—peace talk clothed in every sort of garment, until we thought it was nothing more than a mirage.

The 11th and 12th came around and passed, with still no official confirmation or denial of the armistice. True the absence of aeroplanes and reports of guns made us hopeful. On the 13th, however, someone brought in a paper which had the hoped for news that the armistice was in force—had been signed at 5 AM of the 11th in fact. But then the strange thing was that there was no celebration, no pandemonium. Some shook hands: others, as it is always said, "I told you so"; while others merely sighed and dared not say a word lest they break the magic spell.... We must have had somewhat the feeling of a fireman, who after years of service—his nerves always alert to catch the first sound of the alarm leading him to every sort of danger, is suddenly discharged and no more to think of those alarms and dangers.

During the first days of the Armistice, rumors swirled through the ranks like fallen leaves on the November wind. One rumor had the men immediately packing up their gear and moving out for the warmth and comfort of southern France. Another had the troops rushing headlong into Germany to impose a harsh requital. Neither was true. The Armistice was only a thirty-day cease-fire agreement. According to its terms, either side could breach the agreement on forty-eight hours' notice and renew hostilities. Practically speaking, however, Germany was in no position to continue fighting and additional thirty-day extensions had been incorporated into the original terms of the Armistice to give both sides more time to effectuate a lasting peace. As it turned out, additional time would be sorely needed.

In the weeks leading up to the Armistice, Germany was beset by great internal strife. Under the prolonged stress of war, the German Empire had begun to fracture and was in danger of total collapse. By the early fall of 1918, popular support for the war had all but evaporated. German citizens were focused on more important matters like their own survival, as chronic shortages of food had begun to take a deadly toll. By the end of October, political support for the war had deteriorated as well. On November 9, the Kaiser abdicated the throne. Most German allies had already surrendered. Only die-hard monarchists and a few members of the German Army high command still believed that the war could be successfully prosecuted.

In the Kaiser's absence, an impromptu democratic assembly, called the Council of People's Representatives, assumed the role of governance. The council had scant faith in the military high command—so little, in fact, that a civilian, Mathias Erzberger, had been appointed head of the German delegation in Armistice negotiations. The manner and means of the negotiations did not bode well for Germany. The Armistice meeting was held in Marshal Ferdinand Foch's private railroad car in Compiègne, France. The fact that the negotiations were largely one-sided came as no surprise. The Erzberger-led German delegation had little leverage with which to bargain, and the Allies were in no mood to listen. Instead, the Allies insisted on a number of conditions that would make it extremely difficult, if not impossible, for Germany to renew hostilities.

The German delegation had little choice but to comply. Despite the obvious disparity in bargaining positions, the Germans hoped that an equitable end to the war might still be possible. This wishful thinking was grounded in a series of communiqués between President Woodrow Wilson and the German high command that had taken place in October, in which the Germans were led to believe (purposefully or not) that if they met certain Armistice conditions, a working framework for peace negotiations would to some extent be based on Wilson's Fourteen Points, a plan first proposed in January. Although Wilson made no explicit guarantees as to what terms the treaty would ultimately contain, Germany did not want to be perceived as an obstructionist from the outset of the Armistice process and thereby remove any hope, however slim, of later attaining a just peace.

Among the more important preconditions required of Germany in the Armistice agreement were to immediately cede control of

Alsace-Lorraine to France, to withdraw its armed forces from all territory west of the Rhine, to effectively disarm itself by turning over thousands of artillery pieces, machine guns, airplanes, and submarines, and to allow Allied forces to establish occupied zones at key bridgeheads on the German side of the Rhine River. To the relief of many, no incidents of resistance occurred while a still proud and potentially dangerous German Army gradually made good on those conditions. On the heels of the German withdrawal, the Rainbow Division was carefully maneuvered into position along the Luxembourg border. In doing so, it became clear that each move made by the American army would be as carefully considered as it was considerate of the fragile peace that hung in the balance. To that end, only well-disciplined and experienced troops were selected to enforce the accord.

On November 16, the Rainbow Division learned that it would be part of the newly formed Army of Occupation. On December 3, 1918, British troops were the first element of Allied forces to enter Germany. The Rainbow Division soon followed. According to Byron's diary: "On the 10th we loaded on the cars in the morning—for Germany at last. The trip lasted all day. It was thru hill and valley for the entire distance, many of the roads along the edges of the precipices having beautiful views. We crossed the border into Germany over a bridge in Echternach, a river forming the boundary there. Farther on we passed through Bitburg, Prüm, arriving finally in Lissendorf."

In a letter to Estelle dated December 8, Byron further noted: "We saw here and there Boche soldiers with part or all of their uniforms still on—discharged men. There were many others who had already put on their civilian clothes—probably gladly. The people for the most part seem to have enough to eat." In reality, Byron's assessment of the conditions in Germany at that time was accurate only regarding the relatively well-off section of the Rhine River valley where he was stationed. In many other areas of Germany, the situation was indeed bleak. Like the inhabitants of England, France, and Belgium, many Germans had suffered greatly from privation. Unlike the war-devastated regions of France and Belgium, however, the villages, cities, and countryside of Germany had largely been spared the physically destructive ravages of war. Over the next several days, Byron would bear witness to that fact.

According to Byron's diary, after four years of war, German villages and towns looked none the worse for wear. The cities of Lissendorf, Mayen, and Adenau appeared well kept and unmolested. As the ambulance company continued to wend its way further into Germany, the countryside only grew more beautiful. After their experience of the battle-scarred terrain of France, it seemed as if the men had been magically transported to an enchanted land, where the picturesque ruins of old towers and medieval castles stood guard like ancient sentinels over the grape-terraced hillsides and mist-shrouded valleys. The splendor of the new environs was not lost on Byron:

> If we had ever seen scenery it was this. The best of all, tho' was when we rounded the turn and sighted the Rhine, and the low-lying mountains beyond. We then saw the reason why tourists talked so of the Rhine valley, and why the Germans fought so to defend it. As we rode on down parallel to the river we saw more and more its beauty. The river here is perhaps 400 yards wide. The mountains are a patchwork of every color of green and brown. On many are crumbling ruins. Here and there a village is clustered on the bank, as the river winds in and out.

To the utter surprise of many American soldiers, the beauty of the land was equaled by the charm of its people. Byron, however, had a more guarded view of the cordial greeting received by the men. As further noted in his letter to Estelle on December 8: "They were very decent to us, trying in every way to fraternize with us. Of course, we have strict orders against mixing with them on any but a business basis. I never saw so many kids in my life. There seem to be multitudes everywhere. Most of 'em wear the round fatigue caps of the soldiers. Little children—they scarce know what villanies have been perpetrated by men wearing them."

In subsequent letters written to Estelle and his parents, and in a newspaper interview that would later be published in Michigan, Byron attributed nefarious motives to the German people—describing them as "schemers" who were merely trying to curry favor with the Army of Occupation in hopes of securing more favorable treatment from the Americans. Gertrude Bray showed similar contempt for the civilians she encountered on entering Germany with the Rainbow Division. In a December 9 entry in her diary, Gertrude noted, "They show us no animosity and treat us well. . . . [P]ersonally, I can't bear these people, and I don't even want the children around."

No doubt many Germans did go to great lengths to ingratiate themselves with the Army of Occupation—under the circumstances, who could blame them? After four years of brutal warfare, Germans could hardly be faulted for fearing that their conquerors might want to exact a harsh revenge on them, even personally. Contrary to Byron's and Gertrude's suspicions, however, most Germans were simply glad that the war was over, anxious to make peace with the world so that they could return to normal living.

Unlike Byron, some American soldiers were only too ready to forgive and forget—to such an extent, in fact, that it became necessary for General Headquarters to issue an order prohibiting excessive fraternization between soldiers and local residents. In Byron's words, the order might as well have read: "Love thy neighbor as thyself, just don't get caught doing it." As later noted in a diary entry, liberal interpretation of that order soon led to an outbreak of "the V-disease," which in turn resulted in the cancellation of all leave passes for enlisted men in the unit, costing Byron a much-anticipated trip to Cologne, where he had planned to visit its famous cathedral.

By December 16, the sanitary train found itself comfortably quartered in Bad Neuenahr, a resort town twenty-four miles downstream from the city of Koblenz in the Rhine River valley. Because of its mineral spas, posh hotels, and relatively well-stocked restaurants, American soldiers renamed the town "Good Neuenahr," and for the next four months the grateful men called the town home. For the duration of their stay in Bad Neuenahr, Byron and the rest of the Michigan Ambulance Company were billeted in the Hof Von Holland Hotel. Compared to the barns, sheds, and dugouts that the men had been living in for the past year, the old hotel was the lap of luxury. After settling in, the first order of business was to finally get clean—frequent baths in the mineral springs soon succeeded in ridding the men of the lice and scabies that had been with them since they first entered the trenches of France.

It was in Bad Neuenahr that Byron began to write sections of the book *The History of Ambulance Company 168*. Byron had been asked by Lieutenant Roy Bryson to write an introductory tribute to fallen comrades in the ambulance company as well as the "Dawn of Peace" chapter of the book. Byron had also been selected by Colonel Wilbur Conkling to write the "Champagne" chapter of a similar book, *Iodine and Gasoline*, which recounted the exploits and experiences of the 117th Sanitary Train during the war. For Byron, those writing assignments must have come as a mixed blessing. On the one hand, working on the book was undoubtedly a welcome change of pace from the daily grind of army life. On the other hand, being asked to reflect deeply, possibly for the first time, about what he had witnessed and experienced during the war had the potential to cause him great anguish. Perhaps it was no coincidence, then, that during this period of introspection, Byron would slip into an emotional funk. The first signs of Byron's discontent appeared in a somewhat rambling letter to Estelle on January 9, 1919:

> I can't figure out any possible way that anyone could have been exposed to the amount of knowledge I have been, and know less. I'm stuck on some of the simplest stuff. I've noticed it a hundred times on this "book" deal. . . . I've been getting mighty dissatisfied with myself in recent months. I can't seem to make the grade in some things the way I ought to. . . . So now I'm living along a bit different than I used to. . . . So you see, I've come to the notion that I better not bother any girl seriously until I come a lot closer to making good than I have so far.

The emergence of this disaffection was not without good cause. In endeavoring to write about the horrific battle of Champagne, Byron was required to revisit the war in excruciating detail—a task that couldn't have been more personal or painful. For it was during the battle of Champagne that Byron's best friend in the company, Herbert

Jackson, had been killed—and in the process had in all likelihood inadvertently saved Byron's life. As described by Byron in his diary and in the "Champagne" chapter of *Iodine and Gasoline*, he and Jackson had been temporarily detailed to the 166th Infantry Regiment as litter bearers in anticipation of an all-out assault by German forces. Shortly after midnight on July 15, while the two men slept in a flimsy shack just behind the front lines, the Germans unleashed the forces of hell in one of the largest artillery barrages of the war. On hearing the first German shell screech overhead, Byron and Jackson grabbed their gas masks and made a mad dash for safety. As the two men tore across the open ground trying to reach a dugout, a second deadly shell exploded nearby. In the ensuing chaos, Jackson stopped to help a wagoner who was struggling to control frightened mules. Apparently, Byron did not stop. As Jackson and the wagoner resumed the sprint for cover, they were now positioned behind Byron as the three men attempted to enter the passageway of the dugout. Before they were completely inside, however, a third German shell exploded within five feet of the entrance, cutting down both Jackson and the wagoner, whose bodies almost certainly shielded Byron from the deadly shards of metal. Despite the best efforts of Byron and others to get Jackson to a field hospital, he died quickly—without uttering a word. That disquieting silence would resonate for the rest of Byron's life.

The first evidence of that silence is found in Byron's diary and letters home. Jackson's death must have had a devastating impact on Byron, given the circumstances in which it occurred and the close friendship of the two. It is also likely that Byron struggled with feelings of guilt and self-recrimination, a completely predictable reaction to the death of a comrade in battle. As explained by Dr. Jonathan Shay, a psychiatric expert in treating post-traumatic stress disorder in war veterans, the intense heat of war forges a unique filial bond between men, so that when a soldier dies in combat, his loss is mourned by his brothers-in-arms like a death in the family; some survivors even wish they had died instead.

Yet nowhere in Byron's writings does he mention his feelings about Jackson's death, which may not have been unusual in the context of those times. From Achilles' inconsolable grief over the slaying of his friend Pátroklos in the *Iliad* to Iraq War veterans trying to cope with the horror of seeing a fellow soldier killed by an IED, warriors have always struggled with the death of a friend in battle. It is one of war's eternal laments. Unlike Achilles, however, who openly and unashamedly grieved by wailing aloud, Byron was almost certainly compelled to internalize his grief. According to the conventions of the Edwardian era, the proper and manly thing to do was to keep a stiff upper lip and soldier on.

An interesting question is whether Byron had been asked to write the passages dealing with Jackson's death, or had volunteered to do so as a way to unburdening himself—perhaps out of a sense of duty to Jackson, or possibly even as some form of self-imposed penance. The plausibility of the latter scenario is supported by recent studies in the emerging field of moral injury sustained by soldiers in battle. Moral injury is defined as "perpetrating, failing to prevent, bearing witness to or learning about acts that transgress deeply held moral beliefs and expectations." As a combat medic and deeply religious person, Byron would have been doubly afflicted in this regard. Not only was he exposed to the same horrors of war as infantrymen caught in the throes of battle, he was also immersed in the bloody consequences of that carnage right up to the Red Cross brassard on his sleeves—as he cradled in his arms countless dying soldiers whose last experience of kind words and a tender touch were often his own. That he would later be wracked by self-doubt, guilt, and shame at his inability to do more as a medic to save their lives is entirely possible. That his deeply held religious beliefs would serve to exacerbate those feelings of regret and self-recrimination is equally probable. The corrosive effect of war may have eroded his belief in those sacred ideals, but the dimensions of Byron's soul searching will remain forever untold—he never gave expression to those issues in writing.

Nonetheless, the fact that Byron was finally able to vocalize and communalize his grief over Jackson's death with other members of the ambulance company was undoubtedly a relief for him and others. Byron's heartfelt tribute to Jackson and the other members of the ambulance company killed during the war reads as follows:

In Memoriam

These men are gone, who lived and loved as you and I. But we have found that there are worse things in life than death. We have learned too, the beauty of sacrifice, the joy of generosity, and the inspiration of well-doing.

We have seen the handiwork of God and learned of Him as we never did before. We, who have come through safely, loved these men, and so, keenly must we feel for those who loved them most. Their fight is o'er, ours just begun. We would not aspire to realize the ideals for which they died were we now one whit less than men, unafraid, yet fearing God.

On days when Byron wasn't busy working on the books or teaching classes for enlisted men in the sanitary train's night school, he was transporting seriously ill patients to the base hospital in Koblenz. It was during these trips that Byron saw the disarmament of Germany in progress. As set forth in Byron's letter to Estelle on January 11, 1919:

On the 9th, Sprague and I were lucky enough to take an ambulance to Coblenz, 45 kilometers away. The ride was wonderful—the last 35 kilometers down (or rather up) the Rhine. The weather is far from cold and there is no snow so riding is enjoyable. The scenes on the river are very beautiful. We saw two American patrol boats on the river, on the Rhine! . . . There is a Boche aviation camp here. We saw Boche planes flying overhead for the first time since the Armistice. They are being tested before being turned over to the Allies, as part of the prizes of war.

As encouraging as the sight of German disarmament must have been for Byron, he was nevertheless concerned about the lack of progress in peace negotiations. In his January 11 letter to Estelle, Byron registered some reservation in that regard:

Yes, two months ago today it was all over. The papers say the Peace Conference is to start Monday. Probably it will be held back for some time, waiting for a fixed government to be established over here. We may have to go to Berlin yet. We've lost one man who would have called for the most strict penalties from the Germans—good old Teddy. He was one man in a million who spoke what he thot', and followed in practice what he preached—one who preached preparedness long before the outfit in Washington when war broke out even seriously considered it. Egotistical—very—but mighty sincere.

The "good old Teddy" referred to by Byron was, of course, the former president of the United States, Theodore Roosevelt. The fact that Byron would identify with Roosevelt was somewhat predictable—after all, both were possessed of progressive ideals and strong opinions, and neither was shy about expressing them. That Byron would lament Roosevelt's passing was equally foreseeable—like Byron, Roosevelt had been a frequent critic of President Woodrow Wilson, finding particular fault with his war policy, which he felt was woefully inadequate, to wit: Wilson's diplomatic response to the sinking of the RMS *Lusitania* in 1915 had been too restrained; he had failed to prepare the United States militarily for its entry into the war; and his Fourteen Points proposal to end the war was idealistically misguided and practically unenforceable. With the unexpected death of Roosevelt on January 6, 1919, one of President Wilson's most vocal critics was silenced forever. That, however, did not stop Byron from continuing to express his lack of faith in President Wilson's ability to broker a peace treaty that would impose only the strictest possible penalties on Germany.

In subsequent letters home that spring, Byron described President Wilson's participation in the peace conference as a "fiasco," and even questioned the president's fitness to "perform the duties of his office." It wasn't just President Wilson's perceived deficiencies as a hard-line negotiator that concerned Byron, though. Another unsettling development was beginning to manifest itself in Europe. In a letter to his parents on January 13, 1919, Byron identified the political turmoil in Germany as another unwelcome complication in the effort to negotiate a meaningful peace treaty: "The internal political situation in Germany seems to be getting more complicated daily, rather than clarified. No matter what agreement the Allies may make as to their demands on the Central Powers, they must wait till a fixed government is settled here. I presume the people in the occupied region are better off in reality than those in the other part."

Byron's assessment of the political situation in Germany was correct. In the months leading up to the Armistice, widespread dissatisfaction over chronic food shortages, rampant unemployment, and war fatigue had been building. On October 29, this chorus of discontent had reached a crescendo when the first rallying cries of revolution were heard in Wilhelmshaven, where sailors serving in the German Navy at first refused to obey orders and then mutinied, demanding *Frieden und Brot*. Soon, cries for freedom and bread were heard in neighboring coastal cities as well. Political unrest also cropped up in Hanover, Brunswick, Frankfurt, and Munich, as disparate groups jostled for control of the political apparatus there.

In Berlin, the situation was still relatively stable despite an uncertain mixture of competing political interests. The leading party in control of the German parliament was the Social Democratic Party—a progressive though hardly revolutionary political faction. In the political vacuum that had been created by the Kaiser's sudden departure, Friedrich Ebert, a Social Democrat, assumed the helm of a provisional government. Ebert's unenviable task was to somehow steer a course between the status quo, revolution, and reform. By proposing a series of democratic half measures, Ebert hoped to accomplish this without disregarding the demands of those clamoring for change, or disenfranchising the political elite of Germany. Whether he would ultimately succeed was still very much an open question.

Elsewhere in Germany, the situation was ripe for the spread of Communism. In strike-ridden regions like Westphalia, disgruntled workers and disenchanted soldiers had established Workers and Soldiers Councils to replace local government officials. For months leftist dissidents called Spartacists had been openly advocating revolution against all forms of autocratic rule, and in December 1918, the Communist Party in Germany (KPD) was formed. Finally, on February 6, 1919, when confronted with a Communist-led rebellion in Berlin, Ebert and other members of the provisional government decided to vacate the city, relocating the seat of government to the city of Weimar, where the Weimar Republic was established.

As the long winter of political discontent in Germany turned to spring, the threat of Bolshevism continued to spread. In April, the Communist Party seized control of the newly established Free State of Bavaria, renaming it the Bavarian Soviet Republic. In an effort to prevent the red tide of Communism from staining the political fabric of the entire country, Ebert and the Social Democrats enlisted the support of the Freikorps, a loose confederation of armed citizen militias, composed mostly of disillusioned, battle-hardened soldiers. At this point, Ebert was willing to gamble that by turning the Freikorps loose on revolutionary dissidents, the threat of Communism would be quickly driven from the political landscape. The immediate outcome of the clash with dissidents was never in doubt. In the ensuing bloodbath, the leaders of the fledgling Communist movement, Rosa Luxemburg and Karl Liebknecht, were captured by Freikorps soldiers and murdered before they could be brought before a court of law. Although the threat of Bolshevism mostly shrank from public view, it did not disappear completely—as long as dire economic conditions persisted and people suffered, political dissension in Germany would continue to fester.

The long-term consequences of Ebert's rash decision to bestow a mantel of legitimacy on Freikorps reactionaries would ultimately prove to be the republic's undoing. A dangerous precedent had been set—paramilitarism had been given a role, albeit an unofficial one, in German politics. In the years that followed, marauding groups of uniformed thugs would intimidate and disrupt the fragile democratic process in Germany, eventually setting their sights on the Weimar Republic.

The complexity and potential consequences of this situation seemed to have escaped Byron's notice. His frame of reference was limited to his immediate surroundings. Byron was stationed in a relatively prosperous and peaceful section of the occupied zone, where the management of day-to-day affairs remained largely unchanged due to the presence of Allied forces there. When questioned by Estelle about the political unrest and economic despair that were plaguing the rest of Germany, Byron's narrow-minded response, stridently suspicious of the German people generally, bordered on being uncharacteristically unchristian, if not utterly vengeful. In a letter to Estelle on February 15, 1919, Byron summarily dismissed her concerns.

No, the active Bolshevik trouble is not apparent here, but the continual outcroppings in new places leads me to think that it may appear at any place any time. Oh don't think the Germans are repentant. Not in the least. All of them brag about their successes in the war and say they would have won had it not been for us. And yet so two-faced are they that they feign love for us to gain our early friendship. Do not believe anyone, I don't care who it is who says they are our friends. That is propaganda of the worst sort and you should stamp it as such, and try to keep it from spreading. The whole appeal for leniency in the States is marked in letters a mile high, "Made In Germany"; the people are not starving, they are not poorly clothed, nor are they freezing. They are lying, and the whole difficulty between various factions can be remedied within 48 hours by themselves (when the Allies fall into their trap) and sign an easy peace. But thank God, the English and Belgians aren't theorists at least. The damned ruffians who pulled the stuff they did on the children and women of our allies now coming sobbing around yelping for leniency. Justice must be the word now.

He ended on a condescending final note:

But don't you worry Estelle, it will all come out O.K. at last.

Byron's apparent willingness to condemn the German people generally, and his disdain for those like Estelle and President Wilson who seemed inclined to sympathize with the plight of the average German citizen, was a somewhat predictable reaction, considering his current state of mind. Again, as explained by Dr. Jonathan Shay in *Achilles in Vietnam—Combat Trauma and the Undoing of Character*, a common manifestation of grief in combat is rage and a desire for revenge as a means of keeping faith with the dead and affirming that there is still justice in the world. This phenomenon seems to have found expression in Byron, as evidenced by the harsh characterizations contained in some of his subsequent letters, as well as an apparent inability to appreciate or even consider the possibility that there might be mitigating factors in play that were not within his immediate purview or part of his past experience. The hard edge to Byron's most recent words and feelings represents a sudden and drastic change in character from the thoughtful and enlightened young man who had entered the war wanting to be a missionary.

Byron's sweeping response to Estelle was valid in one respect, though—an increasing number of German soldiers were beginning to perpetuate the myth that they had not actually lost the war but instead had been stabbed in the back by unpatriotic politicians and civilians at home. This fiction, known as *Dolchstoss Von Hinten*, was first articulated by General Erich Ludendorff to justify his own failure as a military commander. In the years following the war, this delusional thinking would gain popular currency as fact among restless and dissatisfied Germans, and would later be used by Adolf Hitler and the Nazi Party to great advantage in discrediting the Weimar Republic.

As to Byron's other impressions about the crisis that was enveloping Germany at that moment, he couldn't have been more mistaken. The war had in fact dealt a devastating blow to German civilians: over eight hundred thousand had died from starvation, privation, and disease, brought on in large part by Britain's naval blockade—the so-called hunger blockade—as well as the loss of manpower essential to cultivate and harvest crops as men left the land to fight in the war.

Byron was equally mistaken in his thinly veiled scorn for the "theorists," as he called them—a team of economic and international political experts assembled by President Wilson to work on plausible scenarios for bringing a just peace to Europe. As would be sadly demonstrated by the outbreak of World War II only twenty years later, the complex problems facing Europe in 1919 needed careful deliberation and a nuanced response—neither of which, to Wilson's chagrin, were given serious expression in the Paris Peace Conference or the Treaty of Versailles.

Byron's belief that the British were determined to impose a harsh peace treaty was also misinformed. Despite public statements by David Lloyd George calling for a full accounting by Germany, the British prime minister was privately concerned that the payment of unduly large war reparations by Germany would hinder the country's ability to recover economically, and thereby imperil the tenuous stability of the Weimar government. Lloyd George recognized that with Bolshevism having already gained a foothold in Austria and Bavaria, a viable Weimar Republic would be needed to keep Communism from spreading to the rest of Europe.

As usual, it did not take long for Estelle to challenge Byron on his cocksure opinion. Byron's letter of February 23 also shows that Estelle had taken exception to his condescending dismissal of her own concerns on the matter. It was a somewhat startling blunder on Byron's part. More than anyone, he should have realized that Estelle was fully capable of arriving at her own conclusions and "not given to bowing at the feet of any man," much less inclined to tolerate his newfound penchant for speaking down to her. That Byron didn't take any of that into consideration before attempting to lecture her was a sign of troubles to come. In offering a qualified apology to Estelle, Byron tried to soften the edges of his rhetoric but still refused to alter the substance of the underlying message:

> I'm mighty sorry if I had given you the impression that I had changed my mind about the Boche in any way whatever. I have been satisfied that you had not been swayed their way by their propaganda, so I had written all sorts of impressions as they came to me. I know as well as I know anything that the spirit of the Boche is not broken—that if anything, they are more bitter than ever toward us,—that every smile covers a sneer. Sometimes I feel as tho' I, with Foch, might have cried a bit that the war did not last a few months longer. We talked so long about knocking them to their knees, all we did was to knock the wind out; when it came back, they were as fresh as ever. Birdie, I don't want to or intend to start a series of talks in defense of my happening to enlist, or in criticizing those who did not. Probably, we at least agree in principle, and, as the war is over, I don't want to start another one now. Probably too, I do often criticize too quickly—Roosevelt had that trouble, and often had a little difficulty explaining himself afterwards.

Then closing the letter on a somewhat ominous note, Byron alluded to changes that both he and Estelle were experiencing:

> We've both formed mental pictures of changes we'll expect to
> find, when we meet we can see how they tally with facts.

It was somewhat predictable, then, that the next letter Estelle
received from Byron was of the Dear John variety. Although they
would soon reconcile, it seemed that Byron was becoming frustrated
at not being able to share his feelings about the war with either Estelle
or his parents without incurring the risk of criticism or disapproval.
The problem first made itself known earlier, in January, when Byron
entered an essay contest in the *Red Cross Magazine*. Each contestant
had been asked to submit a story that realistically depicted the war as
viewed from a soldier's perspective. Byron did his best to be a faithful correspondent—chronicling the war the way he saw it: the coarse
language; the humorous moments; the good, the bad, and the ugly of
it all. His colleagues in the ambulance company loved the story. His
parents, however, on reviewing a draft he had mailed home, didn't
hesitate to express their disapproval of its indelicate nature—and told
him so in no uncertain terms. It must have been a crushing rejection
by those whose opinion he valued most.

As Byron was beginning to painfully learn, war was not an experience easily shared or understood by those who had never been subjected
to its challenges. From the age of Odysseus, soldiers returning home
from war have often felt a sense of estrangement from loved ones and
the community at large. In the months to come, Byron would continue to
turn inward. In a letter to Estelle written on January 28, Byron exhibited
an uncharacteristic sense of disaffection and isolation: "Guess your New
Year's resolution is a worthy one—may you keep it. I made none at all. I
don't know why. God knows I'm living straight as I know it, tho' my views
may be too narrow on some things and too broad on others.... Except for
a few chums, we can confide in no one. You have your folks, and chums
too, and not the sense of sheer loneliness which fills us I'm sure."

Byron's sense of isolation and disconnectedness manifested itself
in other ways too. His once-frequent references to scripture and
church services, as well as his mention of the inspiration and comfort that he drew from religion had all but vanished from his diary
entries and letters home. It was during this winter of disconsolation

that Byron informed Estelle that he no longer felt the calling to do God's work as a missionary. Instead, he intended to become a history and social studies teacher.

Despite Byron's growing sense of disaffection, he soon discovered that he was not alone in his opposition to President Wilson's proposal for a just peace—by the end of June, Wilson's Fourteen Points plan had been rejected at the peace conference in Paris, point by point. Georges Clemenceau of France, David Lloyd George of Great Britain, and Vittorio Orlando of Italy saw little merit in Wilson's idealistic notions about a just peace. Instead, their demands were nationalistically simple—reparations, retribution, disarmament, and acceptance of responsibility by Germany for having started the war were all that mattered. The only provision of Wilson's plan to be adopted by the Treaty of Versailles was the establishment of the League of Nations to mediate future disputes among the nations of Europe.

Byron's fervent wish that "the Boche be brought to their knees" was in perfect accord with Clemenceau's insistence that Germany be punished harshly. Although this hard-line position would later be criticized as unnecessarily vindictive and shortsighted, it was understandable given what Clemenceau, Byron, and others who had been exposed to the ravages of the war had witnessed firsthand. In addition to the unavoidable collateral damage that was the normal by-product of war, many of the cities and villages of France had been deliberately and callously destroyed by the German Army in the course of its retreat. It was part of a scorched-earth policy code-named Operation Alberich in which the German Army sought to make the land as uninhabitable as possible for advancing Allied troops. Perhaps the best description of this wanton destruction was written by one of its perpetrators, German Sturmtruppen Lieutenant Ernst Jünger. In his memoir, *The Storm of Steel*, Jünger recounts the destruction inflicted on French villages by German troops during their retreat from the Somme in March 1917:

> From right to left, the sectors were to be under the command of Lieutenants Reinhardt, Fischer, Lorek and myself. The villages we passed through on our way had the look of vast lunatic asylums.

Whole companies were set to pulling down walls, or sitting on rooftops, uprooting the tiles. Trees were cut down, windows smashed; wherever you looked, clouds of smoke and dust rose from piles of debris. We saw men dashing about wearing suits and dresses left behind by the inhabitants, with top hats on their heads. With destructive cunning, they found the roof-trees of the houses, fixed ropes to them, and with concerted shouts, pulled till they all came tumbling down. Others were swinging pile-driving hammers, and went around smashing everything in their way, from the flowerpots on the window-sills to whole ornate conservatories. As far back as the Siegfried Line, every village was reduced to rubble, every tree chopped down, every road undermined, every well poisoned, every basement blown up or booby-trapped, every rail unscrewed, every telephone wire rolled up, everything burnable burned; in a word, we were turning the country that our advancing opponents would occupy into a wasteland.

After bearing witness to such abject depravity, it was no doubt difficult for Clemenceau, Byron, and others to keep an objective and open mind in trying to implement a fair peace treaty with Germany. Vast expanses of northeastern France had been utterly defiled. Entire villages had been obliterated. Over 250,000 homes were destroyed. Another 500,000 were severely damaged, displacing countless civilians. Food was in short supply—vast stores of crops and livestock had been either destroyed or consumed by German troops. The infrastructure of the region had been gutted, machinery appropriated, and factories razed. Which was exactly the reason President Wilson, on first arriving in France, had refused to tour the killing fields and scenes of destruction wrought by the war. Wilson believed that a dispassionate perspective would be needed to see past the eye for an eye mentality that had all too often blinded the diplomats who were charged with drafting peace treaties. Unfortunately, no other Allies shared Wilson's vision.

The Paris Peace Conference began on January 18, 1919. Delegates from twenty-six countries were invited to participate in negotiations. The Central Powers, however, were excluded from attending. In late April, Germany was finally summoned to the conference and presented with a draft of the proposed peace treaty. The German delegation was dismayed to discover that it scarcely resembled President Woodrow Wilson's Fourteen Points plan as originally proposed in his speech to Congress in January 1918. German reaction to the treaty as drafted was predictable—they found everything about it objectionable—in particular Article 231 or, as it became more widely known, "the War Guilt Clause." The clause was the first paragraph in the "Reparations" section of the treaty, written as a prefatory statement necessary to establish the legal prerequisite of liability, from which financial reparations to the Allies would then flow. Ironically, it was President Wilson's delegates to the peace conference, John Foster Dulles and Norman Davis, who were responsible for drafting what turned out to be the most controversial clause in the treaty. In its entirety, Article 231 reads: "The Allied and Associated Governments affirm that Germany accepts the responsibility of Germany and her allies for causing all the loss and damage to which the Allied and Associated Governments and their nationals have been subjected as a consequence of the war imposed on them by the aggression of Germany and her allies."

On May 5, members of the German delegation were informed that there would be no negotiation over the terms of the treaty, and on May 7 they were further told that they had only fifteen days in which to reply. They responded by finding fault with numerous clauses in a treaty they viewed as being *Diktat*. A brief impasse ensued, after which an ultimatum was issued on June 16—stating in no uncertain terms that if Germany did not sign the treaty within seven days, hostilities would be resumed. In response to the ultimatum, the newly elected president of the Weimar Republic, Philipp Scheidemann, and his entire cabinet resigned rather than sign the treaty. In their place, a new coalition government was hastily assembled, and after being advised by Field Marshal Paul Hindenburg that the German Army was in no position to resume the war, the National Assembly voted to ratify the treaty. On June 28, German foreign minister Hermann Müller and colonial minister Johannes Bell were dispatched to Versailles to sign the treaty.

In its final form, the Treaty of Versailles satisfied no one: the Germans viewed it as undeservedly harsh and begrudged the fact that they had been forced to sign a document that was the creation of a peace conference from which they had been all but excluded; the French were indignant that the treaty was too lenient and resented the fact that Germany had not been completely neutralized by turning the Rhineland into an independent state instead of just a demilitarized zone; in England, Lloyd George and other officials privately remarked that the treaty was neither just nor wise, but they were more concerned with not losing face with a citizenry that they had whipped into a propaganda-induced anti-German frenzy, so after agreeing to some reparations and ensuring that the German Navy had been dismantled, England was anxious to move on as quickly as possible—after all, it had a colonial empire to run; President Wilson returned to the United States discouraged, empty-handed, and confronted by opponents in Congress who had no intention of ratifying the treaty or signing on as a member of the League of Nations.

In the history of the world, there had certainly been worse treatment accorded to the vanquished. The Treaty of Versailles was not so draconian as to require that German soil be tilled with salt, as some French ideologues might have preferred. In the final telling, though, the treaty was as much a failure of process as it was of substance. By essentially excluding Germany from participating in the peace process, the Allies had succeeded only in sowing the seeds of resentment and discontent that would later ripen into the poisonous fruit so insidiously cultivated by Adolf Hitler in his garden of horrors. To what extent the shortcomings of the Treaty of Versailles were responsible for the emergence of the Nazi Party in Germany is still the subject of much debate. That the League of Nations would prove an abject failure, however, in preventing another world war was a factual tragedy in the making from the very moment that the treaty was signed.

In the spring of 1919, though, the specter of another bloodbath in Europe was unforeseen by most. Especially Byron. At that moment, his focus was on more immediate concerns. He had an odyssey of his own to finish.

EPILOGUE

The Journey Home

In some respects, Byron's odyssey after the war was an ordeal more arduous than the war itself. But no soldier's story is complete without recounting what happened when the conflict was over.

On April 9, 1919, the Rainbow Division was relieved of its duties in the Rhine River valley. One week later, members of the Michigan Ambulance Company set sail for the United States on the USS *Leviathan*. Byron was not among those on board. His journey home would take another route.

On March 1, 1919, the U.S. Army had selected Byron to further his education in Europe. Based on his intellect and exemplary record of service during the war, Byron was one of only two thousand soldiers in the American Expeditionary Force who were being accorded the honor. As noted by Byron, it was an emotional parting of the ways:

> For the next two days, I was very busy, here and there, getting my things ready, leaving word about a hundred and one things with different fellows, and having some last talks. It was not all pleasant—the thot' of leaving the fellows, many of whom I had learned to love, almost as brothers, during my over a year and a half with them. I had been through Hell with a lot of 'em and knew the fine stuff inside of them, tho' sometimes the outside was coated over with an appearance which almost hid their true selves.

For the next four months, Byron was enrolled at the University of Edinburgh in Scotland. He found his semester there as intellectually challenging as it was culturally enlightening. Not to mention romantically diverting. After all, spring was in the air, and it doesn't take much to turn the head of a young soldier returning from war—like countless warriors before him, Byron soon succumbed to the timeless call of the siren's song. It was a chance encounter. In the course of paying his respects to the family of his fallen comrade Herbert Jackson (an Englishman), Byron became smitten with Jackson's niece, Jessie Griffiths. The ensuing affair played out like a PG-rated production of the trials of Odysseus on the isle of Calypso. Byron fell hard. Not because of any bewitchment on Jessie's part; she was more a victim of Byron's amorous intentions than a beguiling temptress. The song of longing was in Byron's head. After sending a Dear John letter to Estelle, Byron pursued an all-out courtship of Jessie, spending weekends in his own "Garden of Eden, Birmingham." Before Byron could consummate the affair, however, his parents got wind of his letter to Estelle, and they, like the omniscient gods Zeus and Athena, reached out from afar to break the spell and summon him home.

Byron (*back row, second from left*) as a student at the University of Edinburgh, March 1919. (Photograph by Army Signal Corps.)

On July 19, Byron finally set foot back in the United States. After returning to Jackson and reuniting with his parents, Byron became a local celebrity of sorts, often asked to offer his opinion on the war. It didn't take long for these requests to become tedious and for his rancor to surface. In an interview published in the *Jackson Patriot News* on August 5, 1919, Byron was especially scornful of the German people, anti-English dissidents in Ireland, and the Treaty of Versailles. The intolerant tone of Byron's statements made them border on imperious dicta. He seemed now a far cry from the thoughtful young man who had left Jackson only two years before. The harsh edge to Byron's words and thoughts was not an uncommon phenomenon among returning war veterans. As noted by Willard Waller, a World War I veteran and Columbia University professor, in his book *The Veteran Comes Back*: "There is a core of anger in the soul of almost every veteran, and we are justified in calling it bitterness, but bitterness in one man is not the same thing as the bitterness of another. In one man it becomes a consuming flame that sears his soul and burns his body. In another it is barely traceable. It leads one man to outbursts of temper, another to social radicalism, a third to excesses of conservatism."

In Byron, that simmering sense of dissatisfaction seems to have bubbled to the surface in an outpouring of conservative thinking. There is no written record of his day-to-day interaction with Estelle after returning to Jackson, but given her liberal nature and his new-found conservatism, it is unlikely they saw eye to eye on social and political issues. What is known for certain is that in September 1919, both Byron and Estelle were enrolled as students at the University of Michigan, and it was there that their paths began to diverge. Both would forsake their youthful dream of becoming missionaries—Byron devoting himself instead to the study of political science and history, earning a master's degree in 1922. Estelle, as always, continued to follow her heart—majoring in liberal and performing arts, she also graduated with a master's degree in 1922.

Although Byron's relationship with Estelle had turned into a platonic one, he did eventually find true love. During a Methodist church service at the University of Michigan Byron met another beautiful, strong-willed woman, Helen Jeanette Hulst. On June 22, 1922, the couple was married. Even in the midst of newfound love, though, vestiges of the war continued to roil Byron's world. In this he was not alone. From the time of Odysseus, recently returned veterans have often found themselves the objects of an almost ghoulish public fascination with the challenges of combat. Considering that Byron had never spoken to his parents, Estelle, or Helen about the intimate details of war, he was not about to share his innermost feelings with complete strangers. Still, that did not stop some from inquiring, which caused him to issue fair warning. In an essay titled "Why Won't He Talk about Himself?" written in September 1919 under the nom de guerre Homer Fiske, which Byron would use only for war-related matters, Byron attempted to explain the reticence of most veterans to discuss the war.

> You've noticed haven't you, with growing wonderment, how almost every returned soldier, no matter who, has been mighty reluctant about telling what he did in the Great War, if it was at all hazardous? Isn't it so? Why? You met him, and the first thing that struck you as a good thing to say was "Aren't you glad to be back?" Rather unnecessary question wasn't it? But of course he brightened up, more or less. More if he was just back. And less if back a little longer and a bit bored at the question, he said, "Yes." Then you wandered on in your questioning and started speaking of the awful things he must have seen and endured. Just then he changed the subject. Why? . . . These same fellows who won't talk have said, in a joking way, "If I ever have a boy and he steps off with his left foot, I'll lick him," and, "If there is another war they will have to send for me with a gun," or "One war is all I shall fight." And yet, I'll venture to say, as one who was a member of one of the earliest, hard-fighting, cursingest, crabbiest outfits that came home with three stripes and five stars and only a third of its original roster, that if there were another war today there would be more enlistments in less time than there were for this one. Does that indicate that men like the Army? Ma foi, no! It simply means that there has been instilled in the average American's heart and mind a willingness to suffer from wounds of the flesh, and those worse wounds—those of the

mind from the heartless autocracy of the American Army—in order to see the logical course of right and justice speeded on its way. The ex-soldier does not want to remember the hardships, the fault-finding, the living-dying tearing of the flesh and heart. He does not want to talk about it because it has struck too deep into his soul and mind for any proper expression.

... The average American hates war, hates military machinery, hates killing, hates to be too much the brute. So, he doesn't speak of it. He is not a savage to delight in the mere recital of exploits, neither is he a dramatist to take those scenes to play upon the hearts of his listeners. He is just Jack, or Bill, or Fred, a bit older than before, a bit wilder, yet a bit more prudent, but most of all, he's modest about it. Isn't that what pleases us most?

Homer Fiske

Today, Byron's observations about the reluctance of war veterans to talk about their experiences in combat would be viewed as a well-worn but socially acceptable refrain. In the historical context in which it was written, however, the essay expressed an extraordinary position for a twenty-two-year-old college student to take—in 1919, one simply didn't acknowledge feelings of that sort, much less voice them in public. In the intervening one hundred years, much has happened to raise public awareness of the post-traumatic stress that many veterans struggle with on returning home. In the immediate aftermath of the Great War, however, for an ex-soldier to write about his reluctance to talk about the war ran the risk of being misconstrued—not only as unappreciative of a supportive and naturally curious public but, worse yet, as unpatriotic.

Other writers who had served in the Great War gave expression to similar feelings of resentment at being the object of unwanted curiosity. Most notable among them were Germany's Erich Maria Remarque in his sequel to *All Quiet on the Western Front*, titled *The Road Back*; and Britain's Robert Graves in his postwar classic, *Goodbye to All That*. But Byron's expression of dissatisfaction predated those works by several years, bearing witness to his willingness to speak his mind regardless of popular sentiment or consequence. It appears that Byron's essay was never published. The reasons are unknown—perhaps editors simply deemed it too outspoken for a country still enthusiastic about its role in the war.

On graduating from the University of Michigan, Byron and Helen took up residence in Culver, Indiana, home to Culver Military Academy (CMA), where Byron had been offered a job as a history teacher. The curriculum at CMA was standard prep-school fare. The regimen, however, was exceptional—modeled after West Point right down to the polished brass tunic buttons and spit-shined black leather shoes. In addition to scholastic classes, courses in basic military training were woven into the fabric of academy life. In order for Byron to join the ranks of the faculty, he was required to enlist as a lieutenant in the Officers' Reserve Corps. At first blush, Byron's attraction to such a regimented environment appears inconsistent with his professed desire to leave the unpleasantness of the war and the autocracy of the army in the past. On further reflection, however, in all likelihood he would have viewed the move as professionally and personally advantageous—not only was he being afforded an opportunity to embark on a teaching career at a prestigious school, the position also gave him a foothold on familiar ground in a postwar world that was rapidly changing. For better or worse, CMA represented a sanctuary of sorts. Byron's trunk contained graphic proof of this—etchings depicting the fortress-like ivy-covered halls of the academy, and a mission statement from CMA, "In Step with the Future." In its entirety, the statement reads as follows:

> Out of the ferment of the ages have come vast economic and social changes that must be met by a new type of citizen.
>
> In India a half-starved, half-clad Hindu, the antithesis in viewpoint of present economic ideas, by the influence of an ideal and the reactions of a strange magnetic personality on three hundred millions of people is making a great empire tremble.
>
> In Russia is the iron man's ruthless attempt to transform a society of a hundred and sixty millions by force.

Within the decade our own country has been precipitated into economic and social situations such as it has never had to face before.

The schools of the nation have the greatest challenge and the greatest responsibility they have ever known in the training of tomorrow's citizens. Culver has the vision and the traditions of discipline and service to send out through the sallyport of the School into life, young men trained in the fundamentals that make a nation safe.

It is a patriotic privilege to send Culver boys who will profit most by such training.

The fact that Byron retained among his most cherished belongings a document proclaiming that it was CMA's patriotic duty to prepare a new generation of young men to defend the United States against a host of perceived threats (the foremost of which was apparently Mahatma Gandhi), speaks volumes about the philosophical sea change Byron had undergone. After all, ridding the world of tyranny and oppression was one of the reasons Byron had often given for enlisting. Now, it seemed he subscribed to a viewpoint that the world was such an inherently dangerous place that he was willing to overlook the oppressive colonial policies of a nation like Great Britain in order to defend the American way of life against the supposedly more insidious threat posed by a populist movement for equality and self-determination led by a "half-clad" pacifist half a world away.

What caused this drastic change in Byron's philosophical and political beliefs? It is certainly possible that his prior battle cries of liberty-and-justice-for-all were nothing more than the liberal exhortations of youth, and that his true conservative nature had finally come to the surface after being put to the test by the grim reality of war. On the other hand, it seems far more likely that the corrosive effect of the war had acted as a catalyst in bringing about a fundamental and lasting change in Byron's character. Indeed, the perception that the world is an ever-dangerous place and that there is a compelling need to find a safe haven within it is not an uncommon phenomenon among veterans suffering from war trauma. According to Dr. Jonathan

Shay, an expert in treating PTSD in war veterans, a common reaction on returning home is to stay in combat mode mentally in order to defend against a host of perceived threats. In Byron's postwar battles, it appears that his weapon of choice was his considerable skills as an advocate—for it was at CMA that Byron would create some of his most pointed writing.

Byron's first shot out of the cannon was a small but effective missive, dated January 23, 1923, to Harold De Wolf Fuller, editor of the *Independent*, a weekly magazine published in New York City.

> Dear Mr. Fuller:
>
> Nothing has more heartened me in this day of commercialized sentimentalism than the well-advised veto of the Bursum Pension Bill by President Harding. Your editorial comment in the current (20 January) issue of the INDEPENDENT is exceptionally worthwhile.
>
> As you remark, the path of government is now plain, to handsomely care for, and rehabilitate the disabled. For others, their solemn duty, now—as in 1917–18—is to bear their responsibilities in life, without thought of a mercenary reward for services rendered in the most solemn hour of a nation's life.
>
> For the able-bodied ex-soldier to plead now for either a pension or a stipend is as un-American, in the true sense of the word, as it would have been in 1917–18 to demand a promise of such reward before offering himself for service.
>
> Yours very truly,
>
> Byron F. Field, Lt., C.M.A.

De Wolf Fuller responded immediately in a letter dated January 30, requesting permission to publish Byron's letter. In order to fully appreciate the significance of Byron's letter in support of De Wolf Fuller's editorial comment opposing the Bursum pension bill, it is first necessary to understand the economic, social, and political context in which all three documents were written. The so-called Bursum pension bill was introduced in 1921 and finally enacted into law in 1924 as the World War Adjusted Compensation Act. The three-year contro-versy surrounding the passage of the bill was a tortuous affair that was hardly unique to this war—history is replete with stories of soldiers being sent into harm's way with little or no regard for their fate on safe return.

After this latest war, it was especially difficult for returning Amer-ican soldiers to find gainful employment. In an economy struggling to retool from wartime production to domestic consumption, employ-ment opportunities for veterans were few. After a brief recession, just when it seemed that the job market might improve, the economy was beset by an eighteen-month depression that lasted until July 1921. Under such prolonged and dire circumstances, the $60 severance pay that had been given to soldiers on discharge from the army was exhausted long before most veterans could come close to landing a job. Unlike Byron, who had been comfortably ensconced at the Univer-sity of Michigan, and then CMA, less fortunate veterans were worried about where their next meal would come from. In 1923, when Byron wrote his letter to the *Independent*, this was a grave concern—many of the public welfare programs we take for granted today, like food stamps and unemployment assistance, did not exist at the time. For many unemployed veterans, the only line of assistance available was the one that led to the soup kitchen door.

In an attempt to obtain some measure of relief for veterans, two prior iterations of the Bursum pension bill had been put forth for legis-lative consideration. Both failed, one by presidential veto. By the early spring of 1924, it had become clear that President Calvin Coolidge (a fiscal conservative who had succeeded Harding) was prepared to veto any legislation that called for immediate cash payments to ex-soldiers. Because there was little likelihood that the Senate would override his veto, a compromise bill was drafted that proposed awarding cash pay-ments to veterans, but with an all-important proviso—payment would come due only after a twenty-year period had expired, much like an insurance policy. Coolidge was unmoved by the legislation and vetoed the bill. Congress promptly overrode his veto, and on May 19, 1924, the World War Adjusted Compensation Act became law. In accordance with its provisions, veterans were issued pieces of paper called Bonus

Certificates that would be redeemable in 1945—until that time, struggling ex-soldiers would have to get by any way they could.

In France, ex-*soldats* felt that they too had been abandoned by their government. After their repeated pleas for additional aid had fallen on deaf ears, the men decided to take matters into their own hands. On Armistice Day, November 11, 1924, a procession of disabled war veterans upstaged official ceremonies in Paris by marching down the Champs-Élysées to the Chamber of Deputies, where they presented their petition for increased pension benefits to Premier Édouard Herriot. The assembled human wreckage was truly breathtaking—teary-eyed bystanders looked on in silence.

The symbolic significance of the march was not lost on Byron. Twelve days later, he made it the focal point of an address to an after-church audience of reverent listeners at the Methodist Church in Plymouth, Indiana. Titled "Six Years After the Armistice," Byron's speech began:

> Nine Hundred ten years ago, one of the Basilian Emperors at the height of the Byzantine Empire, after a victory over his Bulgar enemies, put out the eyes of his captives and sent them staring, stumbling down the Rhodope Mountains back into their home valleys. Even the most barbaric contemporaries were filled with horror as they heard of the vindictive fate visited upon these defeated Bulgars by the implacable Basil. The captives numbered 15,000 in all, and were divided into hundreds, each hundred being put under the leadership of one of their number who had been spared one eye in order that he might find the way for his companions and guide them to homes they would never see again. The czar of the Bulgars, who, with his people, was on the walls of the capital to welcome the returning warriors, was stricken unconscious by the very sight of them and died from the effects.
>
> On Armistice Day this year, fifteen thousand of her warriors, victors not captives, marched through the Champs Elysees, under the Arch of Triumph. It was the most ghastly procession of marching soldiers which had been seen since the days of Basil. Yet, this was not an exhibition of the vindictiveness of a savage

monarch; it was the normal result of modern warfare. To be sure some agencies were used that were condemned—poison gas, for example, and bombs that killed innocent people far from the scene of conflict. But the spectacle of these victors was scarcely less pitiable than that of those vanquished from their last battle in the Rhodope Mountains.

Not all of the 15,000 who marched under the Arch of Triumph on Armistice Day had lost their eyes; some were without legs, some without arms, some with faces that even their dearest friends could not look upon without revulsion. An on-looker spoke of the blinded, "who marched hand-locked, unseeing, at the head of the procession, past hordes of silent bare-headed spectators." This visible procession that made its halting way, led by the blind, was but the smallest fraction of those who have suffered in like manner in France and throughout the world, not to speak of the millions who gave their all and never came home at all to the living. It is such a sight as this that makes it possible to see in another great war, to use Secretary Hoover's Armistice Day phrase, "the cemetery of civilization."

Today we are six years removed from the end of the war, ten years and more from its beginning. We can now, in the quiet of a Sunday morning, in a peaceful Indiana village, dispassionately and earnestly consider the underlying element that made the last war inevitable, as it had made hundreds of others inescapable—the war mind of the world.

After eloquently setting the stage for his listeners, Byron did not make an impassioned plea for more and better services for disabled war veterans. Instead he focused on the root cause of such misery— "the pre-dominance of war-as-the-ultimate-in-case-of-international-disagreement" mindset of man—and the need to replace "the war-idea" with a system of negotiation and arbitration as the world's first line of defense against future hostilities. It was a concept of national defense given short shrift by most, and one that undoubtedly put him at odds with many of his cohorts at CMA—in 1924, the legacy of Teddy Roosevelt's "big stick diplomacy" still held powerful sway with most Americans, especially the military. Considering Byron's Christian upbringing, however, it was a proposition in which he had the utmost faith—reliance on methods of reconciliation to resolve disputes was a cornerstone of the Methodist Social Creed that he had been schooled in at Albion College. Being able to explain the applicability of those principles in the context of a detailed discussion of war and international affairs to an audience of churchgoers was a tall order. As reported the following day in the *Plymouth Daily Democrat*, Byron was equal to the task, skillfully explaining his position by recounting the nationalistically driven economic and political factors that had contributed to the outbreak of hostilities in 1914. Then, changing his pitch, Byron continued to preach to the choir of Methodist faithful by singing the praises of the League of Nations. This change of heart was somewhat startling coming from a man who only five years earlier had been utterly scornful of President Wilson's proposal for the League—especially in light of the fact that at that particular moment, the United States was still adamantly opposed to becoming a member of the organization. Ultimately, Byron would be disappointed by his country's inability to rise above its own self-interest and abandon its policy of isolationism—the United States would never join the League of Nations.

In all likelihood Byron's superiors at CMA were equally disappointed in him. The fact that a lowly lieutenant from their institution had given a public speech that called into question the country's official position on international affairs could not have escaped their notice—the speech was published in large part verbatim in the *Plymouth Daily Democrat*, barely a stone's throw from Culver. As it turned out, Byron didn't just break ranks with the established diplomatic wisdom of his country that day—while he was at it, he broke faith with his religion as well, taking exception to the newly drafted position of a subcommittee of the General Conference of the Methodist Church on war—"that we should never fight, no matter the cause." Having just experienced the horrors of war firsthand, Byron was no doubt sympathetic to that heartfelt sentiment. Yet, as he pointed out to his listeners, it was a position that unrealistically "presupposes that a near Utopia has been reached in which none but justiciable causes will occur to mar the relations of men." After suggesting to his audience that the use of force should always be reserved as a regrettable but at times unavoidable option of last resort, Byron closed his remarks with a biblical flourish that was reminiscent of his more sanguine days. "Let us strive to hasten the day when 'the mountain of the Lord's house shall be established in the top of the mountains, and shall be exalted above the hills; and all nations shall flow unto it. And he shall judge among the nations, and shall rebuke many people; and they shall beat their swords into plow-shares, and their spears into pruninghooks; nation shall not lift up sword against nation, neither shall they learn war any more.'"

It now seemed that much of the bitterness that had infected Byron's soul on first returning from war was beginning to dissipate as he focused on more life-affirming matters, like his lovely wife Helen and their newborn son, Byron Fiske Field Jr. Perhaps the most telling expression of Byron's newfound contentment is contained in a Homeric paean written during his days at CMA. Titled "I Have a Rendezvous with Life," Byron's verse was essentially a postlude to Alan Seeger's well-known soldier's poem, "I Have a Rendezvous with Death." In its entirety, Byron's verse reads:

> *"I have a rendezvous with death,"*
> *We said, long years ago,*
> *And thought that every hour we spent*
> *Was loaned us from eternity.*
> *But death came not, somehow,*
> *No matter how we courted her.*
> *"Peace" came instead—and hours*
> *To live and move and love.*
> *I have a rendezvous with life,*
> *A tryst with living things—not dead.*
> *To breathe spring's fragrance,*
> *Bask in summer's sun,*
> *Glory in autumn's radiance,*
> *And revel in winter's snow.*
> *So come life,—gay, stern, changing as the seasons*
> *I'll meet thee as thou art—and glad.*

The fact that Byron was fully prepared to embrace life on whatever terms came his way was a hopeful sign that for the moment, at least, he had been able to leave the turmoil of war in the past.

By 1927, the Roaring Twenties were in full swing—a recent wave of economic prosperity had washed away the postwar blues. Business was back. Jobs were plenty. With a wife and son to support on the respectable but modest salary of a prep-school teacher, Byron decided that it was time to venture beyond the confines of CMA and stake his claim to a more lucrative job in the fast-paced but uncertain world of business. On February 27 that opportunity presented itself when Byron received a telegram from the Midwest public utility giant Commonwealth Edison of Chicago enthusiastically offering him a position in which "the possibilities are what you make them."

Byron's first position at Commonwealth Edison was as the superintendent of training, which was perfectly suited to his skills as a teacher. As the director of training, his achievements did not go

Lieutenant Byron F. Field in uniform, Culver Military Academy, November 1922.

unnoticed—the company newspaper, the *Edison Round Table*, often highlighted his accomplishments. In the civic arena, Byron exemplified the finest ideals of corporate responsibility to the community at large, serving as a member of the board of trustees of his hometown village, Hinsdale, Illinois.

While employed at Commonwealth Edison, Byron continued to serve his country as well. Found among Byron's personal belongings was a document signed by the adjutant general of the U.S. Army on August 6, 1930, appointing him first lieutenant in the Officers' Reserve Corps. Oddly, this appointment did not seek to take advantage of Byron's prior training and experience in the sanitary train—instead he was assigned to military intelligence. Although Byron had absolutely no prior experience in intelligence gathering or analysis, he did possess a skill set that would have been of great interest to the army—he was ideally situated to monitor the latest perceived threat to the security of the country: the suspected infiltration of the American workforce by Communist agitators. The fact that Byron shared these suspicions is reflected in a letter in which he equated unionism with Socialism or, worse yet, Communism. It was a commonly held viewpoint at the time. In the aftermath of the Bolshevik revolution in Russia and the political turmoil that had afflicted much of Germany in the 1920s, the democracies of the Western world were deeply concerned about the spread of Communism and other forms of subversive activity. The United States was not immune from those feelings of dread—many viewed the nascent labor movement as an incubator for the foment of political dysfunction. The record is silent as to what specific function Byron performed in his role as a reserve officer assigned to military intelligence or what, if any, information he was able to garner in that capacity.

What is clear from the record is that during his tenure at Commonwealth Edison, Byron succeeded in establishing himself in the upper echelons of the Chicago business world. For years to come, it was a reputation that would serve him well. By 1929, Byron had been elected vice president of the influential Chicago Junior Chamber of Commerce. Two years later he became the association's president. His duties often required him to preside over formal dinners, business meetings, and various symposiums. According to his wife Helen, it was in the high-octane social milieu of the Chicago business world that Byron began to drink, although not to excess at first. It is impossible to determine now with any degree of certainty what specific impulses caused Byron to begin drinking after thirty-seven years of complete temperance—any written or oral history on the matter disappeared long ago. Still, there remains some evidence from which reasonable inferences can be drawn.

First, it is reasonable to assume that Byron's sudden embrace of alcohol was not the direct result of any psychological trauma he may have sustained during the war, although it is certainly possible, and indeed probable, that latent traumatization from the war might later manifest itself as a contributing factor in Byron's recurring struggles with alcohol. But after returning from France, Byron remained a tee-totaler for fifteen years, during which time he was able to lead a pro-fessionally productive and personally rewarding life. Up to this point, there is not even the faintest hint of alcohol-related problems found in any documentation. To the contrary, as later related by his wife Helen in a journal that she compiled in 1980, these were good years.

During the war, Byron had made the principled choice not to drink with fellow soldiers and superior officers—a decision that he believed (as he wrote in letters to Estelle and his parents) contributed to his being passed over for promotion. Now it appears that, Method-ist strictures notwithstanding, Byron did not intend to forgo oppor-tunities for advancement in the ranks of the corporate world, where spirituous collegiality could often be as important as professional competence in closing a business deal or forging an important per-sonal connection. Again according to Helen, Byron was well liked at Commonwealth Edison, and as a talented and personable employee, his star continued to rise.

On November 1, 1932, he was elevated to the position of assis-tant director of labor relations. This was not an insignificant develop-ment. In the world of corporate America, the emerging field of labor relations was uncharted territory. From time immemorial, it seemed, the prerogative of management to deal with labor issues in the work-place as it saw fit was as absolute as the divine right of kings. With the

DISCUSS ACTIVITIES OF JUNIORS

Durward Howes (left), president of the United States Junior Association of Commerce, who plans to attend the United States Chamber of Commerce meeting at Washington, D. C., April 28, talks over plans for the annual convention which is to take place June 10 to 13 in Des Moines, Iowa, with Byron F. Field, president of the Junior Association of Commerce of Chicago. They met at luncheon in the Old Town Club at the Hotel Sherman on Saturday to outline plans for the future events. [By a staff photographer.]

Byron (*right*) as president of the Junior Chamber of Commerce, Chicago, April 27, 1931.

impending election of Franklin Delano Roosevelt and his promise of a New Deal, all that was about to change. Apparently, the old guard at Commonwealth Edison recognized that a bright young executive would be needed to cope with the demands, as yet unknown, that would flow from this change. In this new position, it would be Byron's job to steer the course of least disruption to the company. To better enable him to do so, in February 1933, Commonwealth Edison decided to give labor relations a larger voice in the formulation of corporate policy, appointing Byron to serve on the company's Advisory Committee. In September, the company followed up Byron's recent promotion by sending him to a national conference on labor relations held in Princeton, New Jersey. Labor relations managers from seventy-four other companies were in attendance, along with college professors and staff members from the Department of Labor—all attempting to discern the mandates of Roosevelt's New Deal legislation. For most of the managers at the conference, the curriculum represented culture shock. Unionization was largely an unknown commodity in American industry. As Byron would later remark in a letter to Professor J. Douglas Brown, director of the Industrial Relations Section at Princeton University, "[A]lmost all the men present, represented a company having almost no union contacts or union problems." After returning from the conference at Princeton, Byron found that his recently acquired expertise was in great demand. On November 13, he was the featured speaker at a meeting of the Industrial Relations Association of Chicago, was tasked with explaining the challenges presented by unionization in the workplace to other executives as well as the requirements of the newly enacted National Industrial Recovery Act (NIRA). As dictated by the new law, implementation of fair-trade codes on businesses was intended to raise wages, create more jobs, and stimulate the economy. From the outset, however, big business hated the act and immediately sought to challenge it in court.

On November 22 and 23, Byron was sent to yet another conference, where he and other labor relations managers discussed the new and perplexing problems of collective bargaining and employee representation in the workplace. On returning from that conference, Byron was again listed as the featured speaker on labor relations issues, this time at a meeting of the National Vocational Guidance Association. By now, Byron's expertise on labor relations and his eloquence as a speaker were apparent to all. In the fall of 1933, he was elected vice president of the Industrial Relations Association of Chicago, becoming president the following year. Byron's reputation as an expert in labor relations was not limited to the Midwest; personnel managers from across the nation often sought his advice, which made for busy times.

There was no limit to the number of new proposals that old-school business managers found threatening—even something as innocuous as the establishment of an employee credit union was viewed with great suspicion. As is apparent from a letter Byron wrote to the manager of personnel at the Philadelphia Gas Works encouraging him to approve the establishment of an employee credit union at the company, Byron's philosophy on workers' rights was more enlightened than that of most labor relations managers at the time. This fact was further underscored in a letter to Professor Brown of Princeton University recounting the various strategies employed by business owners to thwart implementation of the NIRA. Byron's letter reads in part:

> (b)   Many, as in the early N.R.A. days—deluged us with questions as to how or to what extent they could avoid or evade making good on the agreements.
> (c)   Others—an unfortunate goodly number—did not communicate either with the union or with us and flaunted the terms of the agreements, "taking their chances" on the day when the union would uncover their "negligence" and call for an accounting. Naturally, we have had multitudinous troubles with classes "b" and "c." . . .

I recall an A.M.A. Personnel Management Meeting in 1932 in which I was made to feel very uncomfortable following some remarks of mine. I arose to say that "regardless of who pays my salary check I feel that I will earn that check best by trying truly to represent the feelings and aspiration of the employees to the management, rather than chiefly trying to 'sell' the employees on what the management thinks is best for them."

No doubt Byron's philosophy on labor relations was received by most of his conservative corporate brethren as heresy. Nevertheless, it was a forward-looking policy—in years to come, good-faith efforts by both management and unions to mediate and arbitrate workplace issues were destined to become the bedrock of labor relations practices.

On October 19, 1934, Byron sought to put that philosophy up for consideration at the Midwest Conference on Industrial Relations held at the University of Chicago. For its time, the conference was cutting-edge stuff—to quote Byron's opening remarks as the presiding chairman, it was "an experiment." Professors from both the Chicago and Wisconsin schools of economic theory were in attendance, as well as labor relations experts, government officials, and industry executives from across the Midwest. By giving equal consideration to all points of view, Byron and others hoped to find middle ground. The conference had only limited success in achieving its lofty goals. With both sides of the labor relations divide still firmly entrenched, middle ground remained a no-man's-land. Contentious and often bloody labor disputes would continue to occur at factories and manufacturing plants in the Midwest and across the country. Still, it was during this period of great contention that Byron succeeded in establishing himself as an informed voice whose enlightened counsel was much valued in the upper echelons of the business world. Unfortunately, his exalted status did not last—and its undoing was entirely of his own making.

On January 8, 1935, the business section of the *Chicago Daily News* contained the following notice: "Byron F. Field, until recently assistant manager of industrial relations for Commonwealth Edison Company, has resigned to go to New York as industrial relations counsel for the realty advisory board on labor relations of that city. Mr. Field is president of the Labor Relations Association of Chicago and in 1931 was president of the Junior Association of Commerce of Chicago."

The two-sentence announcement was particularly noteworthy for what it did not say. For someone as accomplished and well known as Byron in the inner circles of the Chicago business world, this bare bones statement read more like a death notice than a fond farewell to a colleague who was moving on to greener pastures. And for good reason—according to his wife Helen, Byron had been fired from Commonwealth Edison for drinking on the job. What specific incident or series of events led to his precipitous departure is unknown. As later related by Helen, when Byron began to drink at work, he had the impolitic habit of challenging supervisors he disagreed with in front of subordinate employees. It was a pattern of self-destructive behavior that would continue to plague Byron throughout his business career. As noted in Helen's journal, "From the time Byron lost his job in Chicago, all through the years—it was because of his drinking on the job."

In attempting to discern what factors may have contributed to Byron's sudden embrace of alcohol, there is some evidence to suggest that vestiges of the war had begun to surface and percolate in Byron's world. In an essay titled "Just a Rug," written by Byron only weeks before his departure from Commonwealth Edison, unmistakable threads of melancholy and regret are woven into the fabric of a four-page lament about the passage of time, the passing of old friends, and the presage of change for change's sake. The essay is ostensibly about having to part ways with an old dining room rug that had given every ounce of its fiber in selfless service over the years. The nameless protagonist is sadly resigned to perpetuating a never-ending "cycle of sly deceit"—replacing the battle-scarred old friend with a newer, more fashionable rug, one that would also, invariably, grow old and threadbare, needing to be replaced by yet another new rug whose cut and style was more in keeping with contemporary standards.

As a metaphor, the essay speaks to more substantial concerns in Byron's world—a feeling of regret that with the passage of time much of his life's work had gone unappreciated or, worse yet, like an old rug, in danger of being discarded completely. Dated October 17, 1934, the essay was penned under his old nom de guerre Homer Fiske, a pseudonym that Byron used for war-related matters only. And when viewed in that context, the essay can be read as a soldier's lament about the sacrifice that he and others had made during the Great War, and the fear that those previous labors were about to come undone as militaristic fervor was once again on the march in Germany, where Adolf Hitler and the Nazi Party had recently risen to power.

On the home front an equally disconcerting development was beginning to play out in the U.S. Senate. A special committee, chaired by Senator Gerald P. Nye, had been empaneled to investigate the extent to which a persistent and troublesome rumor was actually true—that the captains of the munitions industry and the financial world had engineered the United States' entry into the Great War in order to reap outlandish profits and to protect financial investments they had made in Great Britain and France. The so-called Nye Committee began its hearings in early September 1934, taking testimony for the next eighteen months from over two hundred witnesses, including J. P. Morgan and Pierre du Pont. In 1936, the committee's work came to an abrupt end when its funding was cut. The issue, however, remained unresolved, and questions concerning the extent to which corporate and personal financial considerations may have influenced the country's decision to enter into the war continued to linger. In the face of such unsettling allegations, it's possible that the realization that they had been duped into war by a group of unscrupulous businessmen—and that war in Europe was once again in the making—would be sufficient impetus to drive Byron and other battle-scarred veterans to drink. Whether that was in fact the case will never be known.

As it turned out, even in the midst of the Great Depression, Byron ended up profiting from his latest misfortune. At this point, his good reputation still preceded him, and he was able to land a lucrative job in New York City as a labor relations expert for the New York Realty Advisory Board. The organization represented a consortium of realty companies in New York City and Long Island. Apparently Byron was very good at his job. As set forth in a letter from the deputy mayor of New York City, Henry H. Curran, Byron's expertise in mediating labor disputes was much appreciated by the administration of Mayor Fiorello LaGuardia. The particular dispute upon which Curran based his opinion was the much-publicized strike by elevator operators and maintenance workers in New York City. The impact of the work stoppage was crippling. In the short term, Mayor LaGuardia had been able to fashion a quick fix by declaring a state of emergency in which city personnel were drafted to operate residential elevators. Finding a permanent solution was left to Byron and negotiators from the building service employees' union. Evidently, Byron acquitted himself well. On March 16, 1936, the labor dispute was settled to everyone's satisfaction.

Byron's time at the realty board was short-lived, however. By the fall of 1936, he had already moved on to another job, at the corporate headquarters of Republic Steel in Cleveland, Ohio. It is unclear if Byron decided to move on from the realty board or was asked to leave. Regardless, he still managed to land yet another well-paid executive position. Like a modern-day parable about the wages of sin, however, Byron's time at Republic Steel would prove to lead to his emotional death. At this point, drinking to excess had become a recurring problem in Byron's life, though it was not yet all consuming, as evidenced by his voluminous writings. Intellectual discourse had always been the litmus test as to Byron's state of mind, and while employed at the New York Realty Board as well as for during his first few months at Republic Steel, Byron was still a proficient though somewhat sporadic writer. An essay titled "150th Anniversary of the U.S. Constitution" stands out. An objection to FDR's attempt to expand the number of justices appointed to the U.S. Supreme Court, the essay was a substantively impressive piece of writing. More important, though, it was the product of a clear mind and even temperament—not the residue of an alcohol-induced rant. It proved to be the last piece of accomplished writing that Byron would produce before a cascade of personal struggles engulfed him—the onset of which coincided with recent events in the workplace, the most notable of which was the Memorial Day Massacre.

May 30, 1937, will forever be remembered as one of the bloodiest chapters in the annals of American organized labor. Although the incident occurred at the South Chicago plant of Republic Steel, the groundwork had been laid months earlier in other locations. By the late winter of 1936, laborers in the United States were not only beginning to organize, they were on the march. In factories and plants across the country, thousands of workers staged strikes, demanding higher wages and improved working conditions. None was more important than the strike that began in December 1936 in Flint, Michigan, where workers belonging to the newly formed United Auto Workers (UAW) union conducted a sit-down strike at the General Motors plant. The work stoppage lasted fifty-six days before General Motors signed an agreement that recognized the UAW as the sole bargaining agent for workers.

After its victory in Flint, organized labor set its sights on U.S. Steel. In late winter of 1937, the Steel Workers Organizing Committee (SWOC) began to exert pressure on the management of U.S. Steel. With lucrative contracts hanging in the balance, U.S. Steel quickly entered into a labor accord with the SWOC. On the heels of that agreement, the SWOC turned its focus from "Big Steel" (U.S. Steel) to the corporations that comprised "Little Steel," of which Republic Steel was the most prominent. Republic Steel was headed by Tom Girdler, an intractable old steel man who wasn't the least bit intimidated by the SWOC. The strike began on May 26, 1937. Both sides dug in for a long siege. It never got that far—four days later, things went terribly wrong.

On May 30, a large group of SWOC members and their families were assembled at a park in South Chicago to celebrate Memorial Day. The main purpose of the gathering was to show union solidarity in support of the ongoing strike at the nearby Republic Steel plant. After listening to speeches, a group of about two hundred men, women, and children left the park, waving American flags and singing union songs as they set out for the gates of Republic Steel. Waiting for them on a rubble-strewn field a short distance from the gates of the plant was a phalanx of 150 Chicago police officers and plant goons. When the police refused to let the marchers pass, angry words were exchanged. Pushing and shoving ensued. Rocks were hurled by frustrated marchers. Then a fusillade of gunfire erupted from the police ranks, after which officers charged the mob. Marchers ran for their lives, but not all escaped. In a matter of seconds, four marchers lay dead, and six more were fatally wounded—several shot in the back. Scores of others were grievously injured. A Paramount cameraman captured much of the carnage on film. The depiction was so graphic that Paramount Studios later refused to show the newsreel footage in theaters for fear that audiences would riot.

Girdler was totally unrepentant about the company's position or the tragic consequences of the confrontation. Questioned by the press about whether he actually believed that the unarmed men, women, and children in the march were intent on breaching the gates of Republic Steel, Girdler sarcastically remarked that "maybe they were out there to catch butterflies."

No doubt this horrific event struck an emotional chord with Byron. For someone who had risked his own life to give aid and comfort to wounded and dying soldiers during the war, even enemy combatants, the hostility and callous indifference shown to the strikers must have been hard for Byron to reconcile. There is no direct evidence to indicate that Byron had any involvement in the formulation of the company's labor relations policy—he was the company's director of training. Given his well-known expertise in the field, however, coupled with the fact that Byron had worked at corporate headquarters in Cleveland

Memorial Day Massacre, South Chicago Republic Steel Plant. These photographs were introduced as evidence at the La Follette Committee hearings in the Senate.

with Girdler, it is hard to imagine that Girdler would not have consulted with him on the matter. A letter written by Byron in 1951 seems to support this conclusion, wherein he cited "the South Chicago Massacre" as having been part of his career in labor relations.

Not surprisingly, it was during his time at Republic Steel that Byron's drinking problems reached new depths. Whether the Memorial Day Massacre had actually served as a triggering mechanism, activating post-traumatic stress disorder that had lain dormant since the war, is unknown. Byron left no record of his struggles. His once prolific writing had stopped completely. From this point forward, he seems to have entered a period of personal darkness. As later related by his daughter Nancy, it was during these years that Byron began to sell off pieces from the valuable coin collection he had inherited from his father in order to finance his drinking habit. Some of those coins Byron had actually collected for his father while stationed in Europe during the war. Nancy also recalled that on nights when Byron failed to come home from work, Helen and their teenaged son Fiske were forced to make the rounds of his drinking haunts to retrieve him—which was never a pleasant task, and at times an unpeaceful one. Coping with the unpredictable and unsettling behavior of an alcoholic father must have been especially confusing and difficult for the adolescent Fiske. When sober, Byron was still capable of commanding enough respect to be elected president of the Lakewood PTA—inebriated, however, he could be prone to inexplicable acts of self-humiliation and public embarrassment, like creating a drunken spectacle at Fiske's high school graduation ceremony. It is entirely understandable that Fiske would harbor conflicting emotions about his father for the rest of his life.

During the Cleveland years Byron finally came to the inescapable conclusion that he had a serious drinking problem and sought help from a promising new organization that had been formed in nearby Akron, Ohio. According to Helen: "He was one of the first 100 men in Alcoholics Anonymous. When we lived in Lakewood, we attended meetings three or four times a week, in all the cities we lived in, whenever he was sober. He helped hundreds of men to stay sober—but he could not, for any length of time. We knew Dr. Smith and Bill Wilson, the founders of A.A. very well."

Over the ensuing years, Byron would help to found two chapters of Alcoholics Anonymous, assuming leadership roles and even appearing on a local radio show to extol the virtues of AA. Despite his best intentions, however, for Byron, the cure never took, and a downward spiral of short-lived jobs inevitably followed. In 1942 Byron was fired from Republic Steel, and then hired as the director of personnel at R. E. Oldsmobile in Lansing, Michigan. After either being fired or asked to leave Oldsmobile, he next worked for the McIntryre Group as a corporate business consultant, followed by a short stint as a low-level supervisor at the Vickers manufactory plant in Detroit, where the hours were exceedingly long and the pay exceptionally low. To add injury to an already disheartening situation, while he was employed at Vickers an accident nearly crippled him permanently. After recovering, Byron next found work at Graham-Paige automotive, another assembly-line plant in Detroit that had been retooled for wartime production. For much of his time at Vickers and Graham-Paige, Byron was separated from the family—living alone in a rented room in Detroit, while Helen remained at the family residence in Lansing with their adolescent daughter Nancy, who attended school there. It was during this period of work-necessitated separation from Byron that Helen took a job as a grinding machine operator on an assembly line at the Nash-Kelvinator plant, hoping to keep the family afloat financially.

The strain that Byron's drinking had placed on his relationship with his wife and children is perhaps best reflected in a series of letters written by his son Fiske to his parents and sister during the Second World War. Although Fiske was far removed from the home scene, stationed at various Army Air Corps bases in the United States and in Attu, Alaska, Helen and Nancy, kept him abreast of Byron's continuing struggles with alcohol. In a letter dated March 19, 1945, Fiske did not mince words in addressing the issue with his father:

> Dad, I'm just sick about your drinking. You are so pathetic when you drink. I hate to think of 673 Palmer [the address of the family's residence] and your coming home like that. It just puts a bad taste in my mouth. . . . There are always fellows getting pitifully drunk. I don't like you to come to mind when I think of them,

Dad. Because it's so much more ludicrous with a middle-aged fellow, and so much more tragic when he happens to be your father. You know you'll keep your good friends and your family; that's been tested often enuff. But as I can see it you're never going to keep on getting jobs as you have. Certainly you must realize that. Can't you absorb yourself in this job now, Dad, and see it thru. It seems to me that having a wife and two children's encouragement and a steady job, should be quite adequate. Plenty of people do a much more reliable job with less, much less.

After Byron was let go by Graham-Paige in 1947, according to Helen, "We left Detroit and drove across country to Seattle to try to start a new life. This was the happiest journey we ever took!" In Seattle, Byron was able to find a good job—when sober he was still an impressive and accomplished figure. This time, he was employed as the director of non-academic personnel at the University of Washington. Then, as always, he was fired for drinking on the job. At that point, Helen filed for divorce. As she related:

> In Oct. 1951, I divorced Byron. He went to San Francisco to get work and left me in Seattle to pack the furniture and put the best pieces in storage, etc. Then I went by train to Vashtis and Arthur's [relatives] in Glendale California. I stopped enroute in San Francisco and saw Byron for about 3 hours. We went out to Golden Gate State Park and had lunch. He had been drinking and I remember how disappointed I was that he couldn't have stayed sober for that short time, when he knew I was coming. He went with me to the train and got on the Pullman with me and kissed me goodbye. That was the last time I saw him. I have never regretted that I got the divorce, nor that I stayed with him as long as I did. We loved one another very much and the "good" times were wonderful and the "bad" times were getting impossible for me to cope with.

As Byron continued to drink, his life trended ever downward. Although he had managed to work briefly in a consulting job for the Pacific Coast Division of Bethlehem Steel in San Francisco, he subsisted on monthly stipends from Social Security, a Veterans Administration need-based pension, food stamps (social welfare programs of which he likely would have disapproved in his more financially stable years), and by selling off pieces of his father's valuable coin and stamp collections. In 1958, he worked as the desk clerk in the newly opened Salvation Army residential rehabilitation facility for struggling alcoholics, but as always the position did not last. Eventually he hit rock bottom—living in transient hotels in San Francisco's Tenderloin District, a very poor section of town. During these years, Byron often received money and clothing from Fiske, but mostly he scraped by on his meager income. Still, he had not given up all hope—filling his days by working as a volunteer at Traveler's Aid, reading books, and going on long walks. He also talked about getting a respectable set of clothes so that he could become more involved in activities at Glide Methodist Church, and he started to attend AA meetings again. He also began to see a psychiatrist, paid for by Fiske, to help "find the right and sure road . . . back to sane living."

Despite his best intentions, Byron's letters reflect his continuing struggles with alcohol. When apparently sober, his letters are clear and concisely written. At other times, his handwriting is shaky, his spelling

Byron, Fiske, and Nancy Field in happier times. This photograph was taken by Helen Field on March 26, 1944, when Fiske was home on leave from service in the Army Air Corps. Helen's inscription reads: "Dad wears his bathrobe to get a laugh—put his war medals on it and walked out as I was taking Fiske's and Nancy's picture!"

faulty, and his letters filled with apologies for having misspent Fiske's hard-earned money on alcohol. On October 29, 1966, Byron mailed Fiske a color snapshot taken of him by the owner of a coffee shop that he frequented on his walks. Though appearing slightly embarrassed and more than a bit weathered by age, he was smiling kindly at the

S.F. CHRONICLE FEB. 9, 1958

Salvation Army Fights Skid Row With New Hotel

The Salvation Army has come up with what it hopes will prove a potent new weapon in its long fight to rehabilitate Skid Row derelicts.

The weapon is a brand new, first-class hotel at 1500 Valencia street, adjacent to the Salvation Army's Men's Social Service Center.

It houses the 115 men who work at re-processing the discarded furniture and clothes in the social service center.

The new men's dormitory, a modern, four-story brick and stucco structure, was opened recently to answer a long-time need in San Francisco's alcoholic rehabilitation program.

For years, derelicts sentenced to the county jail have been released with 15 cents carfare and nothing else. They have naturally gravitated back to Skid Row.

OFF-WORK PROBLEM

Social workers have long felt that alcoholics need close supervision while undergoing treatment.

The Salvation Army has been able to provide jobs for 115 men at its social service

Plants for lobby steps of Salvation Army men's dormitory are watered by desk clerk Byron Field

Byron, Salvation Army, February 9, 1958. (Photograph by *San Francisco Chronicle*.)

camera. It was the last picture taken of him. As noted in the letter that accompanied the photo, on his left hand he was still proudly wearing his "first WW ring on my little finger." To the day he died, reminders of the war would always be with Byron.

On November 13, 1967, Byron was found on a sidewalk not far from his hotel, suffering from a fractured pelvis. There is no written account of how the mishap occurred—hospital and police records were destroyed long ago. In the final telling, though, details of that incident would have provided little additional insight into his decline—for quite some time, it was apparent that Byron's life was destined to end badly. Eleven weeks later, he was dead of complications. Mercifully, his long struggle was over.

Byron, October 1966. Note that he is wearing his World War I ring on the little finger of his left hand.

Nearly fifteen months after Byron's death, Fiske received a personal letter at his office in Manhattan from a woman whose name he didn't recognize. Dated April 24, 1969, the letter read:

Dear Mr. Field,

As you can see the enclosed letter was written a year ago. Your father and I met each other our freshman year at Albion College where my father was director of the music department. As I recall your grandmother attended Albion Conservatory as well—and later your sister. Is that right? I knew your grandparents well. Of course your father and I were quite young—and he young to go off to the war that was to end all wars!

I thot the alumni office at U. of M. would have your father's address (Oddly he and I both received degrees from there in 1922) It has been my fortune to live in many places in many states (I was born in Tacoma, Wash.) and my mother kept my school things at her home. Now it seems time to take inventory of the past and I found these letters, many of them written from France or Edinburgh where your father had a scholarship as you probably know. I also have a picture taken in the trenches in France. In all probability, your grandparents passed on to you many mementos of World War I, but now they are of real historic value. In fact a young friend of mine, working on his Phd. at Princeton wanted them for source material.

When the letter was returned from Ann Arbor, I wrote Mass. Mutual (Your grandfather sold me my life insurance) and they in turn referred me to Mr. Gilbert Byrne, who in turn gave me your address. He told me your father had a tragic accident while living in San Francisco. I hope you were able to be with him.

My husband (with General Electric) was transferred from the N.Y. area to the Boston area a year ago. We lived in Glen Ridge, N.J.—And you? And where is your sister? I know your mother went to South America at one time. I should love to hear from you and know if you would like these mementos—or your sister.

Sincerely,

Estelle Cozine Nelson

Estelle had enclosed a second letter for Fiske's inspection. Mailed almost one year earlier, May 25, 1968, but returned as undelivered, that letter had been addressed to Byron care of the University of Michigan alumni office.

Dear Byron,

I wonder if this will ever reach you and when. I want for a particular reason to get in touch with you. One or two or more mementos from World War I—your son and daughter might wish to keep. At least I'd like to write and ask you about them.

My health has been rather precarious the past five years. And yours?

John is reasonably well—playing golf at this moment. Unexpectedly, we were transferred from the New York to the Boston area just before Christmas. Tried to find your name in the San Francisco telephone book.

Hope the Alumni Office can find your whereabouts. More anon if I can locate you.

As ever,

Estelle (Cozine)
(Mrs. John E. Nelson)

Can you answer pronto ! Have a reason !

On receiving Estelle's letter, Fiske followed up with a telephone call to properly introduce himself. And after speaking with Fiske, Estelle immediately wrote back on May 22, looking to keep that channel of communication open. It was a relationship Estelle would try to foster over the next several years—to quote her words, "I feel as if you should be my nephew at least." Indeed, an unmistakable undercurrent of obligation and fealty runs through all of Estelle's letters—as well as a feeling of immediacy. Having suffered a near-fatal stroke six years before, Estelle was apparently concerned that time might run out before she could "narrow the gap" with Fiske: "Usually I can quickly translate life into 'theatre' and open the curtains with a gay gesture. Today the familiar ropes stick altho the curtain doesn't seem old and faded. You are on the stage, but it's hard to think of you as you must be a grown man. Could you be forty-five? That seems impossible. Maybe Einstein could help me out."

The use of a theatrical metaphor couldn't have been more appropriate for Estelle. After graduating from the University of Michigan in 1922, Estelle taught for two years at Tarkio College in Missouri, then moved to New York City in 1924 to pursue a career in acting. Among Estelle's professional credits were performances at the Provincetown Theatre, Neighborhood Playhouse, and Theatre Guild—all cutting-edge theater companies for their time. After treading the boards of the New York theater scene until her limited funds ran out in 1928, Estelle returned to teaching for one year at Bradley Polytechnic Institute. Then she enrolled in the Yale University School of Drama, graduating in 1930. Any plans to resume her acting career, however, were cut short when she was summoned home to help care for her gravely ill father. Estelle remained in the Midwest to help support her mother and sister, who did not work outside the household, eventually taking a position as an instructor of speech and dramatic arts at Shimer Junior College in Mt. Carroll, Illinois. The job lasted for four years, during which time a young engineer from Colorado walked into her life—John Nelson was working in a nearby Civilian Conservation Corps camp. He and Estelle hit it off immediately, and soon fell in love. In 1935 they were married, and in 1939 a daughter, Martha, was born to them. Unlike Byron's ill-fated marriage to Helen, John and Estelle's life together was a loving, stable, and lasting one.

In attempting to "narrow the gap" with Fiske, Estelle insisted on delivering Byron's war letters, each one of which she had reviewed and annotated, in person. In July 1969, Estelle met Fiske in Manhattan for lunch. Estelle later recalled the meeting as being somewhat "hectic" in that there was so much to discuss and little time in which to do it. Estelle attempted to remedy that situation by trying to stay in touch with Fiske. It was strictly a one-way correspondence. Each Christmas, Estelle sent a card to Fiske with a note attached. Although he never reciprocated, he could never bring himself to destroy the cards either. The fact that Fiske retained the cards until the day he died seems to reflect the conflicting emotions he struggled with concerning his

Estelle Cozine, c. 1925. (Photograph courtesy of Martha Hartmann.)

father. Estelle had evidently picked up on this ambivalence in her brief meeting with Fiske, and in her own small way sought to help Fiske cope with that confusion and pain, writing in her Christmas card of 1974: "We climb life's ladder or path, sometimes taking a wrong turn as did your father. But surely there must be some eternal love somewhere that understands us." Her heartfelt closing, "Fiske, I hope this reaches you," obviously referred to more than just the card itself.

Year after year, Estelle remained faithful to Byron's memory as she continued to reach out to Fiske, even in sickness. In February 1976, after being laid low over the holidays by illness, Estelle included with her card a picture of Byron taken in 1916. Smiling brightly, Byron looked the very embodiment of the hope and idealism that exists in all of us before life exacts its inexorable toll. "Perhaps that is the reason I try to keep in touch with you," Estelle wrote on the accompanying card. "I feel there must be some connection between this world and the next—I feel I owe your father some understanding of all the hazards of this world. I want to tell you that he loves you wherever he is."

In June 1978, Estelle wrote to Fiske for the final time. At the age of eighty-one, she was doing her best to stay "frisky," but as she so aptly put it, "my past is descending on me." Included with her brief note were three mementos that spanned the course of her relationship with Byron. It was the last correspondence that Fiske received from Estelle. It was not her closing tribute, however. Even in death, she remained a faithful friend. Thirty-six years later, Estelle would play a final part in the telling of Byron's story.

It occurred in Denver, Colorado. It was there, on August 4. 2014, that the authors met Estelle's daughter, Martha Hartmann. Possessed of the same candor and kindness that was so characteristic of her mother, Marty filled in little details of Estelle's life as deftly as an artist applying the final brush strokes to a portrait. Soon a more complete picture of Estelle emerged. On viewing that picture in totality, it was apparent that Estelle's relationship with Byron was destined to be a star-crossed affair—with age, Estelle would continue to be a dyed-in-the-wool liberal just as Byron would forever remain a die-hard conservative.

During their brief courtship, however, they still managed to find the bedrock on which to build a lasting relationship—one that has continued to make itself known, even today. To the day he died, Byron carried among his personal belongings Estelle's senior yearbook from Albion College. Byron is nowhere to be found between its covers—and with good cause; he was off fighting the war that was to end all wars. Throughout its pages, though, Estelle is ever-present—it seems that she excelled at everything she did, from athletics to academics. Estelle was also quite simply beautiful. The gleam in her eye and the kindness of her smile capture the very innocence and radiance of youth. That this memory would manage to keep its hold on Byron throughout the years is as understandable as it is self-evident.

Marty revealed that Estelle had likewise held onto a loving memory of Byron all her life. It turned out that after Estelle had met with Fiske and given him all of Byron's letters and mementos from the war, she retained one special keepsake for herself: the silver-etched locket he had so lovingly sent her from Europe during the war. Marty recalled that she had often seen her mother wearing it. Nestled inside was a likeness of Byron, looking out on the world once more—still young, confident, and full of hope. It was the perfect ending to a long journey. In spirit, Byron had finally come home.

Estelle's locket containing photographs of Byron and Harlan Cozine. (Photograph courtesy of Martha Hartmann.)

NOTES

ABBREVIATIONS

BFF: Byron Fiske Field

BFFP: Byron Fiske Field Papers, Bentley Historical Library, University of Michigan, Ann Arbor

DoGB: Diary and Papers of Gertrude Bray, Rhode Island Historical Society, Providence

DP: Donovan Papers, U.S. Army War Collection Archives, Carlisle, PA

EMC: Estelle Miller Cozine

GB: Gertrude Bray

HAC168: Roy Bryson and select members of 168th Ambulance Company, *The History of Ambulance Company 168* (N.p., 1919)

I&G: Wilbur Conkling and select members of 117th Sanitary Train, *Iodine and Gasoline* (N.p., 1919)

JBF: James Bird Field

LW: *Leslie's Weekly Illustrated Magazine*

NAMS: National Archives and Records Administration, College Park, MD, Mopix Section

NYT: *New York Times*

WJD: Lieutenant Colonel William J. Donovan

A NOTE ON THE TEXT

xvi "Homer Fiske." That BFF had purposefully chosen this nom de guerre and was fully aware of the difficulties that often confronted soldiers returning from war is evidenced by the well-thumbed copy of *The Iliad* found among his personal belongings.

CHAPTER 1: ANSWERING THE CALL

1   The events recounted in this chapter concerning BFF's enlistment in
the 1st Michigan Ambulance Company are drawn from an undated
essay, "An Interlude," written by BFF in the years immediately following the war (c. 1923–26), and a letter from BFF to EMC dated May 24,
1917, BFFP.

1   "Potawatomi Curtain." For a discussion of the legend of the Potawatomi
Curtain, refer to Debra Ann Pawlak, *Farmington and Farmington Hills*,
The Making of America (Charleston, SC: Arcadia, 2003), 11–13.

1   "exceptionally cool spring." A description of the unusually cool spring
of 1917 and the corresponding agricultural conditions in southern
Michigan are contained in C. F. Schneider, *Climatological Data*, Michigan Section 32, no. 5 (Washington, DC: U.S. Department of Agriculture, Weather Bureau, 1917), 51–60. See also "Poorest Wheat Crop in
13 Years: Condition of May 1 Shows We Will Have Enough to Feed Ourselves Only," *NYT*, May 8, 1917.

2   "Red Cross corps." BFF's categorization of the American Red Cross
as a "corps" was technically incorrect, although understandable considering the circumstances. The American Red Cross was originally
established in 1881 as a private humanitarian relief organization. Its
founder, Clara Barton, was convinced of the need for such an organization as a result of her work as a volunteer nurse in both the American
Civil War and the Franco-Prussian War. In 1905, the U.S. government
chartered the organization to assist the military in providing medical
care during time of war, and to organize for that eventuality in time
of peace. In assuming this coadjutant role, the American Red Cross
had in effect morphed into a paramilitary organization—although it
was not a medical corps of the U.S. Army per se. During World War I,
its activities included providing much-needed medical supplies to
hospitals and medical units in the field; helping to staff hospitals and
medical units with doctors and nurses who had volunteered their services; and equipping and manning volunteer ambulance companies.
Many of those who served in Red Cross units during the war (ambulance company personnel in particular) wore military-style uniforms.
Henry P. Davison, *The American Red Cross in the Great War* (New York:
Macmillan, 1919).

3   The following terms contained in "An Interlude" require further explanation: "atrocities" refer to Belgian and French civilians killed by invading German troops during the first weeks of the war; "White Papers" and
"Red Papers" refer to a series of official reports issued by the German,
British, and Austro-Hungarian governments shortly after the outbreak of hostilities in Europe. Published within weeks of one another,
each paper purportedly offered an objective (albeit competing) historical summary of the diplomatic events that had compelled each country

to declare war on the other. The German and British justifications were called "White Papers," the Austro-Hungarian justification the "Red Book." The Russian and Serbian justifications (not mentioned by BFF in his essay) were called the "Orange Book" and "Blue Book" respectively. In choosing which particular set of facts or circumstances to emphasize (or ignore) in justifying its respective actions, each nation's position paper was essentially a work of propaganda.

"Princess Pats" refer to a regiment of Canadian infantry more formally known as Princess Patricia's Light Infantry. Named after the daughter of the governor-general of Canada, Princess Patricia of Connaught, the regiment came into existence on August 10, 1914. It was composed primarily of Canadian citizens, although a significant number of enlistees from the United States served in the regiment as well. This was not an uncommon occurrence—by the end of the war, thousands of American citizens had volunteered to serve in various branches of the Canadian Expeditionary Force (CEF). In addition to the CEF, there were several other options available to Americans who were eager to support the Allied cause prior to the United States' declaration of war. One of the most popular was to enlist in one of the privately sponsored ambulance companies that were serving in Europe under French and Italian command—the young Ernest Hemingway was a member of one such company. Other notable examples of foreign military units in which U.S. citizens served prior to April 6, 1917 were the Lafayette Escadrille, a squadron of American pilots that fought under French command (this squadron began its tour of duty in France on March 21, 1916); the French Foreign Legion; and the Royal Flying Corps. Chris Dickon, *Americans at War in Foreign Forces: A History, 1914–1945* (Jefferson, NC: McFarland, 2014).

"Officer Training Camp." In an unquoted paragraph of "An Interlude," BFF also noted an intermediate course of action that was available to American college students who were sympathetic to the Allied cause and wished to begin their basic training, but wanted to wait for a formal declaration of war by the United States before enlisting. For those so inclined, attendance at an Officer's Training Camp during the summer semester break was deemed a desirable option. The first of these ninety-day summer training camps was held in 1915 at Plattsburg, New York. In 1916, with the passage of the National Defense Act and at the urging of former President Theodore Roosevelt and U.S. Army general Leonard Wood (the leading proponents of a national campaign for military readiness called "the Preparedness Movement"), additional officer training camps were established in Gettysburg, Pennsylvania, Pacific Woods, California, Ludington, Michigan, Asheville, North Carolina, Ft. Sheridan, Kansas, and Ft. Ethan Allen, Vermont. To this day, graduates of officer training schools are still referred to as "90 Day Wonders."

5   "packet of letters." Nine letters of recommendation, dated May 23–28, 1917, were found among BFF's personal belongings. The letters were

320 NOTES TO CHAPTER 1: ANSWERING THE CALL

written by various business, educational, and religious leaders in Jackson and Albion, Michigan.

5   "Each ambulance company would be comprised of." For information concerning the composition of the Michigan Ambulance Company as first sworn into service, refer to Harold Stanley Johnson, *Roster of the Rainbow Division: Major General Wm. A. Mann, Commanding* (New York: Eaton & Gettinger, 1917).

5   "experienced driver." In the years leading up to the war, the purchase price of an automobile generally exceeded the financial wherewithal of most families. In 1915, the median annual household income was $687, the average sticker price of an automobile $2,005. Although Henry Ford had originally intended the Model T to provide a less expensive option for the average consumer (approximately $825 in 1908), because the mechanics of the moving assembly line were not fine-tuned or fully operational until 1914, the mass production of inexpensive automobiles (like the Model T) had not been fully realized. As such, the opportunity for most citizens to purchase an automobile and learn to drive was limited. As reflected in BFF's letters, the Field family purchased its first automobile in 1916. The family of his college sweetheart, the Cozines, did not purchase one until the summer of 1917, at which point EMC learned to drive. But the Field and Cozine families were exceptions. It was still very much a horse-drawn world—as set forth in a letter by BFF dated October 5, 1917, in which he fondly recalled the evening of June 5, 1917, when he and EMC had taken the Cozine family horse and buggy for a ride around town because the Cozine family had not yet been "blessed" with a car. When the Cozines did finally purchase one later that summer, BFF was prompted to caution EMC and her father (as inexperienced drivers) not to risk driving their new car on the bustling streets of Detroit to visit him in training camp there. That the ability to drive a "machine" was a relatively rare skill is further underscored in a recruiting poster, "Can You Drive a Car?" in which the American Field Service was seeking to enlist the services of young men capable of driving motorized ambulances in France. See also the January 18, 1917, cover of *LW* for an amusing depiction of a wide-eyed man attempting to learn to drive one of these new-fangled contraptions, and the January 6, 1916, cover of *LW* for an equally intriguing depiction concerning technological challenges presented by automobiles, titled "Knowledge Is Power," in which a young woman is depicted reading an owner's manual as she attempts to fix an automobile. That this scenario was a common one for new drivers (female or not) is recounted in a letter from BFF to EMC dated July 2, 1918, in which BFF commiserated with EMC over her having had to change *four* flat tires on a recent Sunday ride in the family car—agreeing with her (no doubt with a smile on his face) that yes, at least her "shoes won't blow up!" For statistics on automobiles, see U.S. Federal Highway Administration Highway Statistics, annual,

http://www.fhwa.dot.gov/ohim/ohimstat.htm; and "Comparison of Average American Car for Past 8 Years," *Motor Age Magazine*, January 4, 1917, 8. For statistics on income, see *U.S. Department of Labor, Bureau of Labor Statistics*, "The Life of American Workers in 1915," February 2016, https://www.bls.gov/opub/mlr/2016/article/the-life-of-american-workers-in-1915.htm.

5   "a very dangerous and arduous job." For information concerning the extraction, treatment, and transportation of the wounded during battle, refer to *The Medical Department of the United States Army in the World War*, vol. 8, *Field Operations* (Washington, DC: Government Printing Office, 1925).

11   "There had never been anything like it." The scale and ferocity of World War I was truly unprecedented. Major battles devoured manpower at a staggering rate. In the battle of the Somme on the first day of combat, 60,000 British soldiers were cut down by German artillery and machine guns. Five months later, over 420,000 British, 200,000 French, and 650,000 German soldiers were listed as causalities of that prolonged battle. Equally horrifying numbers of soldiers were killed or wounded in other protracted military engagements, like the five battles of Ypres and the nearly yearlong siege of Verdun. By the time the Armistice was declared on November 11, 1918, the combatants had sustained over 34 million casualties—8 million of whom died from wounds or disease. In the face of such overwhelming carnage, the need for medical support was paramount but the scope of the effort daunting. For statistics, refer to Fielding H. Garrison, *Notes on the History of Military Medicine* (Washington, DC: Association of Military Surgeons of the United States, 1922), 199; and Theodore Ropp, *War in the Modern World* (New York: Collier Books, 1979), 248, 250. For discussion of the battle of the Somme, see John Keegan, *The Face of Battle* (New York: Penguin, 1978), 235, 285. For a thorough discussion of the battle of Verdun, refer to Paul Jankowski, *Verdun: The Longest Battle of the Great War* (Oxford: Oxford University Press, 2014).

In an attempt to highlight the indiscriminate loss of life wrought by the war, *LW* used the front cover of its January 25, 1917, edition to place this issue squarely before the American public. In a depiction titled "How Long Must This Continue?" Mars (the all-powerful god of war) is seen towering over desperate men caught in the chaos of battle as he uses his sword to herd countless legions of soldiers and equipment into the smoking breech of a gigantic artillery piece to be disposed of like cannon fodder.

CHAPTER 2: THE WORLD'S GREATEST ADVERTISING ADVENTURE

13   The events recounted in this chapter concerning BFF's enlistment in the 1st Michigan Ambulance Company are drawn from an undated

essay, "An Interlude," written by BFF in the years immediately following the war (c. 1923–26), and a letter from BFF to EMC dated May 24, 1917, BFFP.

14   "Uncle Sam." The finger-pointing depiction of Uncle Sam now commonly associated with U.S. Army recruiting posters was originally created by artist James Montgomery Flagg for the cover of the July 6, 1916, issue of *LW*, titled "What Are You Doing for Preparedness?" Seven months later, as the United States stood on the precipice of war, the illustration was recaptioned "I Want You" and displayed again on the cover of *LW* (February 15, 1917). Once war had been declared on April 6, 1917, the image was co-opted by the War Department, recaptioned "I Want You for U.S. Army," and used on over 4 million recruiting posters. To this day, Flagg's creation remains one of the most iconic works of wartime art ever produced. In order to fully appreciate the impact Flagg's creation had as a recruitment tool, it is first necessary to discuss the enormous influence that cover and poster art played in shaping public opinion at that time. The cover of *LW* (originally *Frank Leslie's Illustrated Weekly Newspaper*) is a prime example of this phenomenon. Over the course of the magazine's existence (1855–1922), the front cover frequently displayed works of art that spoke to a variety of social, political, and patriotic themes in a concise and impactful manner that mere words simply could not match. That the editors at *LW* and other pictorial publications fully understood the persuasive power that attention-grabbing art and photographs had as a messaging tool is evident in an editorial comment titled "Pictures" in the January 4, 1917, issue of *LW*. The editor proclaimed that in the ongoing evolution of news reporting, this particular period of time was "the era of pictures," and that for the past sixty-one years it had been *LW*'s mission as "the great weekly illustrated newspaper of the land" to satisfy America's ever-growing affinity for pictorial news. Although undeniably self-serving, this statement was not so self-aggrandizing as to entirely stretch the bounds of credulity—in the early 1900s, radio broadcasting was still in its infancy, and most Americans relied on newspapers and magazines to provide them with news on current events. With a weekly circulation of over sixty-five thousand (and a claimed readership of five hundred thousand), *LW* was one of the periodicals to which many Americans turned to obtain news of war-related events.

In the initial stages of the war, *LW*'s coverage of news from the front was fairly evenhanded. Beginning in the latter half of 1916, however, and continuing into 1917 as the United States crept ever closer to war, the articles and photographs assumed a subtle but persistent pro-Allied/anti-isolationist bias. This was hardly surprising given that John A. Sleicher, the magazine's managing editor, was a supporter of former president Theodore Roosevelt and the internationalist "Big Stick" diplomacy he had so vociferously championed. In assuming this posture, the magazine had in effect morphed into a de facto (albeit inadvertent) arm of the British propaganda machine, and much of the eye-catching art displayed on the cover of the magazine during this period of time portrayed that inherent bias. On April 13, 1917, six days after the United States declared war on Germany, any pretense that *LW*'s coverage of war-related news was neutral evaporated when President Woodrow Wilson empaneled the Committee on Public Information or, as it was more commonly known, the Creel Committee (after its chairman George Creel). The purpose of the committee was to launch an all-out public relations campaign to influence popular opinion in favor of the war. To that end, commerce and commercial advertising were enlisted to assist the committee in its propaganda assault on the American citizenry. Art was one of the mediums utilized in that effort, and picture periodicals like *LW* served as one of the commercial vehicles used to deliver that patriotic message. Much of the cover art displayed by *LW* during the war was produced by illustrators James Montgomery Flagg, Orson Lowell, Clyde Forsythe, Charles Sarka, Griswold Tyng, and the very talented young Norman Rockwell. For an excellent discussion of propaganda and American art, refer to Robert Cozzolino, Anne C. Knutson, and David M. Lubin, *World War I and American Art* (Princeton: Princeton University Press, 2016). See also George Creel, *How We Advertised America: The First Telling of the Amazing Story of the Committee on Public Information That Carried the Gospel of Americanism to Every Corner of the Globe* (New York: Harper & Bros., 1920). See also the front cover of *Leslie's Weekly*, April 19, 1917, titled "The Call."

14   "war bonds." On April 24, 1917, Congress passed the Emergency Loan Act, which gave the U.S. Treasury Department the authority to issue $5 billion in war bonds. In an effort to promote the sale of these bonds, posters urging citizens to invest in "Liberty Bonds" were displayed in areas commonly frequented by civilians, particularly bus terminals, train stations, government buildings, public thoroughfares, and civic plazas.

16   "security at strategic locations." A photographic depiction of the nation's increased vigilance on the eve of war is contained in the February 22, 1917, issue of *LW*. As depicted on the magazine's front cover, a snow-covered naval militiaman stands guard at the base of the Brooklyn Bridge, the destruction of which would have blocked the entrance to the Brooklyn Naval Yard.

16   "acts of sabotage." For a discussion of German sabotage in the Detroit area, refer to Grant Grams, "Karl Respa and German Espionage in Canada during World War One," *Journal of Military and Strategic Studies* 8, no. 1 (2005).

16   "men who are at the head of this new unit." BFF's statement, as set forth in his letter of May 24, 1917, that he was expecting to meet these men raises an interesting question as to the type of the ambulance company he intended to enlist in. At this point in the war, there were several options available to him. It should be noted that BFF enlisted in and

subsequently served in the 1st Michigan Ambulance Company for the duration of the war. The 1st Michigan Ambulance Company was not, however, a "new unit"—it was a long-standing company in the Michigan National Guard, having served most recently in the Mexican Border War in 1916. There were two other types of ambulance companies in existence at that time that were in fact relatively new, which may account for this apparent misstatement on BFF's part. The first were the privately sponsored ambulance companies staffed by American volunteers. These companies were funded and equipped by organizations like the American Red Cross, the American Field Service, and the Norton-Harjes Volunteer Ambulance Corps, all of which had been serving under French and Italian command from the outset of the war. The second contingent of American ambulance companies that would ultimately see service in France was made up of units that would comprise the fledgling U.S. Army Ambulance Service. This component of the American Expeditionary Force came into existence on June 23, 1917. As to BFF's apparent misstatement, it is possible that he was misinformed as to the long-tenured status of the 1st Michigan Ambulance Company. That seems unlikely, however: BFF was, after all, a bright and relatively well-informed young man, and the 1st Michigan Ambulance Company was a fairly well-known National Guard unit in the Detroit area. It might be that in his discussion with "Mr. Jones" of the "State Red Cross" on the afternoon of May 24, 1917, he had been unofficially told of the impending formation of the fledgling U.S. Army Ambulance Service (the establishment of which was officially announced just four weeks later), and that he was fully expecting to enlist in one of those new units the next day, but was offered an unexpected opening in the 1st Michigan Ambulance Company instead. That this scenario is entirely possible is based on the following facts: at this point in time, established National Guard Ambulance Companies were recruiting in excess of their normal manpower requirements (122 men). The reason for this was twofold: first, it was anticipated that the imposition of new federal medical guidelines would winnow the existing ranks of established National Guard units. That such concerns were not misplaced is evidenced in a letter written by BFF on August 1, 1917, in which he noted that 18 men out of 130 were rejected by army doctors from the ranks of the 1st Michigan Ambulance Company for a host of medical reasons, with the medical fitness of an additional 20 men yet to be determined. As further noted in BFF's letter of that date, according to a recent newspaper article, a total of 250 National Guardsmen from various Detroit-area units had been rejected by federal mustering officers. In the final telling, this figure would turn out to be but a fraction of the total number of guardsmen rejected statewide. As written in a *Detroit Free Press* article on August 2, 1917, 800 National Guardsmen from Michigan had failed to pass muster with army doctors. This number constituted a 14 percent rejection rate—relatively low compared to the 24–28 percent rate of rejection for National Guardsmen from other states whose units had been medically inspected the previous year. The second factor that may have accounted for the overenlistment of personnel by National Guard Ambulance Companies is that at this point in the mustering process (the early summer of 1917), no decision had yet been made as to which ambulance companies would remain mule-drawn (which would require more manpower), and which would become motorized, as set forth in *I&G*, 10. Regardless of the reason BFF described the unit that he was about to enlist in as "new," as a matter of record on May 25, 1917 BFF enlisted in the 1st Michigan Ambulance Company. See "Medical Tests Get 800 Guards: 14 Percent of State Soldiers Rejected for Physical Disabilities—Half of Discharges Are Due to Incorrect Living," *Detroit Free Press*, August 2, 1917, 2. For more detailed information on the formation and function of ambulance companies in World War I, refer to *U.S. Army Medical Department, Office of Medical History*, "World War I: The Ambulance Service," in *The United States Army Medical Service Corps* (Washington, DC: Government Printing Office, 1925), http://history.amedd.army.mil/booksdocs/HistoryofUSArmyMSC/chapter2.html; and "The U.S. Army Ambulance Service: American Ambulance Service in France Prior to April 5, 1917," in the same work, http://history.amedd.army.mil/booksdocs/wwi/fieldoperations/chapter6.html.

16   "too smart to be swayed." The divergent views held by BFF and EMC on the necessity of the United States entering the war was likely a gender-based difference of opinion that was shared by countless other men and women as well. The cover of the January 11, 1917, issue of *LW* seems to support this conclusion. In a depiction titled "Fact and Fiction," Norman Rockwell appears to cast this difference in mindset as both a gender- and age-based divide reflective of the prevailing attitudes of the era. In 1917, in most states, women were still excluded from voting. As depicted in Rockwell's painting, an older (and ostensibly wiser) man is seated on a bench intently scouring a newspaper, presumably reading news of the war or some other item of importance, possibly women's suffrage, another hot-button issue at that time. Seated on the bench next to him is a young woman, staring dreamily off into space with a novel resting on her lap. The none-too-subtle inference being that men (especially elders) are grounded in reality, while women are not—and thus the more important issues in life (like the decision to go to war or exercising the right to vote) are more appropriately dealt with by men.

17   "*Eagle's Wing*." *The Eagle's Wing* was released on December 4, 1916 by Bluebird Photoplays (a subsidiary of Universal Pictures). The movie was touted as a "Thundering Drama with a Thundering Message from the virile pen of Rufus Steele. A Story of National Defense. Presented by a Brilliant Cast." Refer to Turner Classic Movies: http://www.tcm.com/tcmdb/title/495133/The-Eagle-s-Wing/. In April 1917, after public

disclosure of the Zimmermann telegram and the U.S. declaration of war, Bluebird Photoplays emphasized the timeliness of the movie as an additional selling point with exhibitors. See *The Moving Picture World: The Film Exhibitor's Index Guide*, April 28, 1917, 650. Newspaper accounts further reported that six members of President Wilson's cabinet and the National Council of Defense had viewed the film. It should also be noted that Bluebird's use of the words "virile pen" was an apparent attempt to assure its target audience (male viewers) that this story was appropriately masculine ("thundering"), and not written by one of the many female scriptwriters who were common in the film industry at that time. According to the American Film Institute, however, a woman, Maud Grange, wrote the screenplay—Rufus Steele was the film's director. See *American Film Institute Catalog of Feature Films*, http://catalog.afi.com/Catalog/moviedetails/14075. For an excellent discussion of the role the film industry played in shaping public opinion during the war, see Leslie M. DeBauche, *Reel Patriotism: The Movies and World War I* (Madison: University of Wisconsin Press, 1997).

17   "Zimmermann telegram." My account of the Zimmermann telegram is indebted to Barbara Tuchman, *The Zimmermann Telegram* (New York: Viking, 1958).

19   "The use of propaganda as a weapon of war." In September 1914, at the urging of David Lloyd George (chancellor of the exchequer), the cabinet of British prime minister Herbert H. Asquith established the War Propaganda Bureau as a means of counteracting the dissemination of pro-German propaganda to neutral nations. The establishment of Wellington House (as the newly created bureau would soon be known) was done with such complete discretion that its existence went largely unnoticed by most members of Parliament—its impact on shaping public opinion worldwide, however, would be profound and long lasting. Work at the bureau was divided into five geographic/linguistic zones: Scandinavia; Holland; Italy and Switzerland; Spain, Portugal, and South America; and, most important, the United States. The mission of the bureau was to influence popular and political sentiment in neutral countries in favor of the Allied cause. In furtherance of that goal, the bureau enlisted the help of academic experts and historians, such as Arnold Toynbee, Lewis Namier, and James W. Headlam-Morley, to identify issues, events, and audiences that would lend themselves to a particular propagandist message. The creative talents of such writers and artists as novelist Anthony Hope Hawkins and Dutch political cartoonist Louis Raemaekers were also utilized to craft messages. In delivering a particular message to a target audience, the bureau drew on the expertise of media and public relations agents like A. S. Watt and the merchandizing savvy of business magnates like Harry Gordon Selfridge. The ultimate form that an individual piece of propaganda took was varied, including but not limited to pamphlets, newspaper articles, academic papers, books, medals, knickknacks and other war-related

curiosities, photographs, paintings, illustrations, poster art, political cartoons, public rallies, lecture tours, exhibitions, bazaars, songs, the-atrical productions, and motion pictures. For a more extensive discussion, refer to M. L. Sanders, "Wellington House and British Propaganda during the First World War," *Historical Journal* (March 1975): 119–46.

19   "The onslaught of propaganda." From the outbreak of hostilities in August 1914, the United States became the target of an intense propaganda campaign by both sides. Once the country declared war, however, and the Creel Committee had begun its work, the homegrown dissemination of propaganda quickly dwarfed the prior efforts of all of the belligerent nations combined—in a matter of days, more than 20 million posters promoting war-related activities (from the enlistment of recruits to the establishment of Liberty Gardens) were produced and distributed throughout the nation. See Cozzolino, Knutson, and Lubin, *World War I and American Art*, 49, citing Walton Rawls, *Wake Up, America! World War I and the American Poster* (New York: Abbeville, 1988).

19   "The first casualty when war comes is truth." Although this statement has been commonly attributed to Hiram Warren Johnson, the isolationist senator from California, there is no record of him having actually uttered these words on the floor of the U.S. Senate. That he could have done so, however, in the context of another setting is likely, given that words to that effect had been expressed by others throughout the ages, from Samuel Johnson to Rudyard Kipling to Greek dramatist Aeschylus in the fifth century BC.

20   "munitions gap." In Great Britain, the political maelstrom generated by the munitions shortage would come to be known as "the Shell Crisis of 1915." In May 1915, the issue reached crisis proportions, contributing to the dissolution of the liberal government of Prime Minister H. H. Asquith. To rectify the problem, the Ministry of Munitions was established under David Lloyd George. For a thorough discussion of munitions shortages in Great Britain, France, Germany, and Russia, see Hew Strachan, "Shell Shortage," in *The First World War: To Arms*, vol. 1 (Oxford: Oxford University Press, 2001).

20   "turned to American manufacturers." From August 1914 to September 1915, the U.S. government instituted a policy that prohibited American banks from issuing direct loans to belligerent nations. The chief proponent of this ban was William Jennings Bryan (secretary of state), who believed that by denying the combatants the money with which to purchase arms and munitions, an extremely expensive and brutal war could be brought to an end. Interestingly, a similar ban on the sale of armaments and munitions from American manufacturers to combatants was never enacted by the United States. Though laudable in intent, the ban on bank loans began to lose political traction almost from the outset. In October 1914, the ban was softened to permit the extension of credit to belligerent nations that were reluctant to deplete their reserves of gold for purposes of trade, and by September 1915,

fearing that any further loss of business would trigger an economic recession at home, President Woodrow Wilson lifted the ban entirely. Immediately thereafter (October 1915), financier J. P. Morgan organized a syndicate of over two thousand banks to loan $500 million to Great Britain and France. By 1917, American banks were loaning Great Britain $10 million per day to buy goods from manufacturers in the United States. Simply put, war was good for the American economy. See Kendrick A. Clements, "Woodrow Wilson and World War I," *Presidential Studies Quarterly* 34, no. 1 (2004): 62–82. See also front cover of the December 28, 1916, issue of *LW*, titled "The Golden Shower," depicting a blue-collared American worker and top-hatted business mogul standing ankle deep under a shower of gold coins.

23   "blockade . . . waters adjacent to Great Britain and Ireland" To view a copy of the German declaration of naval blockade of shipping to Great Britain and Ireland, issued on February 4, 1915, see Charles F. Horne, ed., *Source Records of the Great War*, vol. 3 (New York: National Alumni, 1923).

23   "sailing under false colors." Compliance with the Cruiser Rules was complicated by the British Navy's use of Q-boats. Q-boats were armed naval vessels disguised to look like merchant ships, often illicitly displaying the colors of neutral nations in an attempt to entice an unsuspecting U-boat captain to the surface and issue fair warning—thereby affording the Q-boat the opportunity to open fire at close range. The most notorious of these Q-boat incidents occurred on August 19, 1915, during which the Q-boat HMS *Baralong* was sailing under cover of U.S. flag, causing the German submarine *U-27* to permit the *Baralong* to get close enough to destroy the U-boat. The twelve German sailors who had initially managed to survive the attack (by abandoning the sinking U-boat) were executed by the crew of the *Baralong* as they floundered helplessly in the water. In the diplomatic wake of the incident, the U.S. response to the illegal use of its flag by the British Navy was muted at best. The German Navy responded by no longer requiring U-boat captains to surface in order to issue fair warning, instituting instead a policy of unrestricted submarine warfare.

23   "In the wake of the disaster." For discussion of events leading up to the sinking of the RMS *Lusitania* and the propaganda battle that ensued, refer to David Ramsay, *Lusitania: Saga and Myth* (New York: Norton, 2002). For film footage of the RMS *Lusitania's* last voyage (depicting passengers boarding the ship and the ship's departure from New York City Harbor, May 1, 1915) refer to film no. 111-H-1221, NAMS.

24   "Great Britain would own the moral high ground." It should be pointed out that not all Americans were convinced that Germany was solely responsible for the disaster. There were those who believed that none of the parties involved had clean hands, including the United States. In President Woodrow Wilson's cabinet, that skepticism was voiced by William Jennings Bryan, secretary of state. In Bryan's view, the practice

of allowing unsuspecting civilians to travel aboard British passenger ships transporting contraband was tantamount to putting women and children on the front lines of combat. Bryan further believed that the U.S. government had a duty to discourage, if not altogether ban, American citizens from traveling on the ships of belligerent nations. Wilson and most of his cabinet did not share this view—differentiating "England's violation of neutral rights . . . from Germany's violation of the rights of humanity." Realizing that he was at irreconcilable odds with the president, Bryan resigned his post as secretary of state on June 8, 1915. In Bryan's judgment, Wilson's reluctance to hold both sides equally accountable for their reckless conduct was an indication that his administration was unduly sympathetic toward Great Britain, and that that bias would eventually cause the United States to enter the war on the side of the Allies. Nearly two years later, he would be proven correct. For a firsthand account of the relationship and ongoing dialogue (including correspondence) between William Jennings Bryan and President Woodrow Wilson from the period of time immediately preceding the sinking of the RMS *Lusitania* up to Bryan's resignation as secretary of state, see William Jennings Bryan and Mary Baird, "War Is Declared in Europe" and "Mr. Bryan's Resignation," in *The Memoirs of William Jennings Bryan* (Chicago: Johnson C. Winston, 1925), 395–414, 415–28.

24 "denied that the *Lusitania* had been transporting contraband." For decades, successive administrations of the British government maintained the fiction that the *Lusitania* had not been carrying military-grade munitions in her hold. In 1982, technology finally stripped the British of the ability to simply dismiss any innuendo to the contrary when a deep-sea salvage company announced plans to explore the ship's wreckage. As set forth in a memorandum written in 1982 by Noel Marshall, head of the North American Department of the British Foreign Office, the truth of the matter was still a closely held secret: "The facts are that there is a large amount of ammunition in the wreck. The Treasury have decided that they must inform the salvage company of this fact in the interests of the safety of all concerned. Although there have been rumors in the press that the previous denial of the presence of munitions was untrue, this would be the first acknowledgement of the facts by HMG." Marshall's memorandum was eventually declassified for public inspection in 2014. See "Revealed: British Officials Feared Sunk WWI Cruise Ship *Lusitania* Could 'Literally Blow Up on Us' in 1982 Salvage Mission," *Daily Mail*, May 1, 2014.

24 "infamous 'Lusitania Medal.'" A British reproduction of the medal was purchased by BFF in Edinburgh in 1919. It was found by the authors among BFF's personal effects. Translated, the front side of medal reads: "Keine Bann Ware" (No Contraband); DER GROSS-DAMPFER LUSITANIA DURCH EIN DEUTSCHES TAUCHBOOT VERSENKT 5 May 1915 (The Liner Lusitania sunk by German submarine May 5, 1915); the back side reads: GERSHAFT

UBER ALLES (Business Over All). Also note the skeleton depicted working in the window of the Cunard Line (CUNARD LINIE) ticket office (FAURKARTEN AUSGABE), and the German ambassador (seen in a top hat) wagging a finger of warning behind a customer in line who is seemingly oblivious to the headline U BOOT GEFAHR (U-boat danger) printed on the back page of the newspaper he is reading.

24   "British propaganda campaign." Each British-produced medal was packaged in a presentation box that had sixteen lines of factually questionable anti-German propaganda printed on the lid, the last line reading: "The picture (reverse design) seeks apparently to propound the theory that if a murderer warns his victims of his intention, the guilt of the crime will rest with the victim not the murderer." For good measure, a leaflet containing additional anti-German propaganda was tucked inside each box. For discussion of the Lusitania Medal, refer to an article written by Phil Dutton (curator of the Imperial War Museum): "How a German Medallion Became a British Propaganda Tool," *Imperial War Museum Review*, no. 1 (1986).

25   "the latest spate of U-boat attacks." Between February 1, 1917, and April 1, 1917, nine merchant ships belonging to maritime companies registered in the United States were sunk by German U-boats and marine mines. The most egregious of these incidents (cited by President Wilson in his address to Congress on April 2, 1917) involved the *Vigilancia* on March 16, the *City of Memphis* on March 17, and the *Illinois* on March 18, 1917.

26   "the world's greatest advertising adventure." This statement was no exaggeration on Creel's part. In the estimation of art historian David Lubin, the unparalleled success of war propagandists had been such that the face of advertising was forever changed—from a sales model that was predicated on words to one that relied on "images with eye appeal." See Cozzolino, Knutson, and Lubin, *World War I and American Art*, 45–55; and Creel, *How We Advertised America*, 4.

CHAPTER 3: MARKING TIME

27   "one of the most prodigious family trees in the New World." The facts in this chapter concerning Field family history are drawn from a self-published genealogical treatise titled *Progenitors and Descendants of Our Grandfather Seldon Field* written by JBF in 1934.

28   "An Interlude." There is no specific date affixed to this essay. It does appear, however, that the essay was written by BFF while employed at Culver Military Academy (1923–26). As to the sentence in the essay highlighted by BFF in quotation marks ("I didn't raise my son to be a soldier"), it referred not only to his parents' reaction on first learning of his enlistment but also to the title of an antiwar song popular at that time. Released in 1915, "I Didn't Raise My Son to Be a Soldier," written in support of the pacifist movement, sold over 650,000 copies. It was

clearly marketed to mothers in particular, meant to strike an emotional chord; inscribed in bold lettering at the top of the sheet music are the words: "A Mother's Plea for Peace." The song's popularity was short-lived. In the spring of 1917 (after the United States had declared war on Germany), public sentiment quickly shifted in favor of war, and the Victor Talking Machine Company ceased distribution of the song. At that point, pro-war songs like George M. Cohan's "Over There" (written on April 7, 1917) became all the rage. For an extensive discussion of music as a tool of propaganda, refer to K. A. Wells, "Music as War Propaganda: Did Music Help Win the First World War?" in *The Parlor Songs Academy: Lessons in America's Popular Music History*, 2004, http://parlorsongs.com/issues/2004-4/thismonth/feature.php. See also *Songs of the Peace Movement of World War I*, https://www.loc.gov/item/has.200197516.

29   "the Powers were one of the oldest families of Quakers." The information contained in this chapter concerning the Power family's migration from England to Rhode Island in the mid-1700s, then to upstate New York, and then to Farmington, Michigan, in 1823, as well as the family's Quaker background, is drawn from Debra Ann Pawlak, *Farmington and Farmington Hills*, The Making of America (Charleston, SC: Arcadia, 2003), 21–37; a six-page handwritten family genealogy by Birdie Ella Power, covering the years 1824 to 1936; and newspaper obituary notices for Amy Power, dated February 29, 1892, and Arthur Power, dated January 13, 1892 (summarizing the Power family migration to Michigan).

29   "In a letter written to Estelle." The description of events leading up to and including Sunday, June 24, 1917, are based on a letter from BFF to EMC dated June 27, 1917, BFFP.

30   "the strict etiquette of the time." In 1969, EMC made a point of commenting on the importance of proper etiquette between young men and women in 1917—writing in red ink on the outside of the envelope containing the abovementioned letter from BFF, "Having graduated from High S., my mother gave me a book on etiquette—pretty strict for those days—*E '69*."

30   "Byron would find great solace in music." During the war, BFF's letters to EMC often contained references to songs and the sentiments they expressed. One letter in particular stood out in that regard. Written on March 13, 1918, from Baccarat, France, it was addressed to EMC's mother and expressed a "wish for those happy songs, for a return to those happy days gone by." Also included in the letter was a sketch of the parlor of the Cozine household, in which BFF depicted himself seated at the piano with members of the Cozine family gathered around.

31   "Dickie was a public figure of almost mythical proportions." Biographical information concerning Dr. Dickie is drawn from Robert Gildart, *Albion College, 1835–1960, A History* (Chicago: Lakeside, 1961).

31   "Dickie began by relating." There is no record of the text of the speech delivered by Dr. Dickie at the Masonic Lodge on June 24, 1917. The words attributed to Dr. Dickie in this chapter (as well as the tenor of the speech) are based on a newspaper article in the *Syracuse Herald* on March 22, 1918, quoting verbatim a similar speech on *Kultur* delivered by Dickie to a meeting of businessmen in Syracuse, New York.

31   "a monster who has outdone Attila." The lurid extremes used by propagandists to justify U.S. entry into the war is graphically depicted on the May 3, 1917, cover of *LW*, titled "Despotism against Democracy." In the painting by James Montgomery Flagg, the Hun is depicted as a bloodthirsty (if not lustful) barbarian in the process of assaulting a dignified Lady Liberty (clad head to toe in pure white). See also the recruiting poster titled "Destroy This Mad Brute—Enlist," https://www.loc.gov/pictures/resource/ds.03216/.

31   "The cause of this war was anything but simple." Information on the factors contributing to the outbreak of hostilities in Europe is drawn from Barbara Tuchman, *The Guns of August* (New York: Ballantine Books, 1962); Holger Herwig, "Military Doomsday Machine? The Decisions for War, 1914," *Journal of Military and Strategic Studies* 13, no. 4 (2011).

34   "German soldiers did in fact execute." In order to properly contextualize the callous disregard displayed by German soldiers toward civilians in Belgium and France, it is necessary to discuss the German plan of attack. Known as the Schlieffen Plan (after its architect Field Marshal Alfred Von Schlieffen), the plan called for the German Army to invade France by way of Belgium, then sweep south to take Paris, all within six weeks—which in theory would force France to sue for peace before Russia could mobilize its army and launch an attack on Germany from the east. Speed was the all-important element in the success of the plan. In their haste to adhere to this daunting deadline, German troops took little time to differentiate between combatants and innocent civilians caught in the path of the onrushing army. For a detailed examination of the atrocities committed by German soldiers in Belgium and France during the first days of the war, the propaganda that attended those atrocities, and the differing accounts filed by American war correspondents concerning them, refer to John Horne and Alan Kramer, *German Atrocities, 1914: A History of Denial* (New Haven: Yale University Press, 2001).

35   "speaking out against." Refer to William H. Thomas, *Unsafe for Democracy: World War I and the U.S. Justice Department's Covert Campaign to Suppress Dissent* (Madison: University of Wisconsin Press, 2008).

36   "ministers numbered among those who had changed their minds." For a discussion of changing views in the Methodist Church concerning the propriety of the war, refer to Raymond Forest Brown, "The Church Protests against War," in "The Development of the Social Creed of the Methodist Church" (PhD diss., Boston University, 1942), 141–65.

37 "mainly the same as the Commencement speech." The commencement baccalaureate sermon referred to by BFF in his letter to EMC as being "mainly the same" as the speech given by Dr. Dickie at the Masonic Lodge was titled "*Kultur* versus Culture." Delivered on June 17, 1917, the speech is referenced in the Albion College newspaper the *Pleiad*, June 5, 1917, 1. See also the October 30, 1917, edition of the *Pleiad*, reporting on a similar speech delivered by Dr. Dickie, titled "The Peculiarities of the German People," to record crowds at Albion College in support of the Liberty Loan Campaign on October 23 and 24, 1917. It should also be noted that EMC's father, Harlan Cozine, is mentioned in the article as being the music director at the meeting. In yet another newspaper account (contained in the July 10, 1917, edition of the *Ludington Daily News*) Dr. Dickie was reportedly scheduled to deliver a speech titled "Kaiserism and *Kultur*" at a Methodist Church Camp Meeting.

38 "Four Minute Men." The label "Four Minute Men" was derived from an agreement between the Committee on Public Information and motion picture theater owners wherein volunteer speakers (approved by the committee) were allowed to deliver patriotic speeches to movie audiences during intermissions—provided those speeches did not exceed four minutes in length (the average time it took projectionists to change a movie reel). In an effort to ensure that the speaker program did not to wear out the goodwill of theater owners and their ticket-paying customers, the committee gave prospective speakers a template and content guidelines to follow, and encouraged them to practice and time their speeches at home prior to appearing onstage. These guidelines were strictly enforced by the committee—those who could not adhere to this time limit or failed to confine their speeches to authorized content, were promptly removed as speakers. Refer to Committee on Public Information, Division of Four Minute Men, *Purpose and Plan of the Four Minute Men* (Washington, DC: Government Printing Office, 1917). For a thorough discussion of the Four Minute Men and various other campaigns to drum up public support for the war, refer to Robert Wells, "Mobilizing Public Support for War: An Analysis of American Propaganda during World War I" (paper presented at the Annual Meeting of International Studies Association, New Orleans, March 24–27, 2005). See also George Creel, "The Four Minute Men," in *How We Advertised America: The First Telling of the Amazing Story of the Committee on Public Information That Carried the Gospel of Americanism to Every Corner of the Globe* (New York: Harper & Bros., 1920), 84–99; and Alfred Cornebise, *War as Advertised: The Four Minute Men and America's Crusade* (Philadelphia: American Philosophical Society, 1984), 154.

CHAPTER 4: PASSING MUSTER

39 "From the time of its inception." Benson J. Lossing, *The Pictorial Fieldbook of the War of 1812* (New York: Harper & Bros., 1868), 278n.2.

39 "Michigan militiamen had never failed to answer the call to duty." In an effort to encourage young men to enlist, military recruiters and pro-war propagandists emphasized this time-honored tradition. The militia-bedecked cover of the October 20, 1917 edition of *LW* speaks to that patriotic theme.

40 "report to their home station." Refer to "125, 000 Guards Now Mobilized," *Detroit Free Press*, July 15, 1917, reporting on the executive order calling militiamen for federal service. See also "31st Ready, Will Leave by August 1," *Detroit Free Press*, July 16, 1917, reporting on the 31st Infantry Regiment, and the 1st Michigan Ambulance Company answering the call to duty at the Detroit Armory.

40 "At 9:00 that morning." My description of BFF's experience in reporting for duty on Monday, July 16, 1917, relies on his letters to EMC dated July 13, 17, 1917, BFFP; and "Rookies," in *HAC168*, 3–4. For the remainder of BFF's stay in Detroit (July 17–August 12, 1917), this chapter's account draws on letters from BFF to EMC dated July 18, 26, 1917; August 1, 6, 12, 1917; and letter from BFF to Professor Harlan Cozine dated July 23, 1917, BFFP.

40 "Captain Robert Baskerville." For background on Baskerville, see "Baskerville, Robert J.," in *The Book of Detroiters: A Biographical Dictionary of Leading Living Men of the City of Detroit*, 2nd ed., ed. Albert Nelson Marquis (Chicago: A. N. Marquis, 1914), 40.

41 "could not afford to put him up at a hotel." For perspective on the expense of staying at a hotel, refer to (1) the letterhead of stationery from the Henry Clay Hotel (used by BFF to write to EMC on August 1, 1917), in which room rates at the hotel are listed as ranging from $1.25 to $2.50 per night; and (2) the cost of a furnished room at the YMCA in Chicago as advertised in *Association Men: Official Magazine of North American Young Men's Christian Association*, March 1922, 249: "50 cents to $1.00 a day." It should also be noted that even at this relatively inexpensive price, a room at the YMCA still would have depleted BFF's limited funds, as evidenced in a letter written by BFF on October 7, 1917, in which he noted that his salary as a buck private was $30 per month before taxes.

43 "Helping to guide Byron." For background on Dr. Ballin, see Irving I. Edgar, "Dr. Max Ballin," parts 1–3, *Michigan Jewish History* 10, no. 1 (1970): 18–24; 11, no. 2 (1971), 13–19; 18, no. 2 (1978): 3–6.

45 "pocket-sized edition of the New Testament." In addition to being a source of spiritual inspiration, the pocket Bible also served as a travel log. BFF used the blank pages inside the back cover of the Bible to note (in chronological order) each location where he was stationed during the war.

45 "rejected for various medical reasons." Other than mentioning the concern that his eyesight would not pass muster with army doctors, BFF's letters do not refer to any other medical tests administered during the mustering process. At that time, the usual battery of medical tests

conducted on recruits consisted of screening for obvious disqualify-
ing conditions, like infectious diseases (e.g., tuberculosis and syphilis)
and, muscular-skeletal debilities (e.g., inguinal and abdominal her-
nias, severe scoliosis). That is not to say, however, that other, more
exacting tests were not contemplated. In the summer of 1917, the U.S
Army (with the help of psychiatric experts) began to develop psychological tests designed to identify recruits who were mentally unfit for
service. Prior to this war, any number of ad hoc screening methods
had been employed in an attempt to weed out mentally defective
recruits. Due to the unusually grueling nature of this war, however (in
particular the recognition of shell shock as an injury of war), and the
large number of men who would soon be entering combat, the army
sought to employ a more precise method of assessing the intellectual
and emotional suitability of recruits to withstand the rigors of modern
warfare, and to allocate that manpower in the most efficient manner
possible. To that end, a series of experimental tests were conducted on
Regular Army and National Guard units during the summer of 1917.
These new tests were called the Alpha Test (for literate recruits) and
the Beta Test (for illiterate recruits). Although there is no direct evidence to indicate that the 1st Michigan Ambulance Company (or other
Detroit-based National Guard units) participated in the preliminary
studies conducted during this time frame, there is some evidence in
BFF's letters to suggest that the mental fitness of recruits to serve was
an issue of which he was aware. Specifically, in a letter to EMC's father,
Harlan Cozine, dated July 23, 1917, BFF made a point of noting that
"as companies go, . . . our men are considerably better than the average in intelligence," followed by a letter to EMC on August 1, 1917, in
which he informed her that he had finally been medically accepted for
service, remarking that "it seems the sportive features of this monkey aren't quite prominent enough to keep the doctors from allowing
him to be a soldier," implying perhaps ("sportive" as a synonym for
behavioral) that he had been subjected to some form of psychological/
mental assessment. See BFF letters dated July 23, 1917, and August 1,
1917. See also Charles Yoakum and Robert Yerkes, *Army Mental Tests*
(New York: Henry Holt, 1920); Robert Cardona and Elspeth Ritchie,
"Psychological Screening of Recruits Prior to Accession in the US Military," in *Recruit Medicine: Textbook of Military Medicine* (Washington,
DC: Office of the Surgeon General, U.S. Department of Army, 2006),
297–309.

CHAPTER 5: THIS IS NO SUNDAY SCHOOL

49 In this chapter, my description of BFF's experiences in Camp Grayling
    from August 12, 1917, to September 11, 1917, is based on letters from
    BFF to EMC dated August 13, 15, 18, 19, 23, 26, 27, 28, 29, 30, 1917; Sep-
    tember 2, 4, 5, 6, 7, 8, 10, 1917, BFFP; and "In Camp," in *HAC168*, 5–6.

50   "the men entertained themselves." As set forth in BFF's letters and *HAC168* at 5, while the Michigan Ambulance Company was training at Camp Grayling, during the evenings the atmosphere in camp more closely resembled the youthful exuberance of a scout jamboree than the grim-faced determination of soldiers girding themselves for war. The fact that such convivial settings were but a momentary diversion from the unrelentingly cruel conditions that awaited the men in France did not deter publicists and recruiters from playing on the emotions engendered by the portrayal of such congenial (but fleeting) moments in camp to drum up support for the war. For an example of this promotional sleight of hand, see the depiction titled "Over There"—created by Norman Rockwell for the January 31, 1918, cover of *Life* magazine (later used as the cover for the musical score to George M. Cohan's stirring war song, "Over There"). Whether it had been Rockwell's original intent or not, when viewed in retrospect, this endearing camp vignette assumes an almost regretful tone as it captures the unbridled enthusiasm and naivete of recruits like BFF and his Camp Grayling tent mates whose innocence would soon be extinguished in the hellfire of war.

53   "exploits of Herbert Jackson." "Soldier Weds: Gets 30 Days Manual Labor," *Detroit News*, August 31, 1917.

54   "joy derived from the new fad of kissing." Refer to "As Advertised," *Life*, August 30, 1917, 332.

56   "Camp Mills was located on a tract of land." My description of BFF's experiences in Camp Mills from September 13, 1917, to October 17, 1917, is based on "At the Eastern Mobilization Camp," in *HAC168*, 7–9; "Camp Mills," in *I&G*, 7–9; and letters from BFF to EMC dated September 13, 17, 20, 26, 28, 1917; and October 2, 4, 5, 7, 10, 12, 14, 15, 17, 1917.

57   "ten-mile marches." For a head-to-toe depiction of the gear that a foot soldier was required to carry, refer to the front cover of the August 24, 1916, issue of *LW* titled "The U.S.A. Fighting Man's Burden."

57   "sleep with the flaps of their tents open." Refer to Esmond R. Long, "Tuberculosis in World War I," in *The Department of the United States Army in the World War: Communicable and Other Diseases*. (Washington, DC: U.S. Government Printing Office, 1928), 9:171–202.

57   "the camp would be shut down." "Abandon Camp Mills Because of Weather: Secretary Baker Announces Department's Decision—Lack of Blankets Denied," *NYT*, December 15, 1917.

57   "spectators turned out to cheer." "Three Brigades in Review: 40,000 Visitors Watch Troops Marching at Camp Mills," *NYT*, October 1, 1917.

58   "Nebraska must be a good sized town." *I&G*, 12.

60   "scarcely a household in America . . . didn't have a recording of McCormack's 'Mother Machree.'" This statement was practically if not actually true. As reflected in the Victor Talking Machine advertisement displayed on the back cover of the September 30, 1917, issue of *LW* (extolling McCormack's life story and beautiful voice), as the great tenor of his time, McCormack was under an exclusive recording

contract with the Victor Company. That BFF numbered among those who were great admirers of John McCormack's musical prowess is evidenced by the piano sheet music found among BFF's personal belongings, including these songs popularized by McCormack: "Macushala," "Mother Machree," "Roses of Picardy," "The Barefoot Trail," "The Old Refrain," "The Trumpeter," and "The Rainbow of Love."

60   "there is no room in the country for hyphenated Americanism." The fact that former president Theodore Roosevelt was a staunch advocate of American patriotism and fierce critic of President Woodrow Wilson's isolationist policies is amply illustrated on the cover of the July 27, 1916, issue of *LW*. A scowling, saber-wielding Teddy Roosevelt is clad in his Rough Rider uniform, ready as always to join the fray. The word *Americanism* is boldly inscribed on the blade of Roosevelt's sword. The illustration's title, "Not Too Proud to Fight," is a none-too-subtle reference to a speech that President Wilson had delivered to group of immigrants at a naturalization ceremony in Philadelphia on May 10, 1915 (two days after the sinking of the RMS *Lusitania*), in which Wilson had in essence said that is permissible (indeed, preferable) for men of principle "who were too proud to fight" to turn the other cheek, as opposed to debasing their standards by entering into an unethical conflict. Although the speech was originally titled "Americanism and Foreign Born," it would be referred to as Wilson's "Too Proud to Fight" speech. Needless to say, it became fodder for critics of Wilson's isolationist policy.

60   "continued to fan the flames of suspicion." On the matter of so-called hyphenated Americans and the lengths to which some immigrants went in order to avoid detection by nativist Americans, an interesting postscript attaches to Dr. Samuel Dickie, president of Albion College, in that regard. While Dr. Dickie was busy traveling the country imploring young men to march off to war, he was not himself an American citizen. Records reflect that Dr. Dickie was born in Buford Township, Canada, in 1851 to parents who had emigrated from Scotland in 1849. The Dickie family then immigrated to Lansing, Michigan, in 1858. At no point thereafter did Dr. Dickie's parents ever apply for U.S. citizenship, and it was not until 1921, when Dr. Dickie applied for a U.S. passport (at the age of seventy) that his status as a noncitizen came to light publicly. That most of those, including BFF, who had listened to Dr. Dickie's impassioned speeches were ignorant of this fact is almost certain. Dr. Dickie's failure to apply for U.S. citizenship, despite having lived in the country for many years and having twice run for elective office during that period of time, is somewhat perplexing. To further confuse the issue is the fact that although Dr. Dickie's lack of citizenship reportedly kept him from running for president of the United States on the National Prohibition Party ticket in the 1890s, it did not deter him from making an unsuccessful run for governor of Michigan in 1886, or from subsequently being elected mayor of the city of Albion in 1896.

In analyzing this apparent discrepancy, it is important to note that the Michigan Constitution requires only that a candidate for public office be registered to vote in Michigan for four continuous years prior to an election, as opposed to the U.S. Constitution requirement that a candidate for president be a natural-born citizen. Still, that factor alone does not adequately explain Dr. Dickie's failure to apply for citizenship until 1921. There is, however, another factor to be considered, one unique to those times, that may shed some light on Dr. Dickie's apparent oversight—in the late 1800s, as ever-increasing numbers of European immigrants entered the country, antipathy toward "hyphenated Americans" gained considerable political traction with longstanding nativist citizens who felt threatened by the in-coming tide of immigration. Under such circumstances, it is reasonable to assume that as long as Dr. Dickie continued to harbor political aspirations, he would have wanted to keep his Canadian and Scottish roots hidden from the electorate. Needless to say, applying for U.S. citizenship in a timely fashion would have served to highlight Dr. Dickie's "suspect" status as a so-called hyphenated American, possibly jeopardizing his political career. It should be further noted that such concerns are not so far-fetched as might be imagined today—the fact that Dr. Dickie was of Anglo descent did not exempt him from being scrutinized as a hyphenated American. To the contrary, as noted by BFF in a newspaper interview in 1919, prior to the war, he and many other soldiers held as much enmity, if not more, toward Great Britain than they did for Germany. Lingering resentment toward the British Empire over the Revolutionary War and the War of 1812 was still a very real sentiment in the United States at that time. Although this hypothesis concerning Dr. Dickie's delinquent status as an American citizen amounts to no more than mere conjecture based on a few disparate facts, it is nevertheless an intriguing possibility. The explanation offered by Dr. Dickie in 1921 regarding his belated application for U.S. citizenship, however, is even more fanciful. In an affidavit he filed in support of his passport application (which had recently been rejected under the Travel Control Act, enacted during the war to regulate the issuance of passports for all foreign travel), Dr. Dickie averred that based on talk around the Dickie household when he was a child, he had been led to believe that his father was a naturalized U.S. citizen, which he further believed automatically conferred naturalized citizenship on himself and his brother, and that it was not until he applied for a U.S. passport in 1921 that he was finally apprised of his status as a noncitizen. For a man of Dr. Dickie's education, sophistication, and vast experience in dealing with the complexity and technicalities of government and political affairs, this after-the-fact explanation stretches the bounds of credulity. A more plausible explanation is that he simply finally got caught—for decades Dr. Dickie's bald assertion that he was a U.S. citizen had been accepted at face value, and he was not expecting the background requirements of the Travel Control Act to be so exacting and strictly enforced. Regardless of the actual truth of the matter, the extent to which Dr. Dickie's Scottish and Canadian roots may have influenced his objectivity and ardent belief that the United States should enter the war on the side of Great Britain is certainly an interesting question for consideration. See "The Man Who Would Be President," *Brantford Expositor*, June 3, 2006, 1, 11; and "The Mayor Who Wasn't a U.S. Citizen," *Morning Star*, March 30, 1997, 5.

61   "benefit concerts." "Benefits at Theatres Aid War Charities: John McCormack Sings for Soldiers and Sailors at Vaudeville Performance at Playhouse," *NYT*, May 20, 1918; "$11,000 for 69th Regiment: John McCormack Gives Recital for Dependents of Soldiers," *NYT*, October 1, 1917.

61   "lavish extravaganza." "'Cheer Up' Show at the Hippodrome: An Early Wartime Play Full of Khaki, Flags, and Marching," *NYT*, August 24, 1917.

63   "It may have been marginally better pay." After graduating high school in 1915 and prior to enrolling in Albion College in 1916, BFF worked for eight months as a primary school teacher. Refer to teacher's contract between BFF and school board, Jackson County, Michigan, dated November 12, 1915, BFFP.

63   "in anticipation of the worst-case scenario." In an effort to persuade as many enlisted men as possible to purchase War Risk Insurance, the army produced a promotional movie, *His Best Gift*, which emphasized the benefit and security derived from purchasing a government-issued insurance policy. As portrayed in the dramatized film, a married soldier, on first enlisting in the army, initially refuses to buy war-risk insurance, but prior to shipping out has a dream in which he is blinded in battle and on returning home becomes a financial burden to his wife; the next morning, the soldier has finally come to his senses and immediately rushes off to buy war insurance. Whether or not the melodramatic film had any impact on influencing recruits to purchase insurance is open to conjecture—that the War Risk Insurance program was a success, however, is well-established fact—by the end of the war, 90 percent of the soldiers and sailors who served in World War I (3.4 million) would apply for over $30 billion in coverage under the War Insurance Act. To view *His Best Gift*, refer to Army Signal Corp film, ref. no. 111-H-1542, reels 1 and 2, NAMS. For statistics on the War Risk Insurance program, see "Army 90 Percent Insured: More than 30,000,000,000 of Government Insurance Already Taken," *NYT*, August 30, 1918, 10.

66   "one of the first units to depart for France." The sanitary train's departure for France was unremarkable in all respects except one—the fate that awaited the incoming National Guard unit that would take its place at Camp Mills. For that unit, the 15th New York Infantry Regiment, the series of events that unfolded would end up highlighting one of the great social injustices in America at that time—institutional racism. At the outset of this discussion, it should be noted that at no point in BFF's

war-related writings does he ever mention the issue of race relations or describe interactions with black soldiers. His failure to comment on the matter speaks volumes as to the racial segregation that existed in the U.S. Army at that time—a practice that was implemented in all branches of U.S. government. As such, it is unlikely that BFF would have had the opportunity to observe or interact with black soldiers—there simply were no black soldiers within his immediate area. In Camp Mills a notorious incident involving elements of the Rainbow Division occurred just one week after BFF and other members of the Michigan Ambulance Company had departed for France. In late October 1917, the 15th New York Infantry Regiment (a National Guard unit from Harlem) reported to Camp Mills, where several units in the Rainbow Division were still awaiting orders to depart for Europe. The 15th New York had been transferred to Camp Mills as the result of a racially motivated altercation that had just occurred at Camp Wadsworth, South Carolina, where the all-black regiment had initially been sent for training. The men of the 15th had not instigated that altercation—to the contrary, any fair reading of the record reveals that they were the victims. Nevertheless, the regiment was immediately sent north to ease racial tensions. At this point in the mustering process, army administrators had not yet made a final decision as to where the 15th would ultimately be assigned—Colonel William Hayward, the regiment's white commander, had hoped that on being transferred to Camp Mills, the African American unit would get the opportunity to serve in combat alongside their white National Guard counterparts in the Rainbow Division. He would be sorely disappointed. Not only would the regiment not be made part of the Rainbow Division, it would not even get the opportunity to fight under American command. It was a regrettable but not totally unexpected outcome considering the pronounced ethnic, regional, and cultural differences that existed among Americans at that time. In assembling the Rainbow Division, it was difficult enough for army administrators to combine local units into the same regiment (for example, units from Brooklyn and Manhattan in the 165th Infantry Regiment), let alone meld vastly disparate regiments from across the country into one division. It was only weeks earlier, in late August, that this ugly truth made itself known when the 4th Alabama Infantry Regiment, a National Guard unit from rural Alabama, arrived at Camp Mills. The 4th Alabama came north with a rebel-sized chip on its shoulder. It did not take long before the unit was involved in an altercation with New York City's storied Irish regiment, the Fighting 69th. There had never been any love lost between the two units—the animus dating back to the Civil War. By no means, however, did soldiers from Alabama's 4th restrict their animosity toward northerners to just the Fighting 69th, or limit the expression of that dissatisfaction to the confines of Camp Mills. On subsequent trips into nearby villages on Long Island and Manhattan, soldiers from the 4th became embroiled in racially motivated attacks on black doormen, porters, and civilians. When the all-black New York 15th suddenly arrived at Camp Mills, the situation only worsened as the Alabamans took exception to serving alongside black soldiers and didn't hesitate to make their displeasure known. Not surprisingly, the Fighting 69th sided with their fellow New Yorkers against the Alabamans, and a number of skirmishes erupted, one so violent that a detachment of military police was required to intervene at point of bayonet. To remedy the situation, the New York 15th was moved once again—units were dispersed to nearby armories and other training camps until arrangements could be made to transport them overseas. In the meantime, the remaining units of the Rainbow Division that were still at Camp Mills shipped out for France. It was an expedient but hardly equitable outcome—as one commentator would later remark, "[B]lack was not a color of the rainbow." On December 27, the New York 15th finally embarked for France. After being redesignated the 369th Infantry Regiment, the unit became part of the all-black 93rd Division that would fight under French command. Known as the Harlem Hellfighters, the men of the New York 15th would go on to distinguish themselves with great courage, honor, and sacrifice during the war. Refer to Albert M. Ettinger, *A Doughboy with the Fighting 69th* (New York: Pocket Books, 1992), 8–10; Stephen Harris, *Harlem's Hell Fighters: The African American 369th Infantry in World War I* (Washington, DC: Potomac Books, 2003); Hamilton Fish, *Memoirs of an American Patriot* (Washington, DC: Regnery Gateway, 1991); Michael L. Lanning, "The Great War," in *The African-American Soldier: From Crispus Attucks to Colin Powell* (New York: Citadel, 1997), 129–48. As to the segregationist policy of the Wilson administration, see Jean Edward Smith, *FDR* (New York: Random House, 2007), 99–100.

CHAPTER 6: OVER THERE

69 "The British embargo continued unabated." As set forth in an internal report to the British War Cabinet titled "Memorandum in Regard to the Present Position of the Blockade, January 1st, 1917," the embargo had put a virtual stranglehold on the German people—by the end of the war, more than eight hundred thousand Germans would die from starvation.

69 "the Kaiser threw diplomatic caution to the wind." It took little more than forty-eight hours for fallout from the German declaration to manifest itself. On February 3, 1917, the American freighter *Housatonic* was sunk by a German U-boat—later that day President Wilson announced to a joint session of Congress that diplomatic relations with Germany had been severed. See "Relations with Germany Are Broken Off," *NYT*, February 3, 1917.

69 "the impact of the blockade on Great Britain." See William S. Sims, "When Germany Was Winning the War," in *The Victory at Sea* (London: John Murray, 1920), 1–39.

70   "Vatican tried." "German Catholics Tried Peace Move," *NYT*, June 3, 1917; "Ready for Parleys on Alsace in 1917," *NYT*, March 5, 1920; "Pope Is in Accord with Harding Plan: Views of 1917 Unchanged," *NYT*, August 29, 1921.

70   "convinced that its submarine strategy." "Germany Now Sees War's End in Fall: Official Berlin Figures Give England Only 5,000,000 Tons of Shipping," *NYT*, July 2, 1917; "3 American Ships Sunk by U-Boats," *NYT*, June 2, 1917.

70   "Pershing's attempt to censor the news." For a thorough discussion of the censorship controversy and the unauthorized Associated Press release reporting on the U-boat attack on the first U.S. troopship convoy to sail for France, see George Creel, "The Censorship Bugbear" and "The Fourth of July Fake," in *How We Advertised America: The First Telling of the Amazing Story of the Committee on Public Information That Carried the Gospel of Americanism to Every Corner of the Globe* (New York: Harper & Bros., 1920), 16–27, 28–44; "Pershing's First Force Is in France; General Praises Troops After Visit; Entire Port Put in American Control," *NYT*, July 1, 1917; "News of Our Men Held Up in Paris," *NYT*, July 2, 1917; George Creel, "Official Announcement by U.S. Government Press Bureau regarding Destroyers," June 1917, in *Sources of Records of the Great War*, vol. 5, ed. Charles F. Horne (New York: National Alumni, 1923).

72   "The first day at sea was relatively peaceful." My description of BFF's experiences during the voyage to France is based on "Voyage," in *I&G*, 15–21; "In Neptune's Domain," in *HAC168*, 9–11; and letters written by BFF to EMC dated October 25, 1917, and to JBF dated October 25, 1917, BFFP.

74   "received orders from their superior officers to destroy." Henry J. Reilly, *Americans All: The Rainbow at War* (Columbus, OH: F. J. Heer, 1936), 65.

75   "Life belts were worn." Army Signal Corps film footage of 42nd Division troops aboard the USS *Tenadore* receiving tobacco rations, exercising on deck, attending religious services on deck, lifeboat drills, and entertainment. See also gunnery drills aboard the USS *George Washington* and USS *DeKalb*, ref. no. 111-H-1382, reel 1, NAMS.

77   "German spy, traveling under cover" Reilly, *Americans All*, 75–76.

78   "another Victoria." It would appear that this particular exchange between BFF and EMC concerning the issue of women's suffrage was prompted in part by the much-publicized events unfolding in Washington, DC, at that time: Alice Paul and six fellow suffragettes were sentenced to prison on the charge of "obstructing traffic," stemming from their persistent (yet peaceful) demonstrations in front of the White House in support of a constitutional amendment guaranteeing women's suffrage. Paul and her confederates in the National Woman's Party remained incarcerated (often under brutal conditions) at the Occoquan Workhouse in Virginia until November 27, 1917. For a more detailed discussion, see Katherine H. Adams and Michael L. Keene, *Alice Paul and the American Suffrage Campaign* (Champaign: University

of Illinois Press, 2008); "Miss Alice Paul on Hunger Strike: Suffragist Leader Adopts This Means of Protesting against Washington Prison Fare: Now in Jail Hospital: Threatens to Starve to Death Unless Better Food Is Provided for Six Companions," *NYT*, November 7, 1917.

78 "the Social Creed." Raymond Forest Brown, "Social Relations," in "The Development of the Social Creed of the Methodist Church" (PhD diss., Boston University, 1942), 166–97.

CHAPTER 7: CULTURE SHOCK

83 "Saint-Nazaire was shrouded in cold gray drizzle." My description of the conditions in Saint-Nazaire and the Rainbow Division's arrival in France on November 1, 1917, is drawn from "France," in *I&G*, 22–25; and Leslie Langille, "The President Lincoln and Coetquidian," in *Men of the Rainbow* (Chicago: W. B. Conkey, 1933), 40–45. As to the medical lecture concerning venereal disease, there is no record of which officer actually delivered that warning prior to the 168th Ambulance Company departing the USS *Pastores*. There is little doubt, however, that it was done. In this chapter, I have taken poetic license by assigning that task to First Sergeant Francis Gallagher, the 168th Ambulance Company's "top cutter." I have tried to craft that scene in the spirit of other accounts (Langille, "The President Lincoln and Coetquidian," 41) and, more important, in accordance with the letter of the law as set forth in U.S. Army regulations at that time.

84 "the policy of the U.S. Army." For an excellent discussion of venereal disease in the U.S. Army in World War I, refer to Allan Brandt, *No Magic Bullet: A Social History of Venereal Disease in the United States since 1880* (Oxford: Oxford University Press, 1985), 96–121.

85 "army-regulated houses of prostitution." From the onset of the Mexican Revolution (1910), the U.S. Army stationed troops along the border between Mexico and Texas (as well as New Mexico) to ensure that hostilities between rebel fighters and Mexican federal forces remained on the southern side of the border. Nonetheless, in some instances, fighting did take place on American soil between rebel forces and U.S. soldiers. For the most part, however, interactions between American soldiers and Mexican residents were amicable—in the view of some, a little too cordial. On the cover of October 23, 1913, edition of *LW*, titled "Trouble in Mexico," a U.S. soldier is depicted intently eyeing an attractive young Mexican woman.

88 "the Michigan Ambulance Company was the first unit to disembark." See film footage of USS *Tenadores* docking at Saint-Nazaire, and troops disembarking and marching to base camp. Ref. no. 111-H-1439, NAMS.

89 "nothing short of culture shock." Perhaps the most enduring (and entertaining) expression of the cultural awakening experienced by American soldiers stationed in France is the song "How Ya Gonna Keep 'Em Down on the Farm (After They've Seen Paree?)." Written and

published in February 1919, the lyrics contemplate a domestic scene in which returning American soldiers will "never want to see a rake or a plow / and who the deuce can parley vous a cow?" when they could be "jazzin' around and paintin' the town." Performed by the legendary vaudeville entertainer Nora Bayes and Lieutenant James Reese Europe's world-renowned "Harlem Hellfighters" 369th Infantry Regimental Band, this catchy new song became a popular hit in the United States. For Lieutenant Europe and other black soldiers who had served in France, the sentiment expressed in the lyrics must have held special resonance. Like their white counterparts, black soldiers had been exposed to the more liberal attitudes of French society generally—of far greater importance to African American soldiers, however, was the fact that they had experienced less racial discrimination while stationed in France. This disparity in treatment would have a profound and lasting impact on black soldiers returning from the war. For further discussion on this point and the "Red Summer" of 1919 refer to the epilogue's endnotes.

91   "turpitude of soldiers." See William Howard Taft, *Service with Fighting Men: An Account of the Work of the American Young Men's Christian Association in the World War* (New York: Association, 1922), 109, 118.

91   "quickly the savage comes to the surface." "The Militiaman's Morals," *Literary Digest*, December 18, 1916; "Army Life Improving Health," *Literary Digest*, June 22, 1918.

91   "My dearest Birdie, you need not worry." Letter from BFF to EMC dated December 6, 1917. For a more explicit discussion of the venereal disease problem, see also letter from BFF to JBF dated November 24, 1917, BFFP.

92   "For God's sake, Raymond, don't show this to the President." One of the most notable proponents of the Progressive Era reform movement was Raymond B. Fosdick. After graduating from Princeton University (1906), and then New York Law School (1908), Fosdick began his work as a social reformer by investigating the white slave traffic in New York City. Fosdick was a friend and confidante of Woodrow Wilson, dating back to their days at Princeton University, and also had a close working relationship with John D. Rockefeller Jr. During Fosdick's long career in urban social work, he became an acknowledged expert in the fields of poverty, unemployment, prostitution, city government, police systems, and military vice. During World War I, Fosdick was commissioned by the War Department to study conditions at army and navy training camps. It was in this capacity that Fosdick empaneled the Committee on Training Camp Activities and then launched a social purification crusade to purge red-light districts from American cities and from the immediate vicinity of military training camps and bases. According to Fosdick, by the end of 1917, his hard-charging social purity crusaders had shut down 110 red-light districts. In the decades after the war, Fosdick continued to champion a myriad of public service and

philanthropic causes, the most notable being the Rockefeller Foundation. When viewed through the prism of contemporary moral standards, Fosdick's dauntless efforts during the war to implement his social purity agenda assumes almost cartoonish proportions—whether that unabashed idealism and unbridled zeal was later recognized by the great American satirist and cartoonist Al Capp in naming his well-intentioned but hapless big-city do-gooder police inspector "Fearless Fosdick" (a thinly veiled parody of Dick Tracy) is unknown. It nevertheless is an intriguing possibility to consider. Refer to Ronald Shaffer, "Social Purity and the Great Crusade," in *America in the Great War: The Rise of the War Welfare State* (Oxford: Oxford University Press, 1994), 98–108. See also Horace Green, "America: The Criminal's Happy Hunting Grounds," *LW*, July 9, 1921, 56, hailing Raymond B. Fosdick as "the greatest American authority on crime."

CHAPTER 8: THE HANDWRITING ON THE WALL

93   "In order to create room." My descriptions of BFF's experiences in Vaucouleurs, France, from November 4, 1917, to December 12, 1917, are drawn from letters written by BFF to EMC dated November 11, 16, 23, 1917, and December 3, 6, 29, 1917; letters from BFF to JBF dated November 25, 29, 1917, and December 3, 1917, BFFP; "Vaucouleurs," in *HAC168*, 11–14; and "France," in *I&G*, 25–29.

94   "iron meals." Franz A. Koehler, *Special Rations for the Armed Forces* (Washington, DC: Office of the Quartermaster General, 1958).

98   "My present life . . . religious worker." BFF's intention to become a missionary was in part grounded in a pledge he had taken at a meeting of the Epworth League at Albion College. The Epworth League was a young-adult organization in the Methodist Church that was part of a larger youth social services movement common to Protestantism at that time. Foreign mission work (global evangelism) was one of the social service/religious vocations promoted by these organizations. Some of the organizations even asked prospective missionaries to stand and take a pledge—apparently, BFF and EMC were both impressionable and devout enough to do so. Letter from BFF to EMC dated December 6, 1917, referencing the taking of that pledge "when neither of us knew exactly what it all meant." EMC annotated this in 1969, remarking, "This [inclination] was the result of religious affiliation rather than aptitude for me."

98   "'for the want of a nail' wars had been lost." For a thorough discussion of the logistics of supplying U.S. troops in France, refer to Johnson Hagood, *The Services of Supply: A Memoir of the Great War* (New York: Houghton Mifflin, 1927). See also Frank Freidel, "Supplying the Troops," in *Over There* (Ithaca, NY: Burford Books, 1964), 72–83.

99   "sheer incompetence of its lines of communication." Letter from Colonel Johnson Hagood, C.A.C. Chief of Coordination, Section G.S., 1st

Army to Chief of Staff, A.E.F. "Subject: Requirements of Advance Section," November 15, 1917, in Freidel, *Over There*, 74.

99   "a state of disarray." Hagood, *The Services of Supply*, 53.

99   "system of narrow-gauge railroad tracks." Refer to Army Signal Corps film footage of construction and operation of narrow gauge railroad system in France by U.S. troops, ref. no. 111-H-1498, reels 1, 2, NAMS.

100   "Byron took particular note of Napoleon's tomb." "Byron Field Describes Many Beauties and Wonders of Paris," *Jackson Patriot News*, November 25, 1917.

100   "in a town held by the Germans." Regarding the lack of geographic references in letters: in keeping with the army's strict rules on censorship, BFF's letters to EMC and his parents do not mention the specific location where he was encamped at any given time, or give any information as to nearby landmarks from which the Germans would be able to deduce from intercepted mail where a particular division was located. As such, at this particular time, Byron's letters are devoid of any details concerning Vaucouleurs generally or Joan of Arc historical sites specifically. Nevertheless, it is evident from the "Humoresque Section" of *HAC168* that Byron was obsessed with all things Jean d'Arc while stationed in Vaucouleurs. For someone with Byron's religious zeal, it is hard to imagine that he would not have been—Vaucouleurs was home to the ruins of Baudricourt Castle and Chapelle Castrale, both prominent sites in the life of Joan of Arc. It was at Baudricourt Castle in 1429 that Joan of Arc implored Sir Robert de Baudricourt to intercede on her behalf with the dauphin of France, Charles Valois, for permission to raise an army to expel the English from France. And it was in the crypt at Chapelle Castrale that Joan of Arc knelt and prayed for divine guidance before embarking on that quest. The fact that Byron and other self-fashioned crusaders in this latest war on French soil would want to visit both sites before marching off to battle is set forth in an essay written by Byron six years after the war ended. In a wonderfully romantic reminiscence titled "Vaucouleurs," Byron recounted his own visit to the crypt. Although Byron did not specifically mention that he and other soldiers actually knelt and prayed where Joan of Arc had previously sought inspiration, with the prospect of death in battle looming only days away, it would not have been unexpected if they had. "For Sale," in *HAC168*, 66.

100   "Before retiring." *HAC168*, 13.

CHAPTER 9: THE VALLEY FORGE HIKE

103   "on the morning of December 12." My description of BFF's experiences during the 117th Sanitary Train's hike from Vaucouleurs to Rolampont is drawn from letters written by BFF to EMC dated December 22, 24, 29, 1917; letter to JBF dated December 26, 1917, BFFP; "The Hike," in *I&G*, 38–44; and "The Long Walk," in *HAC168*, 14–16.

107   "Christmas packages from home" The transmittal of letters between soldiers at the front and loved ones at home in a timely manner was a difficult undertaking for army administrators—the shipment of packages even more so. As reflected on a Christmas package shipping label that BFF had saved for posterity, the size and weight restrictions imposed by the army was strictly enforced. Each package could measure no larger than nine by four by three inches and weigh no more than three pounds. See the depiction by Norman Rockwell for the front cover of December 22, 1917, issue of *LW* titled "They Remembered Me!" portraying a young soldier opening a Christmas package.

107   "a second series of Liberty Bonds." During the war, the Treasury Department issued four series of Liberty Bonds to help finance the war. A fifth bond, called the Victory Liberty Loan, was issued after the war. Posters urging citizens to buy war bonds relied on the usual patriotic themes. Most of these themes were relatively tame compared to the worst-case scenario displayed on two Liberty Bond posters produced in 1918, in which Americans were essentially warned that dire consequences could result from their failure to buy bonds—that the war would end up at their doorstep. The first of these posters depicted the Statue of Liberty silhouetted in a fiery conflagration as enemy bombers flew overhead. The other depicted a green-eyed, blood-soaked Hun peering menacingly over the Atlantic Ocean at the United States—titled "Beat Back the Hun with Liberty Bonds," this poster is one of the most lurid pieces of poster art produced during the war. Also refer to Army Signal Corps film footage depicting Charlie Chaplin, Douglas Fairbanks, Mary Pickford, and others at Liberty Loan campaigns and parades, ref. no. 111-H-1133, reel 2, NAMS.

109   "knitting a woolen 'helmet.'" The Knit Your Bit campaign mentioned by BFF and EMC was highlighted on the cover of the December 1, 1917, issue of *LW* titled "The Santa Claus of 1917."

109   "I've seen enough boozing to last a life-time." In a cruel twist of fate, BFF would become an alcoholic later in life. Whether his recurring battles with alcoholism were due in part to the trauma he experienced during the war will never be known—the definitive answer to that question went to the grave with him. The fact that alcoholism is now recognized as a symptom commonly associated with post-traumatic stress disorder does, however, suggest that that experience may have been a contributing factor in BFF's postwar struggles.

113   "hobnail boot . . . Pershing Boot." For an excellent and exhaustive discussion of the footwear worn by soldiers in the AEF during World War I, refer to *The Medical Department of United States Army in the World War*, Vol. 6, *Sanitation*, "Footwear" (Washington DC: Government Printing Office 1926) 626–35.

113   "five pairs of socks with boards tied to his ankles." Diary entries of WJD, December 26, 1917; December 27, 1917, DP.

CHAPTER 10: REMEMBER JESUS CHRIST

117 "quartered in drafty Adrian barracks." My description of Byron Field's experiences while stationed in the training sector at Rolampont from December 26, 1917, to February 16, 1918, is drawn from letters written by BFF to EMC dated January 1, 2, 3, 4, 6, 18, 29, 1918, and February 2, 7, 10, 1918; letters written to JBF dated January 4, 9, 17, 20, 27, 29, 1918, and February 3, 8, 11, 1918, BFFP; "Training," in *I&G*, 45–52; and "Rolampont," in *HAC168*, 16–18.

119 "Baskerville put the men through their early-morning paces." Refer to Army Signal Corps film footage of 42nd Division in training at Rolampont, December 26, 1917 to February 16, 1918, ref. no. 111-H-1259, NAMS. The footage includes scenes of infantry training, mortar training, artillery training, and members of the Michigan Ambulance Company washing up in the river.

CHAPTER 11: BAPTISM BY FIRE

127 "caught the train out of Rolampont for the front." My description of BFF's experiences while stationed at Baccarat from February 17, 1918, to March 22, 1918, is drawn from letters by BFF to EMC dated February 27, 1918, and March 5, 7, 20, 1918; letters to JBF dated March 1, 18, 22, 1918; diary entries by BFF dated March 4–17, 1918, BFFP; "Training," in *I&G*, 52–60; and "The Crucible of Fire—Baccarat Front," in *HAC168*, 21–24.

129 "knock the enemy's balloons from the sky." For Army Signal Corps film footage of operation of an observation balloon, see ref. no. 111-H-1356, reel 2, NAMS; and for a German plane being shot down after strafing and setting an American observation balloon on fire, see ref. no. 111-M-51, reel 2, NAMS.

129 "German 'Archy' is terrifying at first acquaintance." Eddie Rickenbacker, "An Eventful 'D' Day," in *Fighting the Flying Circus* (Philadelphia: J. B. Lippincott, 1919), 280–81.

131 "walked over and shared cigarettes." See the depiction of a French infantryman (*chasseur à pied*) and an American doughboy taking a break to enjoy a cigarette and a moment of camaraderie together. This depiction appeared on the front cover of *LW* on February 16, 1918—only two days before Byron and the ambulance company marched into Gerbéviller and engaged in a similar gesture of goodwill (*I&G*, 54).

133 "stationed in Lunéville." See Army Signal Corps film footage of 42nd Division in Lunéville sector, February 11, 1918–March 23, 1918, ref. no. 111-H-1262, reels 1, 2, 3, NAMS.

134 "the designated role of the YMCA." General Order No. 26-II-1, published on August 28, 1917.

134 "obtain reading and writing materials." Throughout the war, many of BFF's letters home were written on stationery bearing the YMCA logo.

134 "The woman assigned to run the YMCA hut in Baccarat was Gertrude Bray." DoGB, entry March 4, 1918, 14.

137 "they have their own music." The uniqueness of this is further evidenced in a December 3, 1917, letter from BFF to JBF in which BFF requested that JBF mail him a packet of piano sheet music and an old hymnal as there was "not a note" of printed music to be found at the Y huts.

137 "The bad weather brings the men inside . . . our canteen is a very popular place." Despite the great popularity of YMCA huts with the troops as places of much-needed respite, there were occasions when even the relative calm of a Y hut did not lend itself to unfettered feelings of bonhomie. As related by GB: "[T]here is a good deal of antagonism between the men from New York and the men from Alabama. It arose over some trouble in camp at home, and it breaks out here frequently and I dislike to have the two sides get to arguing in my canteen, for you never know who has a hand grenade in his pocket and this room is too small to be throwing them around and not damage somebody." DoGB, entry April 3, 1918, 25.

139 "carried wounded back from the front line." For a comprehensive discussion of the methods employed in combat for the care and evacuation of the sick and wounded, refer to "Medical Service of the Division in Combat," in *The Medical Department of the United States Army in the World War*, vol. 8, *Field Operations* (Washington, DC: Government Printing Office, 1925), 105–55.

140 "Terrific bombardment" Diary entry by WJD, March 7, 1918, DP.

143 "The 75s and 90s, and 150s and 320s." For a thorough discussion of the development and use of artillery in World War I, refer to Bruce I. Gudmundsson, *On Artillery* (Westport, CT: Praeger, 1993).

145 "sustaining over four hundred casualties in the gas attack." For an excellent discussion of the use of poison gas in World War I, refer to Corey J. Hilmas, Jeffery K. Smart, and Benjamin A. Hill Jr., "History of Chemical Warfare," in *Medical Aspects of Chemical Warfare* (Washington, DC: Government Printing Office, 2008), 9–42.

CHAPTER 12: THERE MUST BE A KIND GOD ABOVE

147 "The Rainbow Division's ten-day march to the rear." My description of BFF's experiences while stationed in the Baccarat sector from March 22, 1918, to June 24, 1918, is drawn from letters by BFF to EMC dated March 2, 7, 1918, April 19, 29, 1918, May 28, 1918, June 8, 24, 1918; letters to JBF dated April 1, 7, 8, 11, 18, 1918, May 1, 5, 11, 19, 27, 1918, June 9, 12, 27, 1918; diary entries by BFF dated March 22, 1918, April 12, 16, 1918, May 26, 1918, June 3, 9, 19, 20, 1918, BFFP; "Baccarat," in *I&G*, 61–72; and "Crucible of Sacrifice," in *HAC168*, 24–25.

147   "After a week of marking time in Domptail." In Domptail, Byron and other members of the Michigan Ambulance Company got the opportunity to interact with East Indian colonial soldiers who were being housed in the same cantonment as the sanitary train. See *I&G*, 62; and diary entry by BFF, March 23, 1918. During the war, 130,000 Indian soldiers assigned to Force A of the Indian Expeditionary Force served on the western front in France and Belgium—9,000 of whom would die in loyal service to the British Empire. See "India in First World War," in *Commonwealth War Graves Commission Report*, June 18, 2010.

154   "Alabamans went in search of them." The fact that these impromptu excursions behind enemy lines were hardly isolated or secretive affairs is evidenced by YMCA worker GB's knowledge of them. As noted in her diary entry of May 7, 1918, "[T]he Alabama boys like little private raids . . . they were gone about an hour and half, lost five men. . . . [T]he next night another party went over and brought back five prisoners with no loss to themselves." DoGB, entry May 7, 1918, 35.

156   "Byron and other medical personnel." It is evident from BFF's diary and letters and from the writings of other medics that they felt they had been deliberately targeted by German forces. Under the circumstances, it was an understandable reaction—whether or not it was an accurate perception of what had actually occurred is, of course, a case-specific factual determination. As a general proposition, it is far more likely that in the midst of a large-scale and fast-moving battle in which long-distance weapons were frequently employed, medical personnel were for the most part the inadvertent recipients of misdirected fire or collateral damage, not the victims of deliberate action on the part of German soldiers.

158   "reporting on the flowers that were presently in bloom in France." BFF was not alone in his ability to find some small measure of pastoral respite in the simple blooming of a flower or the trill of a songbird—other soldier-writers, from poet Siegfried Sassoon to novelist Ernest Hemingway, would also mention these life-affirming occurrences in their war-related writings. The ability of nature to renew itself in the midst of the utter devastation wrought by modern warfare was viewed by some as a sign of hope, even of God's eternal forgiveness. In keeping with that sentiment, in a letter written by WJD to his mother-in-law, Susan Rumsey, on Mother's Day, May 12, 1918, WJD marveled, "At day break this morning a patrol returned. They brought no prisoners with them, only a bouquet of tulips and forget-me-nots gathered in No Man's land. Incredible, isn't it?" Indeed, it was—the religious connotations associated with the return of spring in the middle of a battle-withered war zone was apparent to noncombatants as well. In Norman Rockwell's illustration on the cover of the March 30, 1918, issue of *LW*, titled "Easter," a young soldier is depicted kneeling before a lily that has managed to take root and blossom from the detritus of war. The religious symbolism is unmistakable—in tending to the lily, the soldier pours

water from his helmet as if to cleanse himself and his little patch of the world of sin. See also Paul, Fussell, *The Great War and Modern Memory* (Oxford: Oxford University Press, 1975), 255–76; and letter from WJD to Mrs. Susan Rumsey, dated May 12, 1918, DP. With respect to the war and its effect on artistic expression in the United States, it should be noted that the interpretation of war-related events by various other artists was not nearly so sanguine as Rockwell's. Especially for the modernists, the war assumed chaotic and nightmarish dimensions. Modernist Claggett Wilson in particular held a surrealistic view grounded in personal experience—a highly decorated veteran of the war, Wilson had been gassed and wounded twice in combat. Titled "Flower of Death—The Bursting of a Heavy Shell—Not as It Looks, but as It Feels and Sounds and Smells," Wilson's work stands in stark contrast to Rockwell's relatively benign vignettes of war. For a more thorough discussion of the effect of the war on American art and culture, see Robert Cozzolino, Anne C. Knutson, and David M. Lubin, *World War I and American Art* (Princeton: Princeton University Press, 2016).

160 "the Saxophone Sextette." DoGB, entry May 12, 1918, 36. For Army Signal Corps film footage of YMCA activities in France, refer to ref. no. 111-H-1530, reels 1, 2, NAMS.

160 "Yesterday we performed for the 'movies.'" The film clip in question was taken on April 26, 1918, in Bertrichamps by the Army Signal Corps. Due to the angle of the camera and its distance from the column of men as they marched past, it is not possible to identify BFF and Horace Sprague. For Army Signal Corps film footage of the 42nd Division in Baccarat sector from March 21, 1918, to June 21, 1918, refer to ref. no. 111-H-1299, reels 1, 2, NAMS. For annotated Army Signal Corps film footage of the 42nd Division in Lunéville and Baccarat sector, refer to ref. no. 111-M-42, reels 3, 4, NAMS.

161 "straight talk on religion" Francis, Duffy, "The Religion Our Soldiers Brought Back to Us," *Red Cross Magazine*, January 1919, 50.

162 "Byron's perception of Carpentier's alleged deficiencies." BFF's guarded view of other religious denominations was not unique. In the early 1900s, religious sectarianism was an unfortunate but common state of affairs in the United States—in particular as manifested by Protestant nativists toward Catholic and Jewish immigrants. Of course, the fact that this practice was to some extent a cultural norm does not excuse that conduct, it does help to put that behavior in historical context. Fifty years later (1969), in the course of reviewing a letter written by BFF to EMC on September 1, 1918 (in which BFF described his pup-tent mate Harry Livingstone as "a big good hearted Jew boy"), EMC would hasten to write in the margin of that letter, in bright red ink, "old usage!"—an obvious good-faith attempt to explain (or mitigate) BFF's insensitive characterization to subsequent readers. That these offensive characterizations were in common usage by white nativist Protestants is perhaps best exemplified by some of the correspondence between Franklin and

Eleanor Roosevelt dating from this period, which was less than exemplary in that regard. The fact that the Roosevelts were later able to evolve beyond this narrow-minded manner of speaking and thinking is amply evidenced by their subsequent roles as the principal architects of the most progressive and all-encompassing political and social agenda in the history of the country. See Jean Edward Smith, *FDR* (New York: Random House, 2007), 148–49. That BFF, however, was never able to exorcise these sociopolitical demons from his manner of thinking and speaking is set forth in a letter from Helen Hulst Field to BFF in 1954, in which she asked BFF to please refrain from making disparaging remarks about Catholics and Jews in front of their daughter Nancy for fear of offending her.

162   "Carpentier would be awarded the Distinguished Service Cross." Allison Reppy, "Father George Carpentier," in *Rainbow Memories: Character Sketches and History First Battalion—42nd Division* (Melbourne Beach, FL: Carey, 1919), 34.

163   "German artillery barrage of the Rouge Bouquet Forest." My description of Sergeant Abram Blaustein's actions is based on "Blaustein Dug for Hours and Rescued Comrades Buried When Huns Shelled 165th Inf. Dugout," *Brooklyn Eagle*, December 29, 1918, 52; and "Blaustein Tells How He Won War Cross," *Reform Advocate: American Jewish Journal*, May 31, 1919, 420–22. See also Stephen Harris, "In the Wood They Call Rogue Bouquet," in *Duffy's War* (Washington, DC: Potomac, 2006), 153–76.

163   "wide range of reactions displayed by soldiers." S. C. Linden, and E. Jones, "'Shell Shock' Revisited: An Examination of the Case Records of the National Hospital in London," *Medical History* 58, no. 4 (2014): 519–45.

164   "acts of insubordination or cowardice." Peter Leese, *Shell Shock: Traumatic Neurosis and the British Soldiers of the First World War* (New York: Springer, 2002).

164   "In addition to those who were actually wounded." George C. Marshall, *Memoirs of My Services in the World War, 1917–1918* (Boston: Houghton Mifflin, 1976), 96. Also letter from MPO Harry S. Lane to GB dated August 6, 1918, in which Lane confided that after being "under shell fire for a month, a fellow's nerves go bad on him." DoGB, box 2.

165   "faint purple light." A. S. Helmer, "Rouge Bouquet: From the Depths," *American Legion Magazine* 26, no. 1 (1939): 48–50.

165   "refused to accept his medal." Letter from WJD to Ruth Donovan dated March 11, 1918, DP.

CHAPTER 13: A SCENE THAT WOULD SHOCK THE WORLD FOR ALL ETERNITY

169   My description of BFF's experiences during the battle of Champagne is based on letters by BFF to EMC dated June 24, 1918, July 2, 7, 1918; letters to JBF dated July 3, 6, 10, 18, 1918; diary entries of BFF dated

June 22, 1918, to July 19, 1918, BFFP; "Champagne," in *I&G*, 73–86; "Champagne Front," in *HAC168*, 26–32; "The Champagne-Marne Operation," in *The Medical Department of the United States Army in the World War*, vol. 8 (Washington, DC: Government Printing Office, 1925), 343–56; "From Champagne to the Marne," in James Cooke, *The Rainbow Division in The Great War, 1917–1919* (Westport, CT: Praeger, 1994), 97–98, 103–13. For Army Signal Corps film footage of the 42nd Division in the Esperance and Souain sectors, Châlons-sur-Marne, refer to ref. no. 111-H-1276, reel 2, NAMS. For Army Signal Corps film footage of an advance dressing station and an ambulance blown off the road by German artillery, refer to ref. no. 111-H-1304, reels 2, 3, NAMS.

172   "Gourard was magnificent." For MacArthur's description of the battle of Champagne, refer to Douglas MacArthur, *Reminiscences* (New York: McGraw Hill, 1964), 63–66.

174   "Gourard's 'stand or die' speech." Leslie Langille, *Men of the Rainbow* (Chicago: W. B. Conkey, 1933), 82-83.

176   "I am writing you a few lines." Hamilton Fish, *Memoir of an American Patriot* (Washington, DC: Regnery Gateway, 1991), 25–31; "Capt. Fish in the Fighting: His Helmet Hit by Shrapnel—Narrow Escape from a Shell," *NYT*, August 20, 1918, 7.

181   "They came over in French uniforms." Stephen Harris, *Duffy's War* (Washington, DC: Potomac, 2006), 228.

181   "Alabama soldiers killing wounded and defenseless soldiers." Lawrence O. Stewart, *Rainbow Bright* (Philadelphia: Dorrance, 1923), 70–71.

182   "Again, it becomes absolutely impossible." Langille, *Men of the Rainbow*, 90–91.

CHAPTER 14: THE RIVER OF BLOOD

185   My description of BFF's experiences during the battle of Château-Thierry is based on diary entries by BFF covering July 24 to August 2, 1918, BFFP; "Chateau Thierry," in *I&G*, 87–97; "Chateau Thierry," in *HAC168*, 33–37; "Aisne-Marne Offensive," in *The Medical Department of the United States Army in the World War*, vol. 8 (Washington, DC: Government Printing Office, 1925), 357–430; and Henry J. Reilly, *Americans All: The Rainbow at War* (Columbus, OH: F. J. Heer, 1936), 480–85, as related by Colonel David S. Fairchild, chief surgeon, 42nd Division. For a dramatic depiction of the battle of Château-Thierry, refer to newsreel footage titled *The Turn of the Tide* from the *Supreme Thrills* series by RKO-Pathé (1931). This film is narrated by Floyd Gibbons, a war correspondent for the *Chicago Tribune* who was assigned to the AEF. The fact that Gibbons often went in harm's way to bring his readers a firsthand account of action at the front is evidenced by the patch that he wore over his left eye, which he lost in the battle of Belleau Wood, where he was shot three times, once in the head. Ref. no. 111-M-103,

NAMS. For Army Signal Corps footage of the 42nd Division at Château-Thierry and Épieds, see ref. no. 111-H-1363, NAMS.

186 "barge balloons were deployed in a defensive array." *I&G*, 74. It should also be noted that interconnecting cables, from which a series of descending cables hung, were often strung between the balloons, in effect creating a web to deter enemy aircraft from attacking at lower altitudes, reducing a pilot's ability to accurately drop bombs on intended targets.

186 "While at our old station." Letter from WJD to Ruth Donovan dated July 24, 1918, DP.

186 "both sides engaged in strategic bombing." The practice of long-distance bombing, or "strategic bombing," as it would later be called, started in May 1915 when German airships (zeppelins) first began to attack targets in Great Britain. In theory, the justification for the bombardment of targets far removed from the field of battle (as compared to "tactical bombing" of troops in combat) was that in modern mechanized warfare, it was necessary to attack not only enemy troops actually engaged in battle, but also an opposing army's lines of supply: its transportation system and industry of war. In practice, the destructive impact of these raids on the industrial war machine of an opponent was minimal at best, which was not surprising given the state of the art at that time. At first, the limited speed and maneuverability of zeppelins made them vulnerable to counterattack by British airplanes and anti-aircraft guns. In an attempt to remedy that, in 1916, the Germans began to use fleeter and more elusive long-range bombers called Gothas. The Gotha "Giants" were huge affairs capable of flying at an altitude of fifteen thousand feet, far above the range of British fighters and anti-aircraft guns. At that increased altitude and speed, however, it was difficult for a pilot and crew to drop bombs on intended targets with any degree of accuracy. Still, the overall effect on civilian morale was debilitating. It should also be noted that while all this was occurring in the skies over England, British armed forces were responding in kind as the Royal Naval Air Service began to launch long-range bombing raids on factories, railheads, and cities in Germany. In October 1917, the British War Cabinet decided to increase the number of long-range bombing attacks on targets in Germany—assigning that task to Wing No. 41 of the Royal Flying Corps, which was stationed at an airfield near Nancy, France. In June 1918, the size of the unit was further expanded, redesignated the Independent Air Force of the Royal Air Force. By the end of the war, the Independent Air Force consisted of eleven squadrons that conducted raids day or night. As was the case with the long-range German air offensive, the strategic effectiveness of the British raids was limited. The effect on civilian morale, however, was devastating—the number of German civilians killed or wounded during these attacks was 746 and 1,843 respectively. That some bomber pilots had no qualms whatsoever about endangering innocent civilians

who lived or worked in the immediate vicinity of intended targets is evidenced by an excerpt from the diary of Major W. R. Read:

> As soon as Sgt. Keen dropped (the bombs) I looked over the side for the effect. It looked terrible. I had told Sgt. Keen to aim for the middle of the town. Personally when I go to a German town I am all out to bomb the town and—although it sounds awful to say so—to kill and cause as much destruction as possible in preference to bombing railway junctions or docks. . . . When one thinks of all the atrocities the Huns have committed in this war one learns to hate them and wants to kill them.

The fact that Allied forces (which included AEF air units) fully intended to launch bombing raids of German cities on an even larger and more injurious scale is reflected in a letter from JBF to BFF, dated December 17, 1918, in which he mentioned having discussed that grim possibility with a member of one of those air squadrons (Willis Bryant, a friend of BFF) who had recently mustered out of service at the conclusion of the war. As related in the letter, Bryant's squadron "would have gone to Berlin on that big raid if the [war] had not ended when it did. There were 500 machines in the party." For an excellent discussion of the Independent Air Force, refer to Andrew Whitmarsh, "British Strategic Bombing, 1917–1918: The Independent Force and Its Predecessors," https://www.academia.edu/8630931/British_strategic_bombing_1917-1918_The_Independent_Force (Major Read quote at 10–11). For an equally informative discussion of the German air campaign against Great Britain, see Ian Castle, *London, 1914–17: The Zeppelin Menace* (Oxford: Osprey, 2008).

186 "wreaking havoc, fear, and dissent." The fact that German bombing raids had succeeded in demoralizing the civilian population is reflected in a diary entry of YMCA worker GB dated June 9, 1918, in which she described the drone of an approaching airplane as "sinister and terrifying," forever ruining her ability to appreciate moonlit nights—especially opportune times for bombing raids due to increased visibility for pilots and bombardiers. DoGB, entry June 9, 1918, 52.

186 "Paris Gun." The so-called Paris Gun, or Kaiser Wilhelm *Geschütz* (Emperor William's Gun), was an ultra-long-range artillery piece manufactured by the Krupp armaments foundry. During the war, there were purportedly five guns in existence. The barrel of each gun measured over 130 feet in length, and was capable of firing a 230-pound projectile a distance of sixty miles, which required a trajectory that reached the stratosphere. Despite the gun's impressive long-distance capability, its accuracy and effectiveness as a tactical weapon were severely limited. As such, the super-gun was largely used as a strategic weapon of war—much like a Gotha long-range bomber, the cannon's primary value lay in its ability to harass, terrorize, and demoralize the civilian

population of large metropolitan areas. In using the gun in this fashion, from March 1918 to August 1918, the Germans managed to kill or wound 256 and 650 French civilians respectively. The most notorious incident involving the use of the gun occurred on Good Friday, March 29, 1918, when a projectile fired from the gun crashed through the roof of the cathedral Saint-Gervais-et-Saint-Protais in Paris, killing 88 parishioners who were attending a church service. See the dramatic depiction of the destruction at St. Gervais, entiltled "The Crowning Atrocity," *LW*, April 20, 1918. See also Henry W. Miller, *The Paris Gun: The Bombardment of Paris by the German Long-Range Guns and the Great German Offensives of 1918* (London: George G. Harrap, 1930).

188   "tended the fields." Refer to Army Signal Corps film footage for a depiction of French soldiers on leave from the front cutting wheat and operating an American harvester in the ruins of Vaux and Château-Thierry, Aisne-Marne Offensive, July 18–August 6, 1918. Ref. no. 111-H-1365 reels 1, 2, NAMS.

188   "Parisians girded themselves for the worst." Although the series of attacks commonly referred to as the Spring Offensive, or *Kaiserschlacht*, had failed to achieve its ultimate military objective, it did succeed in wreaking death and destruction across much of France, and in the process seriously wounded the French psyche. As reflected in a depiction on the April 13, 1918, cover of *LW*, "Doing His Bit," the murderous and ruinous specter of invading German forces left an indelible impression on both French and American citizens.

189   "the Allied counteroffensive." The obliteration of the village of Vaux during the first days of the battle of Château-Thierry provides graphic proof that Allied forces were also responsible for destroying French villages during the prosecution of the war. In the course of displacing the German troops ensconced there, on July 1, 1918, American artillery unleashed a withering four-hour barrage that reduced the once thriving village to a pile of rubble. To view U.S. Army Signal Corps photograph of ruins see "Starting Some Yankee Rough Stuff," *LW*, September 28, 1918, 411, which includes a photograph of Vaux captioned "Dust to dust is the way of war."

193   "the dead were left to fester." The inability of troops engaged in a fast-moving and far-ranging battle to bury the dead was brought into horrible relief during the battle of Château-Thierry. In the heat of combat, divisional troops could not be spared for the task. At Château-Thierry, the bodies of German, French, and American soldiers lay festering in the hot July sun for ten days or more. The stench from the blackened and bloated corpses became intolerable. The overall effect on the men was demoralizing. The potential health risk presented by these unsanitary conditions added to their woes. As reflected in a memorandum from Colonel J. W. Grissinger, chief surgeon, 1st Corps, AEF, to chief surgeon, SOS, AEF, dated October 21, 1918:

The stench was terrific but the worst feature was that of fly breeding. The bodies of both men and horses soon become a mass of maggots and flies bred by millions—the surrounding country was infested with them. The result was a widespread outbreak of enteric disease that fortunately carried with it no mortality. Men were usually sick only a few days and were not seriously ill. A few however showed blood and mucus in the stools and were real dysentery. Bacteriologically, Flexner and Shiga bacilli were isolated as well as paratyphoid. It is therefore apparent that a serious outbreak of real dysentery was narrowly averted. It is not certain that flies were responsible for this outbreak but the presumptive evidence is strong.

To address the problem, the surgeon of 1st Corps requested that a special unit of soldiers be organized for the purpose of burying the dead. This unpleasant task was assigned to soldiers from a Pioneer Infantry unit, which subsequently cleared the dead from the fields of Château-Thierry. In future battles, this procedure would be adopted by other corps commanders as well, which resulted in the dead being buried in a timely fashion. The Pioneer soldiers assigned to this onerous task performed their duty faithfully throughout the war, often at great peril to themselves—due to their close proximity to the front lines several of these soldiers were killed in the course of carrying out their assignment. To read the memorandum from Grissinger in its entirety, refer to, http://www.worldwar1.com/dbc/burial.htm, found at Doughboy Center.

193   "great khaki-colored snake." Artilleryman Lawrence Stewart described the column as "a long brown serpent twisting evenly down the road." *Rainbow Bright* (Philadelphia: Dorrance, 1923), 74.

193   "the ruins of Épieds." For a vivid description of ruins of Épieds, see Hervey Allen, *Toward the Flame: A Memoir of World War I* (New York: Farrar & Rinehart, 1926), 128–29.

195   "literally covered with killed and wounded." Reilly, *Americans All*, 350.

196   "romantically remembered." Douglas MacArthur, *Reminiscences* (New York: McGraw Hill, 1964), 66–69.

197   "Meurcy Farm, where German troops were ensconced." For a tactical discussion of the 165th Infantry Regiment assault on Meurcy Farm, refer to David Fivecoat, "A Beautiful War Machine: Irish Offensive Operations," in "Fine Conduct under Fire" (MA thesis, U.S. Military Academy, 1993), 59–68.

197   "before the sun rode at mid-heavens." Francis Duffy, "Battle of the Ourcq," in *Father Duffy's Story: A Tale of Humor and Heroism, of Life and Death with the Fighting 69th* (New York: George Doran, 1919), 158–206.

198   "The evacuation of wounded in 1918." Arlington Lecklider, letter, "Army Medical Equipment 1918 versus 1968," *USARV Medical Bulletin*

(September/October 1968), U.S. Academy of Health Sciences, Stimson Library, Fort Sam Houston, TX.

200 "Many stretcher bearers were wounded or killed." Stewart, "Chateau Thierry," in *Rainbow Bright*, 73–84.

201 "unwitting bed partners." Leslie Langille, *Men of the Rainbow* (Chicago: W. B. Conkey, 1933), 101–22.

202 "born to be hanged." Letter from WJD to Ruth Donovan, August 9, 1918, DP.

203 "cited for bravery in the battle." Allison Reppy, *Rainbow Memories: Character Sketches and History First Battalion—42nd Division* (Melbourne Beach, FL: Carey, 1919), 34.

CHAPTER 15: THE DEVIL'S BUSINESS

205 My description of BFF's experiences in this chapter is based on diary entry by BFF dated August 21, 1918; letter from BFF to JBF dated August 1, 1918; and letter from BFF to EMC dated August 5, 1918, BFFP.

205 "played the organ in a Y. service." The partially destroyed church mentioned by BFF in the above-listed letters is Saint Medard, a thirteenth-century Gothic church located in the village of Epeids, where the Michigan Ambulance Company was stationed during the battle of Château-Thierry. On May 20, 2014, the authors visited the village of Épieds and were given access to the interior of Saint Medard by the mayor of Épieds. Inside the church, the authors found the pump organ played by BFF on July 28, 1918.

207 "observations made by Captain Alan Chesney." Refer to "A Report on Epidemic of Influenza Occurring at Post APO 704, AEF," undated memo, box 7, entry 1011, RG 112, National Archives and Records Administration, College Park, MD, later republished in Alan M. Chesney, and F. W. Snow, "A Report of an Epidemic of Influenza in an Army Post of the American Expeditionary Force in France," *Journal of Laboratory and Clinical Medicine* 6, no. 2 (1920). See also G. Soper, "The Influenza Pandemic in American Camps, September 1918," memo dated October 9, 1918, box 23, entry 29, RG 112, National Archives and Records Administration, College Park, MD. See also Carol R. Byerly, "The U.S. Military and the Influenza Pandemic 1918–1919," *Public Health Reports* 125, suppl. 3 (*2010*): 82–91.

208 "Harry Lane . . . flu." Letter from Harry S. Lane to GB dated September 24, 1918, DoGB.

208 "Paleozoic monsters." Francis Duffy, *Father Duffy's Story: A Tale of Humor and Heroism, of Life and Death with the Fighting 69th* (New York: George Doran, 1919), 233.

209 "If it is a secret, all the world seems to know it." Ibid., 228.

209 "I never hear confessions in a church." Ibid., 109.

211 "Last Hero." Anthony Cave Brown, *The Last American Hero: Wild Bill Donovan* (New York: Times Books, 1982), 833.

211 "became just lustful for German blood." Letter from WJD to Ruth Donovan, August 7, 1918, DP. As reflected on the September 21, 1918, cover
of *LW*, apparently WJD was not alone in his disdain for the duplicity of
some German soldiers. In a depiction titled "Kamerad," German forces
were portrayed as being unscrupulously treacherous, even in surrender. As further explained by the editors below the depiction, this
scenario represented "[o]ne of the simplest of the Hun's treacherous
murder traps. In towns from which the Hun has been driven all manner of devilish contrivances have been found such as gas-filled bulbs
and loaves of bread loaded with bombs."

213 "a decision that would haunt them." David C. Homsher, "Was the
Rainbow Division Tarnished?" *Military Collector & Historian* 58, no. 3
(2006): 158–62n9, citing letter of Clark Jarrett, dated February 18,
1997, recounting conversation with his grandfather Lieutenant Paul
Jarrett of the 166th Ohio Infantry Regiment re: ordering the execution
of German prisoners in the Meuse-Argonne Offensive who could not
be sent to the rear. For a chilling account of the execution of twenty-
two unarmed German soldiers by U.S. Marines in battle, refer to William March, *Company K* (New York: Smith & Haas, 1933), 122–38. In his
book, written as a series of quasi-factual vignettes involving members
of a fictionalized infantry company (Company K), March said that the
actions depicted therein were based on events that he had participated
in personally or witnessed firsthand. During the war, March (born William Edward Campbell) served as a sergeant in Company F, 5th Brigade
of Marines, 2nd Division, AEF. Wounded twice in the battle of Belleau
Wood, March received the French Croix de Guerre, the Distinguished
Service Cross, and the Navy Cross for valor. To this day, *Company K* is
still widely considered one of the most realistically stark depictions
of war ever written. According to March's account, the execution of
the unarmed and frightened German soldiers amounted to a pitiable
slaughter, carried out by reluctant infantrymen on a captain's orders.
On the first Sunday after the execution, the soldiers who were involved
in the execution were ordered to attend church by the sergeant who
had commanded them during the commission of the act. One of the
soldiers who had participated in the slaughter was so consumed by
guilt that he committed suicide after the war (221–22). Long after the
war ended, March too would be afflicted by unpredictable and recurring episodes of post-traumatic stress syndrome. See Philip D. Beidler's
introduction to a later edition of *Company K* (Tuscaloosa: University of
Alabama Press, 1984), viii.

214 "as much a sobering depiction of self as it was of foe." For those inclined
to paint with broad brush strokes in an attempt to demonize the combatants of one side (or the other), the photograph in the text serves
as an emotional reality check. Taken on August 10, 1918, this photograph captures soldiers from New England's 26th "Yankee" Division in
an unguarded moment only days after the battle of Château-Thierry.

A long line of half-clad doughboys wait to take their first shower in months. Stripped of the trappings of combat, these soldiers are exposed for who they actually are—baby-faced young men caught in the clutches of war—in stark contrast to the image normally conjured up by propagandists in which the enemy is portrayed as an older, more sinister creature. Yet it is beyond all doubt that these young innocents are indeed killers, having just ferociously proved that in the battle of Château-Thierry.

214 "some look from five to ten years older." DoGB, entry September 9, 1918.

215 "battle fatigue." James Jones, *WW II: A Chronicle of Soldiering* (New York: Grossett & Dunlap, 1975), 113, 116.

CHAPTER 16: THE FIRST ALL-AMERICAN AFFAIR

217 My description of BFF's experiences during the Saint-Mihiel Offensive is based on diary entries by BFF from September 5 to September 15, 1918, BFFP; "St. Mihiel," in *I&G*, 98–106; "Saint Mihiel Salient," in *HAC168*, 38–41; "The Saint Mihiel Operation, Fourth Corps," in *The Medical Department of the United States Army in the World War* (Washington, DC: Government Printing Office, 1925), 484–97; Henry J. Reilly, *Americans All: The Rainbow at War* (Columbus, OH: F. J. Heer, 1936), 560–75; Francis Duffy, "The Saint Mihiel Offensive," in *Father Duffy's Story: A Tale of Humor and Heroism, of Life and Death with the Fighting 69th* (New York: George Doran, 1919), 232–60. For film footage of 42nd Division troops in Saint-Mihiel Offensive, refer to Army Signal Corps, ref. no. 111-H-1327, NAMS.

217 "day of fresh comprehension." "Labor Day, 1918," *NYT*, September 2, 1918.

218 "Gengault Aerodrome." For film footage of 94th Aero Squadron (Lieutenant Eddie Rickenbacker and the Hat in the Ring Squadron), refer to Army Signal Corps, ref. no. 111-H-1479, reel 1, NAMS.

220 "Criticism of YMCA workers." After the war, the discontent expressed by some ex-soldiers toward the YMCA was so pronounced that it became the subject of intense press scrutiny. In an attempt to quell that dissent and restore the organization's good name, John R. Mott, general secretary of the American YMCA, requested that the secretary of war conduct a formal inquiry. In January 1919, the Inspector General's Office initiated an investigation, culminating in 1923 with the issuance of a final report that exonerated the YMCA of widespread malfeasance. Among those who testified in favor of the YMCA mission in France and its performance during the war, were AEF generals John J. Pershing, James G. Harbord, and Johnson Hagood. See John J. Pershing, *My Experiences in the World War* (New York: Frederick A. Stokes, 1931), 1:108; James G. Harbord, *The American Army in France, 1917–1919* (Boston: Little, Brown, 1936), 370, 474–77; and Johnson Hagood, *The Services of*

Supply: A Memoir of the Great War (New York: Houghton Mifflin, 1927), 86–90. Still, there were war veterans who remained unconvinced by the report and continued to voice their displeasure. See Thomas Boyd, *Through the Wheat* (New York: Charles Scribner's Sons, 1923), 42–43; William March, *Company K* (New York: Smith & Haas, 1933), 195–97; Leslie Langille, *Men of the Rainbow* (Chicago: W. B. Conkey, 1933), 145. See also "Y.M.C.A. Errors as Our Soldiers Have Seen Them," *NYT*, January 6, 1919, 1, 4; and "Orders Y.M.C.A. Inquiry: Baker Directs Inspector General of Army to Look into Charges," *NYT*, January 7, 1919, 10.

221   "recipe for an army-sized ration of doughnuts." DoGB.

221   "the Germans were . . . withdrawing." "Germans Belittle Loss of St. Mihiel," *NYT*, September 16, 1918; "Says We Exaggerate St. Mihiel Success: Berliner Lokal-Anzeiger Still Insists It Was Not Such a Great Victory," *NYT*, September 19, 1918.

222   "Following closely behind Patton's tanks." As set forth in *HAC168* (39), some ambulance drivers were so determined to follow orders (staying as close as possible to the Tank Corps in order to evacuate anticipated casualties) that they advanced directly behind the tanks in a position ahead of the first line of infantry, at times even slipping in between the tanks. That such courageous action was not without considerable risk is evidenced by an incident in which one of the ambulance crews assigned to cover Tank Corps 327 (commanded by Captain Compton in conjunction with Lieutenant Colonel Patton) narrowly escaped serious injury when its vehicle was severely damaged by an exploding shrapnel shell during the assault (94).

222   "No tank is to be surrendered." Lieutenant Colonel George S. Patton Jr., "Special Instructions for the 326 Bn.," September 8, 1918, box 10, Patton Papers, Library of Congress, Washington, DC.

222   "Patton had assiduously prepared for this day." Alan Axelrod, "The Great War and the New Weapon," in *Patton: A Biography*, Great Generals Series (New York: Macmillan, 2006), 43–59; Stanley P. Hirshson, "The Suicide Club," in *General Patton: A Soldier's Life* (New York: Harper Perennial, 2002), 90–131; Martin Blumenson, "The Great War," in *Patton: The Man Behind the Legend, 1885–1945* (New York: William Morrow, 1985), 93–116.

224   "excerpts from the captured letters." Letter from WJD to Ruth Donovan dated September 21, 1918, DP.

225   "A great number also look relieved." Army Signal Corps film footage depicting German soldiers captured during the Saint-Mihiel Offensive, ref. no. 111-M-347, NAMS.

225   "letter written to his mother." Franz Blumenfeld, letter to mother dated October 14, 1914, in Philipp Witkop, *German Students' War Letters*, trans. Annie F. Wedd (New York: E. P. Dutton, 1929), 20.

227   "the Boche shot at me." Letter from George S. Patton Jr. to George Patton Sr. dated September 20, 1918, Patton Papers.

CHAPTER 17: DEATH VALLEY

229   My description of BFF's experiences in the Meuse-Argonne Offensive is drawn from diary entries by BFF from October 1 to October 20, 1918, BFFP: "The Argonne Drive," in *I&G*, 107–14; "The Argonne-Meuse Front," in *HAC168*, 42–44; "Meuse Argonne Operation, Second Phase," in *The Medical Department of the United States Army in the World War* (Washington, DC: Government Printing Office, 1925), 667–89. For Army Signal Corps film footage of the Meuse-Argonne Offensive, September 26—November 11, 1918, depicting traffic congestion, ruins, German defenses, and captured enemy materiel, refer to ref. nos. 111-H-1405, reel 1; 111-H-1424, reels 1, 2, 3; and 111-H-1406, NAMS.

230   "Nigger Jack." Everett T. Tomlinson, "In The Spanish War," in *The Story of General Pershing* (New York: D. Appleton, 1919), 74. See also Richard O'Connor, "A Silver Star for San Juan Hill," in *Black Jack Pershing* (New York: Doubleday, 1961), 36–52.

231   "proud of his service with the 10th Cavalry." Pershing's record on racial equality was mixed. In attempting to assess the overall merit of that position, the most frequently cited examples are that Pershing twice proudly served as an officer in the all-black 10th Cavalry Regiment; that he declared at the outset of World War I that in his opinion, the only combat-ready American military unit was the 10th Cavalry Regiment; and that he insisted that black soldiers not be relegated to noncombat roles in the army (which in previous wars had consisted of serving mostly in supply and communication units). Pershing's detractors, however, point to a less well-known action on his part that proves that he did in fact discriminate against black soldiers during the war: he permitted the 93rd Division, which was comprised of black units, to be dispersed among French Army units to replenish their depleted ranks. This criticism appears valid when viewed in the context of his repeated refusal to allow white combat divisions of the AEF to be dispersed in similar fashion. Some of Pershing's harshest critics have even gone so far as to imply that his initial promotion of the 10th Cavalry Regiment as being combat-ready was nothing more than a calculated statement on his part to set the stage with the beleaguered French Army for the subsequent transfer of the 93rd Division to fight under French command. This accusation seems unwarranted, however, given that the 10th Cavalry was never part of the American Expeditionary Force, having been stationed on the Mexican border for the entirety of the war. A more plausible explanation for Pershing's regrettable action is that he was a reluctant realist. With a war to fight and an army to hold together, it was undoubtedly easier for Pershing to accede to the racist practices of the army (and Wilson administration) than it was to cause dissension in the ranks by putting a division of black soldiers on an equal footing with white counterparts. (A memorandum written by a French liaison officer assigned to AEF HQ, relating AEF-held concerns

to the French army about the alleged limitations of black soldiers in combat, and inadvisability of treating those men as equals seems to support this conclusion). When weighed against the totality of his record, whether that action alone is enough to condemn Pershing as a racist in practice is open to debate. The discriminatory result of his action, however, is not subject to interpretation—the 93rd Division had, in effect, been orphaned by the American Expeditionary Force. In the words of Colonel William Hayward, the white commander of the New York 15th Infantry Regiment from Harlem, the AEF left the all-black 93rd Division "on the doorstep of the French, pulled the bell and went away." The sting of abandonment was felt by other members of the 93rd Division as well, evidenced by the fact that the division chose the blue French Helmet as its insignia. It should be noted that soldiers of the 93rd Division distinguished themselves with great valor and honor throughout the war. Refer to Arthur W. Little, *From Harlem to the Rhine* (New York: Covici-Friede, 1938), 145–46 (quote attributed to Hayward). See also Stephen L. Harris, *Harlem's Hell Fighters: The African-American 369th Infantry in World War I* (Washington, DC: Potomac Books, 2003).

232 "a full-throated argument." Richard O'Connor, "The Jaws of Saint Mihiel," in *Black Jack Pershing* (New York: Doubleday, 1961), 277–98.

235 "a haunted forest." Letter from George S. Patton Jr. to wife Beatrice Ayer Patton dated September 20, 1918, Patton Papers, Library of Congress, Washington, DC.

235 "a natural fortress." Hunter Liggett, *A.E.F.: Ten Years Ago in France* (New York: Dodd, Mead, 1928), 167.

236 "Who is with me?" Martin Blumenson, *Patton: The Man Behind the Legend, 1885–1945* (New York: William Morrow, 1985), 113.

236 "the tank corps established its reputation." Letter from George S. Patton Jr. to wife Beatrice Ayer Patton dated October 10, 1918, Patton Papers.

237 "relieve Pershing of command." O'Connor, "The Longest Toughest Battle," in *Black Jack Pershing*, 299–321.

237 "Foch refused." Ferdinand Foch, *Memoirs of Marshal Foch* (New York: Doubleday, Doran, 1931), 436.

238 "Germany has made her most effective counter-attack." Letter from WJD to Ruth Donovan dated October 8, 1918, DP.

239 "stew of dead things—Boche and American." Letter from WJD to Ruth Donovan dated October 23, 1918, DP.

240 "I went to their machine gun positions." Ibid.

240 "bird's-eye view." Eddie Rickenbacker, "Seeing the War," in *Fighting the Flying Circus* (Philadelphia: J. B. Lippincott, 1919), 307.

241 "Messengers I sent." WJD letter. Ibid.

242 "There also existed." Major Lloyd D. Ross, quoted in Henry J. Reilly, *Americans All: The Rainbow at War* (Columbus, OH: F. J. Heer, 1936), 518–19.

243   "give me Cote de Chatillion" Douglas MacArthur, *Reminiscences* (New York: McGraw Hill, 1964), 75.

243   "hated Summerall ever since." Robert Eichelberger, *Dear Miss Em: General Eichelberger's War in the Pacific, 1942–1945* (Westport, CT: Praeger, 1972), 32.

243   "Officers fell and sergeants leaped to command." MacArthur, *Reminiscences*, 76.

244   "sanitary train sustained more casualties." During the war, 82 officers and 520 enlisted men assigned to the Medical Department of the AEF were killed in action. See Jonathan H. Jaffin, "Medical Support for the American Expeditionary Forces in France during the First World War" (MA thesis, U.S. Army Command and Staff College, 1991), 100.

244   "Mother Springer." Letter from BFF to EMC dated November 16, 1918.

245   "God used me to my satisfaction." Letter from Eva Alice Springer to Mrs. Annie R. Atwater, president of Christian's Women's Board of Missions, dated December 7, 1918, archives of the Disciple of Christ Historical Society, Nashville, TN.

CHAPTER 18: ENOUGH TO NARROW ONE'S MIND FOREVER

247   My descriptions of BFF's experiences in the 42nd Division advance on Sedan are based on diary entries of BFF from November 1 to November 11, 1918, BFFP; "The Race to Sedan," in *I&G*, 115–22; and "Meuse-Argonne Operation, Third Phase," in *The Medical Department of the United States Army in the World War* (Washington, DC: Government Printing Office, 1925), 737–53.

250   "the long-awaited liberation of Sedan." James G. Harbord, *The American Army in France, 1917–1919* (Boston: Little, Brown, 1936), 455–60.

251   "plain talk." Richard O'Connor, "Victory, Peace and Departure," in *Black Jack Pershing* (New York: Doubleday, 1961), 328, citing Pershing diary entries of November 3 and 6, 1918.

252   "ambition of the First Army." John J. Pershing, *My Experiences in the World War* (New York: Frederick A. Stokes, 1931), 2:381.

252   "Pershing was determined." O'Connor, "Victory, Peace and Departure," in *Black Jack Pershing*, 327–31.

253   "MacArthur had gone forward." MacArthur, *Reminiscences*, 77–79.

254   "The division set out on a futile errand." Harbord, *The American Army in France*, 459.

254   "intervened with a vengeance." Liggett would later recall that it was the only time in the war he completely lost his temper. Hunter Liggett, *A.E.F.: Ten Years Ago in France* (New York: Dodd, Mead, 1928), 227–30.

254   "recriminations." MacArthur, *Reminiscences*, 80.

254   "tactical atrocity." Liggett, *A.E.F.*, 230. See also, Joseph T. Dickman, *The Great Crusade* (New York: D. Appleton, 1927), 193.

255   "giving the French a clear path to Sedan." MacArthur, *Reminiscences*, 79.

256   "these senseless deaths." American troops had no sooner returned
from Europe and the euphoria of peace worn off than citizens began to
question the necessity of having sent soldiers into harm's way on the
final day of the war—in particular the six-hour period that stretched
between the signing of the Armistice at 5 a.m. (which was promptly
communicated to all commanders) and the official cessation of hostilities at 11 a.m. One of those demanding answers was Royal C. Johnson,
Republican congressman from South Dakota. As it turned out, Johnson was uniquely qualified to ask those questions—not only was he a
skilled cross-examiner, having served as a county prosecutor and then
the attorney general of South Dakota prior to being elected to Congress,
he was also personally and painfully acquainted with the great sacrifice
made by soldiers in combat—his own story of selfless duty to country is an especially instructive one. As an isolationist congressman, on
April 5, 1917, Johnson had voted against the United States entering the
war. Once war was declared, however, Johnson immediately answered
his country's call to duty, leaving his seat in the House of Representatives to enlist as a private in the 313th Infantry Division, eventually
rising to the rank of lieutenant by the end of the war. On September 25,
1918, in the battle of the Argonne Forest, he was severely wounded in
the assault on Montfaucon, for which he was subsequently awarded the
Distinguished Service Cross and the Croix de Guerre for heroism. On
returning from the war, Johnson promptly resumed his seat in Congress,
and in June 1919, in response to a public outcry for a full accounting of
what many viewed to be the needless deaths of American soldiers on
the last day of war, as chairman of Subcommittee No. 3 of the House of
Representatives Select Committee on Expenditures in the War Department, Johnson began to take sworn testimony from Generals Pershing, Liggett, Conner, Bullard, Summerall, and others concerning their
actions, or lack thereof, to protect the lives of American soldiers. During
the hearings, Johnson's questioning was deferential but tough—lasting
for four contentious sessions before finally ending in February 1920.
Under Johnson's cross-examination, Pershing and others maintained
that they had simply acted in accordance with orders issued by overall commander Field Marshal Ferdinand Foch (specifically, that it was
tactically necessary to maintain pressure on German forces until the
last possible moment) and bristled at the inference that they had reck-
lessly and even ambitiously sent soldiers into harm's way knowing
that the war was already in effect over. Johnson's subcommittee found
the explanation offered by Pershing et al. to be unconvincing at best,
disingenuous at worst, and the committee's draft report said so in no
uncertain terms, categorizing the eleventh-hour loss of life as a "needless slaughter." Although the subcommittee's draft report was initially
approved for adoption by the overarching Select Committee on War
Expenditures, politics soon interceded, and Johnson was persuaded to
modify the harsh conclusions contained in the report. On March 3, a

more politically palatable version of the report was issued, which con-
cluded that although the loss of American life on November 11 was
undeniably tragic, it was nevertheless justifiable. Refer to Joseph Persico, *Eleventh Month, Eleventh Day, Eleventh Hour: Armistice Day 1918,
World War I and Its Violent Climax* (New York: Random House, 2004).
See also U.S. House of Representatives, *Hearings before Subcommittee
No. 3 of the Select Committee on Expenditures in the War Department,*
66th Cong., 1st, 2nd, 3rd sess. (Washington, DC: Government Printing
Office, 1920, 1921).

CHAPTER 19: THE DAWN OF PEACE

257   My descriptions of BFF's experiences during the period between
       November 11, 1918, and March 3, 1919, are drawn from diary entries by
       BFF from November 11, 1918 to March 3, 1919; letters from BFF to EMC
       dated December 8, 1918, January 7, 11, 28, 1919, February 7, 23, 1919,
       and March 13, 1919; letters from BFF to JBF dated November 19, 22, 25,
       1918, December 2, 8, 11, 18, 25, 29, 1918, January 4, 13, 17, 23, 28, 30,
       1919, February 2, 5, 9, 14, 16, 23, 25, 1919, March 1, 2, 6, 1919, April 3,
       20, 1919, and May 24, 1919, BFFP; "To the Rhine" and "Bad Neuenahr,"
       in *I&G*, 123–31, 132–38; "The Dawn of Peace," in *HAC168*, 45–61.
258   "Germany was beset by great internal strife." Thomas Childers, *The
       Nazi Voter: The Social Foundations of Fascism in Germany, 1919–1933*
       (Chapel Hill: University of North Carolina Press, 1983), 29–34, 34–49.
259   "The Germans were led to believe." To read the series of communi-
       qués exchanged by President Wilson and officials of the German gov-
       ernment in October 1918, refer to U.S. Army, Historical Division, "The
       Armistice Agreement and Related Documents," in *The United States
       Army in the World War, 1917–1919* (Washington, DC: U.S. Government
       Printing Office, 1948), vol. 10, pt. 1, 4–24.
259   "preconditions required of Germany." To view document, see: Armi-
       stice with Germany, November 11, 1918; Prolonging of Armistice with
       Germany, December 13, 1918; Prolonging of Armistice with Germany,
       January 16, 1919; Prolonging of Armistice with Germany, February 16,
       1919, all on the Library of Congress website, https://loc.gov/.
262   "I can't bear these people." DoGB, entry December 9, 1918, 101–2.
264   "the death of a comrade in battle." Jonathan Shay, "Grief at the Death
       of a Special Comrade" and "Guilt and Wrongful Substitution," in *Achil-
       les in Vietnam: Combat Trauma and the Undoing of Character* (New York:
       Scribner, 1994), 39–67, 69–75.
265   "internalize his grief." It was not until November, just before the Armi-
       stice, that BFF finally informed his parents of Jackson's death—he did
       not want to cause them further worry about his well-being while he
       was still involved in combat. Indeed, on July 18, 1918, just after the
       conclusion of the battle of Champagne, in responding to an innocent
       query in a letter from his parents, BFF said, "[Y]es, I am seeing big

things lately" (victorious action), followed by an emphatic but oblique "No," at the moment it was "hardly" a matter to prompt "thanksgiving" (no doubt a veiled reference to Jackson's death). See also JBF letters to BFF dated November 14, 1918 (reaction on first learning of Jackson's death) and August 9, 1918 ("[W]e are trying to be brave and courageous in all things . . . remember the natural nervous temperament of us both").

265   "moral injury." Shira Maguen and Brett Litz, "Moral Injury in Veterans of War," *PTSD Research Quarterly* 23, no. 1 (2012). See also Courtney Benshoof, "Not on My Watch: Moral Trauma and Moral Injury among Combat Medics" (MA thesis, Georgia State University, 2017).

269   "Social Democrats enlisted the support of the Freikorps." The Freikorps was one of several paramilitary groups that were part of a larger illicit militia movement in the Weimar Republic known as the Black Reichswehr. The Black Reichswehr was a de facto army reserve corps (composed of volunteers) that had been tacitly endorsed by a cadre of high-ranking officers in the existing German Army (Reichswehr) as a means of circumventing the restrictions imposed by the Treaty of Versailles on the size and use of the standing army. During much of the political unrest that wracked the Weimar Republic, elements of this shadow army aligned themselves with various anti-Weimar factions, and were used by those factions in furtherance of their respective agendas. That the Black Reichswehr represented a serious ongoing threat to the vitality of the Weimar Republic, viewing itself as being outside the established rule of law, is evidenced by the existence of an illicit and brazenly notorious shadow government, the *Organisation Consul*, which utilized a clandestine system of courts, called *Feme*, to mete out sentences of retribution (which included over three hundred executions) against those deemed to be traitors or a threat to the advancement of its ultra-nationalistic and militaristic goals. Notable among the Weimar officials and other political figures who were assassinated by these paramilitary terrorists were: Mathias Erzberger (1921), the minister of finance and signer of the Armistice, and Walther Rathenau (1922), the foreign minister. See "Feme Chief Tells of Official Backing," *NYT*, October 27, 1926, 9; "Gessler Defends Black Reichswehr," *NYT*, November 2, 1926, 19; "Feme Revelations Appall Germany," *NYT*, April 29, 1928, 3; Robert G. Waite, *Vanguard of Nazism: The Free Corps Movement in Postwar Germany, 1918–1923* (New York: Norton, 1969).

270   "Byron's willingness to condemn." Shay, *Achilles in Vietnam*, 89–90.

271   "crisis that was enveloping Germany" Derek H. Aldcroft, *From Versailles to Wall Street* (Berkeley: University of California Press, 1981), 13–17.

271   "the British prime minister was privately concerned." D. Lloyd George, *The Truth about the Treaties* (London: V. Gollancz, 1938), 1:404–16; Margaret MacMillan, "Footing the Bill" and "Deadlock over German Terms," in *Paris 1919* (New York: Random House, 2001), 180–93, 194–203.

274 "recounts the destruction." Ernst Jünger, *Storm of Steel* (New York: Penguin, 1920), 127–28.

275 "infrastructure of the region had been gutted." Aldcroft, *From Versailles to Wall Street*, 18–19.

275 "refused to tour the killing fields." MacMillan, *Paris 1919*, 28.

276 "German delegation was dismayed to discover." "Hall of Mirrors," in ibid., 459–83.

EPILOGUE

279 My description of BFF leaving the ranks of the 168th Ambulance Company and reporting to Edinburgh University is based on diary entries by BFF, March 1–8, 1919, BFFP.

280 "Dear John letter." Letter from BFF to EMC dated March 13, 1919, BFFP. Fifty years later, in annotating this letter for BFF's son Fiske, EMC wrote on the envelope of this letter, "Disaster!"

280 "Garden of Eden, Birmingham." BFF diary entry, April 11, 1919, BFFP.

280 "summon him home." Letter from JBF to BFF dated April 15, 1919, BFFP. From the contents of the letter, it is clear that BFF's parents strongly disapproved of his intentions concerning Jessie Griffiths.

281 "rancor to surface." "Conditions in Southern Ireland Are Described by Byron Field Monday," *Jackson Patriot News*, August 5, 1919.

281 "harsh edge to Byron's words." Willard W. Waller, *The Veteran Comes Back* (New York: Dryden, 1944), 109.

283 "similar feelings of resentment." Erich Maria Remarque, *The Road Back* (Boston: Little, Brown, 1931); Robert Graves, *Goodbye to All That* (New York: Vintage, 1929).

284 "Culver Military Academy." Mark Roeder, *A History of Culver and the Military Academy* (iUniverse, 2009).

285 "perception that the world is an ever-dangerous place." Jonathan Shay, "Pirate Raid: Staying in Combat Mode" and "A Peaceful Harbor: No Safe Place," in *Odysseus in America: Combat Trauma and the Trials of Homecoming* (New York: Scribner, 2002), 19–33, 60–64.

286 "editorial comment." Harold De Wolf Fuller, "Facing the Pension Problem," *Independent*, January 20, 1923.

287 "Coolidge . . . succeeded Harding." As evidenced by admission tickets that BFF retained among his personal belongings and a brief article published in the *Culver Citizen* on June 4, 1924, BFF attended and to a limited extent participated in the Republican National Convention in Cleveland, Ohio, during which Calvin Coolidge was nominated. As part of the opening ceremony, BFF presented presiding officials of the GOP with a wooden gavel carved from a branch of the oak tree under which the first convention of the Republican Party was held in Jackson, Michigan, in 1854. Whether BFF was also allowed to make a brief statement (as he had requested in a series of letters leading up to the convention) is unknown.

288   "struggling ex-soldiers." Returning black soldiers would have had an especially difficult time finding work. Yet nowhere in BFF's postwar writings does he mention the plight of black veterans. This omission is particularly noteworthy given that BFF had chosen to make the mistreatment of foreign veterans (ex-*soldats* in France) the focus of a speech he delivered in 1924, but he overlooked the equally notorious treatment of black veterans in the United States. Their well-publicized mistreatment could hardly have escaped his notice, however—his silence on the matter serves to underscore the regrettable fact that the plight of black veterans was scarcely an afterthought in the collective conscience of white America at that time. The issue merits further discussion here, if no other reason than to place the privileged status enjoyed by BFF in historical context. The difficulties that awaited black soldiers on discharge were far more complex than those that confronted their white counterparts—a sluggish economy was only part of the problem. To their great despair, black veterans found that despite their sacrifice and service to country, nothing had changed in terms of racial equality in the United States—if anything, matters had only gotten worse. In the years that followed the release of D. W. Griffith's *The Birth of a Nation* in 1915, the mostly dormant white supremacist philosophy propounded by the Ku Klux Klan in the 1870s, largely confined to the Deep South, had not only been revitalized, it had metastasized—becoming a full-blown national malignancy by 1920. It seemed that no section of the country was immune from the spread of the disease. Proponents of a Klan strategy called "the Decade" launched a campaign of fear that preyed upon the insecurity of disaffected white working-class Americans who were struggling economically during the recession that followed the Great War. Cloaking themselves in a mantle of Protestant fundamentalism and an ultra-exclusive view of patriotism, they issued a figurative call to arms to safeguard the so-called sacred values of traditional "Americanism." Blacks, Jews, Catholics, and immigrants were targeted as the whipping boys of this hateful rhetoric. By 1924, membership in the organization had increased to over 4 million men, which constituted a substantial bloc of voters capable of exerting considerable political pressure on local, state, and federally elected officials. It was hardly surprising, then, that during this time many of the extrajudicial lynchings and whippings of black men by mobs of self-appointed white vigilantes went unredressed by publicly elected officials, from the Deep South to Duluth, Minnesota. The summer of 1919 was an especially egregious period in this reign of terror—forever to be remembered as "the Red Summer," a bloody reference to the race-related bloodshed that stained much of the country. In speaking to this issue and to the frustration experienced by black soldiers on returning home from the war, W. S. Scarborough, president of Wilberforce College, summed up the situation succinctly:

If the negro had not been to camp—if he had not been trained in common with the white soldier; if he had not gone across the seas; if he had not gone "over the top"; and made good; and if he had not expected better treatment on his return to his native land at the hands of those who drafted him and sent him to the trenches, I am sure he would not be so exasperated at the situation. He feels the injustice keenly. The negro officers and men now returning have but one story to tell, and they tell it with bitterness and tears. . . . Many of these men in going to their homes with the laurels of victory won in their country's defense are not permitted to ride in other than Jim-crow cars. Many of them have been assaulted and thrown off the cars by Government officers. . . . Many of them have not only suffered in this way, but have met death, because they sought better treatment. . . . The negro is law-abiding and only occasionally shows retaliatory spirit. Will not the American people come halfway? . . . They ask no favors, but simply a man's chance in the race of life, and an opportunity to develop the powers that God has given them.

In the face of such dispiriting prospects at home, it was not totally unexpected that some black veterans would decide to reverse course and return to the more enlightened environs of France, where they had experienced far less racial discrimination during the war than they were accustomed to at home. In the ensuing years, other black expatriates would also take up residence in France, many becoming part of a vibrant black community in the Montmartre section of Paris. For a graphic description of one of the most gruesome of these extrajudicial killings, refer to the February 1918 edition of the *Crisis*, the official publication of the NAACP. To read the opinion piece by W. S. Scarborough in its entirety, see "Race Riots and Their Remedy," *Independent*, August 16, 1919. See also Carl Sandburg, *The Chicago Race Riots: July 1919* (New York: Harcourt, Brace & Howe, 1919); Cameron McWhirter, *Red Summer: The Summer of 1919* (New York: Henry Holt, 2011); and Rory McVeigh, *Rise of the Ku Klux Klan: Right-Wing Movements and National Politics* (St. Paul: University of Minnesota Press, 2009); William A. Shack, *Harlem in Montmartre: A Paris Jazz Story between the Great Wars* (Berkeley: University of California Press, 2001).

288 "marching down the Champs Élysées." "Two Celebrations: One Marks the Glory of Victory, the Other the Misery of War," *NYT*, November 12, 1924; "French Derelicts of World War Ask for Better Pay—Thousands of Crippled & Blind Veterans Parade in Paris—Petition Presented to Premier Herriot, Who Promises Aid," *Springfield Missouri Republican*, November 12, 1924; "War-Crippled Sadden Paris Armistice Day," *Detroit Free Press*, November 12, 1924; and "Parade of the War Maimed in France" (quoting Basil D. Woon, correspondent of the Universal News Service), *Advent Review and Sabbath Herald*, December 11, 1924.

288   "Six Years After the Armistice." Byron Field, "Six Years After the Armistice" (speech delivered to Meeting of Methodist Men at Plymouth Methodist Episcopal Church, Plymouth, IN, November 23, 1924), BFFP.
290   "As reported the following day." "Six Years After the Armistice," *Plymouth Daily Democrat*, November 24, 1924.
292   "leave the turmoil of war in the past." While at CMA, BFF wrote an essay titled "Vaucouleurs" that is noteworthy in that he chose to write about his peaceful days in Vaucouleurs rather than more harrowing ones during the war. This romantic reminiscence stands in stark contrast to the postwar recollection of other veterans, specifically the so-called Lost Generation of writers and artists, whose reflections of the war and its aftermath were cast in far harsher tones and subject matter. See John Dos Passos, *Three Soldiers* (New York: George Doran, 1921); Ernest Hemingway, *A Farewell to Arms* (New York: Charles Scribner's Sons, 1929). This divergence in viewpoint is of further interest given that both Hemingway and Dos Passos drew on experiences similar to BFF's—that is, as frontline ambulance drivers.
292   "the possibilities are what you make them." Western Union Telegram from Commonwealth Edison Co. to Byron F. Field, February 28, 1927.
292   "Byron's first position." Letter from Guy E. Turlock, manager of Commercial Division, Commonwealth Edison Company dated January 19, 1954, detailing Byron Field's responsibilities as superintendent of training.
293   "his accomplishments." *Edison Round Table*, March 15, 1929, May 15, 1930, July 2, 1934.
293   "hometown village, Hinsdale." Untitled article (presumably from a Hinsdale newspaper) dated February 4, 1928, listing BFF as member of the Village of Hinsdale Board of Trustees.
293   "Officers' Reserve Corps." Presidential Appointment Proclamation, Byron F. Field, First Lieutenant, United States Army, Military Intelligence, August 6, 1930.
293   "not immune from those feelings of dread." In the years that followed World War I, the fear that Bolshevism would be able to gain a foothold in the United States was not uncommon among Americans. This fear was grounded in the belief that if Bolshevism was capable of overthrowing the established political order in Russia (and to a lesser extent in certain parts of Europe), then the open democratic process of the United States would be particularly susceptible to the spread of this contagion. Although there was no evidence to indicate that Bolshevism had gained any serious political traction in the United States, citizens were nevertheless anxious and inclined to view any agent of change, be it labor unions, immigrants, or socialists, as a threat to the status quo. This period of political paranoia would later be called "the Red Scare of 1920." The attorney general of the United States, A. Mitchell Palmer, was among those who were convinced that the spread of Bolshevism presented a real and present danger to the

democratic process of the country. Arguably Palmer had good cause to feel that way; for him, the threat of political dysfunction had literally struck close to home—on June 2, 1919, a pipe bomb had been detonated on the doorstep of his house. Fortunately, the only person hurt by the blast was the anarchist who had planted the device. Nevertheless, the shock of the incident succeeded in dislodging Palmer from his constitutional moorings—at his direction, federal agents assigned to the Justice Department's recently established Bureau of Investigation launched a campaign to eradicate the threat of subversive political activity from the American home front. In carrying out that assignment, agents from the "Radical Division" (as the General Intelligence Division would soon be known) engaged in what was then the most invasive curtailment of civil rights since the enactment of the Alien and Sedition Acts in 1798. Under the supervision of the division's aggressive young chief, attorney J. Edgar Hoover, hundreds of warrantless searches (known as "Palmer raids") were conducted of homes, businesses, and union headquarters. During these raids, thousands of innocent civilians were rounded up, detained, and arrested—in some cases even deported on little or no evidence. At one point, public fear that Communists had been able to infiltrate and subvert the democratic process of the country became so acute that legislators who had been lawfully elected to Congress and state assemblies were precluded from being sworn into those positions on the grounds that they were active members of the Socialist Party. See Robert K. Murray, *Red Scare: A Study in National Hysteria, 1919–1920* (St. Paul: University of Minnesota Press, 1955).

294   "assistant director of labor relations." Internal memo, Commonwealth Edison to Heads of Departments, dated October 31, 1932, appointing Byron F. Field to the position of assistant manager of industrial relations. See also Commonwealth Edison Company Regulation captioned "Changes in Industrial Relations Organization," dated November 1, 1932, announcing appointment of Byron F. Field as assistant manager of industrial relations; and Turlock letter dated January 19, 1954.

296   "serve on the company's Advisory Committee." Departmental correspondence, Commonwealth Edison Company, dated February 18, 1933, appointing Byron F. Field to advisory committee.

296   "featured speaker." Announcement of Industrial Relations Association of Chicago, dated November 13, 1933, listing Byron F. Field as the featured speaker. The topic to be discussed was "Industrial Relations under the N.R.A."

296   "sent to yet another conference." Program for American Management Association Conference on Collective Bargaining and Employee Representation, November 22–23, 1933, Long Beach, NY.

296   "again listed as the featured speaker." Announcement of National Vocational Association of Chicago, dated November 27, 1933, listing Byron F. Field as the featured speaker. The topic to be discussed was "Past

Developments and Present Plans of Adjustment in Personnel Work in Industry."

297   "There was no limit." Letter from BFF to E. A. Nichol, manager of personnel, Philadelphia Gas Works, October 10, 1935.

297   "Byron's philosophy on workers' rights." Letter from BFF to J. Douglas Brown, Princeton University, October 16, 1935, BFFP.

298   "On October 19, 1934." "Report of Midwest Conference on Industrial Relations," October 19, 1934, conducted by the Industrial Relations Association of Chicago and the School of Business at the University of Chicago.

299   "drinking on the job." Helen Hulst Field, "Thoughts and Memories of Helen Hulst Field" (unpublished MS, 1980), book 1, 65.

299   "Just a Rug," Byron F. Field, October 17, 1934, BFFP.

300   "On the home front." One of the leading voices in the chorus of discontent over the outlandish profits that had been reaped by American manufacturers and financiers during the Great War was that of Major General Smedley D. Butler, USMC. Butler was uniquely well informed on the matter. Over the course of a thirty-four-year career, he had become the most highly decorated combat soldier in U.S. military history. Having served in the Spanish-American War, the Mexican Border War, and World War I, he had also become intimately familiar with the great cost exacted by war—in both human and financial terms. On retiring in 1931, Butler assumed the role of a self-appointed civilian ombudsman—traveling the length and breadth of the country to deliver speeches in which he cautioned citizens to guard against those who would seek to profit from war. The most famous of Butler's speeches, "War Is a Racket," was delivered in 1933. The essence of Butler's position was that as surely as the flag follows the dollar around the globe, American soldiers will follow the flag in order to protect that investment. In expounding on this theme, Butler used his own involvement in military expeditions overseas as a means of highlighting the American economic interests gained or protected in each of those engagements. The anti-war-profiteering sentiments and isolationist stance of Butler's speeches were particularly well received by disillusioned war veterans who were struggling in the midst of the Great Depression. See Smedley D. Butler, *War Is a Racket* (New York: Roundtable, 1935).

300   "Nye Committee." For succinct summary of the Senate Munitions Committee, see http://www.senate.gov/artandhistory/history/minute/merchants_of_death.htm.

300   "New York Realty Advisory Board." Letter from BFF to J. Douglas Brown dated October 16, 1935, BFFP.

300   "letter from the deputy mayor." Henry H. Curran to BFF dated December 9, 1937, BFFP.

301   "managed to land yet another well-paid executive position." Unfortunately, the same could not be said for many of Byron's former colleagues in the Rainbow Division who were mired in the depths of

the Great Depression, some utterly destitute and homeless. By the spring of 1932, the situation had become so dire that thousands of disillusioned ex-soldiers marched on Washington, DC, where they assembled, hoping to persuade President Herbert Hoover and Congress to authorize the immediate redemption of the Bonus Certificates that had been issued to them in 1924. Each certificate had a surrender value of $1,000, but that sum was not scheduled to come due until 1945. Citing fiscal austerity as an overriding concern, the Hoover administration was adamant about not redeeming the certificates prematurely, and told the men to go home. The so-called Bonus Army would not be so easily dissuaded, however, and encamped on the Anacostia Flats in a shantytown they named Hooverville, where the men prepared for a long political siege. Despite their best efforts, the campaign by veterans to lobby legislators came to naught. On July 28, Congress adjourned for the summer without taking any action to aid the men. At this point, a substantial portion of the Bonus Army dispersed. Many, however, continued to stay at Hooverville—some simply had nowhere else to go. Finally, the prolonged standoff came to a head when President Hoover called in the U.S. Army to remove them. General Douglas MacArthur assigned that unenviable task to Major George S. Patton Jr. Although soldiers in the Regular Army were being asked to advance on men they had served with during the war, both MacArthur and Patton, convinced that the ranks of the Bonus Army had been infiltrated by Bolsheviks, revolutionaries, and other dissidents, were determined to carry out their orders. With bayonets fixed, Patton's troops marched in and evicted the veterans, in some cases violently. In the wake of such a controversial and well-publicized event, the fact that Byron had not seen fit to author an opinion one way or the other was highly unusual for someone who had made a habit of expressing himself on a great many of the important issues of the day—and was all the more curious given that he had so vociferously objected to the issuance of Bonus Certificates in the first place, even sharing those feelings in print in the *Independent*. Perhaps in the intervening years Byron's stance had softened somewhat, and he now found it easier to simply carry on as always, dealing with his innermost feelings in silence. Others were not so reticent about expressing their feelings. For many, the forcible eviction of the Bonus Army only served to confirm the widely held belief that struggling World War I veterans were getting a raw deal from the government. Indeed, as the Great Depression worsened, the popular sentiment that ex-servicemen had been forsaken by their country became so pervasive that Warner Bros. Studio tapped into that vein of discontent in the hit movie *Gold Diggers of 1933*. In the movie's final song, "Remember My Forgotten Man," Joan Blondell, in the role of a streetwalker, offers a mournful lament for her down-on-his-luck man. Lasting nearly seven minutes, the song is set against a backdrop of scenes depicting the short-lived euphoria of flag-waving military parades; the endless drudgery, danger, and sacrifice of war; and the abject despair of returning veterans (and those dependent on them) now forced to live on the streets and stand in soup lines. The movie ends on this powerful unresolved note. To view the scene containing the song, see *Gold Diggers of 1933*, "Remember My Forgotten Man," Turner Classic Movies Movie Clip, http.//tcm.com/Mediaroom .video/274289/Gold-Diggers-of-1933-Movie-Clip-Forgotten-Man .html. For an excellent discussion of the Bonus Army, from inception to dissolution, refer to the 2006 PBS video presentation *The Bonus Army: An American Experience*. Commissioned by the Disabled Veterans of America, the documentary was written by Paul Dickson and produced by Thomas B. Allan and Robert Uth. http://www.pbs .org/wgbh/americanexperience/features/macarthur-bonus-march -may-july-1932/. See also Daniel J. B. Mitchell, *Pensions, Politics and the Elderly: Historic Social Movements and Their Lessons for Our Aging Society* (New York: M. E. Sharpe, 2000), 74–75.

301   "FDR's attempt to expand." For a thorough discussion of Roosevelt's "court-packing scheme," refer to: Jean Edward Smith, "Hubris," in *FDR* (New York: Random House, 2007), 360–89.

301   "Memorial Day Massacre." The events surrounding the so-called Memorial Day Massacre have been discussed by many writers over the years, from the young Studs Terkel to the La Follette Commission. Among the sources I consulted are Ahmed White, *The Last Great Strike: Little Steel, the CIO, and the Struggle for Labor Rights in New Deal America* (Berkeley: University of California Press, 2016); Dale Richard Perleman, "Little Steel Battles On," in *Road to Rust: The Disintegration of the Steel Industry in Western Pennsylvania and Eastern Ohio* (Charleston, SC: History Press, 2018); John F. Hogan, *The 1937 Chicago Steel Strike: Blood on the Prairie* (Charleston, SC: History Press, 2014); U.S. Senate, *Hearings before a Subcommittee of the Committee on Education and Labor*, 75th Cong., pursuant to S. Res. 266, *The Chicago Memorial Day Incident; June 30, July 1 and 2, 1937* (Washington, DC: U.S. Government Printing Office, 1937); Carol Quirke, "Reframing Chicago's Memorial Day Massacre, May 30, 1937," *American Quarterly* 60 (March 2008): 129–57. See also Paramount newsreel footage of the labor march at the South Chicago plant of Republic Steel, May 30, 1937: NAIL Control No. NWDNM(m)-46.3, ARC No. 7575, NAMS; and interview of Mollie Lieber West (a marcher), "Memories of the Memorial Day Massacre: Excerpt from 'West Interview,'" Loyola University Chicago Digital Special Collections, http://www.lib.luc.edu/specialcollections/items/show/1494.

302   "Girdler...wasn't...intimidated." Girdler was admittedly bitter about the agreement entered into by U.S. Steel. In a speech delivered by Girdler on May 24, 1934, to American Iron and Steel Institute, he said so, declaring that "before I spend the rest of my life dealing with John L.

Lewis, I'm going to raise apples and potatoes." See minutes of American Iron and Steel Institute, 43rd general meeting, New York, NY, as noted in La Follette Committee hearings, pt. 23, p. 9738.

302   "Marchers ran for their lives." One witness to the carnage was steelworker, Nick Kruga, a veteran of the war in France. As related by Kruga: "I never heard so many bullets as those coppers fired. Women and children were screaming all over the place. They were like a herd of cattle panic stricken. I ran till they got me. I saw a woman shot down and the police drag her away." "4 Killed, 88 Injured in Strike Riot," *Cleveland Plain Dealer*, May 31, 1937, 1, 4. Another witness to the mayhem was Lupe Marshall, a social worker, who recalled standing in the front lines with other marchers trying to persuade the police to let them pass when they were attacked for no apparent reason. After being bludgeoned by the police, Lupe was tossed into a police wagon. In short order sixteen other wounded protesters were also crammed into a space that was designed to hold only a few people—when the doors were padlocked shut, the back of the wagon become an insufferable mass of contorted and bloody bodies. One wounded man, whose head Lupe cradled in her lap, died on the long ride to the hospital.

303   "maybe they were out there to catch butterflies," *Youngstown Vindicator*, June 2, 1937, 1.

303   "struck an emotional chord." As noted in the La Follette Committee report, "[W]ounded prisoners of war might have expected and received greater solicitude." See U.S. Senate, *Hearings before a Subcommittee of the Committee on Education and Labor*, report no. 46, pt. 2, p. 37.

303   "hostility and callous indifference." The Memorial Day Massacre was not an isolated incident—it was a pattern of conduct that would contribute to the death of six more protesters outside the gates of Republic Steel plants in Ohio and Pennsylvania as well—two of those victims died as a result of action taken by police and plant security in disbanding a march by pro-union women and children outside the gates of the Republic Steel plant in Youngstown, Ohio, on June 19. At the time of these incidents, Republic Steel was rumored to possess one of the largest privately owned arsenals in the country.

304   "hard to imagine that Girdler would not have consulted with him." The conclusion that BFF may have been consulted in this unfortunate event seems to be supported by three letters found among his personal papers: (1) a September 4, 1936, letter written by Jess Hopkins of the American Iron and Steel Institute to BFF (on learning of BFF's arrival at Republic Steel) in which he encouraged BFF to make himself (and presumably his expertise) available to Joe Voss, the industrial relations manager at Republic Steel (who "will be glad to see you"); (2) a July 14, 1949, letter written by John Tope, an executive at Republic Steel, who "vividly" recalled a meeting at Republic Steel in Cleveland in the "fall of '36" during which BFF had voiced his antipathy toward the New Deal as being "the 'raw deal'" (which would have been in accord with

Girdler's views on the matter); and (3) a October 10, 1951, letter written by BFF to Walter Gordon Merritt (author of *Destination Unknown: Fifty Years of Labor Relations*), in which BFF specifically mentioned "the South Chicago 'Massacre'" as being among the formative experiences in his "25-odd years in open shop, C.I.O., A.F. of L. personnel and labor relations situations, including Republic Steel."

304 "Alcoholics Anonymous." Field, "Thoughts and Memories of Helen Hulst Field," 66.

305 "kept him abreast of Byron's continuing struggles with alcohol." In a letter written by Fiske on April 23, 1945, to his sister Nancy, then fourteen, he sought to help her cope with the frustration, confusion, and anger of having to deal with her father's repeated episodes of drunkenness. "Nancy, I wish I could be there to help you with Dad. But I feel it would be just about as futile nevertheless. All thru high school I felt the same way you do now. I don't blame you at all—disgust is certainly the natural emotion. Naturally, I feel sorry for Dad. He can't be happy, living so miserably. No one can. Nan, I'm sure you won't grow up and marry a fellow who drinks. I certainly hope you don't fall in love with one who does."

305 "Dad, I'm just sick about your drinking." Letter from Byron Field Jr. to BFF, March 19, 1945.

306 "We left Detroit." Field, "Thoughts and Memories of Helen Hulst Field," 62.

306 "I divorced Byron." Ibid., 66–67.

307 "worked as the desk clerk." "Salvation Army Fights Skid Row with New Hotel," *San Francisco Chronicle*, February 9, 1958.

307 "Byron's letters." Letters from BFF to Byron Field Jr., September 5, 1964, December 21, 28, 1964, January 1965, December 14, 29, 1965, January 5, 1966, February 1966, June 1, 1966, September 6, 1966, October 29, 1966, May 21, 1967.

312 "Estelle's professional credits." During EMC's brief acting career, she served as an understudy to the legendary First Lady of the American Theater, Helen Hayes, on Broadway. Apparently, their relationship was such that it was still memorable many years later. In an interview with EMC's daughter Martha Hartmann, conducted by the authors on August 4, 2014, Martha fondly recalled being taken backstage by her mother to meet Miss Hayes after a performance at the Falmouth Playhouse on Cape Cod in the summer of 1954. After being proudly introduced by her mother to Miss Hayes, Martha, who was fifteen at the time, remembered Miss Hayes telling EMC how fortunate she was to have such a lovely daughter. Sadly, Miss Hayes was speaking from experience—only five years before, she had lost her own daughter, Mary, to polio at the age of sixteen.

312 "cutting-edge theater companies." By the time EMC had arrived in New York City in the summer of 1924, the Provincetown Playhouse had been in existence for nine years. The first performances staged by the

Provincetown Players took place in July 1915 on Cape Cod. After two relatively successful summer seasons, the players decided to relocate their fledgling enterprise to more permanent quarters in Greenwich Village. The plays produced at the playhouse dealt with contemporary social issues, which was not surprising given that several members of the theater group were affiliated with the *Masses*, a magazine of political activism that championed Progressive, Communist, and Socialist causes. Two of those members (Max Eastman and John Reed) had been prosecuted under the Sedition Act for their vocal opposition to the war. Perhaps the most notorious example of the theater company's counterculture chutzpah occurred on May 15, 1924, at the premiere performance of Eugene O'Neill's *All God's Chillun Got Wings*—a play that dealt with the racially inflammatory topic of miscegenation (not to mention the scandalous act of a black actor, Paul Robeson, kissing the hand of a white actress, Mary Blair). The play was viewed as a political pariah—in an attempt to prevent its production, the mayor's office had refused to issue a permit allowing the theater to use children in the cast. Undeterred, the production went on as scheduled, with adults playing those parts. In the midst of the controversy, EMC arrived on the Greenwich Village theater scene—playing in O'Neill's next production at the Provincetown Playhouse, the premiere of the *S.S. Glencairn* on November 3, 1924. See Helen Deutsch and Stella Hanau, *The Provincetown: A Story of the Theatre* (New York: Farrar & Rinehart, 1931), 268–69, 276–77, listing EMC as a player in *The Saint* (a new play by Stark Young) performed by the Provincetown Players at the Greenwich Village Theatre, October 11, 1924; and as a singer in the opening performance of Eugene O'Neill's *S.S. Glencairn* at the Provincetown Theatre on November 3, 1924.

312   "instructor of speech and dramatic arts." "Faculty," in *Frances Shimer Junior College Annual Catalogue, 1934–35*.

312   "strictly a one-way correspondence." As part of a note contained in a Christmas card dated December 11, 1975, EMC expressed her dismay at Fiske's repeated failure to reply to any of her cards or letters. "I have never understood how it could be that I've never had a word from you. But I've hoped for your father's sake you are happy these perilous days." In 1976 and again in 1977, EMC expressed similar disappointment at not having heard back from Fiske.

314   "authors met Estelle's daughter." Interview with Martha Hartmann, Denver, August 4, 2014.

BIBLIOGRAPHY

BOOKS

Adams, Katherine H. and Michael L. Keene. *Alice Paul and the American Suffrage Campaign*. Champaign: University of Illinois Press, 2008.

Aldcroft, Derek H. *From Versailles to Wall Street*. Berkeley: University of California Press, 1981.

Allen, Hervey. *Toward the Flame: A Memoir of World War I*. New York: Farrar & Rinehart, 1926.

Axelrod, Alan. *Patton: A Biography*. Great Generals Series. New York: Macmillan, 2006.

Barry, John M. *The Great Influenza: The Story of the Deadliest Pandemic in History*. New York: Penguin, 2005.

Blumenson, Martin. *Patton: The Man Behind the Legend, 1885–1945*. New York: William Morrow, 1985.

Boyd, Thomas. *Through the Wheat*. New York: Charles Scribner's Sons, 1923.

Brandt, Allan. *No Magic Bullet: A Social History of Venereal Disease in the United States since 1880*. Oxford: Oxford University Press, 1985.

Brown, Anthony Cave. *The Last American Hero: Wild Bill Donovan*. New York: Times Books, 1982.

Bryan, William Jennings, and Mary Baird. *The Memoirs of William Jennings Bryan*. Chicago: Johnson C. Winston, 1925.

Bryson, Roy, and select members of 168th Ambulance Company. *The History of Ambulance Company 168*. N.p., 1919.

Butler, Smedley D. *War Is a Racket*, New York: Roundtable, 1935.

Castle, Ian. *London, 1914–17: The Zeppelin Menace*. Oxford: Osprey, 2008.

Childers, Thomas. *The Nazi Voter: The Social Foundations of Fascism in Germany, 1919–1933*. Chapel Hill: University of North Carolina Press, 1983.

Conkling, Wilbur, and select members of 117th Sanitary Train. *Iodine and Gasoline*. N.p., 1919.

Cooke, James. *The Rainbow Division in the Great War, 1917–1919*. Westport, CT: Praeger, 1994.

Cornebise, Alfred. *War as Advertised: The Four Minute Men and America's Crusade*. Philadelphia: American Philosophical Society, 1984.

Cozzolino, Robert, Anne C. Knutson, and David M. Lubin. *World War I and American Art*. Princeton: Princeton University Press, 2016.

Creel, George. *How We Advertised America: The First Telling of the Amazing Story of the Committee on Public Information That Carried the Gospel of Americanism to Every Corner of the Globe*. New York: Harper & Bros., 1920.

Davison, Henry P. *The American Red Cross in the Great War*. New York: Macmillan, 1919.

DeBauche, Leslie M. *Reel Patriotism: The Movies and World War I*. Madison: University of Wisconsin Press, 1997.

Deutsch, Helen, and Stella Hanau. *The Provincetown: A Story of the Theatre*. New York: Farrar & Rinehart, 1931.

Dickon, Chris. *Americans at War in Foreign Forces: A History, 1914–1945*. Jefferson, NC: McFarland, 2014.

Dos Passos, John. *Three Soldiers*. New York: George Doran, 1921.

Duffy, Francis. *Father Duffy's Story: A Tale of Humor and Heroism, of Life and Death with the Fighting 69th*. New York: George Doran, 1919.

Eichelberger, Robert. *Dear Miss Em: General Eichelberger's War in the Pacific, 1942–1945*. Westport, CT: Praeger, 1972.

Ettinger, Albert M. *A Doughboy with the Fighting 69th*. New York: Pocket Books, 1992.

Field, James B. *Progenitors and Descendants of Our Grandfather Seldon Field*. N.p., 1934.

Fish, Hamilton. *Memoir of an American Patriot*. Washington, DC: Regnery Gateway, 1991.

Foch, Ferdinand. *Memoirs of Marshal Foch*. New York: Doubleday, Doran, 1931.

Freidel, Frank. *Over There: The American Experience in World War I*. Ithaca, NY: Burford Books, 1964.

Fussell, Paul. *The Great War and Modern Memory*. Oxford: Oxford University Press, 1975.

Garrison, Fielding H. *Notes on the History of Military Medicine*. Washington, DC: Association of Military Surgeons of the United States, 1922.

Gildart, Robert. *Albion College, 1835–1960: A History*. Chicago: Lakeside, 1961.

Graves, Robert. *Goodbye to All That*. New York: Vintage, 1929.

Gudmundsson, Bruce I. *On Artillery*. Westport, CT: Praeger, 1993.

Hagood, Johnson. *The Services of Supply: A Memoir of the Great War*. New York: Houghton Mifflin, 1927.

Harbord, James G. *The American Army in France, 1917–1919*. Boston: Little, Brown, 1936.

Harris, Stephen. *Duffy's War*. Washington, DC: Potomac, 2006.

——. *Harlem's Hell Fighters: The African American 369th Infantry in World War I*. Washington, DC: Potomac, 2003.

Hemingway, Ernest. *A Farewell to Arms*. New York: Charles Scribner's Sons, 1929.

Hirshson, Stanley P. *General Patton: A Soldier's Life*. New York: Harper, 2002.

Hogan, John F. *The 1937 Chicago Steel Strike: Blood on the Prairie*. History Press, 2014.

Horne, John, and Alan Kramer. *German Atrocities, 1914: A History of Denial*. New Haven: Yale University Press, 2001.

Jankowski, Paul. *Verdun: The Longest Battle of the Great War*. Oxford: Oxford University Press, 2014.

Johnson, Harold Stanley. *Roster of the Rainbow Division: Major General Wm. A. Mann, Commanding*. New York: Eaton & Gettinger, 1917.

Jones, James. *WW II: A Chronicle of Soldiering*. New York: Grossett & Dunlap, 1975.

Jünger, Ernst. *Storm of Steel*. New York: Penguin, 1920.

Keegan, John. *The Face of Battle*. New York: Penguin, 1978.

Langille, Leslie. *Men of the Rainbow*. Chicago: W. B. Conkey, 1933.

Lanning, Michael L. *The African-American Soldier: From Crispus Attucks to Colin Powell*. New York: Citadel, 1997.

Leese, Peter. *Shell Shock: Traumatic Neurosis and the British Soldiers of the First World War*. New York: Springer, 2002.

Liggett, Hunter. *A.E.F.: Ten Years Ago in France*. New York: Dodd, Mead, 1928.

Little, Arthur W. *From Harlem to the Rhine*. New York: Covici-Friede, 1938.

Lloyd George, David. *The Truth about the Treaties*. London: V. Gollancz, 1938.

Lossing, Benson J. *The Pictorial Field-book of the War of 1812*. New York: Harper & Brothers, 1868.

MacArthur, Douglas. *Reminiscences*. New York: McGraw Hill, 1964.

MacMillan, Margaret. *Paris 1919*. New York: Random House, 2001.

March, William, *Company K*. New York: Smith & Haas, 1933.

Marquis, Albert N., ed. *The Book of Detroiters: A Biographical Dictionary of Leading Living Men of the City of Detroit*. 2nd ed. Chicago: A. N. Marquis, 1914.

Marshall, George C. *Memoirs of My Services in the World War, 1917–1918*. Boston: Houghton Mifflin, 1976.

McVeigh, Rory. *Rise of the Ku Klux Klan: Right-Wing Movements and National Politics*. St. Paul: University of Minnesota Press, 2009.

McWhirter, Cameron. *Red Summer: The Summer of 1919*. New York: Henry Holt, 2011.

Miller, Henry W. *The Paris Gun: The Bombardment of Paris by the German Long-Range Guns and the Great German Offensives of 1918*. London: George C. Harrap, 1930.

Mitchell, Daniel J. B. *Pensions, Politics and the Elderly: Historic Social Movements and Their Lessons for Our Aging Society*. New York: M. E. Sharpe, 2000.

Murray, Robert K. *Red Scare: A Study in National Hysteria, 1919–1920*. St. Paul: University of Minnesota Press, 1955.

O'Connor, Richard. *Black Jack Pershing*. New York: Doubleday, 1961.

Pawlak, Debra Ann. *Farmington and Farmington Hills*. Making of America Series. Charleston, SC: Arcadia, 2003.

Perleman, Dale Richard. *Road to Rust: The Disintegration of the Steel Industry in Western Pennsylvania and Eastern Ohio*. Charleston, SC: History Press, 2018.

Pershing, John J. *My Experiences in the World War*. 2 vols. New York: Frederick A. Stokes, 1931.

Persico, Joseph. *Eleventh Month, Eleventh Day, Eleventh Hour: Armistice Day 1918, World War I and Its Violent Climax*. New York: Random House, 2004.

Ramsay, David. *Lusitania: Saga and Myth*. New York: Norton, 2002.

Rawls, Walton. *Wake Up, America! World War I and the American Poster*. New York: Abbeville, 1988.

Reilly, Henry J. *Americans All: The Rainbow at War*. Columbus, OH: F. J. Heer, 1936.

Remarque, Erich Maria. *The Road Back*. Boston: Little, Brown, 1931.

Reppy, Allison. *Rainbow Memories: Character Sketches and History First Battalion—42nd Division*. Melbourne Beach, FL: Carey, 1919.

Rickenbacker, Eddie. *Fighting the Flying Circus*. Philadelphia: J. B. Lippincott, 1919.

Roeder, Mark. *A History of Culver and the Military Academy*. Indiana: iUniverse, 2009.

Ropp, Theodore. *War in the Modern World*. New York: Collier Books, 1979.

Sandburg, Carl. *The Chicago Race Riots: July 1919*. New York: Harcourt, Brace & Howe, 1919.

Shack, William A. *Harlem in Montmartre: A Paris Jazz Story between the Great Wars*. Berkeley: University of California Press, 2001.

Shaffer, Ronald. *America in the Great War: The Rise of the War Welfare State*. Oxford: Oxford University Press, 1994.

Shay, Jonathan. *Achilles in Vietnam: Combat Trauma and the Undoing of Character*. New York: Scribner, 1994.

———. *Odysseus in America: Combat Trauma and the Trials of Homecoming*. New York: Scribner, 2002.

Sims, William S. *The Victory at Sea*. London: John Murray, 1920.

Smith, Jean Edward. *FDR*. New York: Random House, 2007.

Stewart, Lawrence O. *Rainbow Bright*. Philadelphia: Dorrance, 1923.

Strachan, Hew. *The First World War: To Arms*. Vol. 1. Oxford: Oxford University Press, 2001.

Taft, William Howard. *Service with Fighting Men: An Account of the Work of the American Young Men's Christian Association in the World War*. New York: Association, 1922.

Thomas, William H. *Unsafe for Democracy: World War I and the U.S. Justice Department's Covert Campaign to Suppress Dissent*. Madison: University of Wisconsin Press, 2008.

Tomlinson, Everett T. *The Story of General Pershing*. New York: D. Appleton, 1919.

Tuchman, Barbara. *The Guns of August*. New York: Ballantine Books, 1962.

———. *The Zimmerman Telegram*. New York: Viking, 1958.

Waite, Robert G. *Vanguard of Nazism: The Free Corps Movement in Postwar Germany, 1918–1923*. New York: Norton, 1969.

Waller, Willard W. *The Veteran Comes Back*. New York: Dryden, 1944.

White, Ahmed. *The Last Great Strike: Little Steel, the CIO, and the Struggle for Labor Rights in New Deal America*. Berkeley: University of California Press, 2016.

Witkop, Philipp. *German Students' War Letters*. Translated by Annie F. Wedd. New York: E. P. Dutton, 1929.

Yoakum, Charles, and Robert Yerkes. *Army Mental Tests*. New York: Henry Holt, 1920.

NEWSPAPERS AND PERIODICALS

Advent Review and Sabbath Herald. "Parade of the War Maimed in France," December 11, 1924.

American Legion Weekly. "Bottling Up the Boche," August 29, 1919; "Rouge Bouquet: From the Depths," January 1939.

Brantford Expositor. "The Man Who Would Be President," June 3, 2006.

Brooklyn Eagle. "Blaustein Dug for Hours and Rescued Comrades Buried When Huns Shelled 165th Inf. Dugout," December 29, 1918.

Chicago Daily News. "LaSalle Street Notes," January 8, 1935.

Cleveland Plain Dealer. "4 Killed, 88 Injured in Strike Riot," May 31, 1937.

Creel, George, U.S. Government Press Bureau. Press release, June 1917. In *Source of Records of the Great War*, vol. 5, edited by Charles F. Horne. New York: National Alumni, 1923.

Culver Citizen. June 24, 1924.

Daily Mail. "Revealed: British Officials Feared Sunk WWI Cruise Ship Lusitania Could 'Literally Blow Up on Us' in 1982 Salvage Mission," May 1, 2014.

Detroit Free Press. "31st Ready, Will Leave by August 1," July 16, 1917; "Medical Tests Get 800 Guards: 14 Percent of State Soldiers Rejected for Physical Disabilities—Half of Discharges Are Due to Incorrect Living," August 2, 1917; "First Michigan Ambulance Corps of Detroit at Grayling Mobilization Camp," September 2, 1917; "War-Crippled Sadden Paris Armistice Day," November 12, 1924.

Detroit News. "Soldier Weds—Gets 30 Days Manual Labor," August 31, 1917.

Edison Roundtable. Commonwealth Edison, Chicago, 1929, 1930, 1934.

Independent. "Race Riots and Their Remedy" (W. S. Scarborough), August 16, 1919; "Facing the Pension Problem," January 20, 1923.

Jackson Patriot News. November 25, 1917; August 8, 1919.

Literary Digest. "The Militiaman's Morals," November 18, 1916; "Army Life Improving Health," June 22, 1918.

Ludington Daily News. "Dr. Samuel Dickie at Camp Services," July 10, 1918.

Morning Star. "The Mayor Who Wasn't a U.S. Citizen," March 30, 1997.

Motor Age Magazine. January 4, 1917.

New York Times. "Relations with Germany Are Broken Off," February 3, 1917; "Poorest Wheat Crop in 13 Years: Condition of May 1 Shows We Will Have Enough to Feed Ourselves Only," May 8, 1917; "3 American Ships Sunk by U-boats," June 2, 1917; "Germans Impatient for U-boat Results," June 3, 1917; "German Catholics Tried Peace Move," June 3, 1917; "Pershing's First Force Is in France: General Praises Troops After Visit; Entire Port Put in American Control," July 1, 1917; "News of Our Men Held Up in Paris—Washington Believed to Have Asked French and British Censors to Delay Cables," July 2, 1917; "Germany Now Sees War's End in Fall: Official Berlin Figures Give England Only 5,000,000 Tons of Shipping," July 2, 1917; "'Cheer Up' Show at the Hippodrome: An Early Wartime Play Full of Khaki, Flags, and Marching," August 24, 1917; "$11,000 for 69th Regiment: John McCormack Gives Recital for Dependents of Soldiers," October 1, 1917; "Three Brigades in Review: 40,000 Visitors Watch Troops Marching at Camp Mills," October 1, 1917; "Miss Alice Paul on Hunger Strike: Suffragist Leader Adopts This Means of Protesting against Washington Prison Fare: Now in Jail Hospital: Threatens to Starve to Death Unless Better Food Is Provided for Six Companions," November 7, 1917; "Abandon Camp Mills Because of Weather: Secretary Baker Announces Department's Decision—Lack of Blankets Denied," December 15, 1917; "Benefits at Theatres Aid War Charities: John McCormack Sings for Soldiers and Sailors at Vaudeville Performance at Playhouse," May 20, 1918; "Capt. Fish in the Fighting: His Helmet Hit by Shrapnel—Narrow Escape from a Shell," August 20, 1918; "Army 90 Percent Insured: More than 30,000,000 of Government Insurance Already Taken," August 30, 1918; "Labor Day, 1918," September 2, 1918; "Germans Belittle Loss at St. Mihiel," September 16, 1918; "Says We Exaggerate St. Mihiel Success," September 19, 1918; "Y.M.C.A. Errors As Our Soldiers Have Seen Them," January 6, 1919; "Orders Y.M.C.A. Inquiry: Baker Directs Inspector General of Army to Look into Charges," January 7, 1919; "Ready for Parleys on Alsace in 1917," March 5, 1920; "Pope in Accord with Harding Plan," August 29, 1921; "Two Celebrations: One Marks the Glory of Victory, the Other the Misery of War," November 12, 1924; "Feme Chief Tells of Official Backing," October 27, 1926; "Gessler Defends Black Reichswehr," November 2, 1926; "Feme Revelations Appall Germany," April 29, 1928.

Pleiad (Albion College newspaper). October 30, 1917; June 17, 1918.

Plymouth Daily Democrat. November 24, 1924.

Red Cross Magazine. "The Religion Our Soldiers Brought Back to Us," January 1919.

Reform Advocate: American Jewish Journal. "Blaustein Tells How He Won War Cross," May 31, 1919.

San Francisco Chronicle. "Salvation Army Fights Skid Row with New Hotel," February 9, 1958.

Syracuse Herald. "Kaiserism Arraigned by Dr. Dickie," March 22, 1918.

DIARIES, PERSONAL JOURNALS, ESSAYS, AND LETTERS

Bray, Gertrude. Journal, letters, and papers of Gertrude Bray. Rhode Island Historical Society, Providence.

Donovan, William J. Diary and letters of Lieutenant William J. Donovan. Donovan Papers. U.S. Army War Collection Archives, Carlisle, PA.

Field, Byron F. Diary, letters, papers, books, and photographs. The Field Collection. Bentley Historical Library, University of Michigan, Ann Arbor.

Field, Helen Hulst. "Thoughts and Memories of Helen Hulst Field," January 1980. Authors' collection.

Springer, Eva Alice. Letters dated October 23 and December 7, 1918. Archives, Christian Women's Board of Missions, Nashville, TN.

GOVERNMENT REPORTS, DOCUMENTS, AND ARCHIVAL MATERIAL

Committee on Public Information, Division of Four Minute Men. *Purpose and Plan of the Four Minute Men*. Washington, DC: Government Printing Office, 1917.

Hilmas, Corey J., Jeffery K. Smart, and Benjamin A. Hill Jr. "History of Chemical Warfare." In *Medical Aspects of Chemical Warfare*. (Washington, DC: Government Printing Office, 2008).

Koehler, Franz A. *Special Rations for the Armed Forces*. Washington, DC: Office of the Quartermaster General, 1958.

Medical Department of the United States Army in the World War. Washington, DC: Government Printing Office, 1925.

Paramount News film footage, Memorial Day, Chicago, 1937. National Archives and Records Administration, College Park, MD.

Pershing, John J. *Final Report of Gen. John J. Pershing, Commander in Chief, American Expeditionary Forces*. Washington, DC: Government Printing Office, September 1919.

Records of the Office of the Chief Signal Officer. Motion picture footage of American Expeditionary Force in France. Record Group 111, Mopix Section. National Archives and Records Administration, College Park, MD.

Schneider, C. F. *Climatological Data*, Michigan Section 32, no. 5 Washington, DC: U.S. Department of Agriculture, Weather Bureau, 1917.

Songs of the Peace Movement of World War I. Library of Congress. https://www.loc.gov/item/has.200197516.

Songs of World War I. Library of Congress. https://www.loc.gov/item/has.200197499.

Soper, G. "The Influenza Pandemic in the American Camps, September 1918." Memo dated October 9, 1918. Box 23, entry 29, RG 112, National Archives and Records Administration, College Park, MD.

U.S. Army, Historical Division. *The United States Army in the World War, 1917–1919*. Washington, DC: Government Printing Office, 1948.

U.S. Army Signal Corps. Photographs. National Archives and Records Administration, College Park, MD.

U.S. House of Representatives. *Hearings before Subcommittee No. 3 of the Select Committee on Expenditures in the War Department*. 66th Cong., 1st, 2nd, 3rd sess. Washington, DC: Government Printing Office, 1920, 1921.

U.S. Senate. *Hearings before the Special Committee Investigating the Munitions Industry*. 73rd[–74th] Cong. Pursuant to S. Res. 206, a resolution to make certain investigations concerning the manufacture and sale of arms and other war munitions. Washington, DC: U.S. Government Printing Office, 1934.

U.S. Senate. *Hearings before a Subcommittee of the Committee on Education and Labor*. 75th Cong. Pursuant to S. Res. 266; The Chicago Memorial Day

Incident; June 30, July 1 and July 2, 1937. Washington, DC: Government Printing Office, 1937.

REPORTS, ACADEMIC JOURNALS, THESES, AND DISSERTATIONS

Benshoof, Courtney. "Not on My Watch: Moral Trauma and Moral Injury among Combat Medics." MA thesis, Georgia State University, 2017.

Brown, Raymond Forest. "The Development of the Social Creed of the Methodist Church." PhD diss., Boston University, 1942.

Byerly, Carol R. "The U.S. Military and the Influenza Pandemic of 1918–1919." *Public Health Reports*, 2010 125, suppl. 3 (2010).

Cardona, Robert, and Elspeth Ritchie. "Psychological Screening of Recruits Prior to Accession in the US Military." In *Recruit Medicine: Textbook of Military Medicine*. Washington, DC: Office of the Surgeon General, U.S. Department of Army, 2006.

Chesney, Alan M., and F. W. Snow. "A Report of an Epidemic of Influenza in an Army Post of the American Expeditionary Forces in France." *Journal of Laboratory and Clinical Medicine* (1920).

Clements, Kendrick A. "Woodrow Wilson and World War I." *Presidential Studies Quarterly* 34, no. 1 (2004).

Dutton, Phil. "How a German Medallion Became a British Propaganda Tool." *Imperial War Museum Review* 1 (1986).

Edgar, Irving I. "Dr. Max Ballin." Parts 1–3. *Michigan Jewish History* 10, no. 1 (1970); 11, no. 2 (1971); 18, no. 2 (1978).

Fivecoat, David. "A Beautiful War Machine: Irish Offensive Operations." In "Fine Conduct under Fire." MA thesis, U.S. Military Academy, 1993.

Grams, Grant. "Karl Respa and German Espionage in Canada during World War One." *Journal of Military and Strategic Studies* 8, no. 1 (2005).

Herwig, Holger. "Military Doomsday Machine? The Decisions for War, 1914." *Journal of Military and Strategic Studies* 13, no. 4 (2011).

Homsher, David C. "Was the Rainbow Division Tarnished?" *Military Collector & Historian* 58, no. 3 (2006).

Jaffin, Jonathan H. "Medical Support for the American Expeditionary Forces in France during the First World War." MA thesis, U.S. Army Command and Staff College, 1991.

Lecklider, Arlington. Letter, "Army Medical Equipment 1918 versus 1968." *USARV Medical Bulletin* (September/October 1968). U.S. Academy of Health Sciences, Stimson Library, Fort Sam Houston, TX.

Linden, S. C., and E. Jones. "'Shell Shock' Revisited: An Examination of the Case Records of the National Hospital in London." *Cambridge Journals Medical History* (October 2014).

Maguen, Shira, and Brett Litz. "Moral Injury in Veterans of War." *PTSD Research Quarterly* 23, no. 1 (2012).

Quirke, Carol. "Reframing Chicago's Memorial Day Massacre, May 30, 1937." *American Quarterly* 60 (March 2008).

"Report of Midwest Conference on Industrial Relations." University of Chicago, October 19, 1934.

Sanders, M. L. "Wellington House and British Propaganda during the First World War." *Historical Journal* (March 1975).

Wells, Robert. "Mobilizing Public Support for War: An Analysis of American Propaganda during World War I." Paper presented at Annual Meeting of International Studies Association, New Orleans, 2005.

Whitmarsh, Andrew. "British Strategic Bombing, 1917–1918: The Independent Air Force and Its Predecessors." https://www.academia.edu/8630931/British_strategic_bombing_1917-1918_The_Independent_Force.

CPSIA information can be obtained
at www.ICGtesting.com
Printed in the USA
BVHW051518210323
660848BV00015B/707